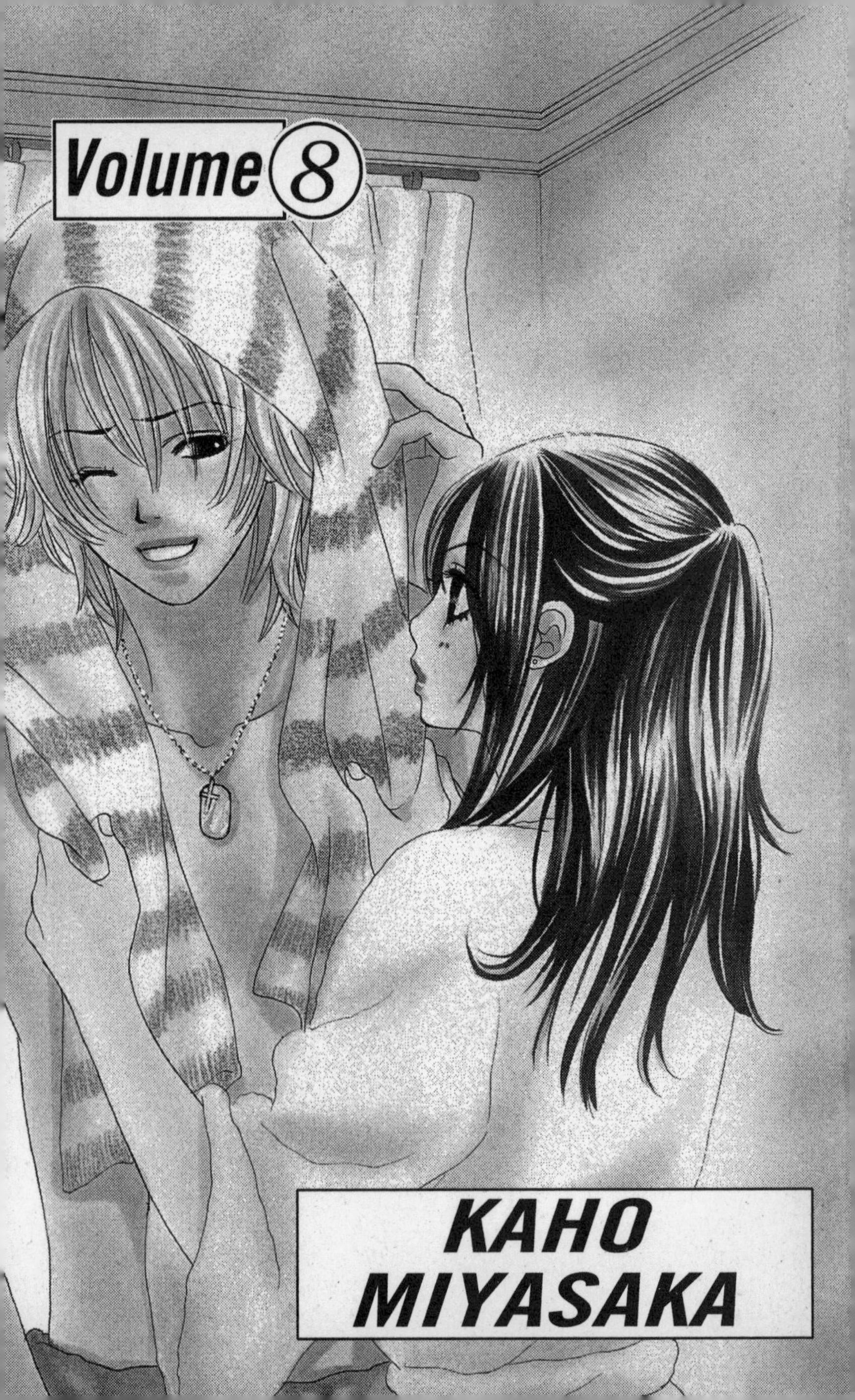
Volume 8
KAHO MIYASAKA

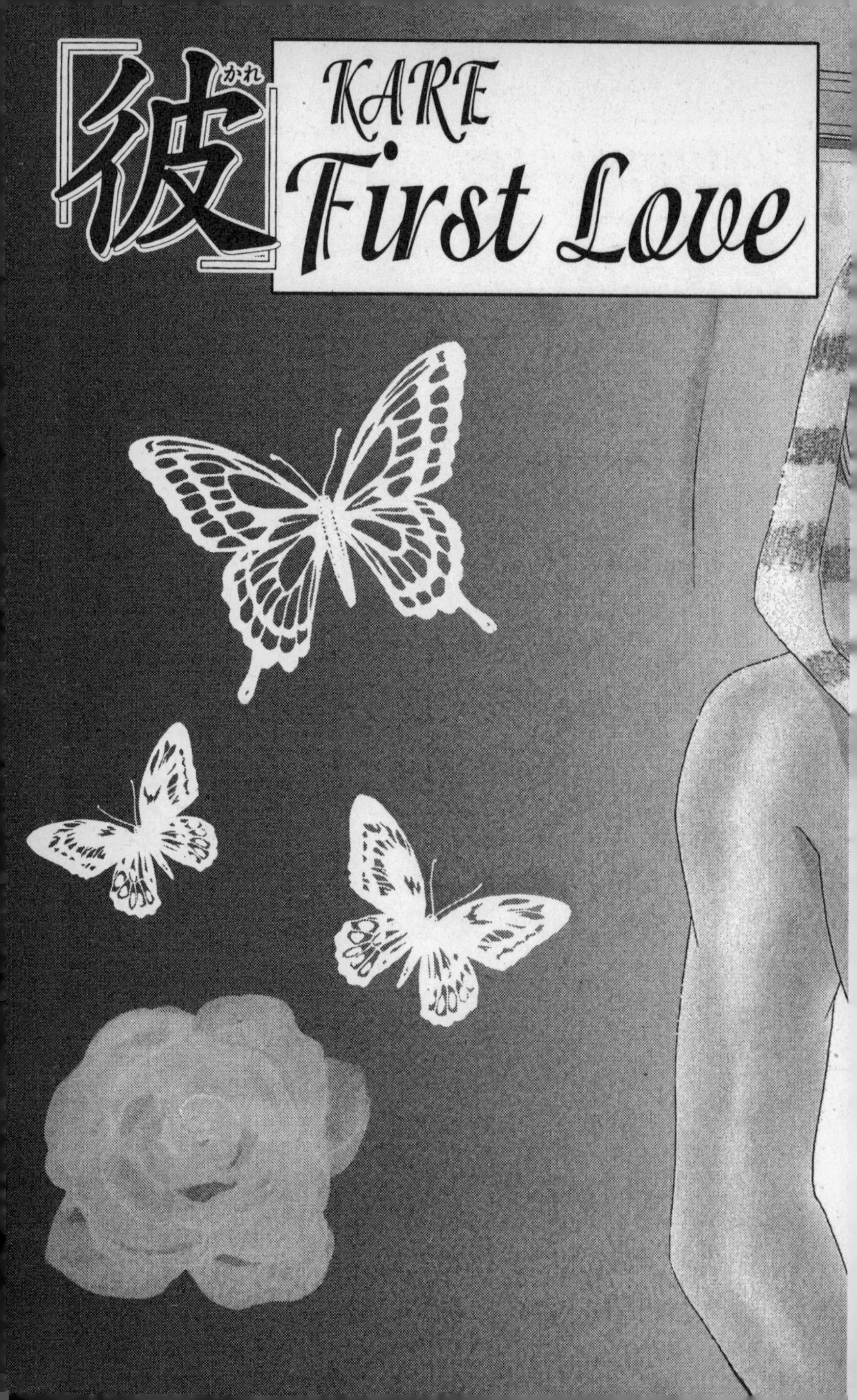
「彼」かれ
KARE
First Love

Characters and Story Digest

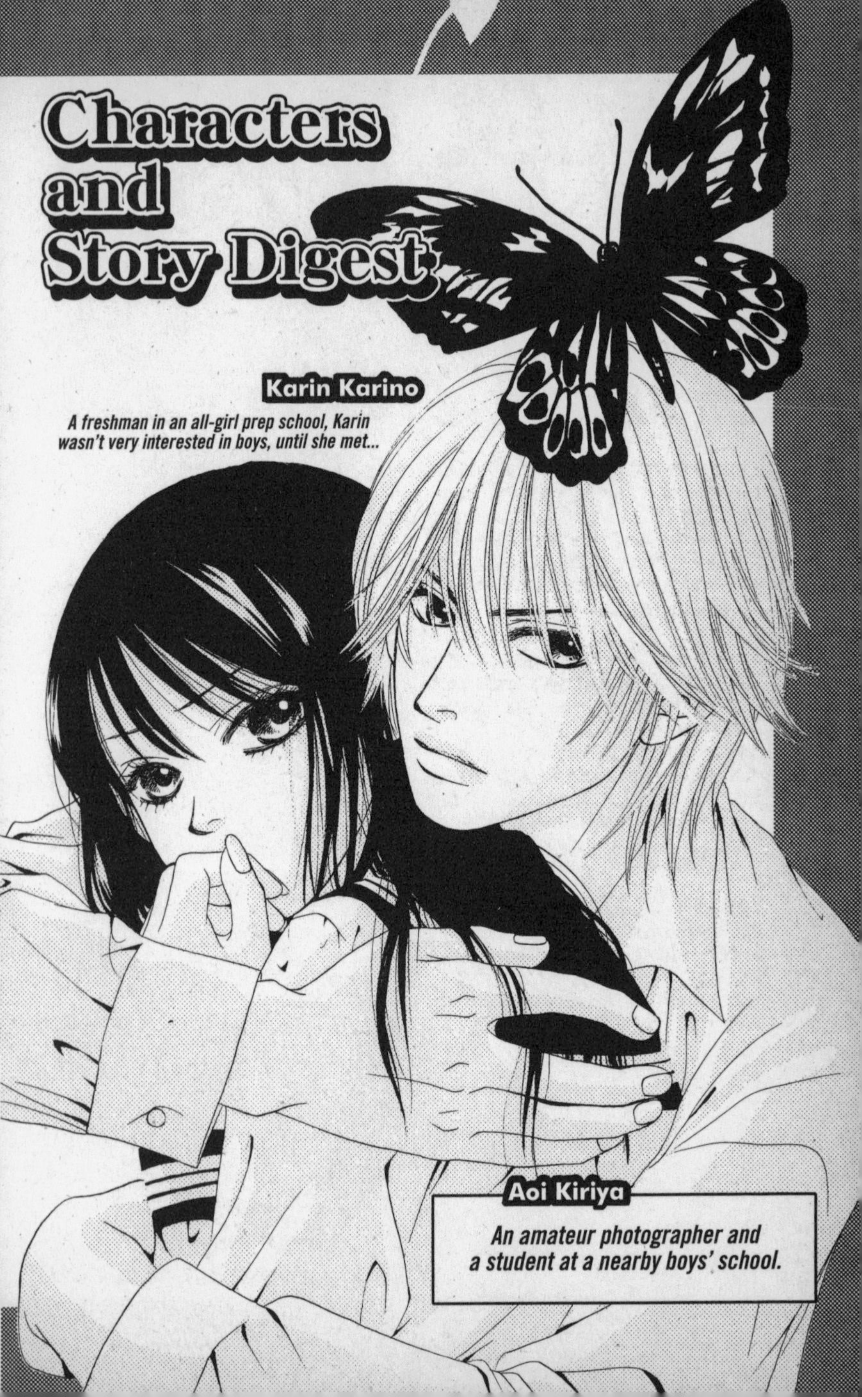

Karin Karino

A freshman in an all-girl prep school, Karin wasn't very interested in boys, until she met...

Aoi Kiriya

An amateur photographer and a student at a nearby boys' school.

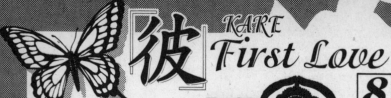

「彼」 KARE First Love 8

Karin chose an all-girls' school because she was never really comfortable around boys. It might not have been bliss, but she managed. Everything changed the morning she met Kiriya and fell in love.

For their first summer vacation together, the two went to Okinawa with their friends and stayed on the same beach where Kiriya's older brother died. They spent the night together, but Karin drank too much to calm her nerves... and the vacation ended with her virginity intact.

When Karin accompanied Kiriya to visit the set of his idol, a photographer and director named Shinji Takagi, some video footage of Karin ended up being used in a TV commercial without her consent. At first this caused a fight between the lovers, but in the end it brought them closer together and they quietly consummated their relationship...

Karin was then asked to model for Shinji again, and once on-set she learned that Shinji's assistant, Saori, was Kiriya's ex-girlfriend. Karin decided to trust Kiriya and move on optimistically, but Saori clearly has a problem with her... Why?!

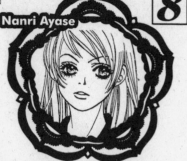

Nanri Ayase

Karin's classmate. She recently broke up with her married boyfriend.

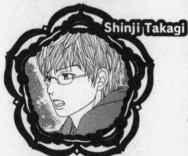

Shinji Takagi

A professional photographer who works in many genres. He was Yuji's colleague.

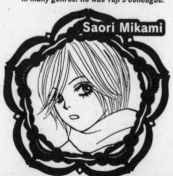

Saori Mikami

Shinji's assistant; she was Kiriya's first girlfriend...

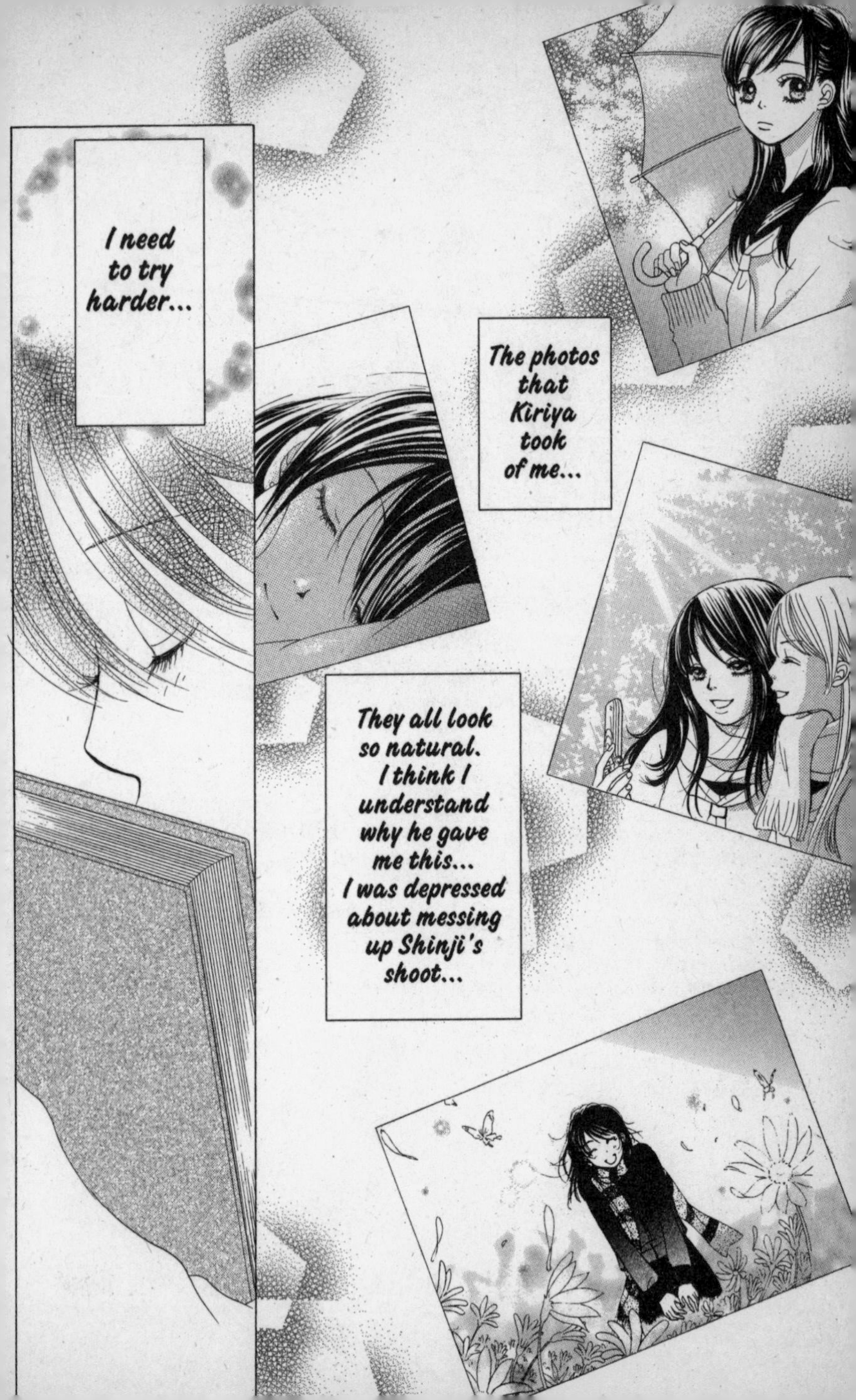
The photos that Kiriya took of me...
They all look so natural. I think I understand why he gave me this... I was depressed about messing up Shinji's shoot...
I need to try harder...

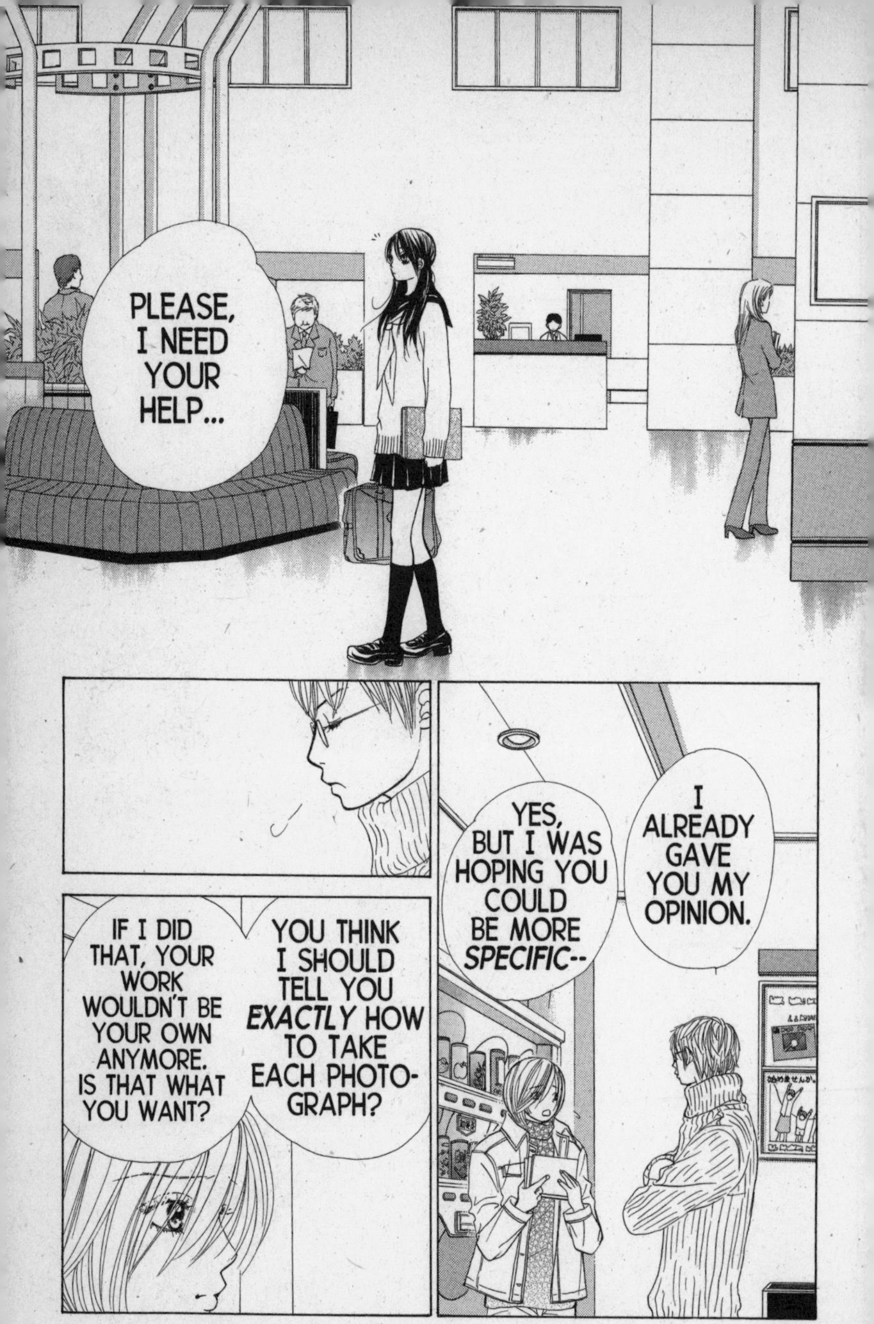
PLEASE, I NEED YOUR HELP...
I ALREADY GAVE YOU MY OPINION.
YES, BUT I WAS HOPING YOU COULD BE MORE *SPECIFIC*--
YOU THINK I SHOULD TELL YOU *EXACTLY* HOW TO TAKE EACH PHOTOGRAPH?
IF I DID THAT, YOUR WORK WOULDN'T BE YOUR OWN ANYMORE. IS THAT WHAT YOU WANT?

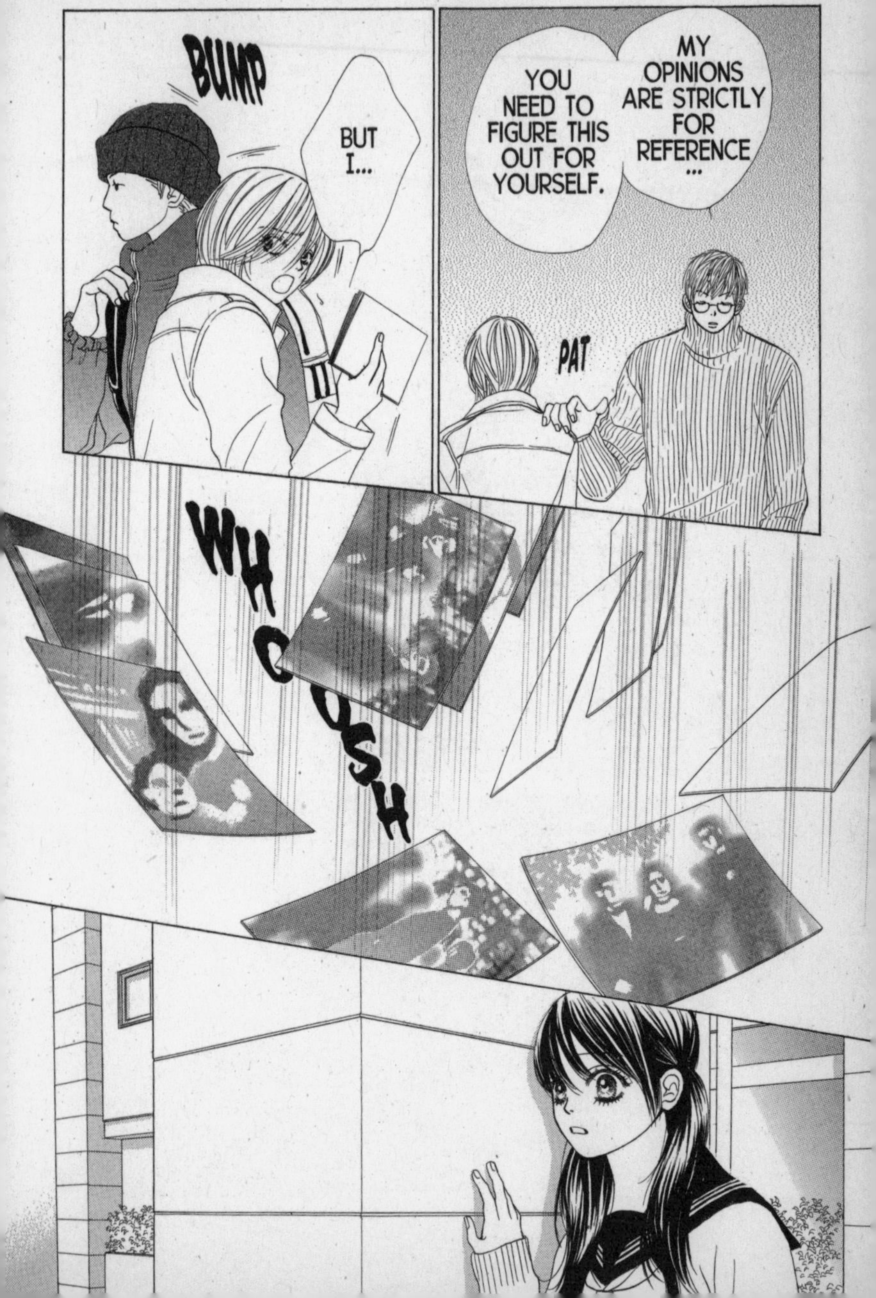
MY OPINIONS ARE STRICTLY FOR REFERENCE ...
YOU NEED TO FIGURE THIS OUT FOR YOURSELF.
PAT
BUT I...
BUMP
WHOOSH

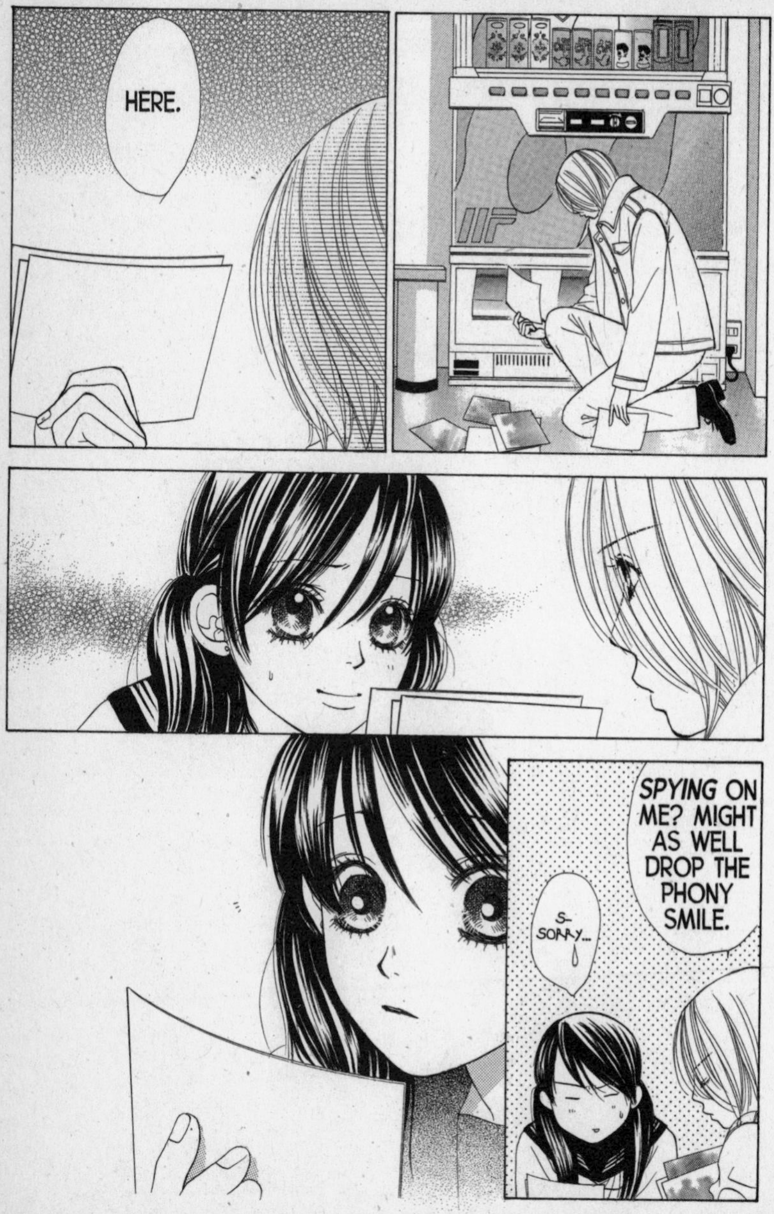
HERE.
SPYING ON ME? MIGHT AS WELL DROP THE PHONY SMILE.
S-SORRY...

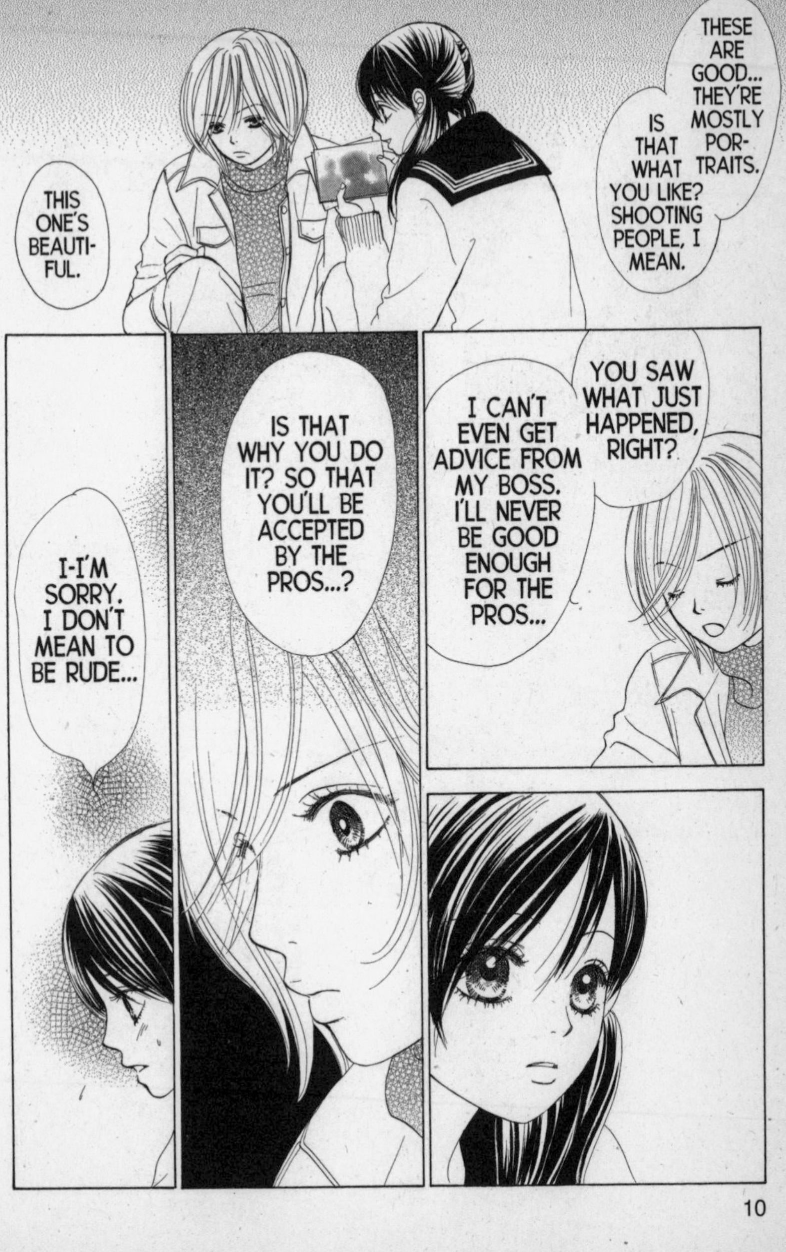
THESE ARE GOOD... THEY'RE MOSTLY POR-TRAITS.
IS THAT WHAT YOU LIKE? SHOOTING PEOPLE, I MEAN.
THIS ONE'S BEAUTI-FUL.
YOU SAW WHAT JUST HAPPENED, RIGHT?
I CAN'T EVEN GET ADVICE FROM MY BOSS. I'LL NEVER BE GOOD ENOUGH FOR THE PROS...
IS THAT WHY YOU DO IT? SO THAT YOU'LL BE ACCEPTED BY THE PROS...?
I-I'M SORRY. I DON'T MEAN TO BE RUDE...

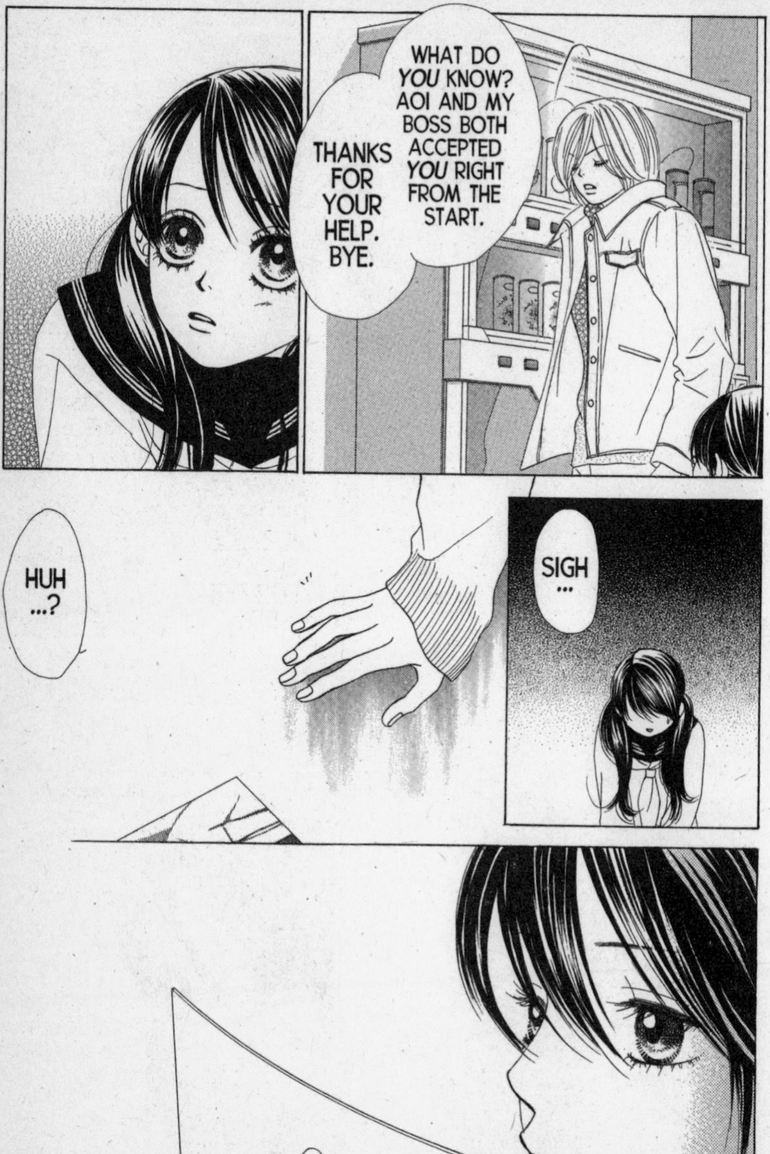
WHAT DO YOU KNOW? AOI AND MY BOSS BOTH ACCEPTED YOU RIGHT FROM THE START.
THANKS FOR YOUR HELP. BYE.
SIGH...
HUH...?

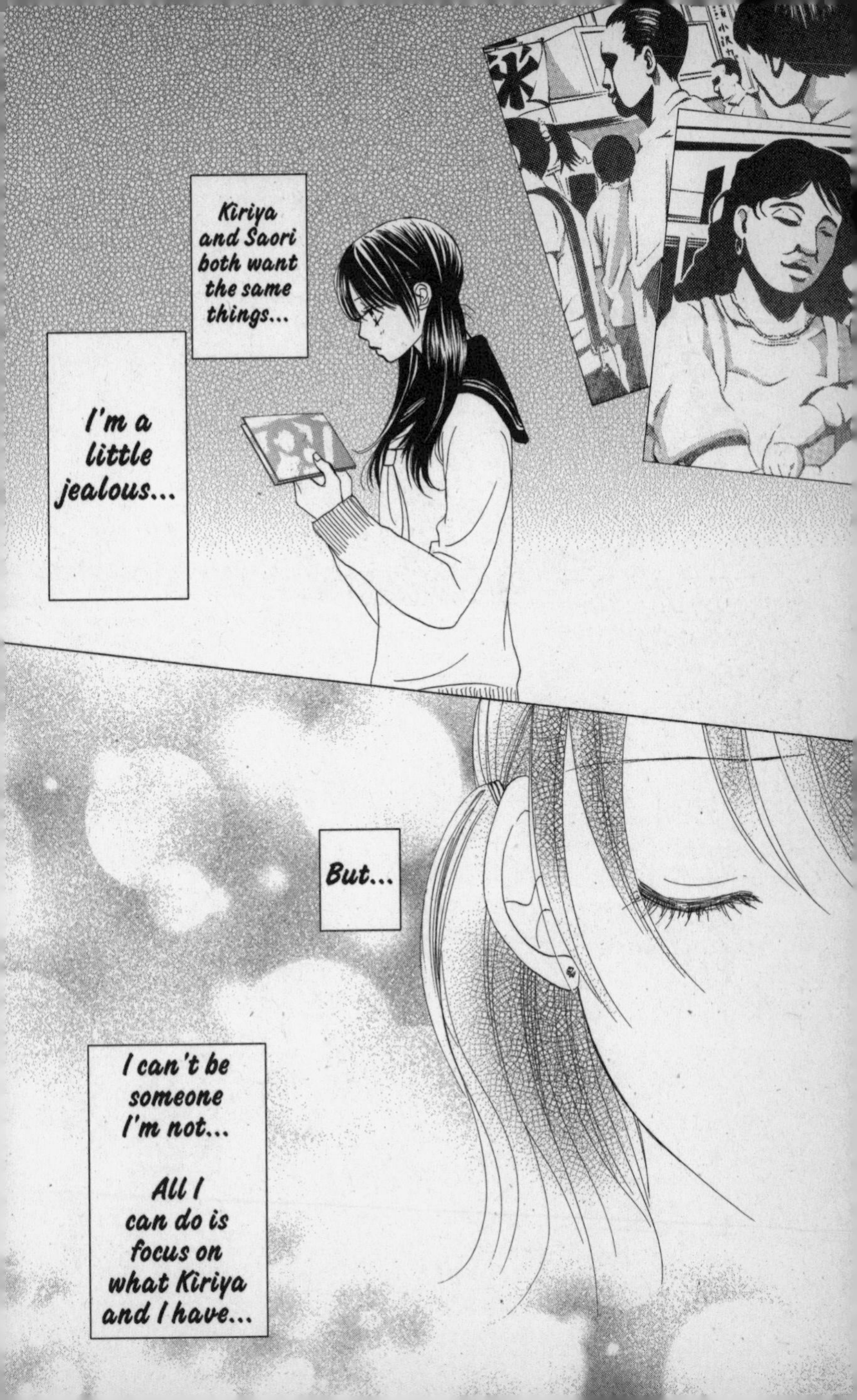

Kiriya and Saori both want the same things...
I'm a little jealous...
But...
I can't be someone I'm not...
All I can do is focus on what Kiriya and I have...

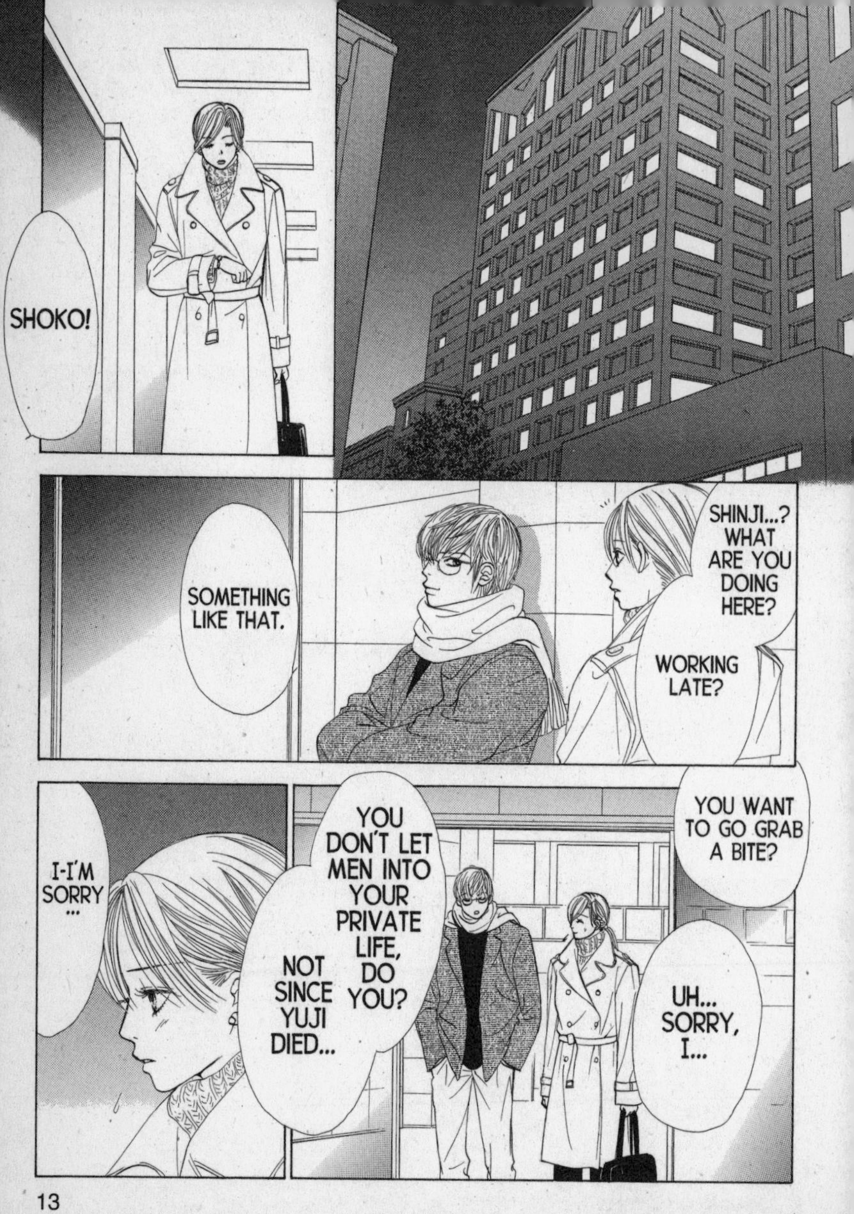
SHOKO!
SHINJI...? WHAT ARE YOU DOING HERE?
WORKING LATE?
SOMETHING LIKE THAT.
YOU WANT TO GO GRAB A BITE?
UH... SORRY, I...
YOU DON'T LET MEN INTO YOUR PRIVATE LIFE, DO YOU?
NOT SINCE YUJI DIED...
I-I'M SORRY...

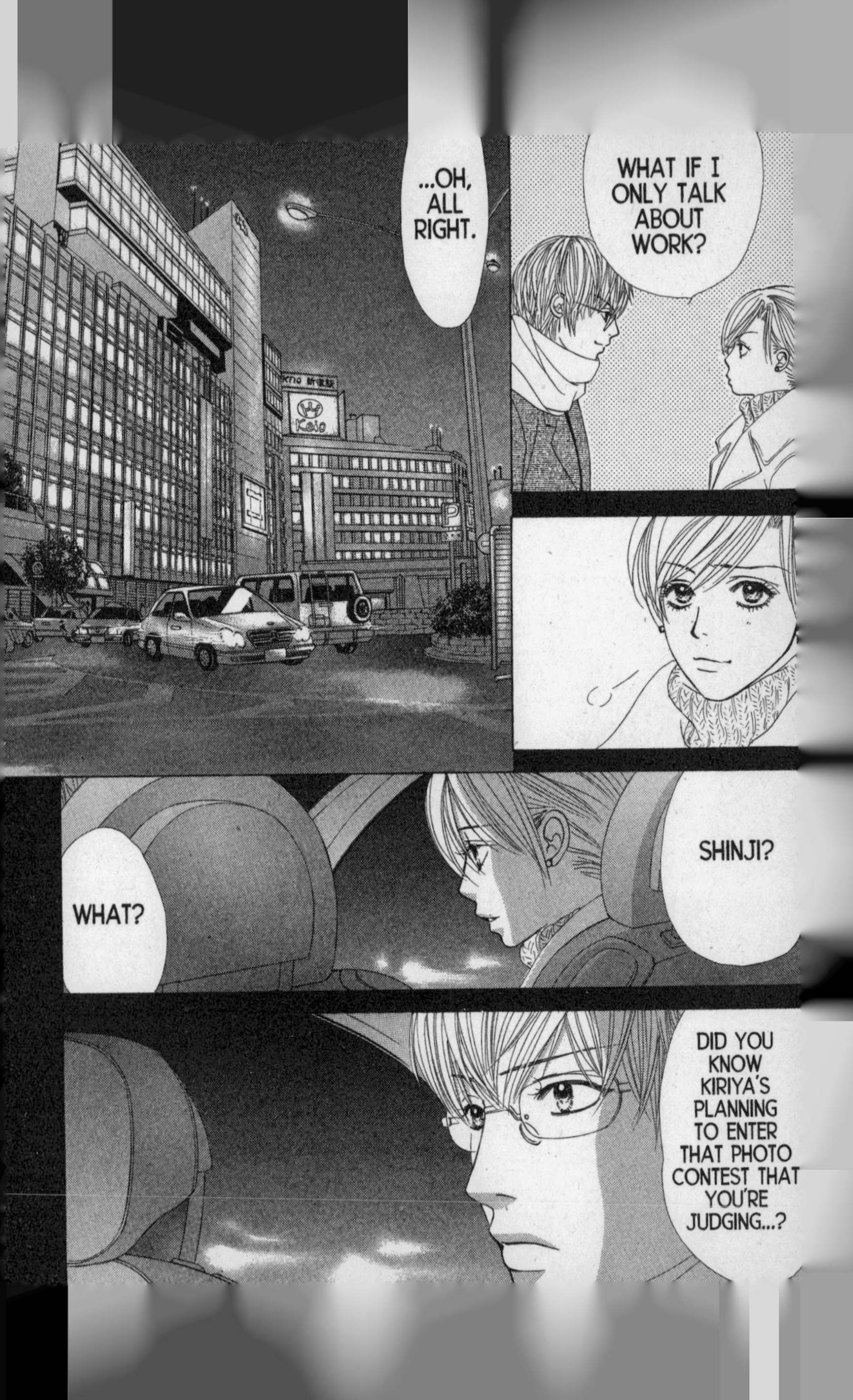
WHAT IF I ONLY TALK ABOUT WORK?
...OH, ALL RIGHT.
Keio
SHINJI?
WHAT?
DID YOU KNOW KIRIYA'S PLANNING TO ENTER THAT PHOTO CONTEST THAT YOU'RE JUDGING...?

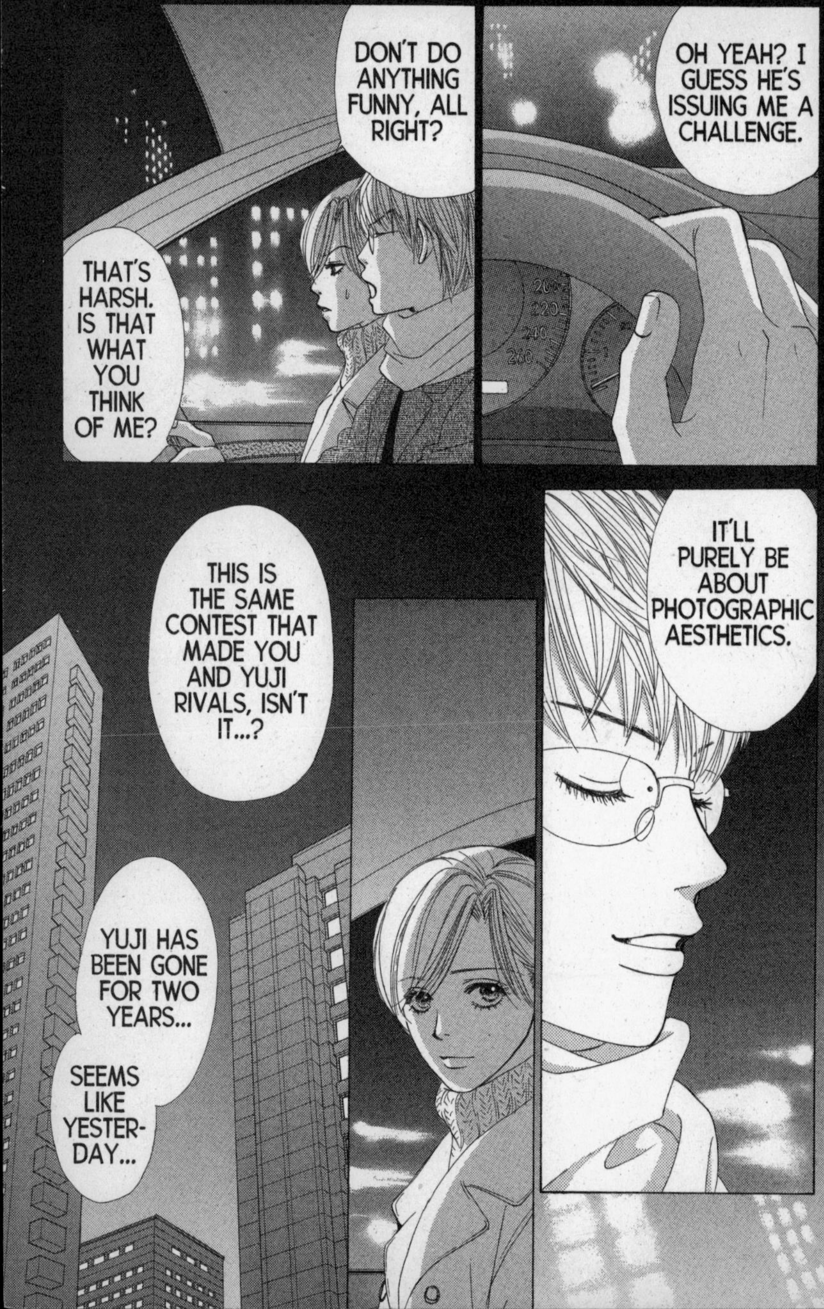
OH YEAH? I GUESS HE'S ISSUING ME A CHALLENGE.
DON'T DO ANYTHING FUNNY, ALL RIGHT?
THAT'S HARSH. IS THAT WHAT YOU THINK OF ME?
IT'LL PURELY BE ABOUT PHOTOGRAPHIC AESTHETICS.
THIS IS THE SAME CONTEST THAT MADE YOU AND YUJI RIVALS, ISN'T IT...?
YUJI HAS BEEN GONE FOR TWO YEARS...
SEEMS LIKE YESTER-DAY...

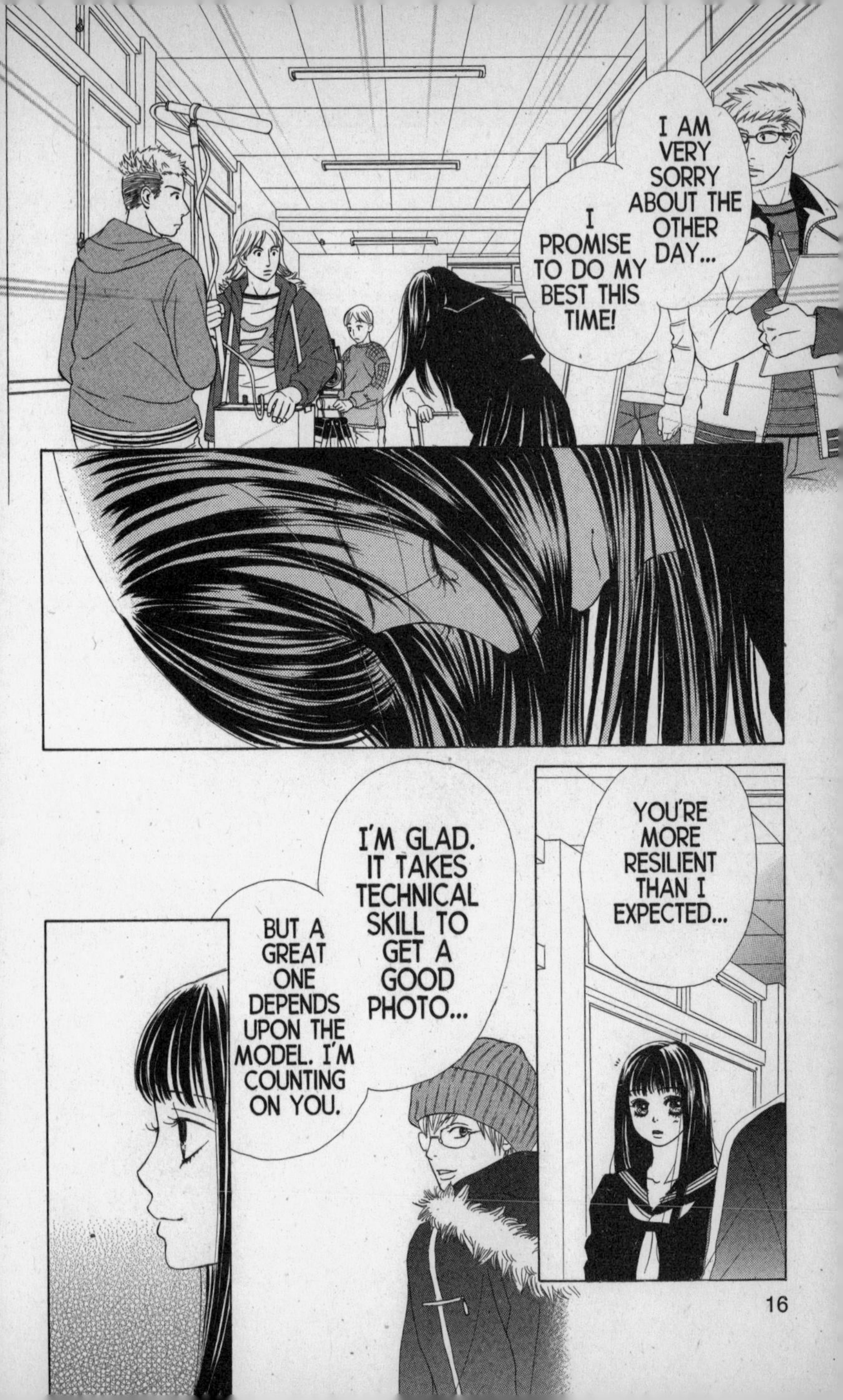
I AM VERY SORRY ABOUT THE OTHER DAY...
I PROMISE TO DO MY BEST THIS TIME!
YOU'RE MORE RESILIENT THAN I EXPECTED...
I'M GLAD. IT TAKES TECHNICAL SKILL TO GET A GOOD PHOTO...
BUT A GREAT ONE DEPENDS UPON THE MODEL. I'M COUNTING ON YOU.

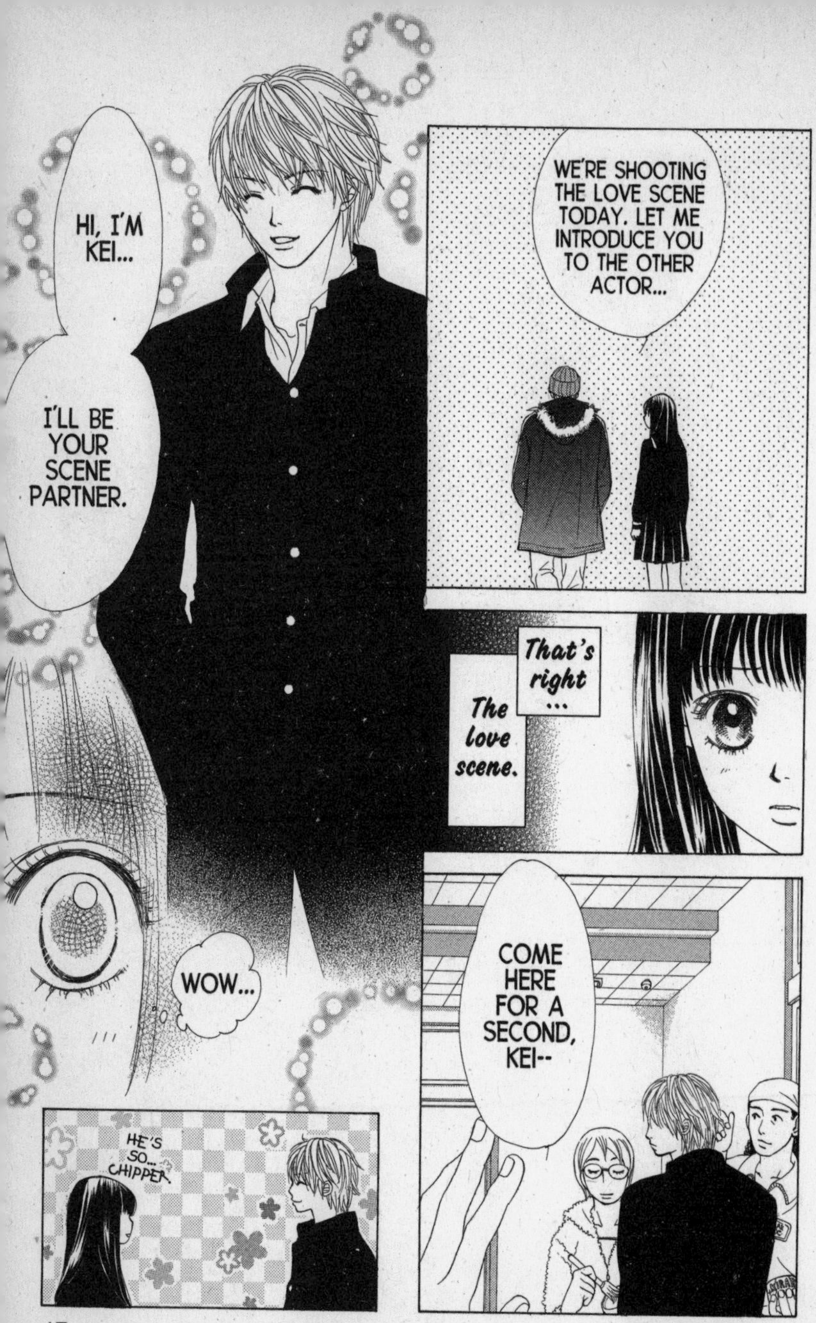
WE'RE SHOOTING THE LOVE SCENE TODAY. LET ME INTRODUCE YOU TO THE OTHER ACTOR...
That's right...
The love scene.
COME HERE FOR A SECOND, KEI--
HI, I'M KEI...
I'LL BE YOUR SCENE PARTNER.
WOW...
HE'S SO... CHIPPER.

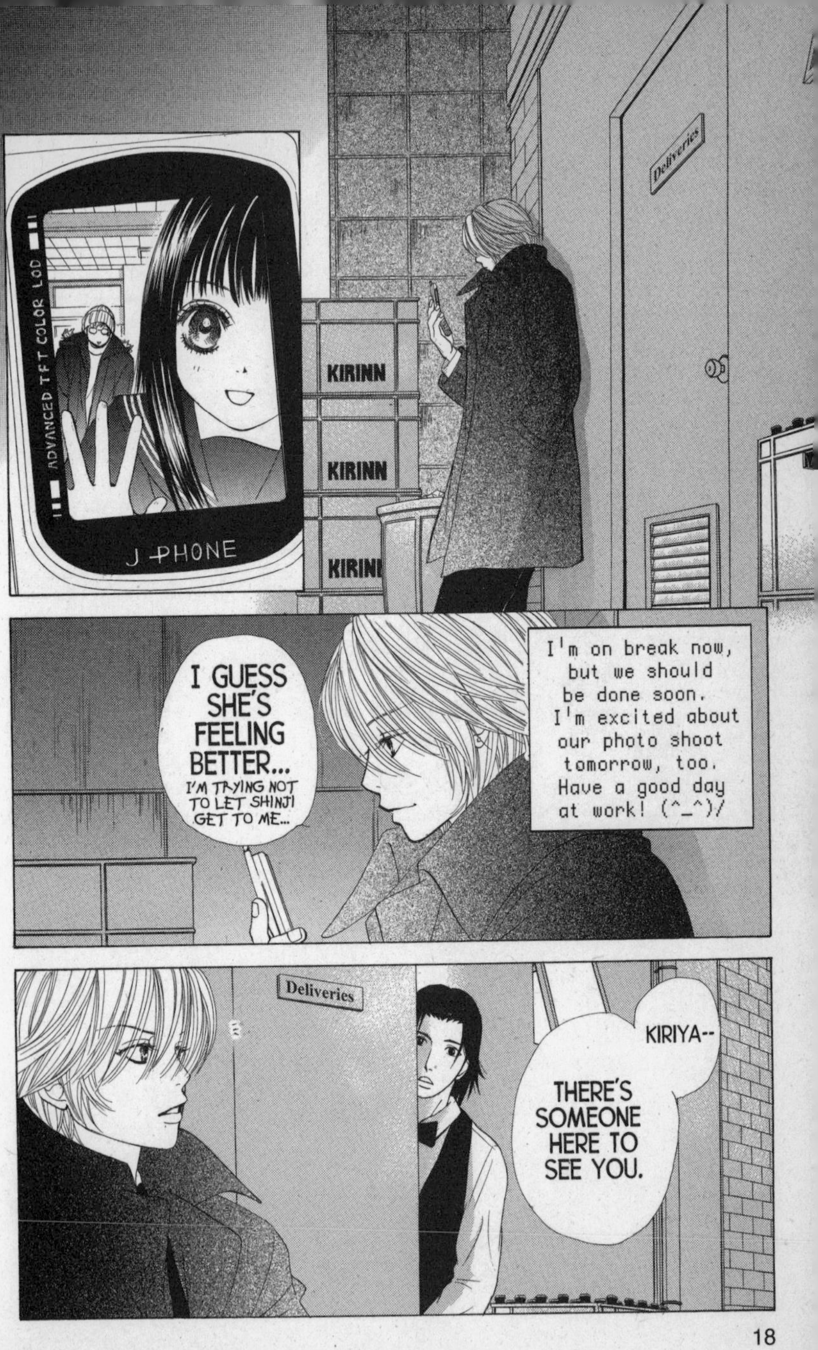
Deliveries
KIRINN
KIRINN
ADVANCED TFT COLOR LCD
J-PHONE
I'm on break now, but we should be done soon. I'm excited about our photo shoot tomorrow, too. Have a good day at work! (^_^)/
I GUESS SHE'S FEELING BETTER...
I'M TRYING NOT TO LET SHINJI GET TO ME...
KIRIYA--
THERE'S SOMEONE HERE TO SEE YOU.
Deliveries

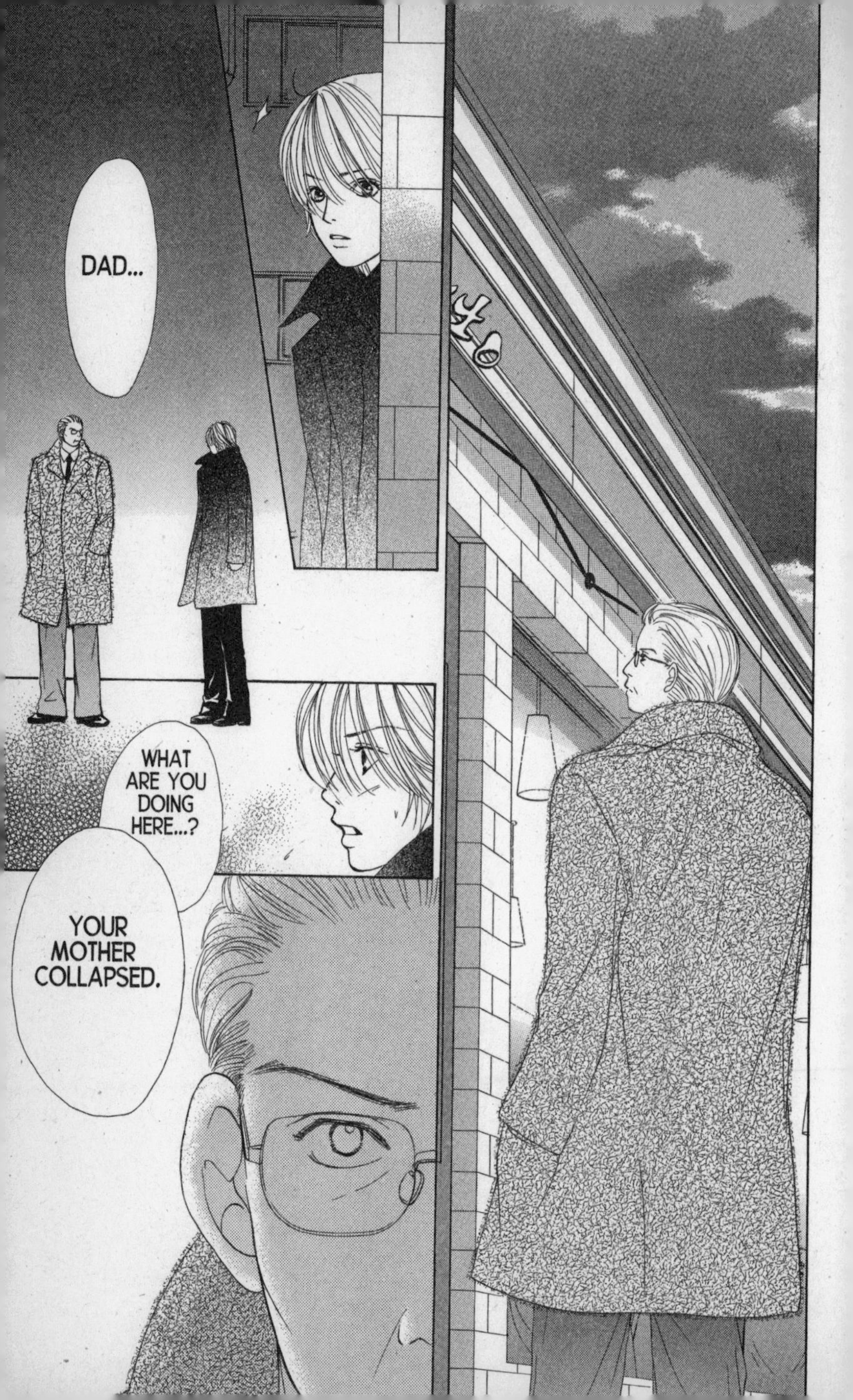
DAD...
WHAT ARE YOU DOING HERE...?
YOUR MOTHER COLLAPSED.

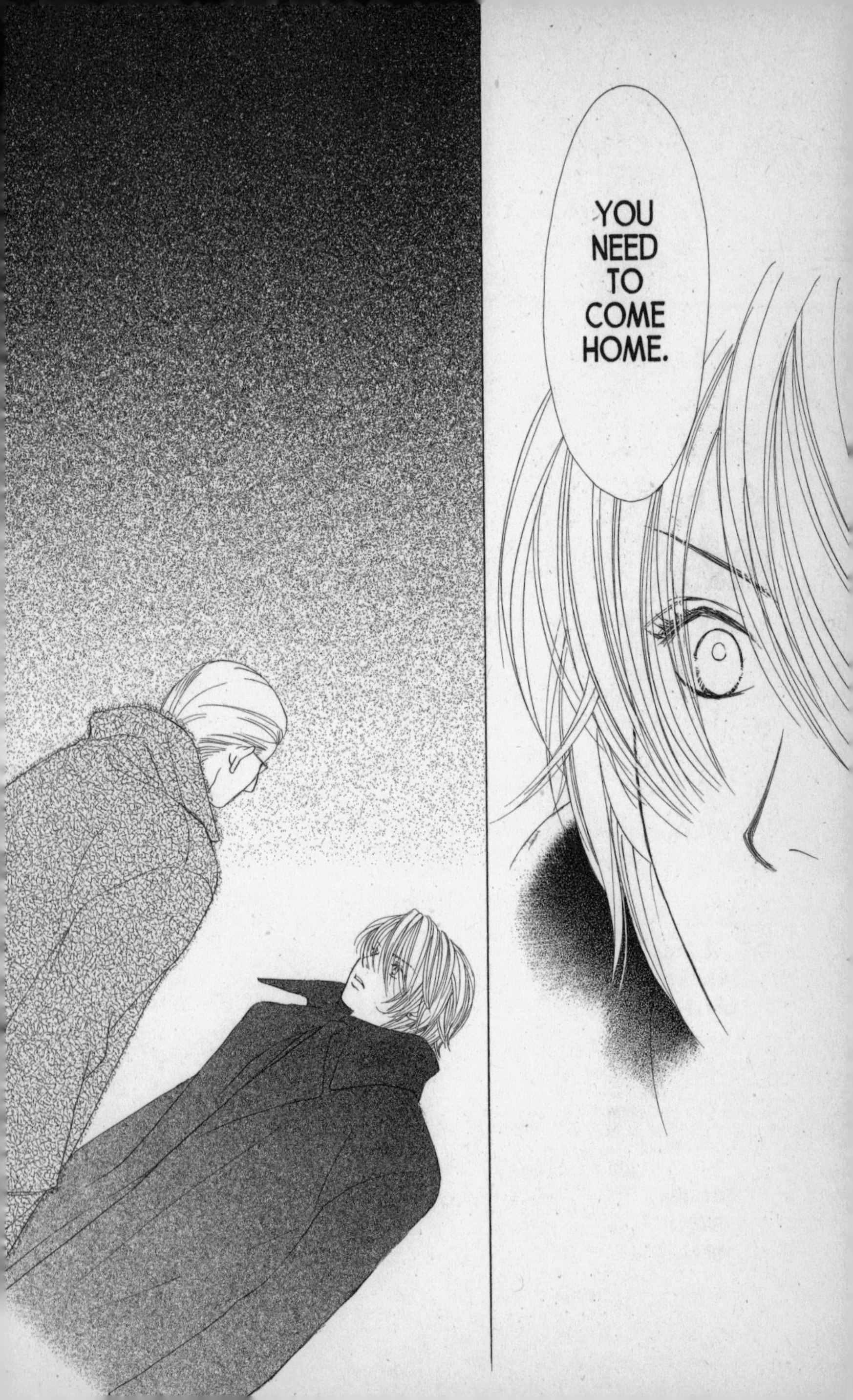
YOU NEED TO COME HOME.

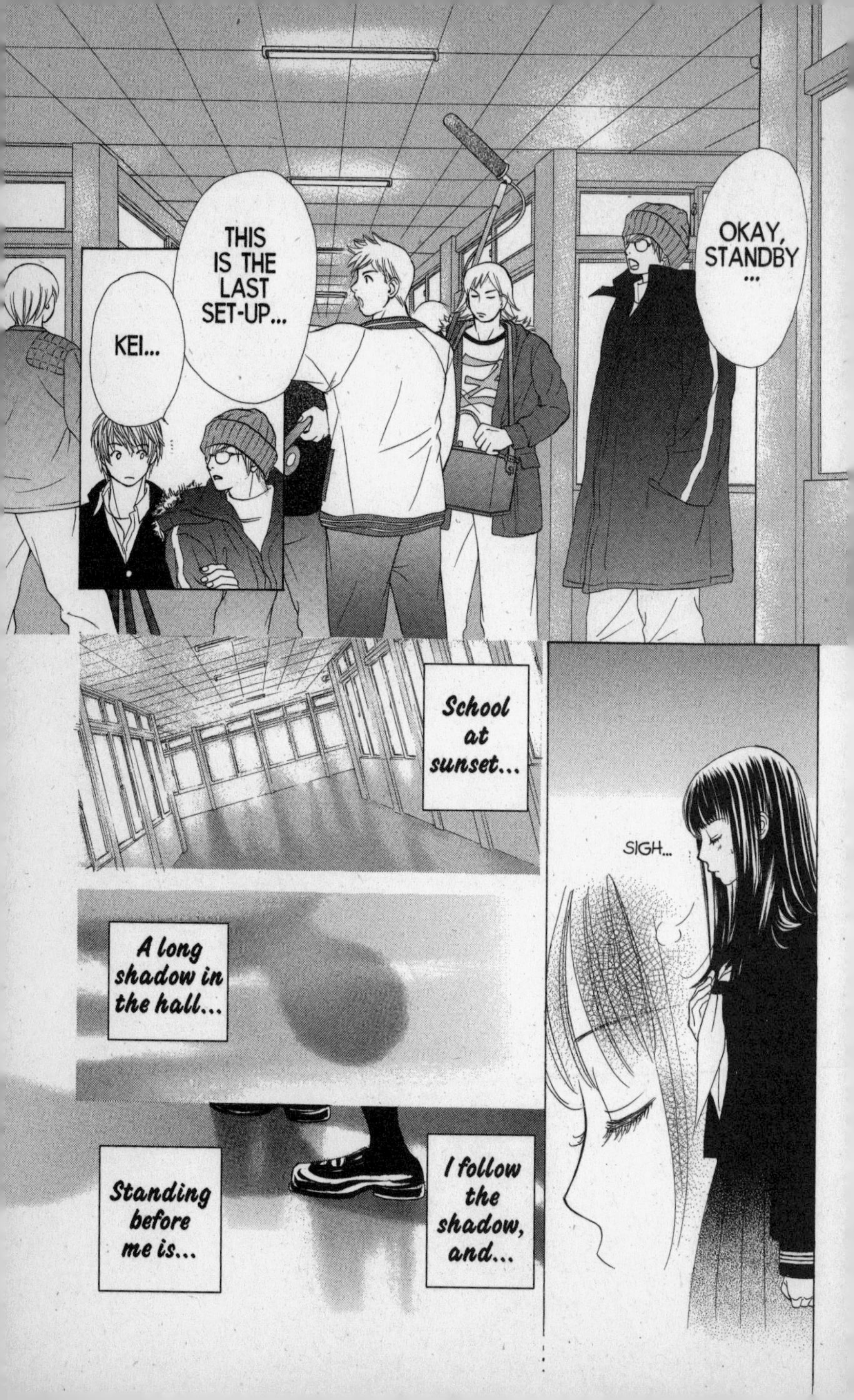
OKAY, STANDBY...
THIS IS THE LAST SET-UP...
KEI...
SIGH...
School at sunset...
A long shadow in the hall...
I follow the shadow, and...
Standing before me is...

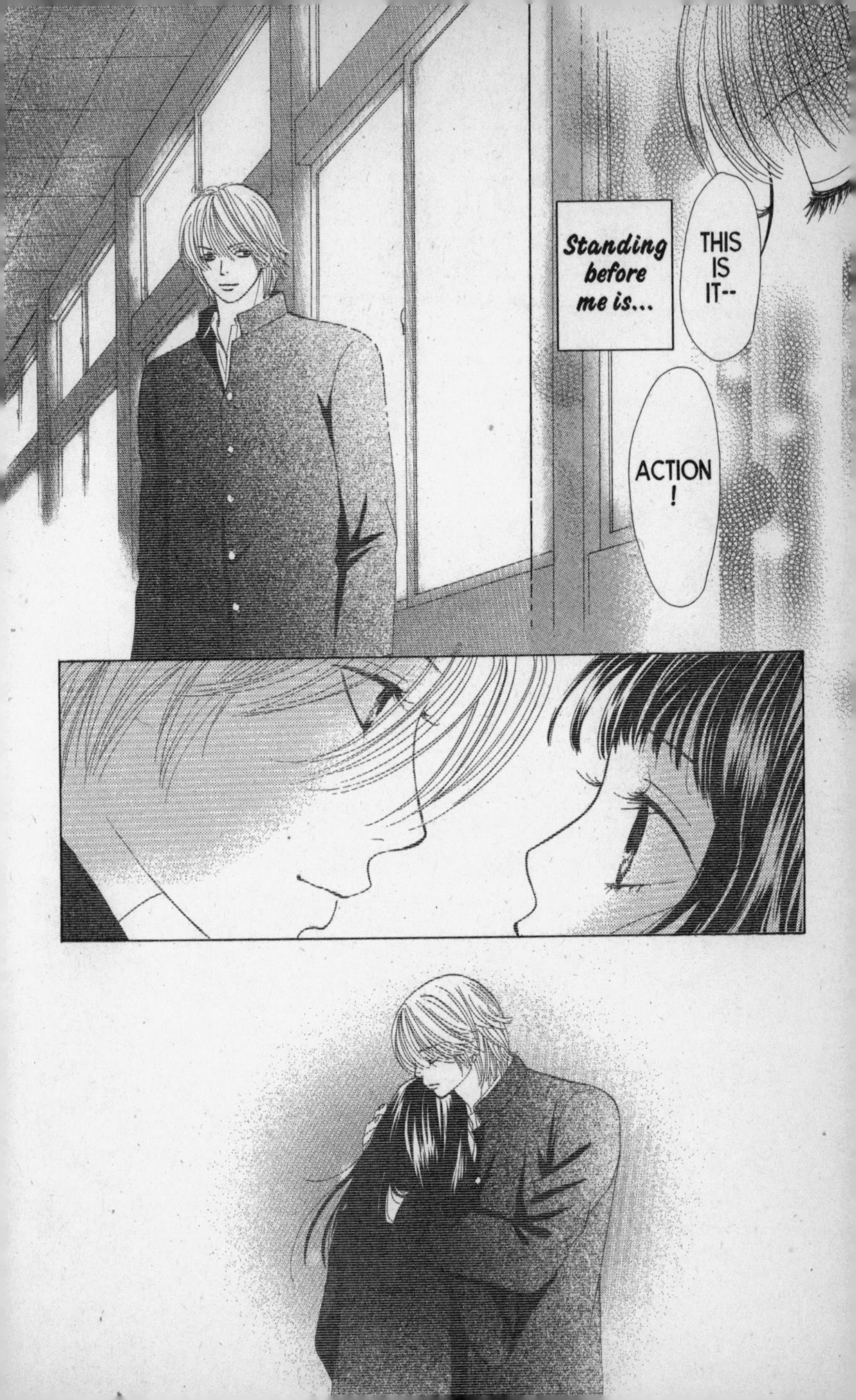
THIS IS IT--
ACTION!
Standing before me is...

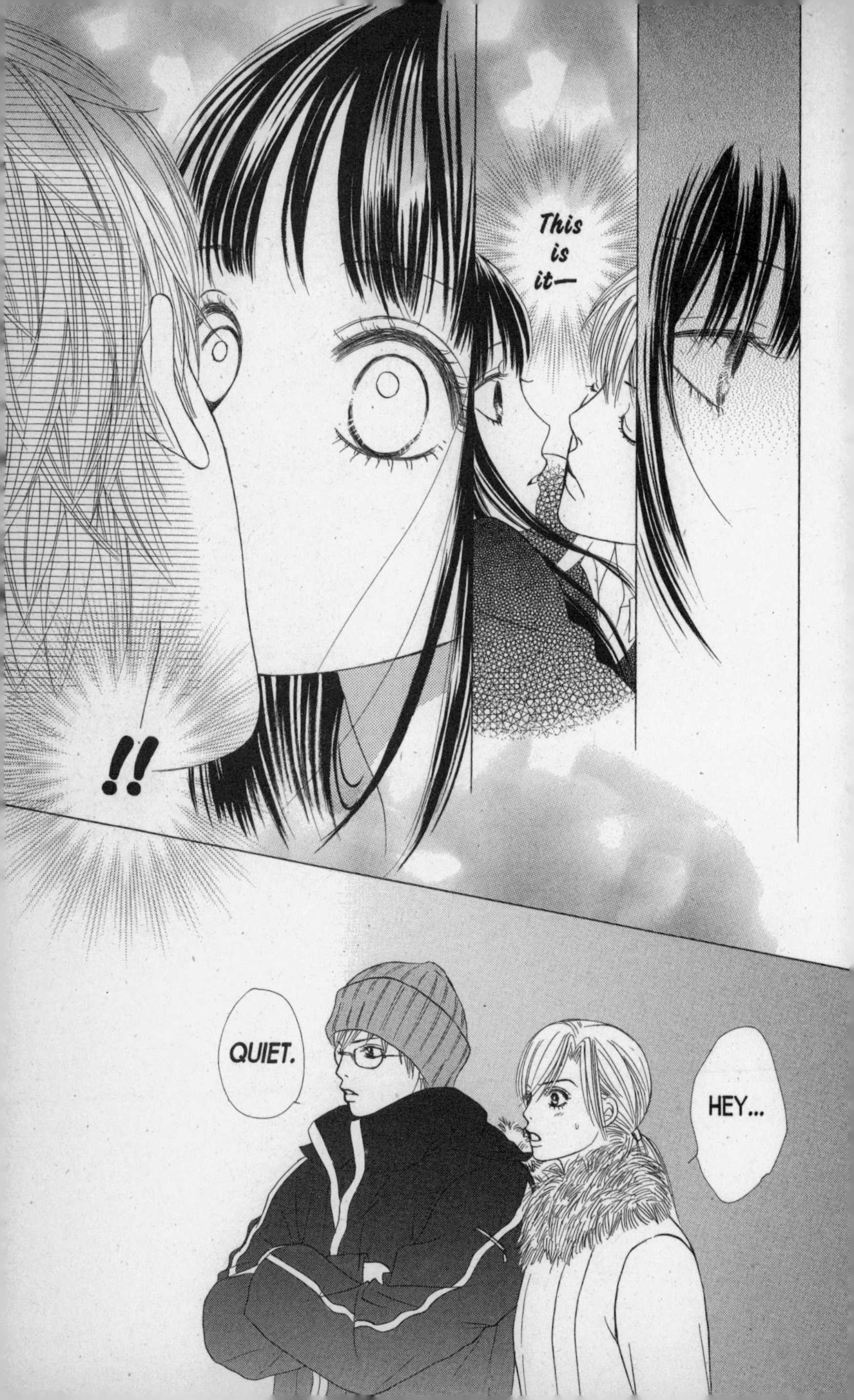
This is it—
!!
HEY...
QUIET.

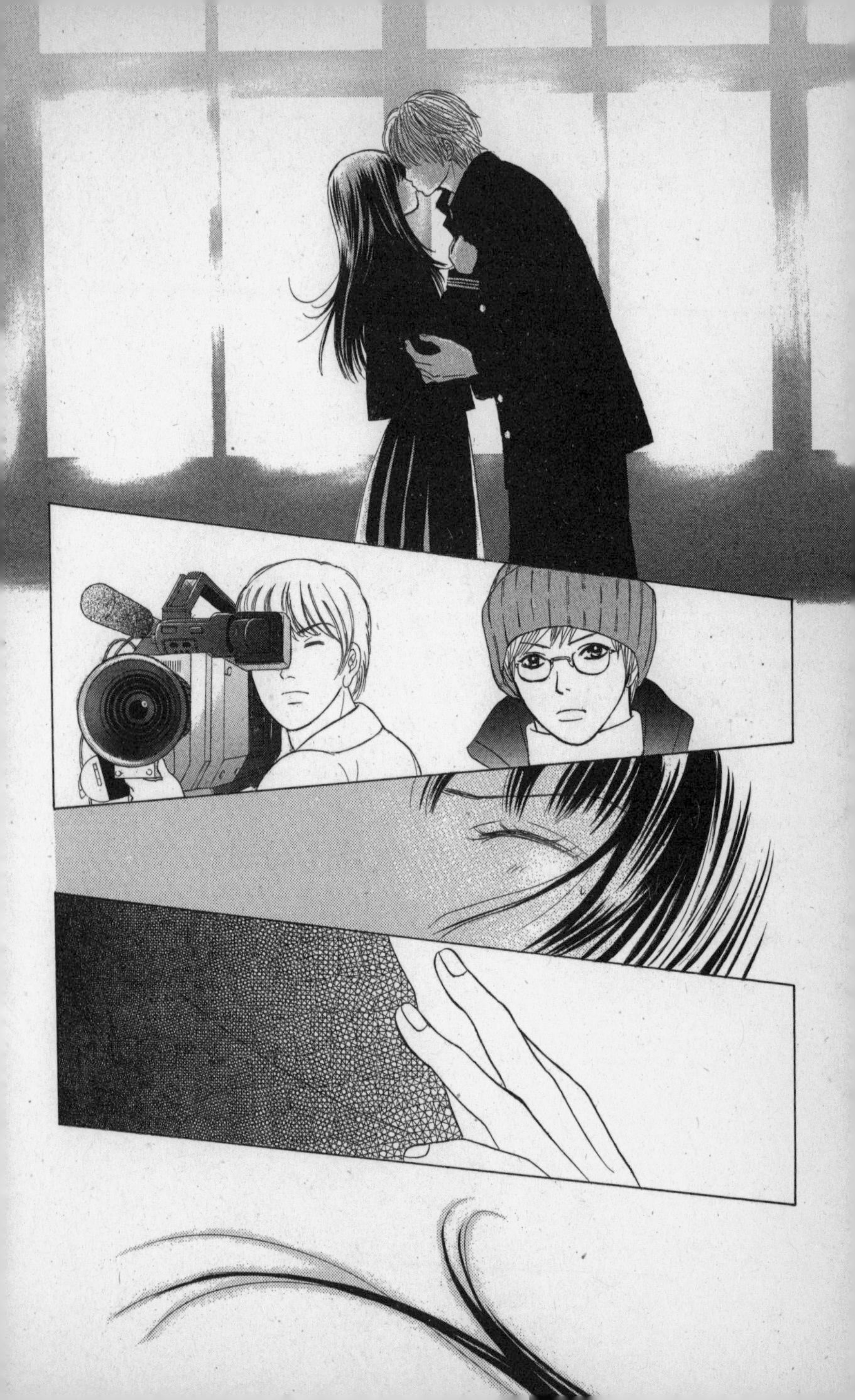

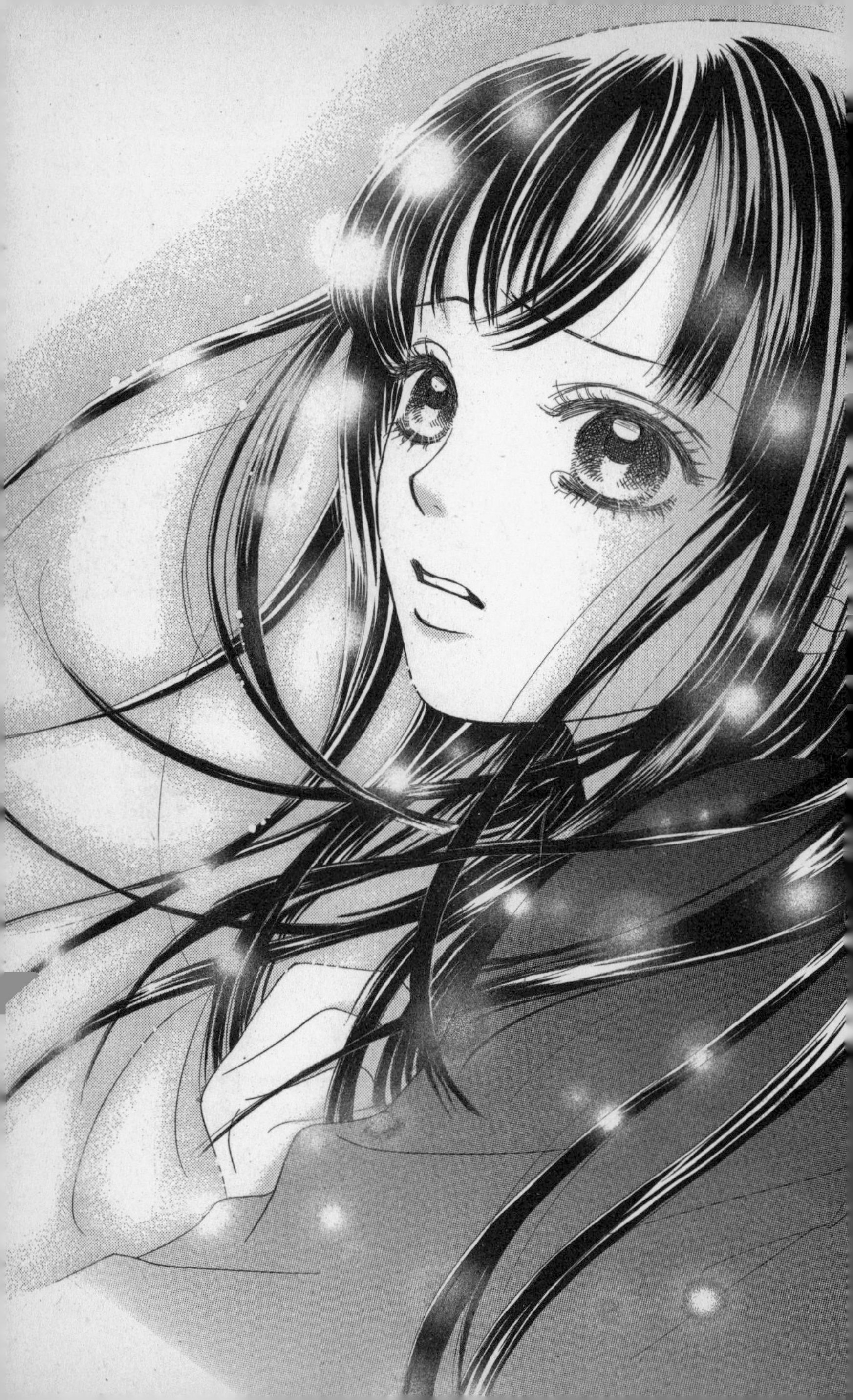

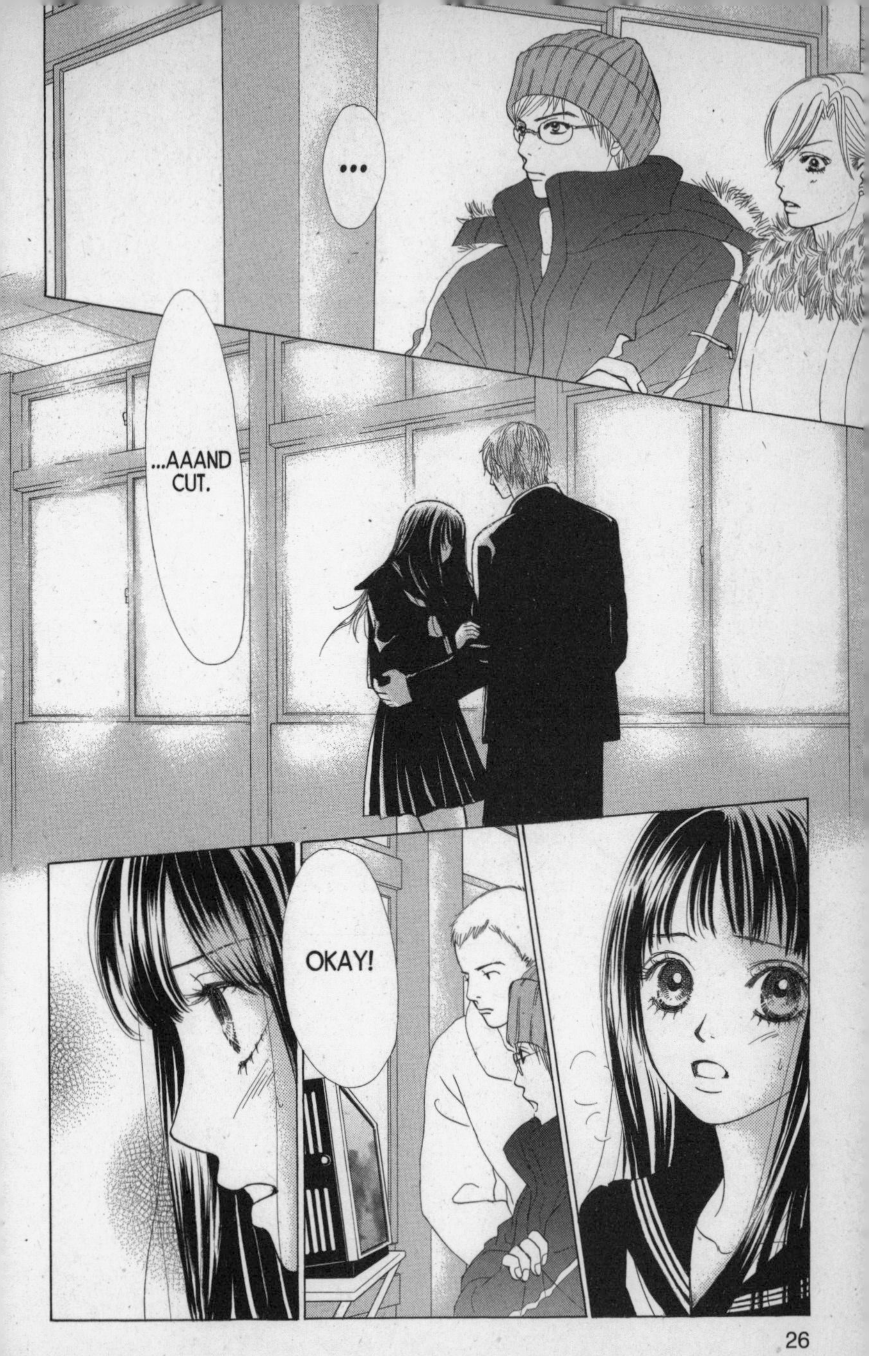
...
...AAAND CUT.
OKAY!

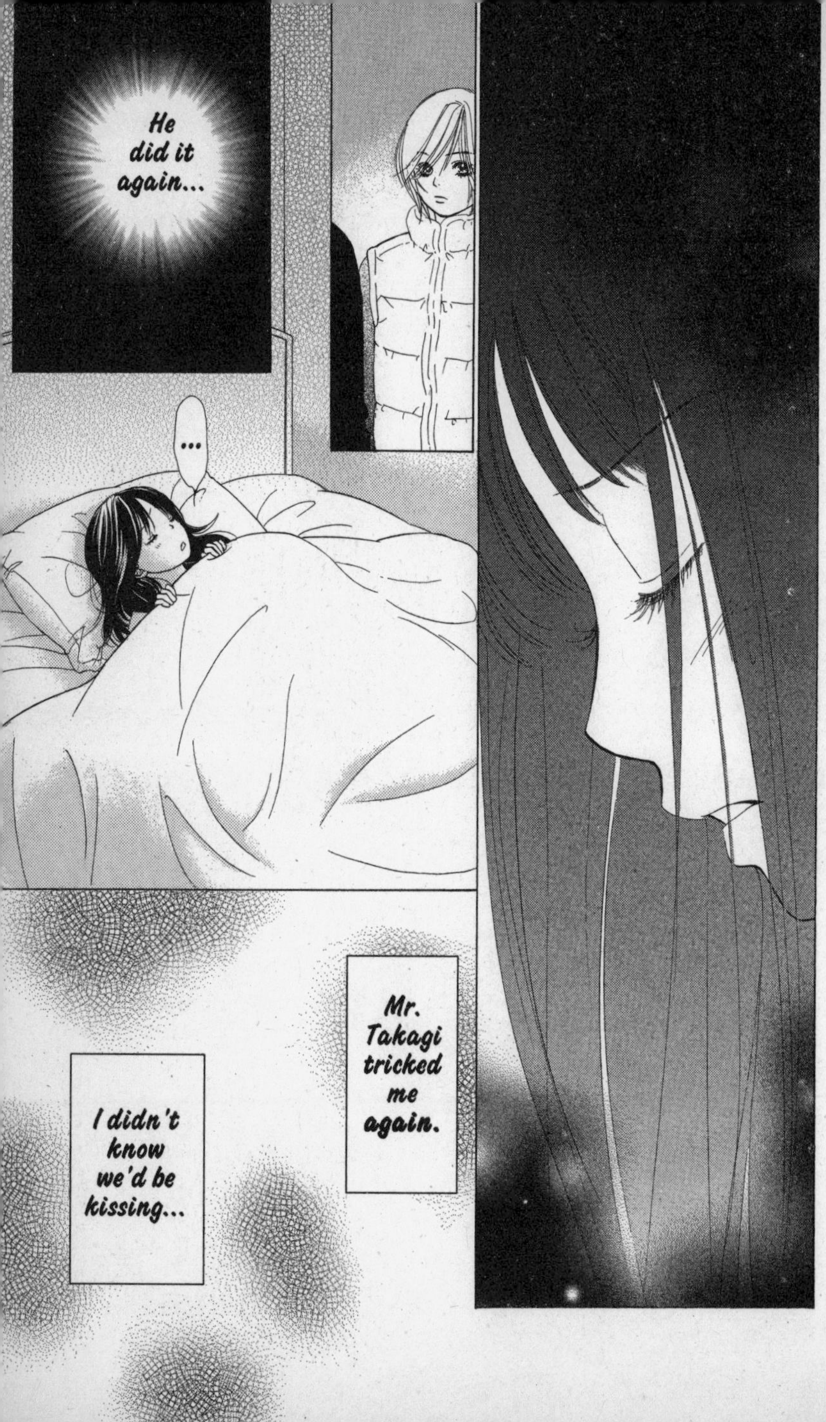
He did it again...
...
Mr. Takagi tricked me again.
I didn't know we'd be kissing...

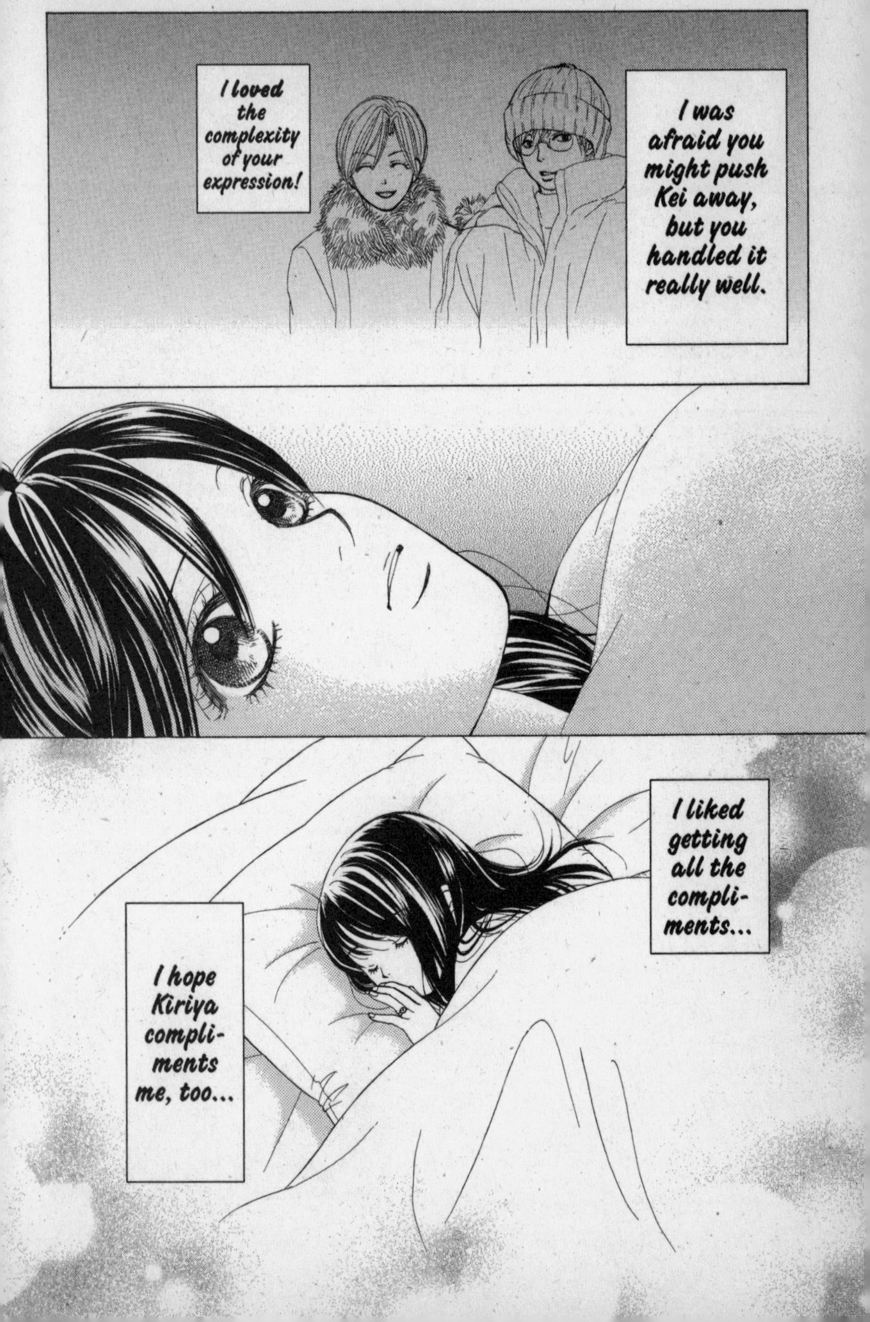
I was afraid you might push Kei away, but you handled it really well.
I loved the complexity of your expression!
I liked getting all the compli-ments...
I hope Kiriya compli-ments me, too...

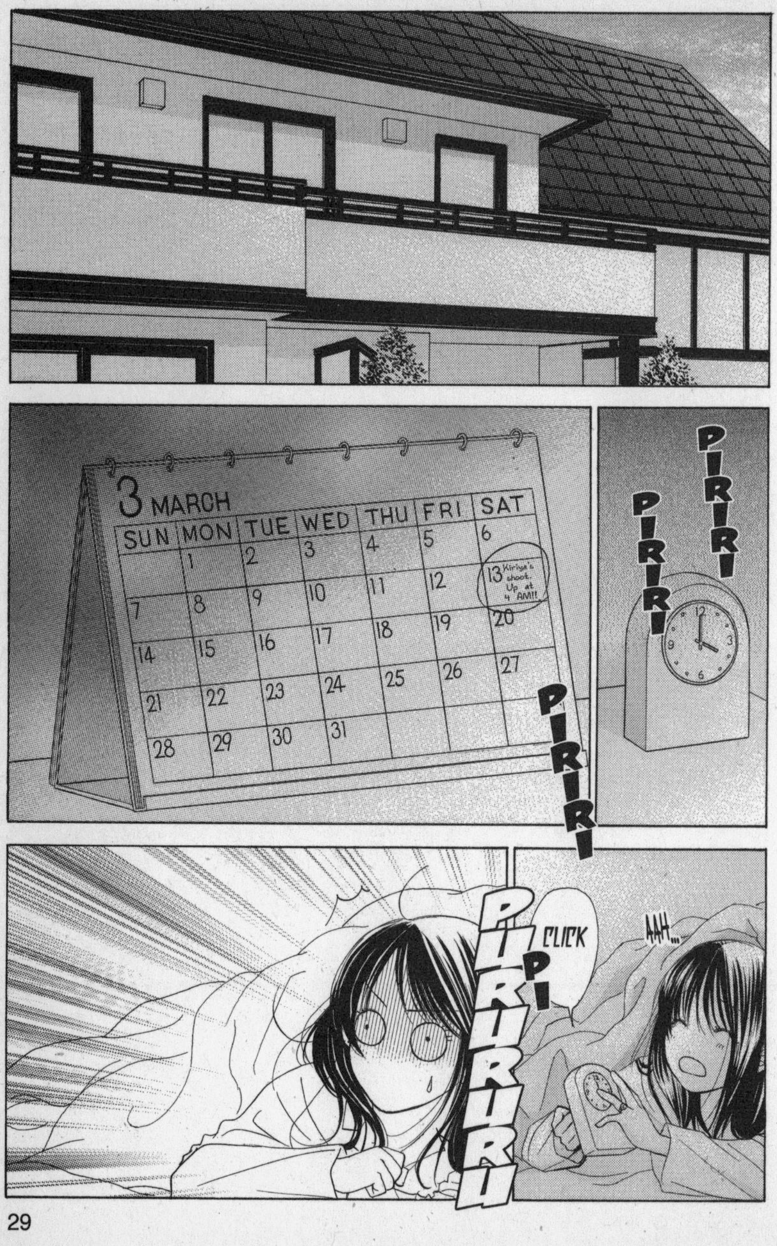
PIRIRI
PIRIRI
3 MARCH
SUN MON TUE WED THU FRI SAT
13 Kiriya's shoot. Up at 4 AM!!
PIRIRI
AAH...
PIRURURURU
CLICK
PI

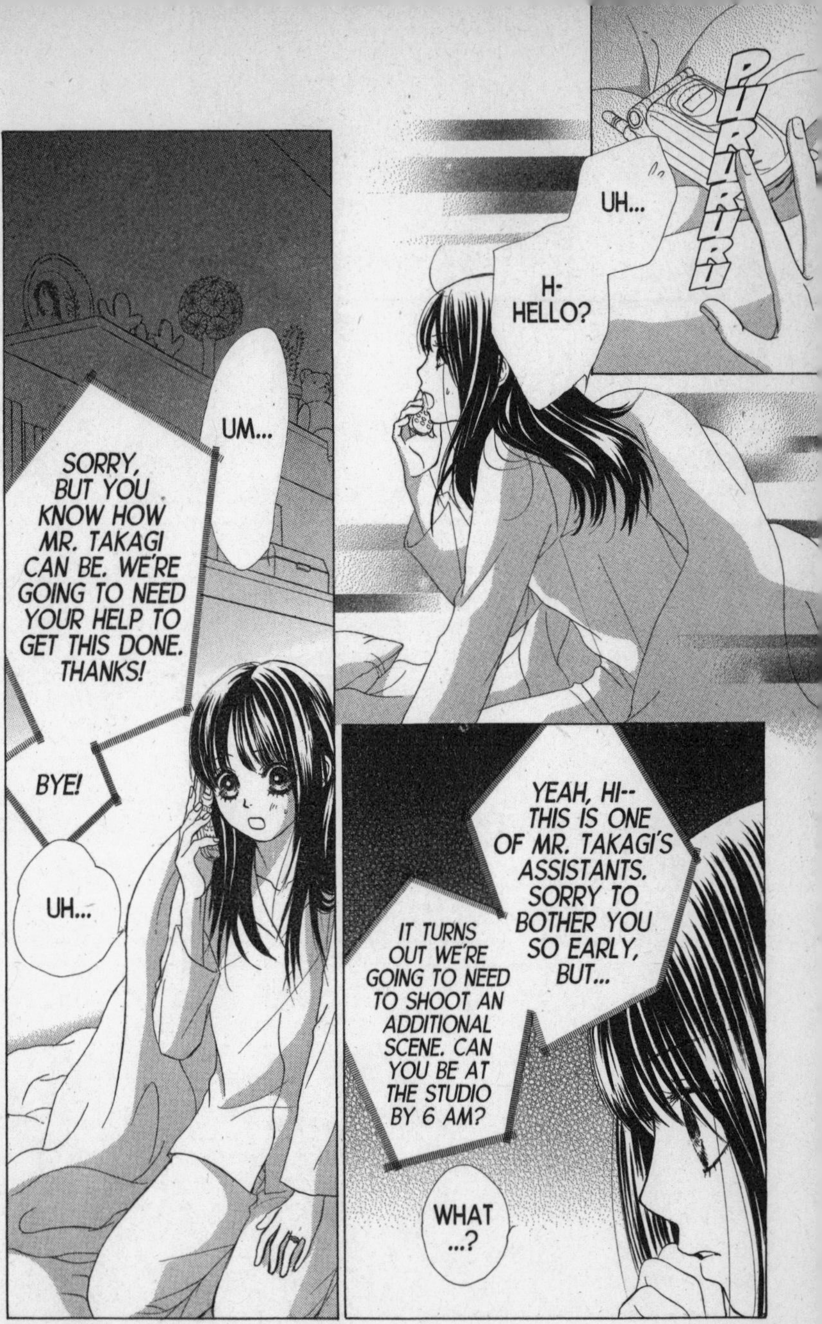
PURURURU
UH...
H-HELLO?
YEAH, HI-- THIS IS ONE OF MR. TAKAGI'S ASSISTANTS. SORRY TO BOTHER YOU SO EARLY, BUT...
IT TURNS OUT WE'RE GOING TO NEED TO SHOOT AN ADDITIONAL SCENE. CAN YOU BE AT THE STUDIO BY 6 AM?
WHAT ...?
UM...
SORRY, BUT YOU KNOW HOW MR. TAKAGI CAN BE. WE'RE GOING TO NEED YOUR HELP TO GET THIS DONE. THANKS!
BYE!
UH...

But Kiriya's shoot is today...

ED	THU	FRI	SAT
	4	5	6
	11	12	13 *Kiriya's shoot. Up at 4 AM!!*
	18	19	20
	25	26	27

RRRR—

...

PERFECT.

HOW WAS THAT?

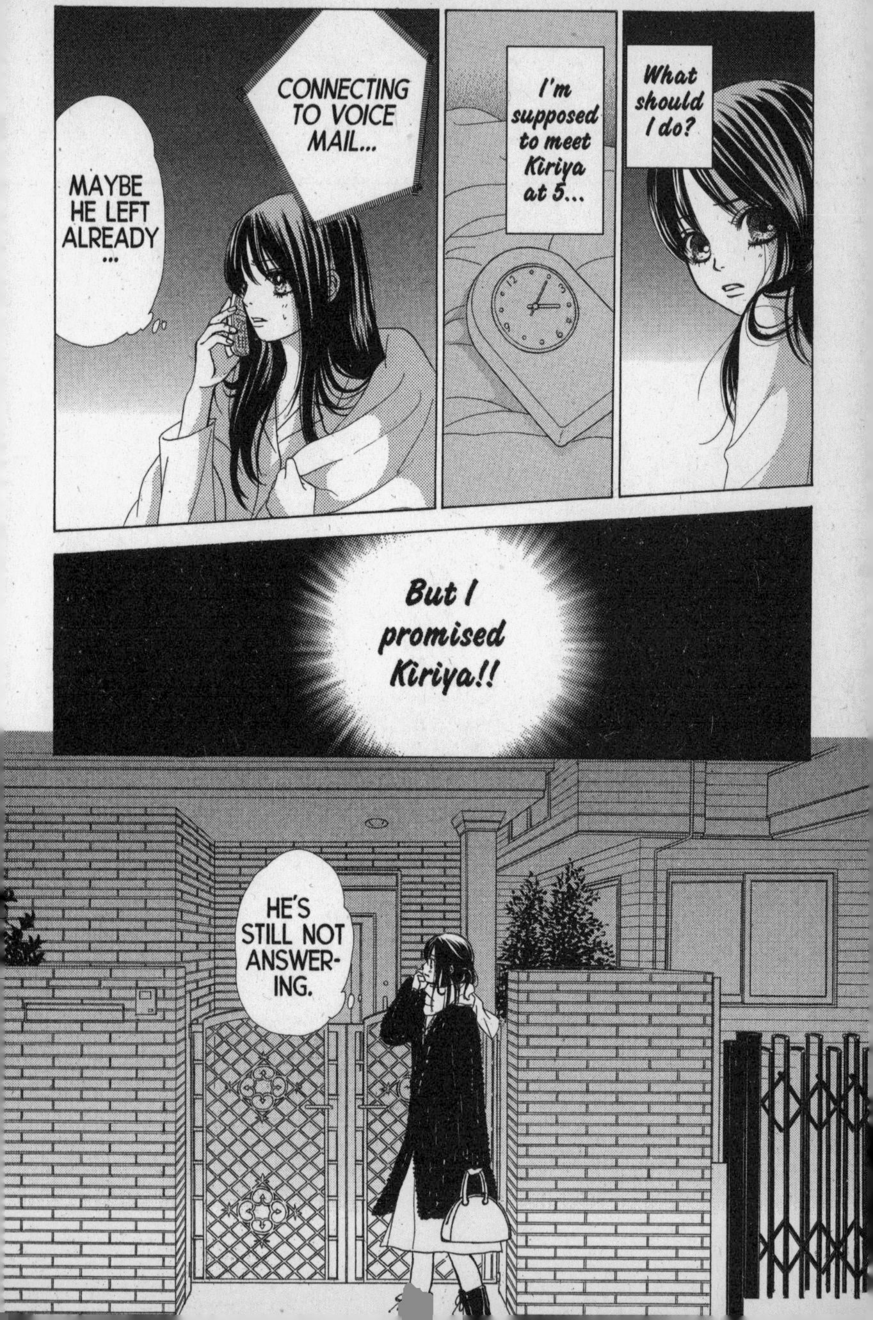
What should I do?
I'm supposed to meet Kiriya at 5...
CONNECTING TO VOICE MAIL...
MAYBE HE LEFT ALREADY...
But I promised Kiriya!!
HE'S STILL NOT ANSWER-ING.

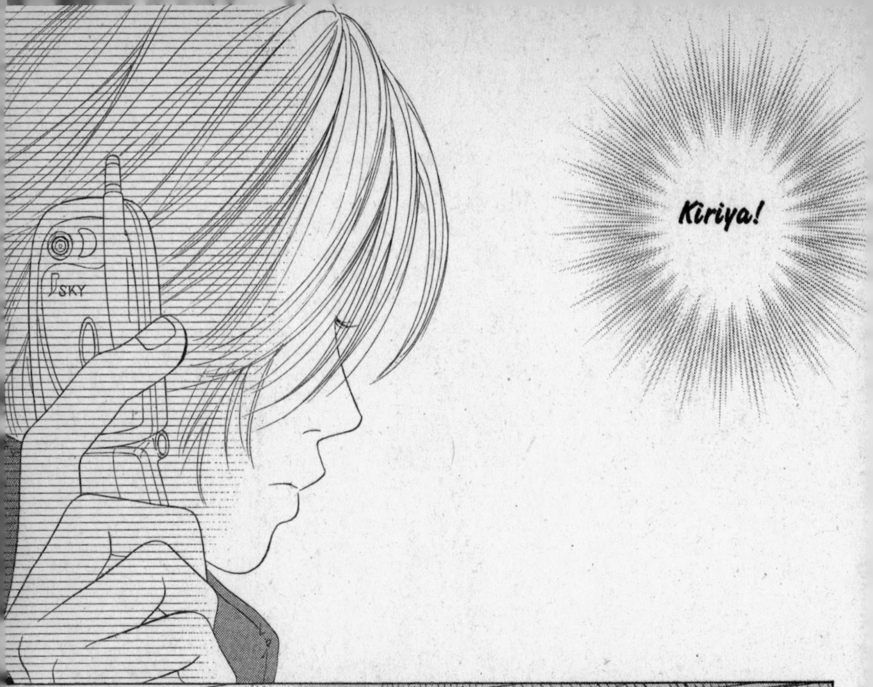
Kiriya!
SKY
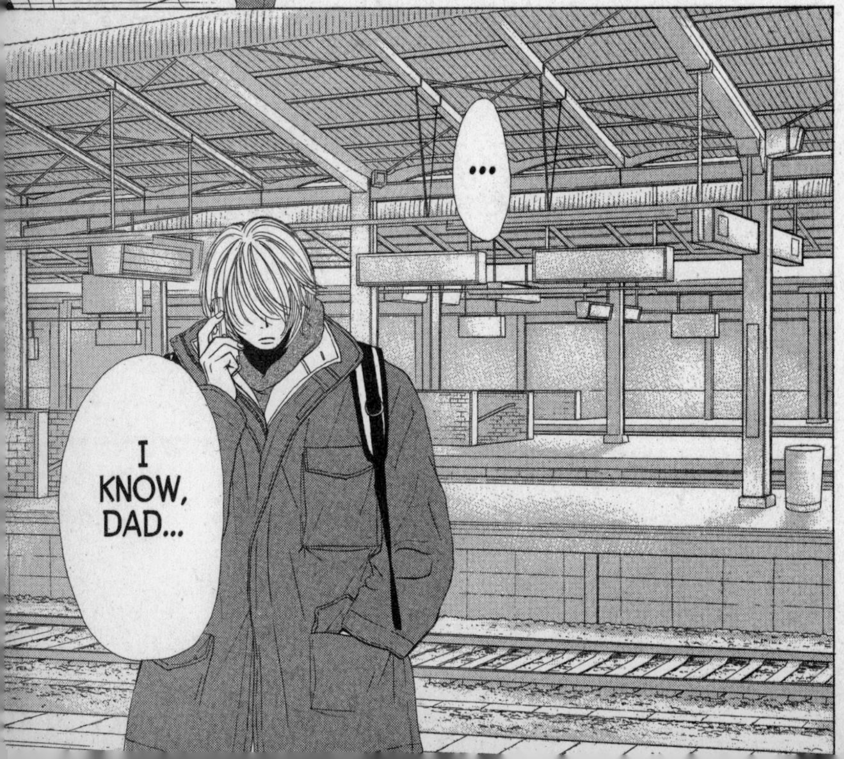
...
I KNOW, DAD...

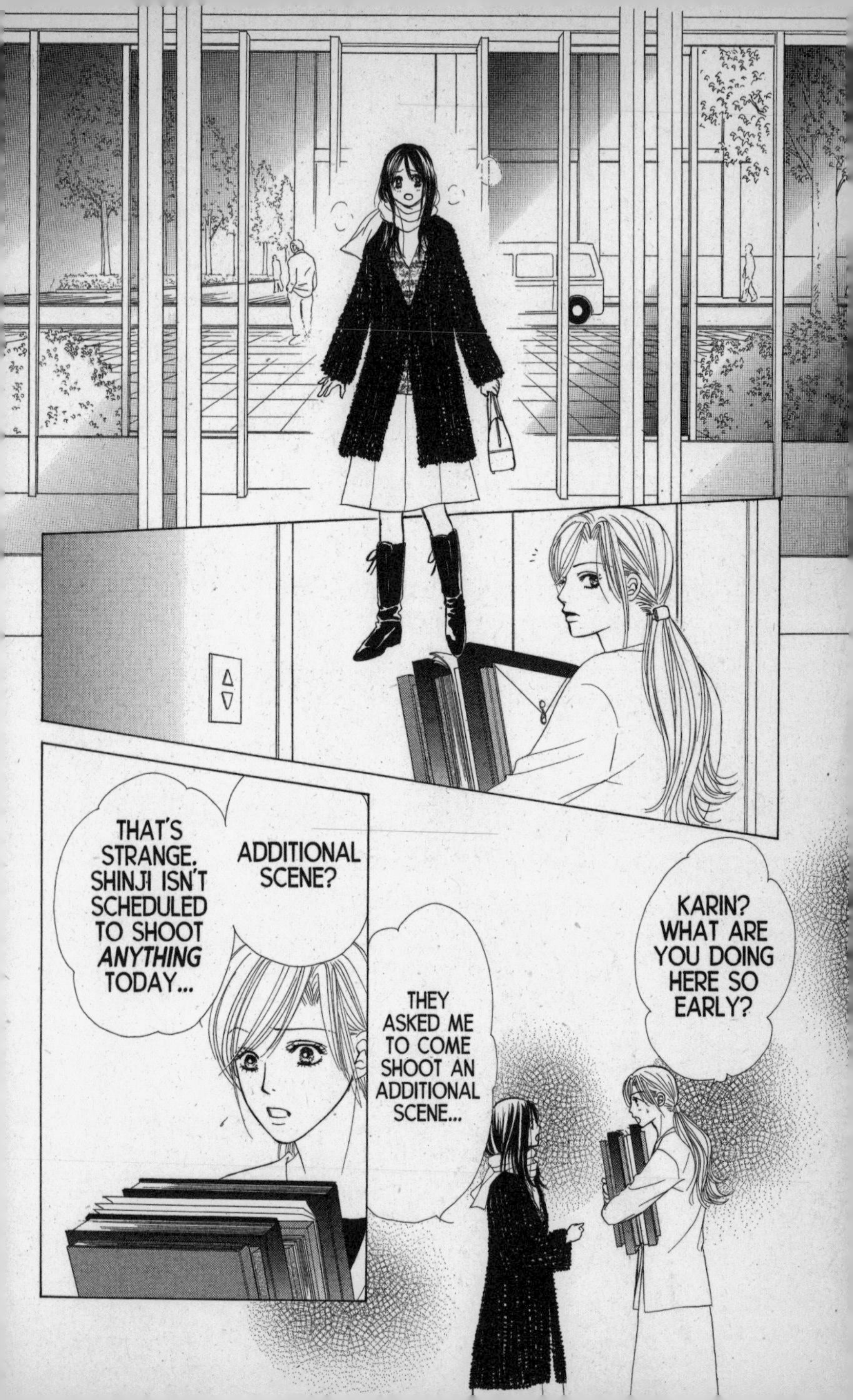
KARIN? WHAT ARE YOU DOING HERE SO EARLY?
THEY ASKED ME TO COME SHOOT AN ADDITIONAL SCENE...
ADDITIONAL SCENE?
THAT'S STRANGE. SHINJI ISN'T SCHEDULED TO SHOOT *ANYTHING* TODAY...

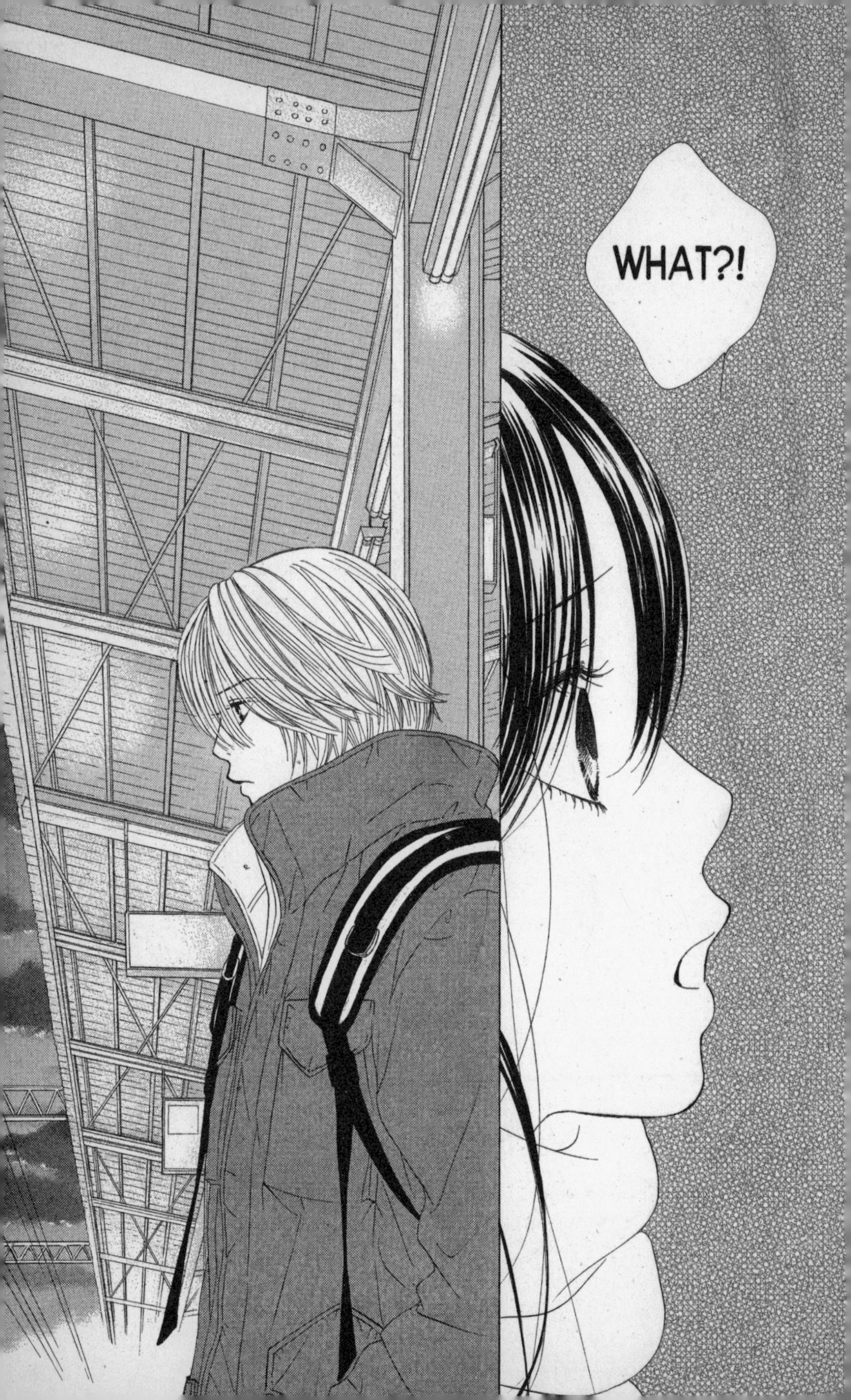
WHAT?!

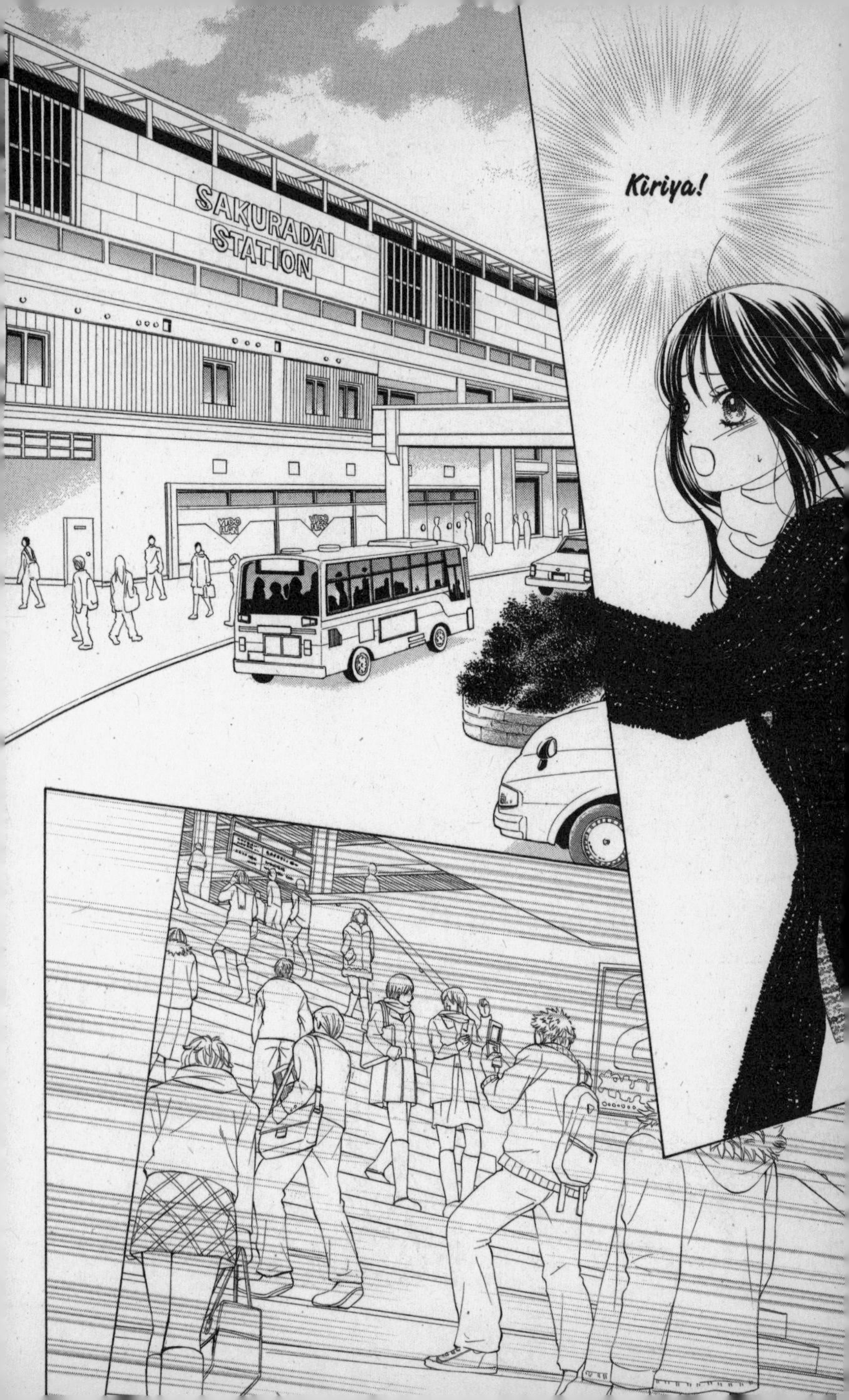
SAKURADAI STATION
Kiriya!

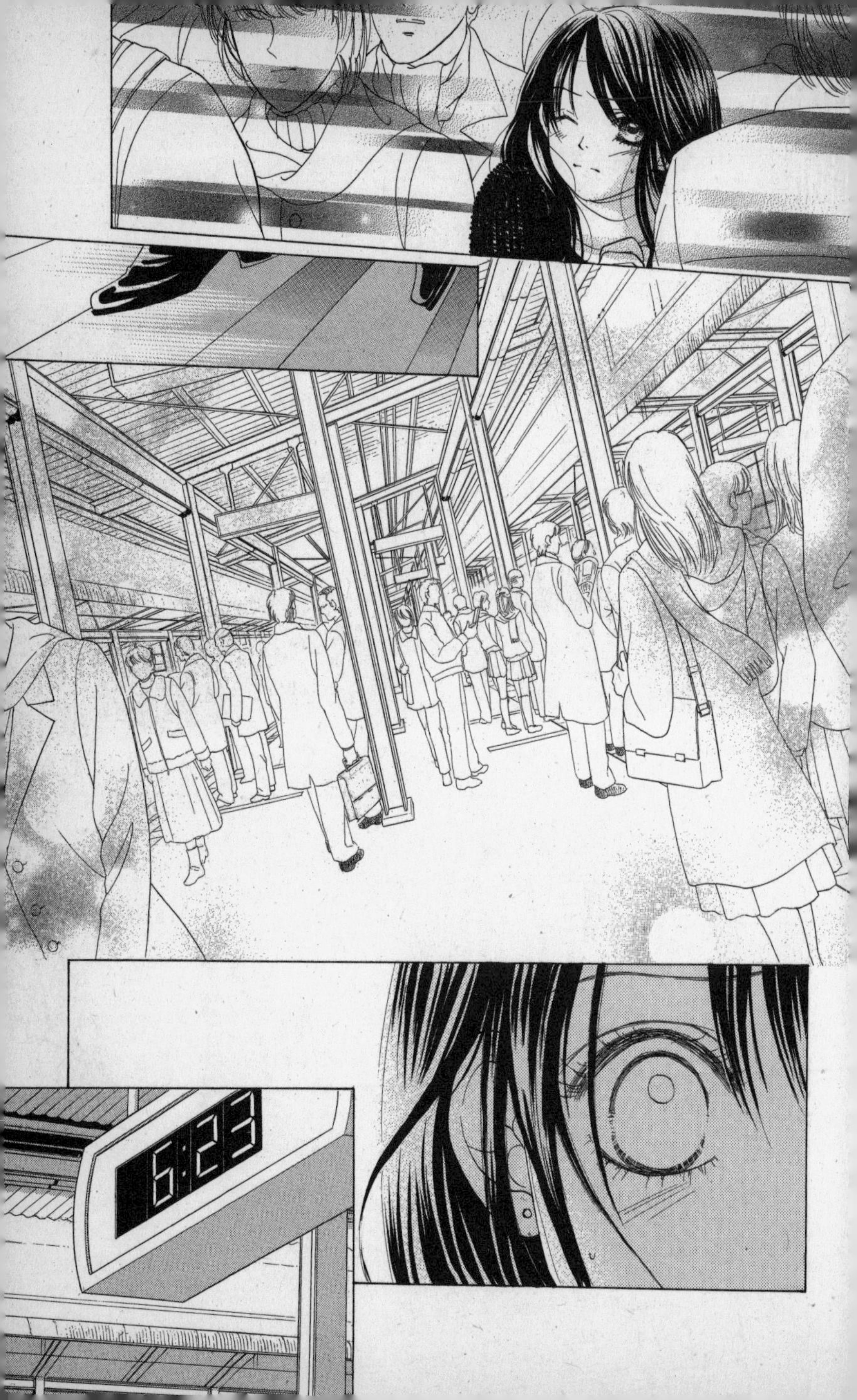
6:23

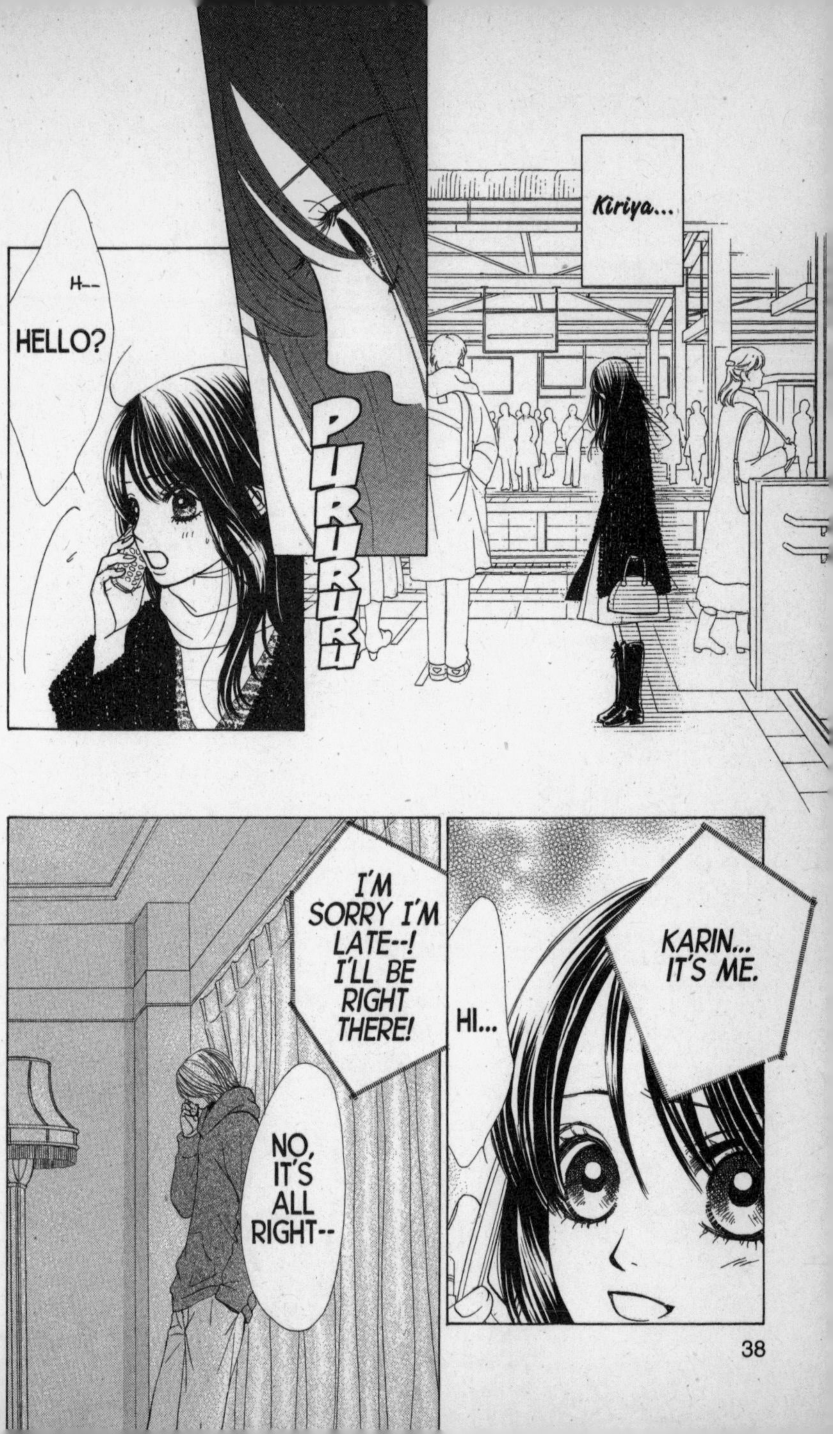
Kiriya...
PURURURU
H--
HELLO?
KARIN... IT'S ME.
HI...
I'M SORRY I'M LATE--! I'LL BE RIGHT THERE!
NO, IT'S ALL RIGHT--

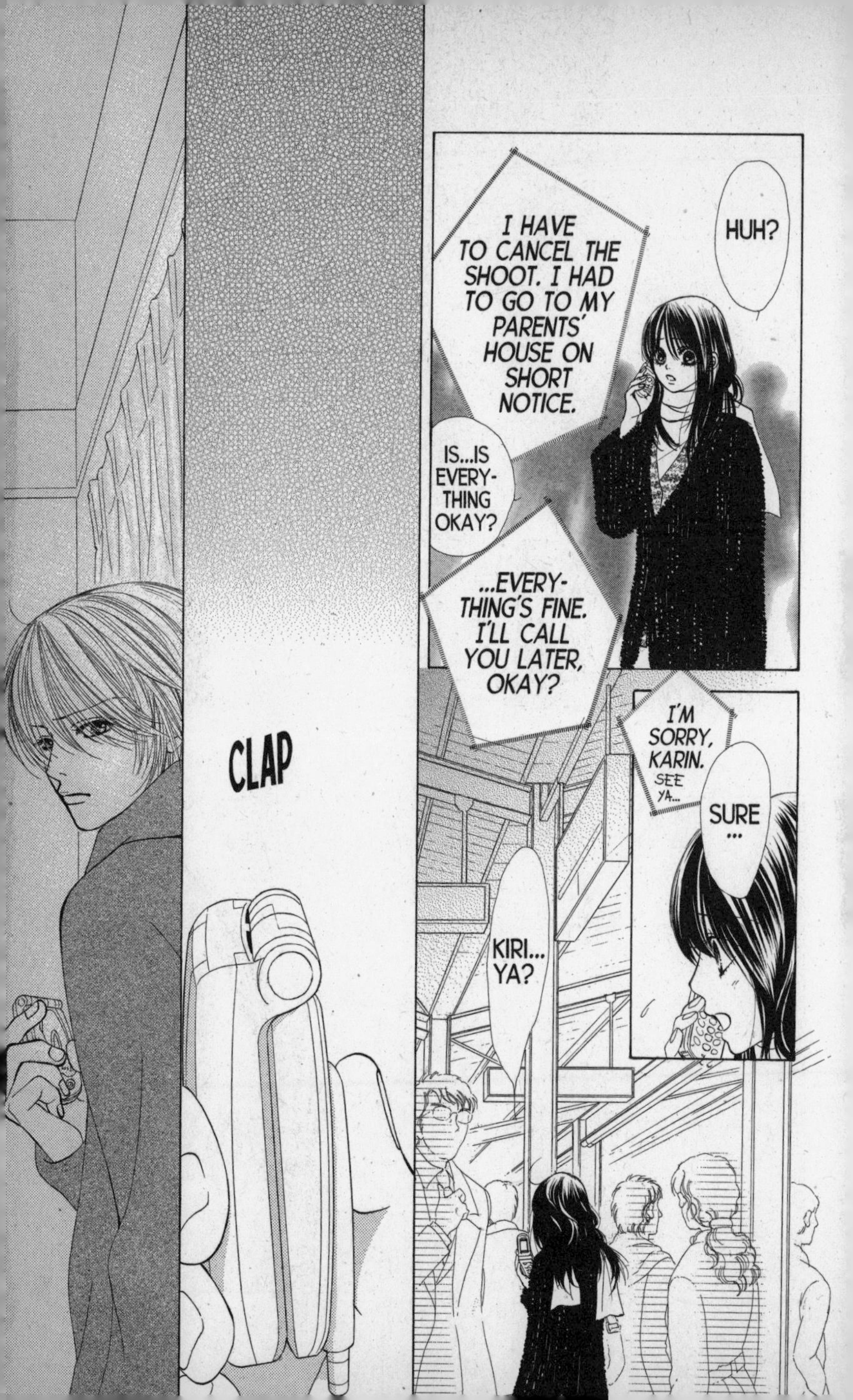
HUH?
I HAVE TO CANCEL THE SHOOT. I HAD TO GO TO MY PARENTS' HOUSE ON SHORT NOTICE.
IS...IS EVERYTHING OKAY?
...EVERYTHING'S FINE. I'LL CALL YOU LATER, OKAY?
I'M SORRY, KARIN.
SEE YA...
SURE...
KIRI... YA?
CLAP

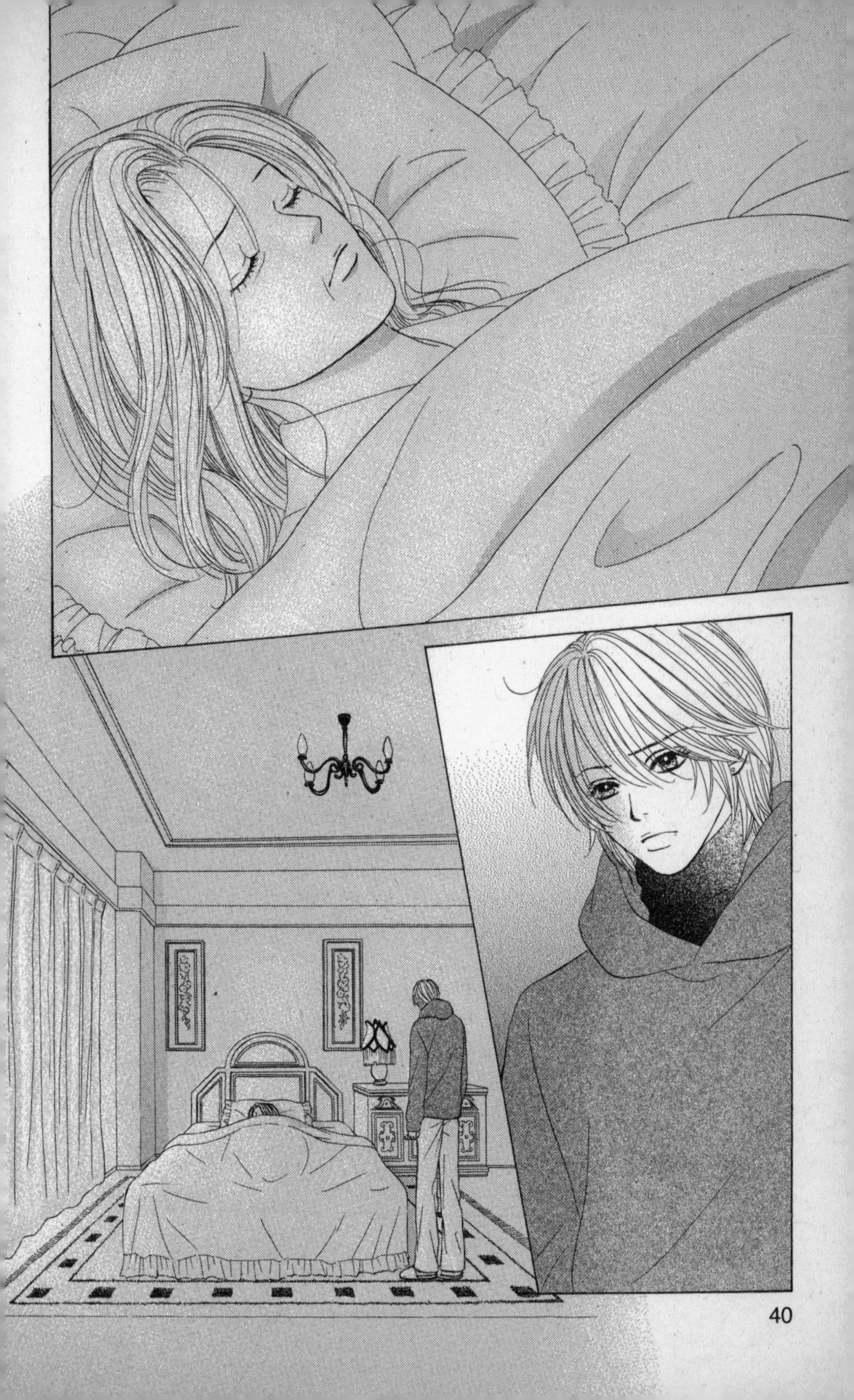

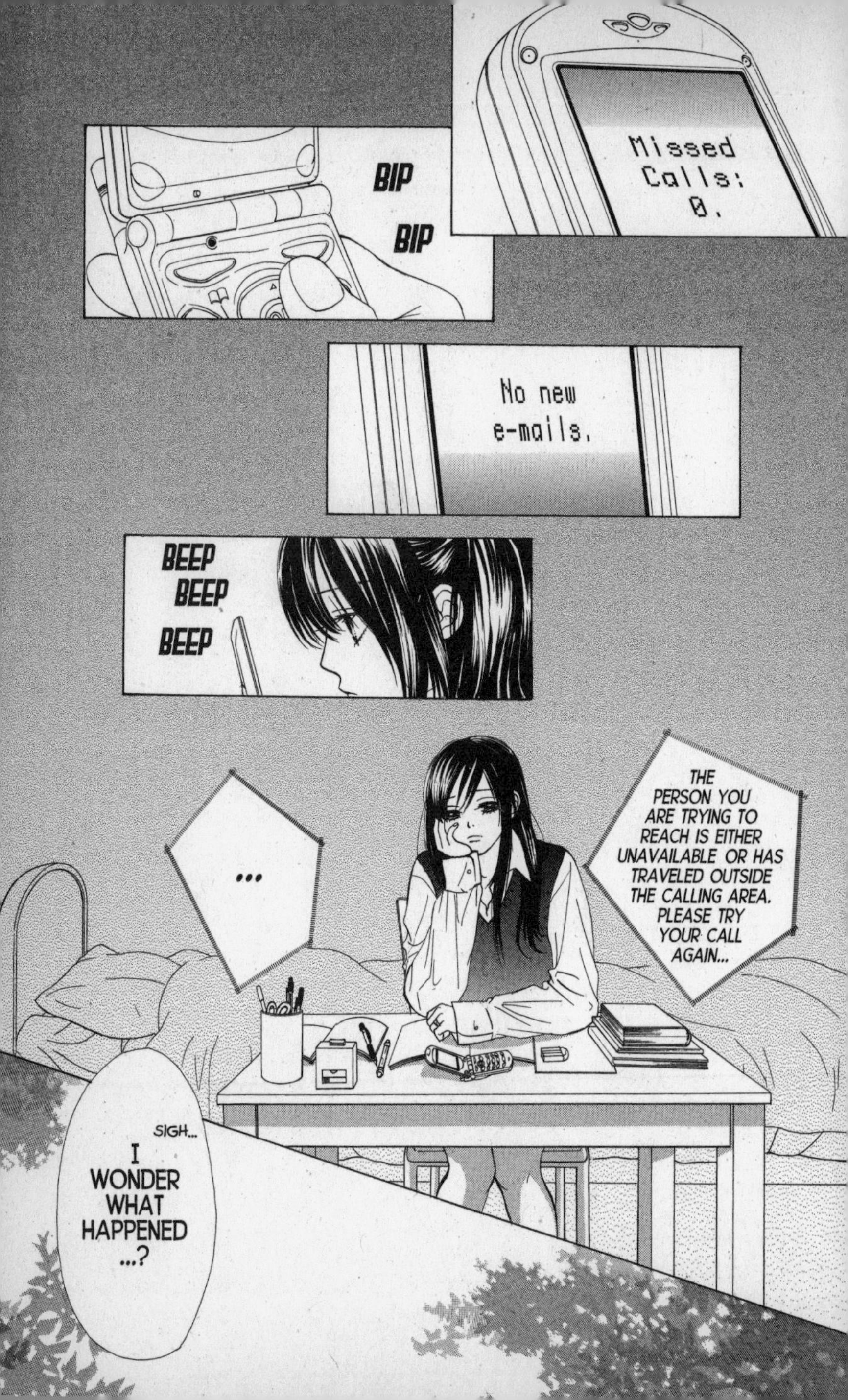
Missed Calls: 0.
BIP
BIP
No new e-mails.
BEEP
BEEP
BEEP
THE PERSON YOU ARE TRYING TO REACH IS EITHER UNAVAILABLE OR HAS TRAVELED OUTSIDE THE CALLING AREA. PLEASE TRY YOUR CALL AGAIN...
...
SIGH...
I WONDER WHAT HAPPENED ...?

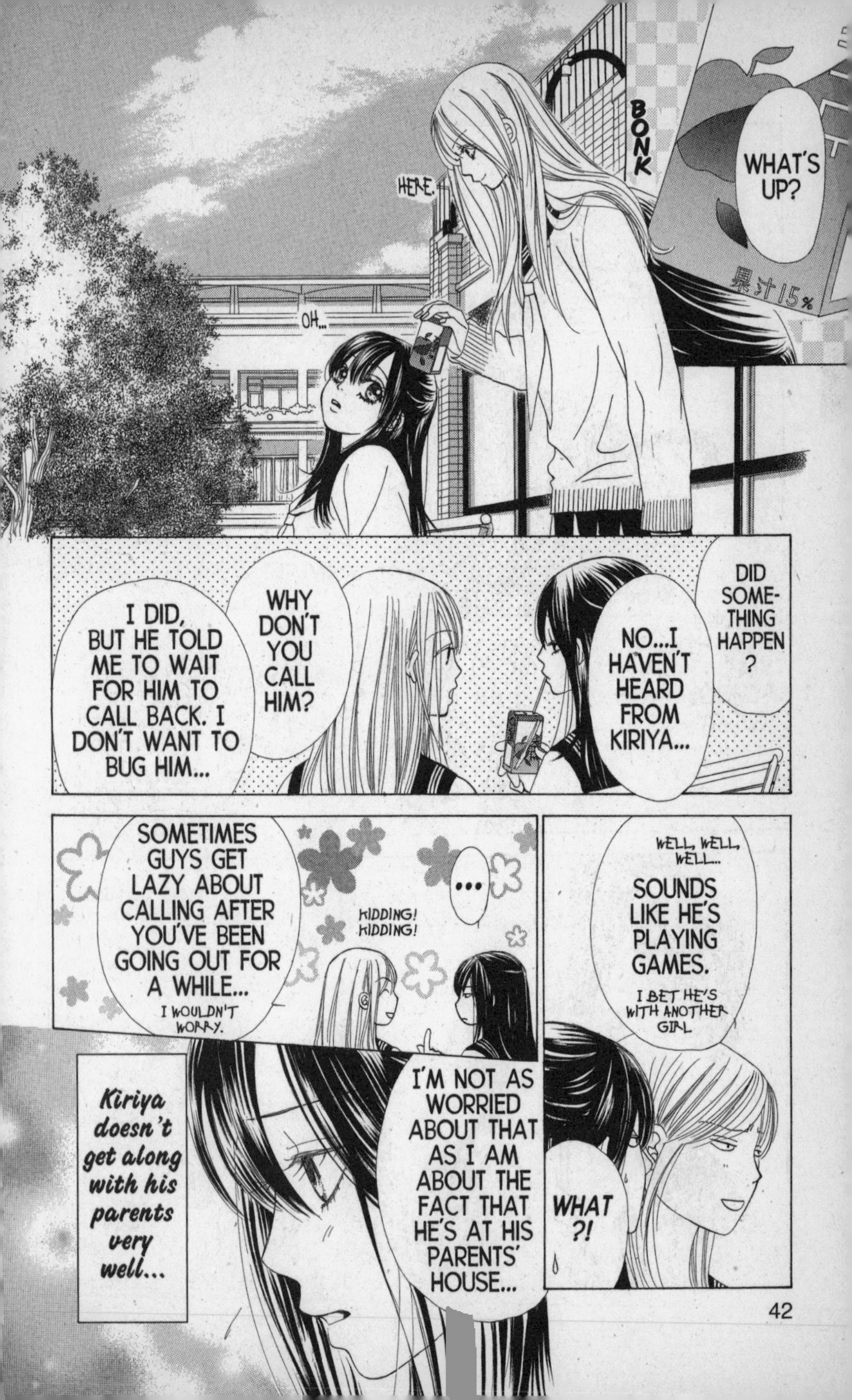
WHAT'S UP?
BONK
果汁15%
HERE.
OH...
DID SOMETHING HAPPEN?
NO...I HAVEN'T HEARD FROM KIRIYA...
WHY DON'T YOU CALL HIM?
I DID, BUT HE TOLD ME TO WAIT FOR HIM TO CALL BACK. I DON'T WANT TO BUG HIM...
WELL, WELL, WELL...
SOUNDS LIKE HE'S PLAYING GAMES.
I BET HE'S WITH ANOTHER GIRL
...
KIDDING! KIDDING!
SOMETIMES GUYS GET LAZY ABOUT CALLING AFTER YOU'VE BEEN GOING OUT FOR A WHILE...
I WOULDN'T WORRY.
WHAT?!
I'M NOT AS WORRIED ABOUT THAT AS I AM ABOUT THE FACT THAT HE'S AT HIS PARENTS' HOUSE...
Kiriya doesn't get along with his parents very well...

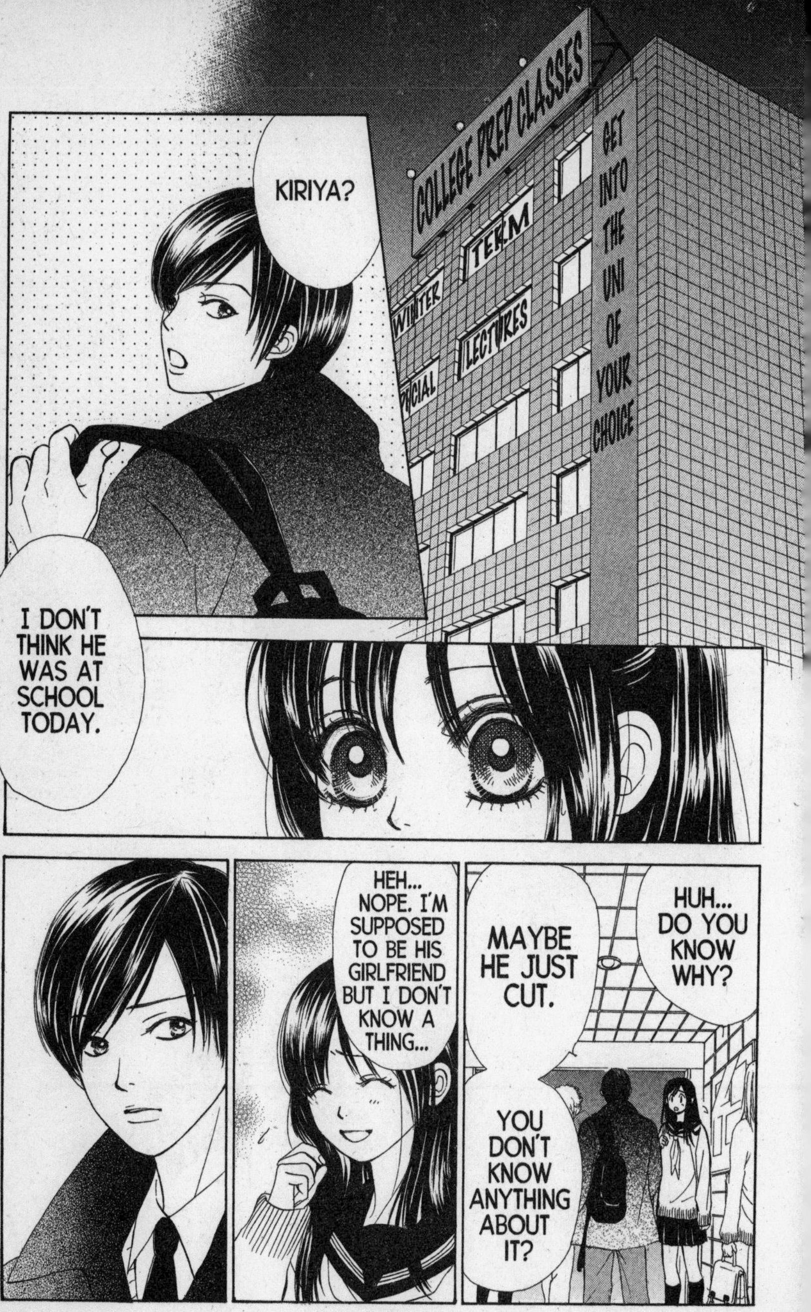
COLLEGE PREP CLASSES
WINTER
TERM
LECTURES
GET INTO THE UNI OF YOUR CHOICE
KIRIYA?
I DON'T THINK HE WAS AT SCHOOL TODAY.
HUH... DO YOU KNOW WHY?
MAYBE HE JUST CUT.
YOU DON'T KNOW ANYTHING ABOUT IT?
HEH... NOPE. I'M SUPPOSED TO BE HIS GIRLFRIEND BUT I DON'T KNOW A THING...

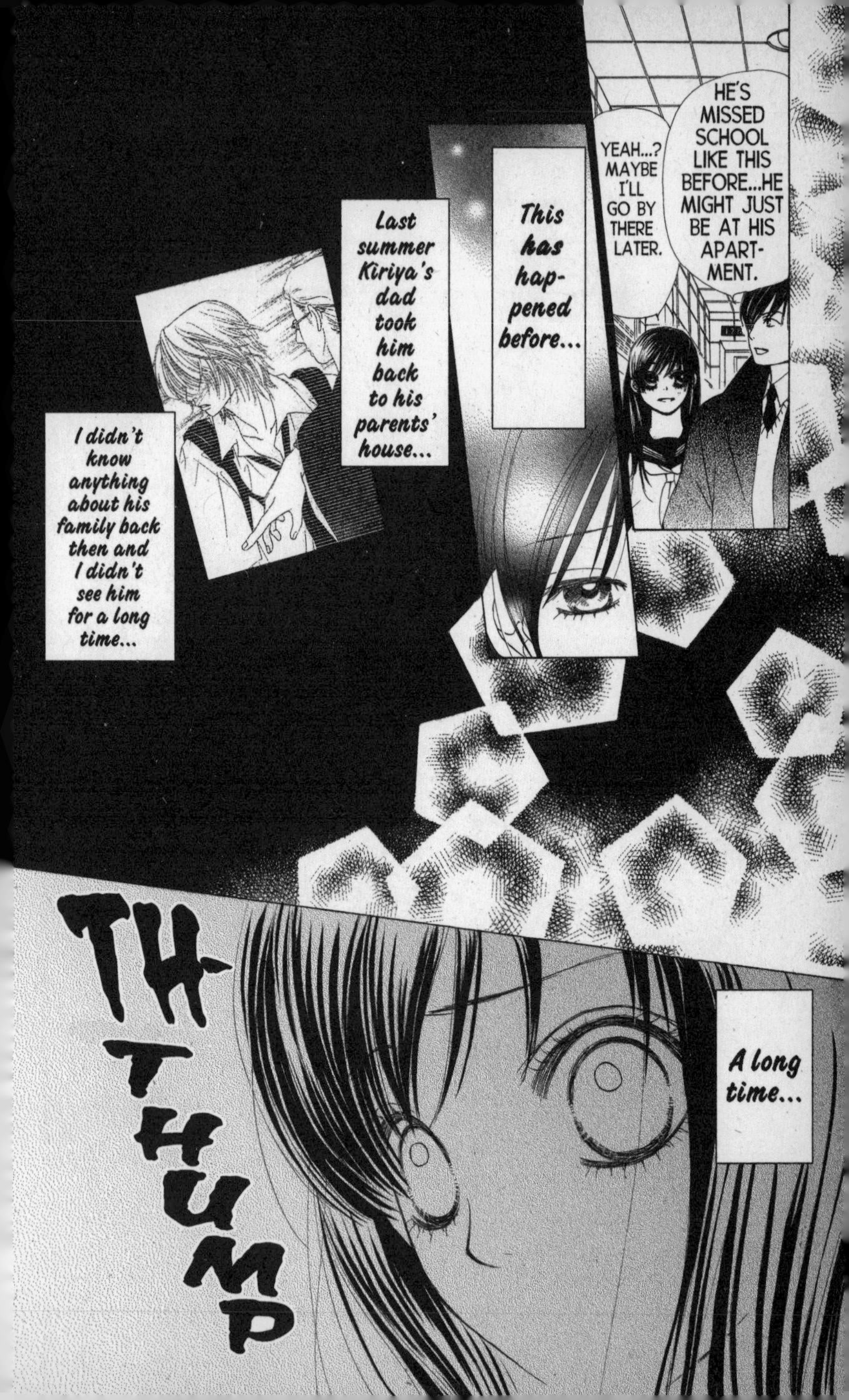
HE'S MISSED SCHOOL LIKE THIS BEFORE...HE MIGHT JUST BE AT HIS APARTMENT.
YEAH...? MAYBE I'LL GO BY THERE LATER.
This has happened before...
Last summer Kiriya's dad took him back to his parents' house...
I didn't know anything about his family back then and I didn't see him for a long time...
A long time...
THTHUMP

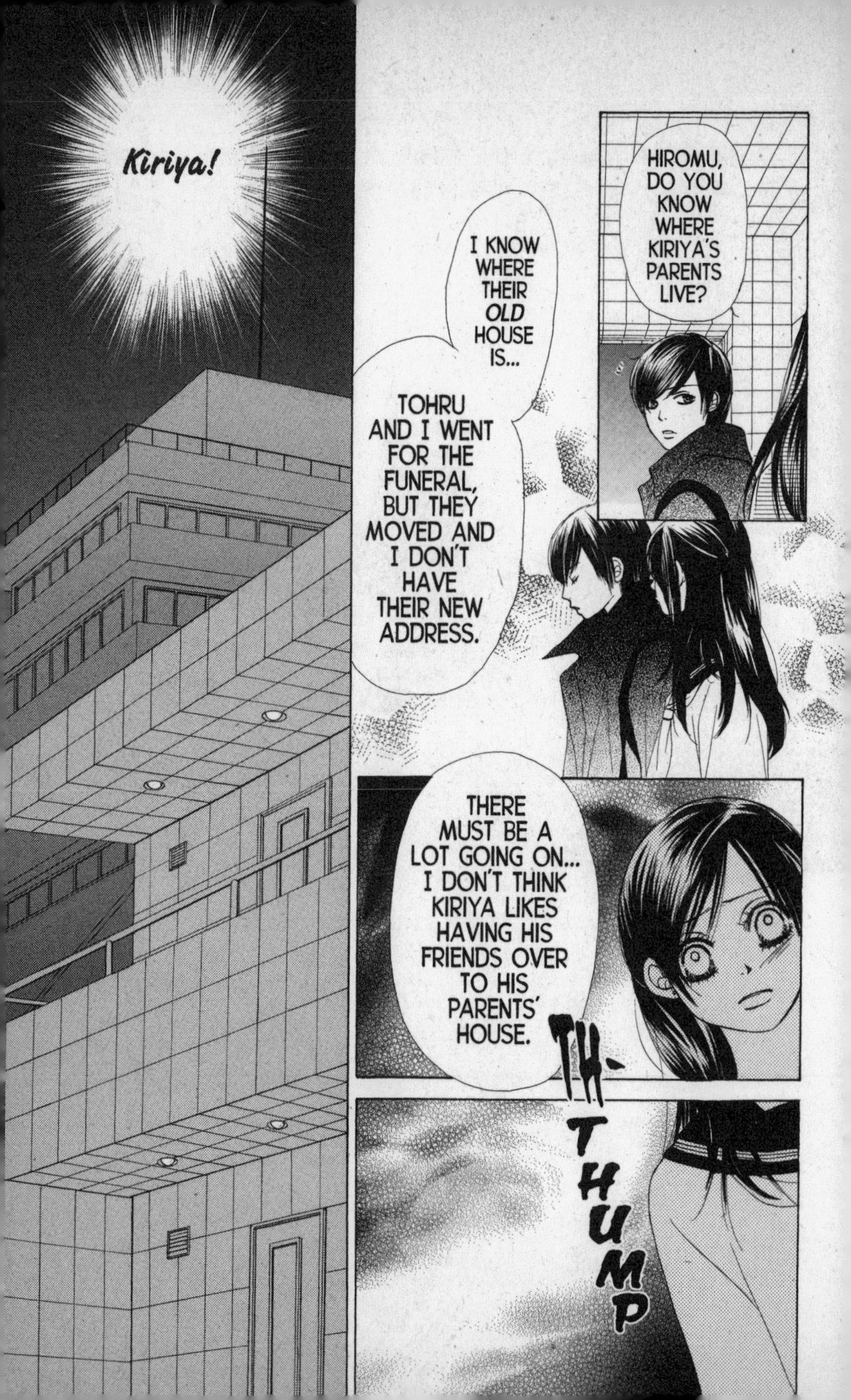
HIROMU, DO YOU KNOW WHERE KIRIYA'S PARENTS LIVE?
I KNOW WHERE THEIR *OLD* HOUSE IS...
TOHRU AND I WENT FOR THE FUNERAL, BUT THEY MOVED AND I DON'T HAVE THEIR NEW ADDRESS.
THERE MUST BE A LOT GOING ON... I DON'T THINK KIRIYA LIKES HAVING HIS FRIENDS OVER TO HIS PARENTS' HOUSE.
TH-THUMP
Kiriya!

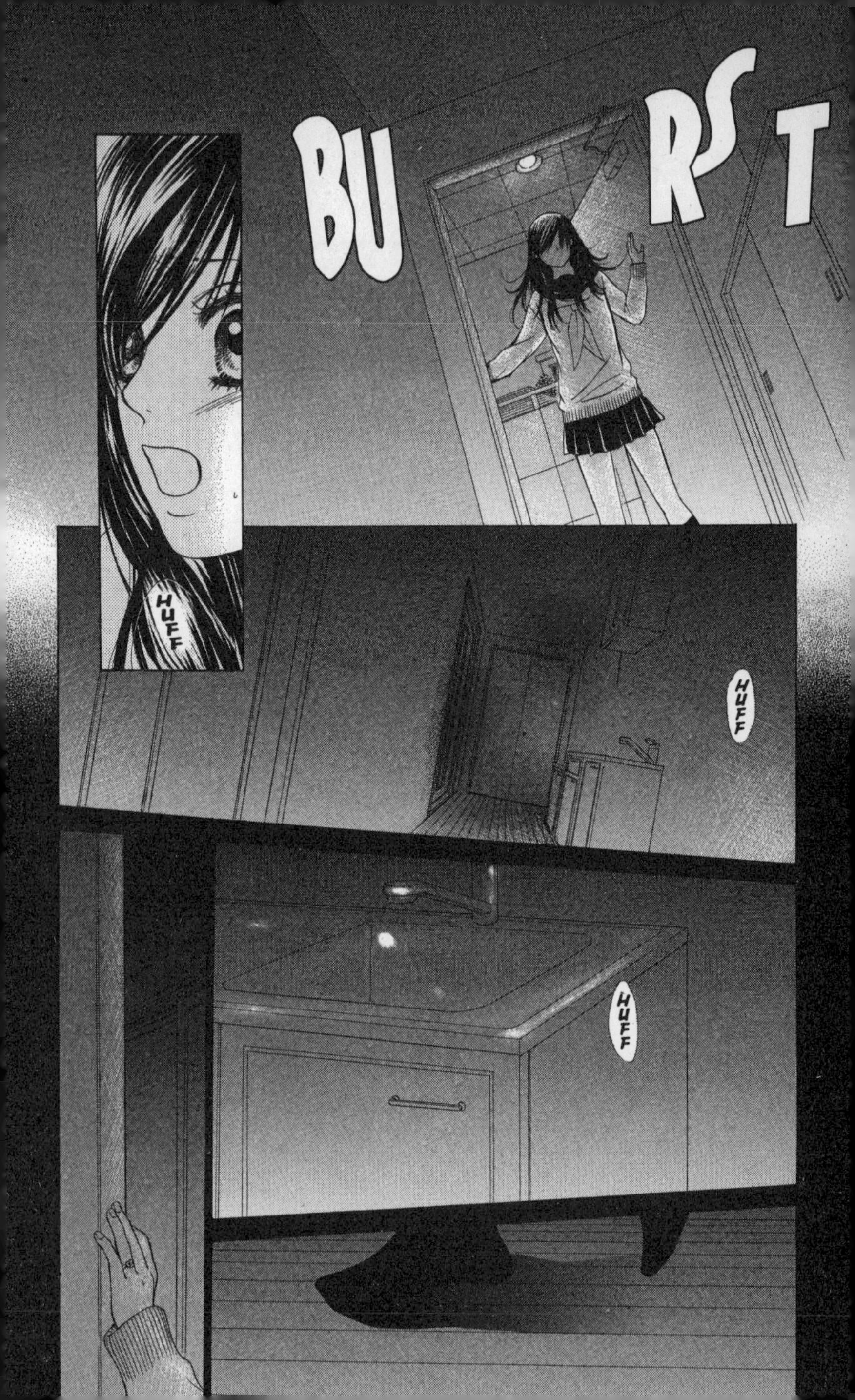
BURST
HUFF
HUFF
HUFF

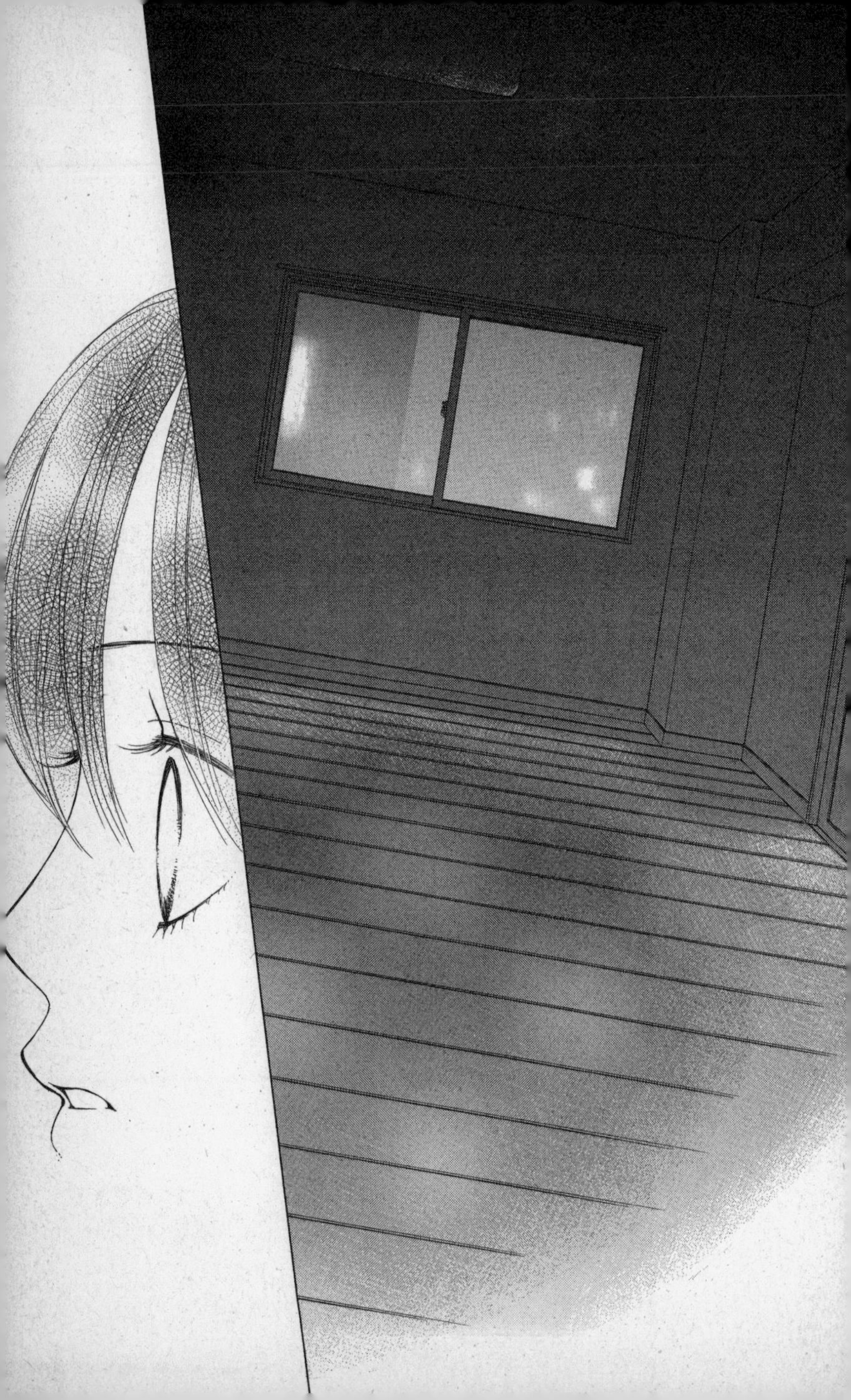

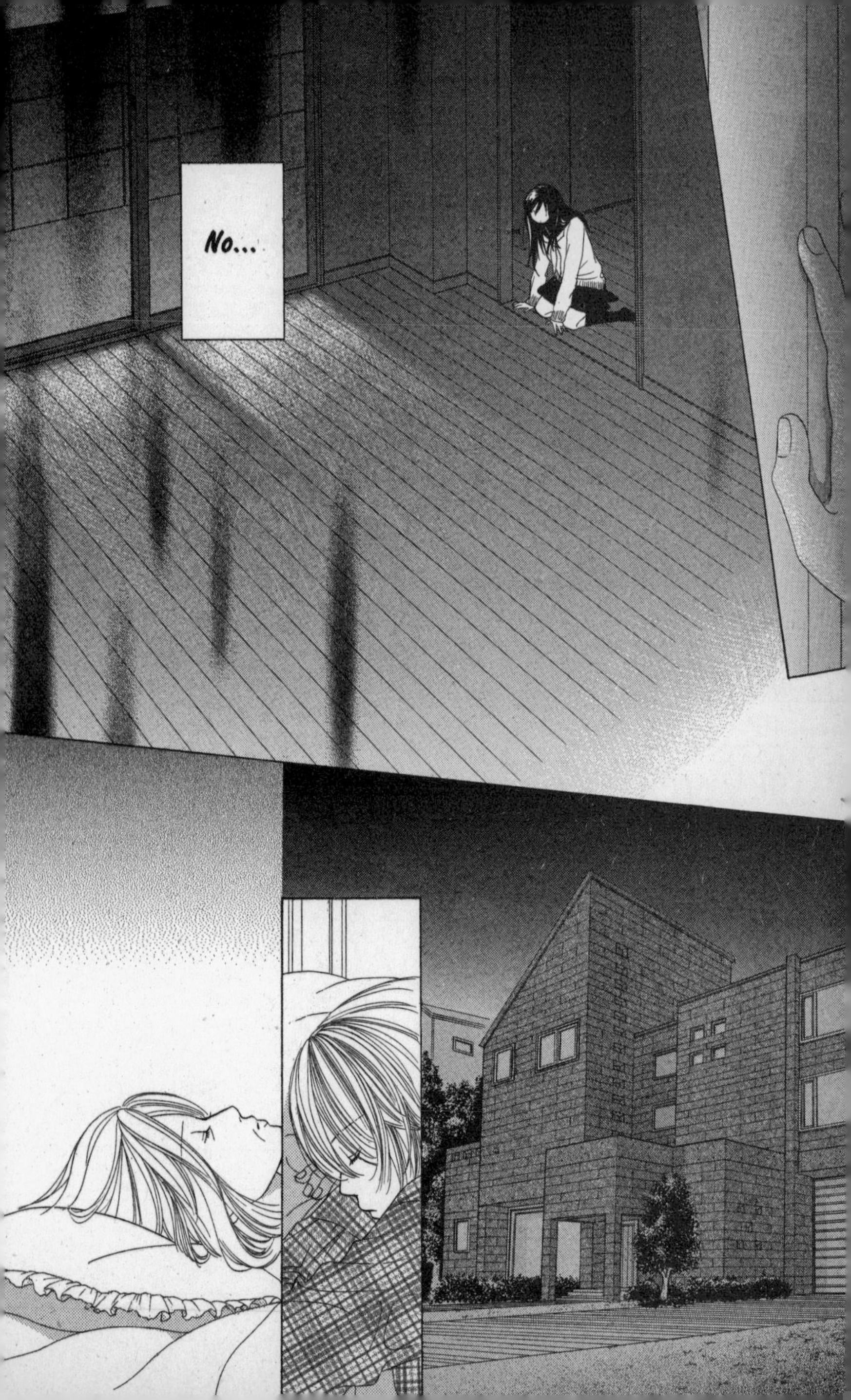
No...

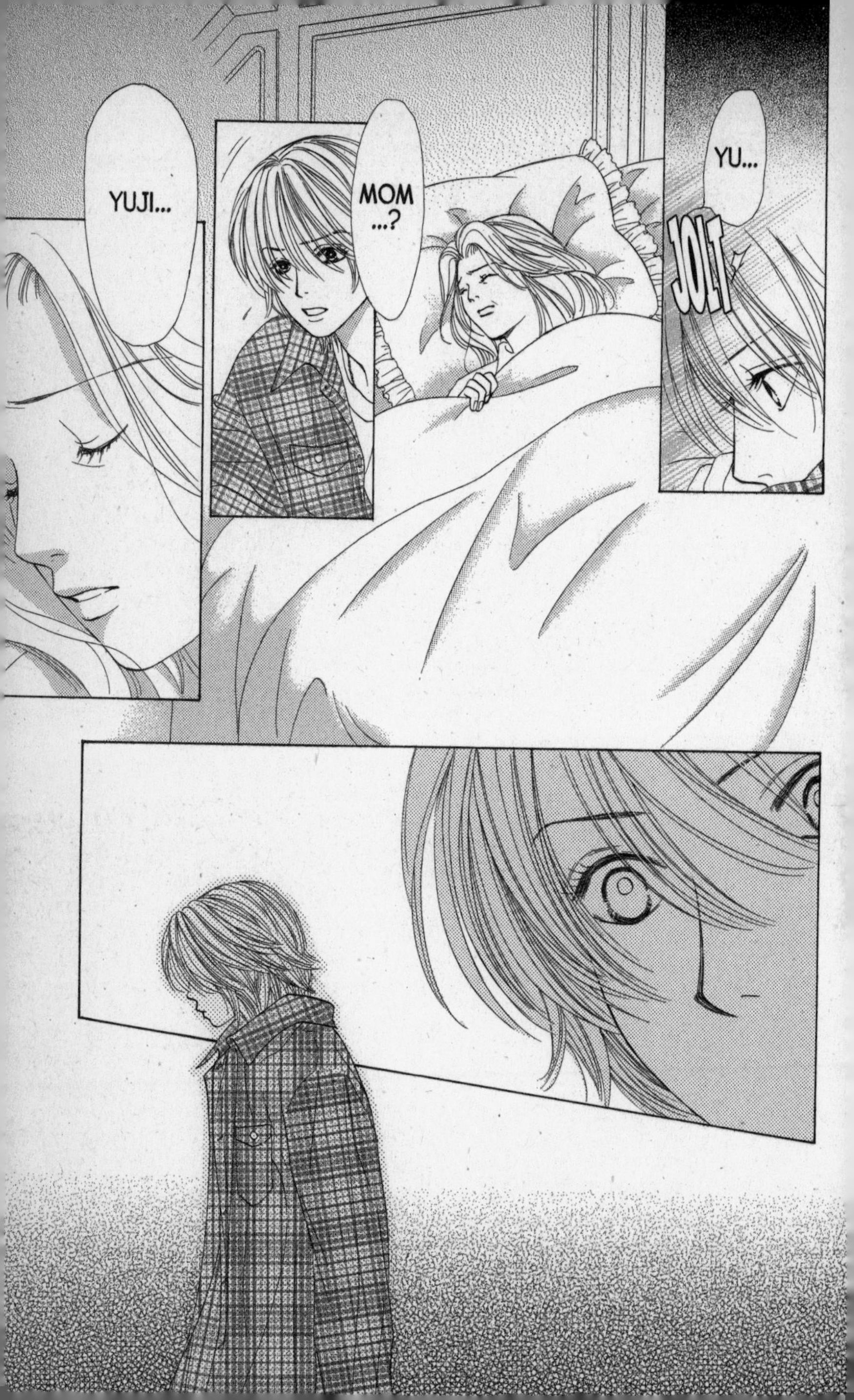
YU...
JOLT
MOM ...?
YUJI...

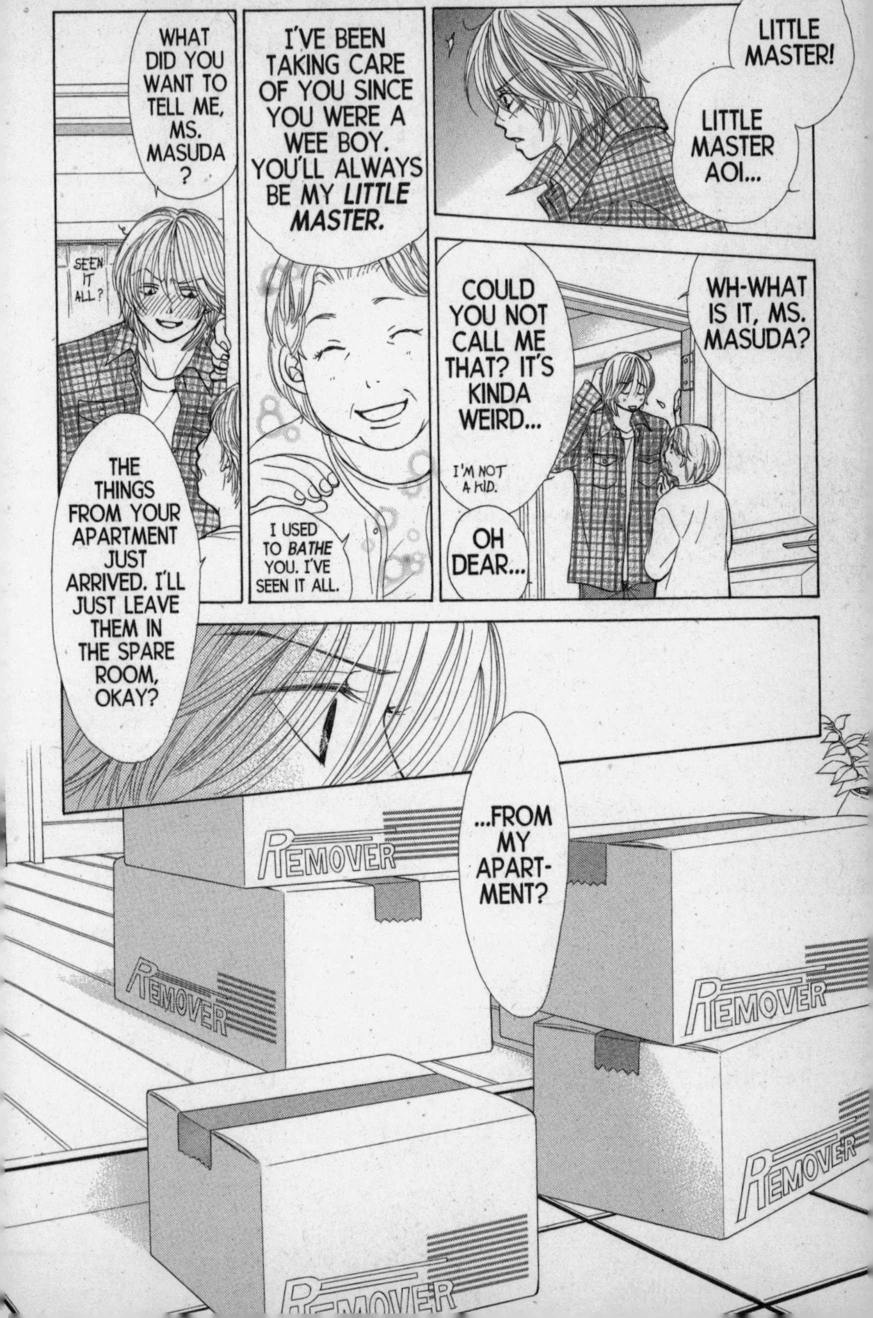
LITTLE MASTER!
LITTLE MASTER AOI...
WH-WHAT IS IT, MS. MASUDA?
COULD YOU NOT CALL ME THAT? IT'S KINDA WEIRD...
I'M NOT A KID.
OH DEAR...
I'VE BEEN TAKING CARE OF YOU SINCE YOU WERE A WEE BOY. YOU'LL ALWAYS BE MY *LITTLE MASTER.*
I USED TO *BATHE* YOU. I'VE SEEN IT ALL.
WHAT DID YOU WANT TO TELL ME, MS. MASUDA?
SEEN IT ALL?
THE THINGS FROM YOUR APARTMENT JUST ARRIVED. I'LL JUST LEAVE THEM IN THE SPARE ROOM, OKAY?
...FROM MY APARTMENT?
REMOVER
REMOVER
REMOVER
REMOVER

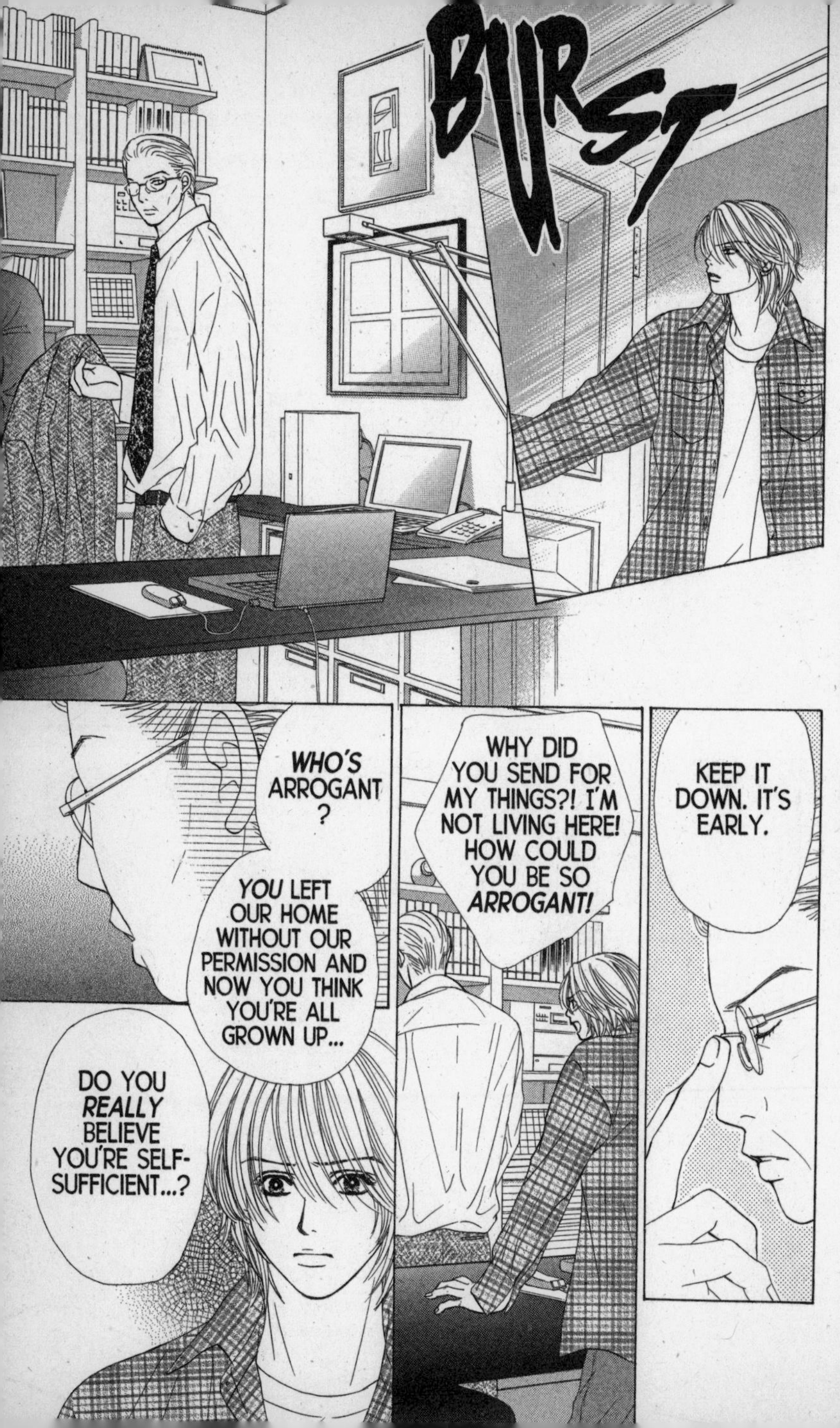
BURST
KEEP IT DOWN. IT'S EARLY.
WHY DID YOU SEND FOR MY THINGS?! I'M NOT LIVING HERE! HOW COULD YOU BE SO *ARROGANT!*
WHO'S ARROGANT?
YOU LEFT OUR HOME WITHOUT OUR PERMISSION AND NOW YOU THINK YOU'RE ALL GROWN UP...
DO YOU *REALLY* BELIEVE YOU'RE SELF-SUFFICIENT...?

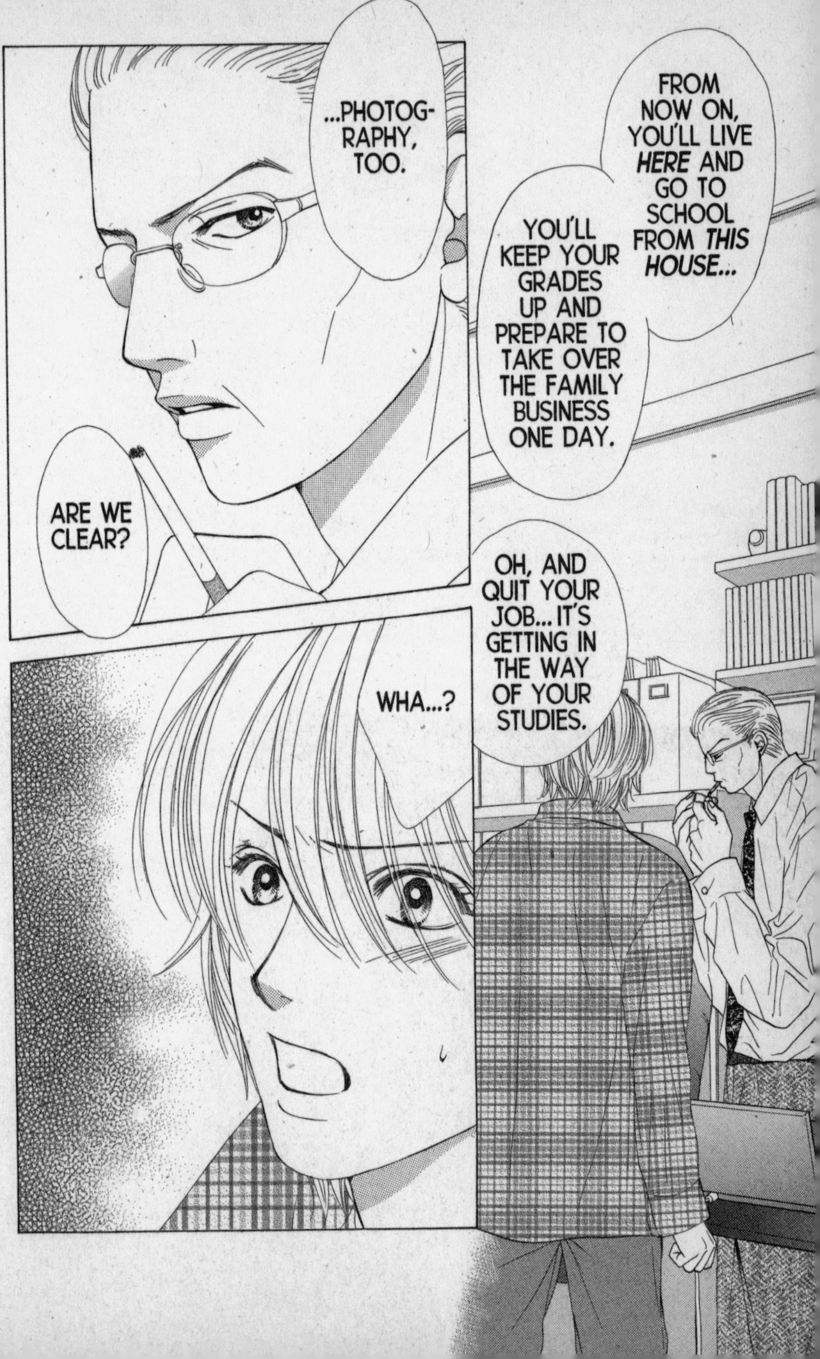
FROM NOW ON, YOU'LL LIVE *HERE* AND GO TO SCHOOL FROM *THIS HOUSE...*
YOU'LL KEEP YOUR GRADES UP AND PREPARE TO TAKE OVER THE FAMILY BUSINESS ONE DAY.
OH, AND QUIT YOUR JOB... IT'S GETTING IN THE WAY OF YOUR STUDIES.
...PHOTOG-RAPHY, TOO.
ARE WE CLEAR?
WHA...?

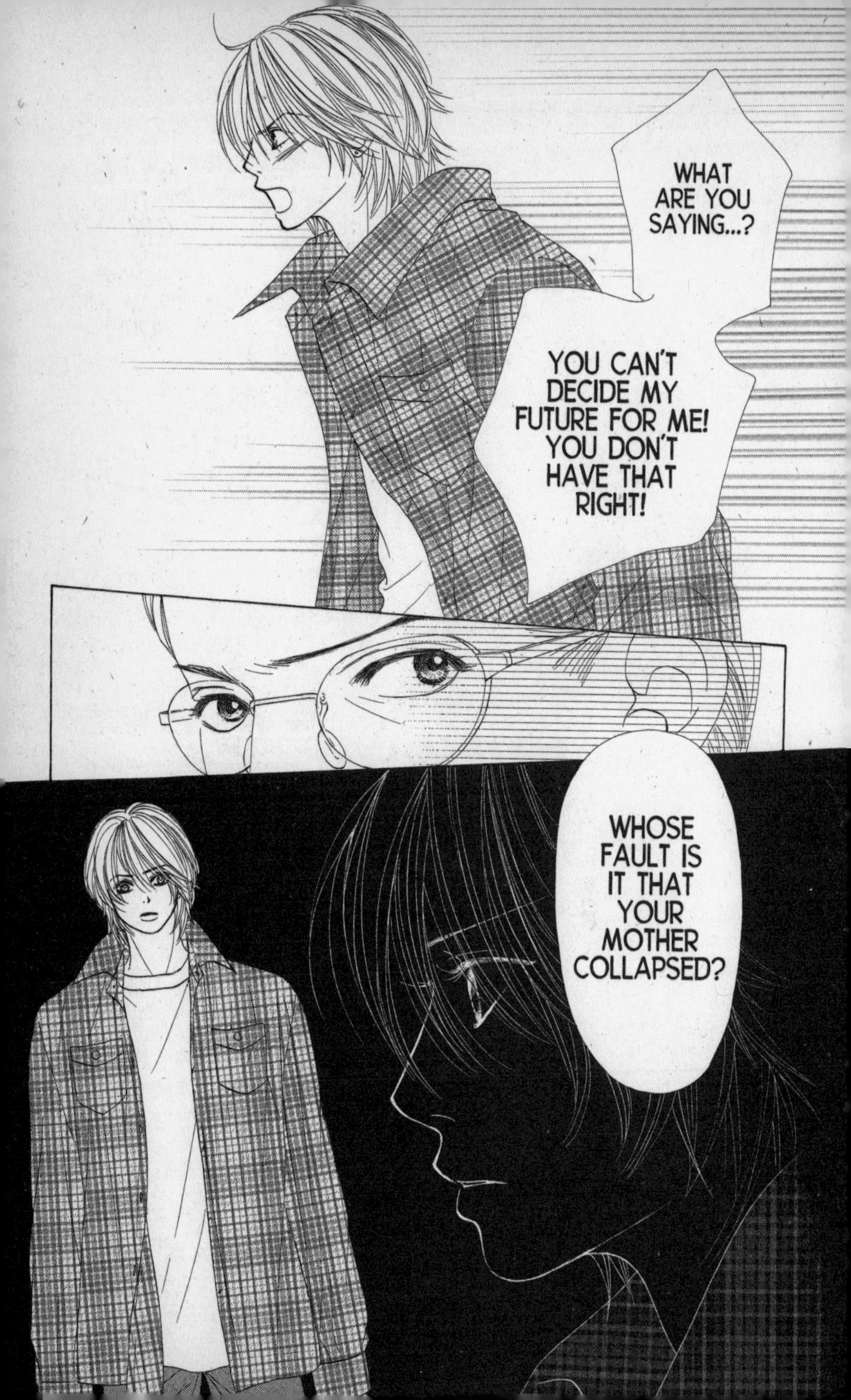
WHAT ARE YOU SAYING...?
YOU CAN'T DECIDE MY FUTURE FOR ME! YOU DON'T HAVE THAT RIGHT!
WHOSE FAULT IS IT THAT YOUR MOTHER COLLAPSED?

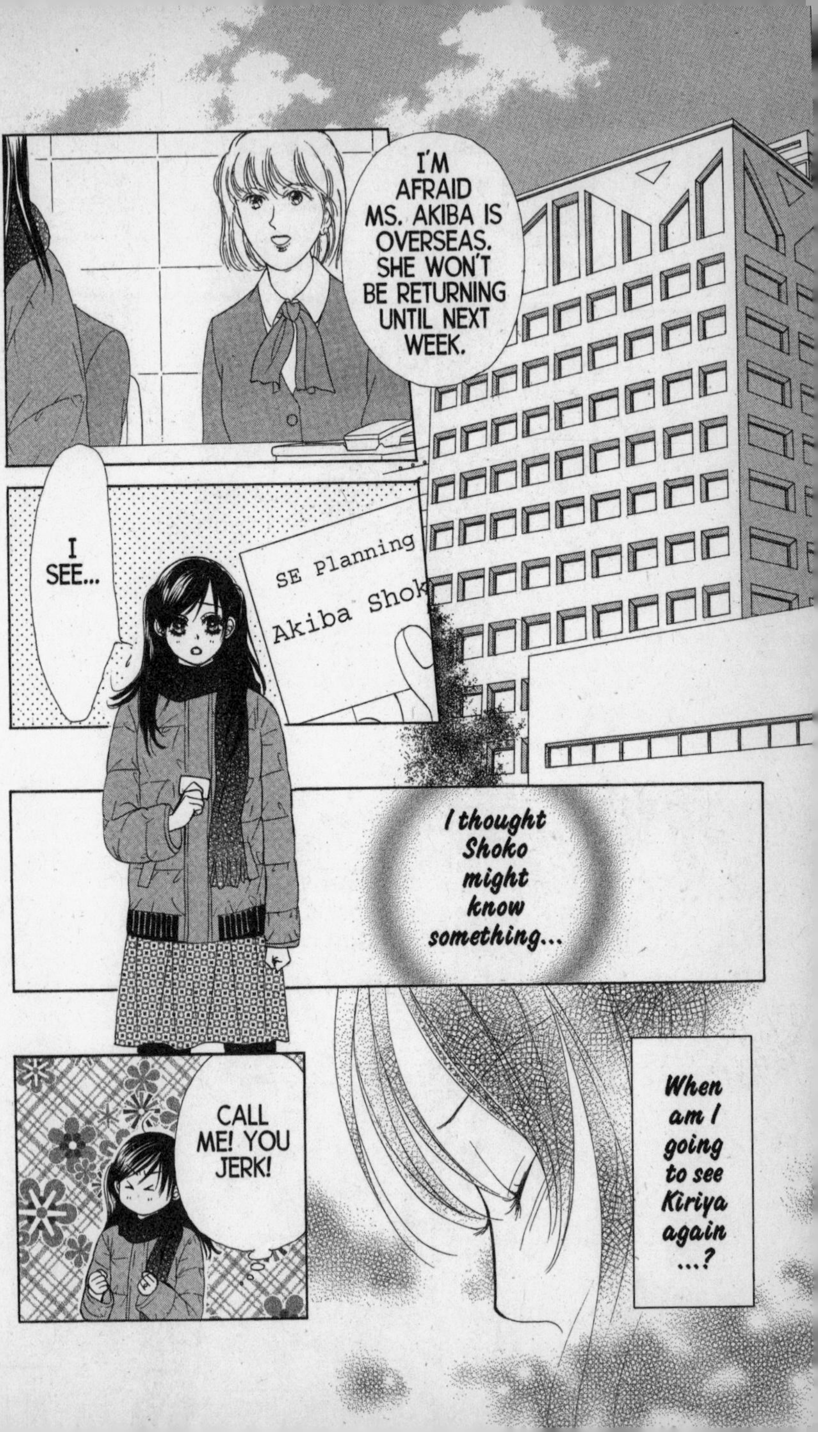
I'M AFRAID MS. AKIBA IS OVERSEAS. SHE WON'T BE RETURNING UNTIL NEXT WEEK.
I SEE...
SE Planning
Akiba Shok
I thought Shoko might know something...
CALL ME! YOU JERK!
When am I going to see Kiriya again ...?

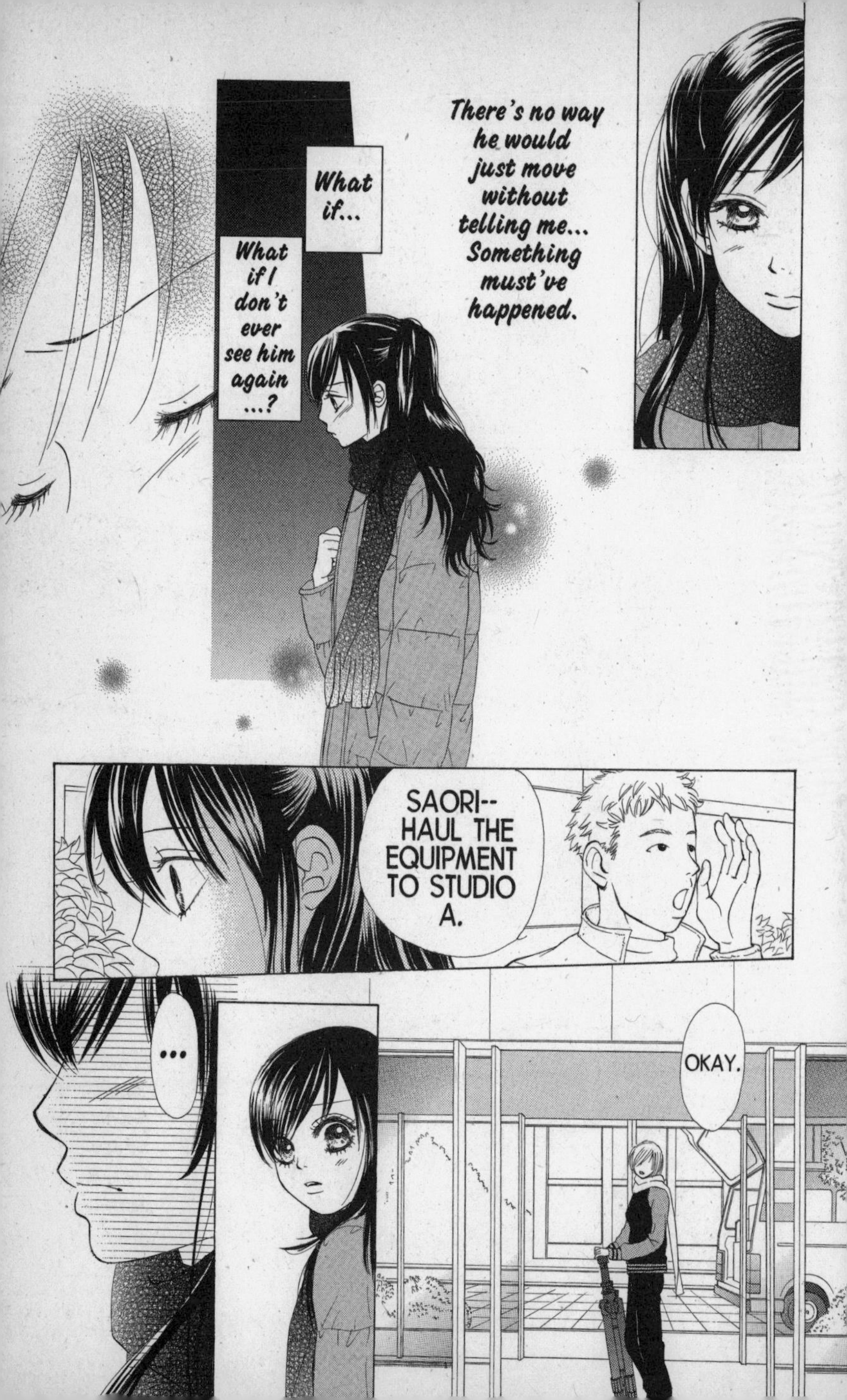
There's no way he would just move without telling me... Something must've happened.
What if...
What if I don't ever see him again ...?
SAORI-- HAUL THE EQUIPMENT TO STUDIO A.
OKAY.
...

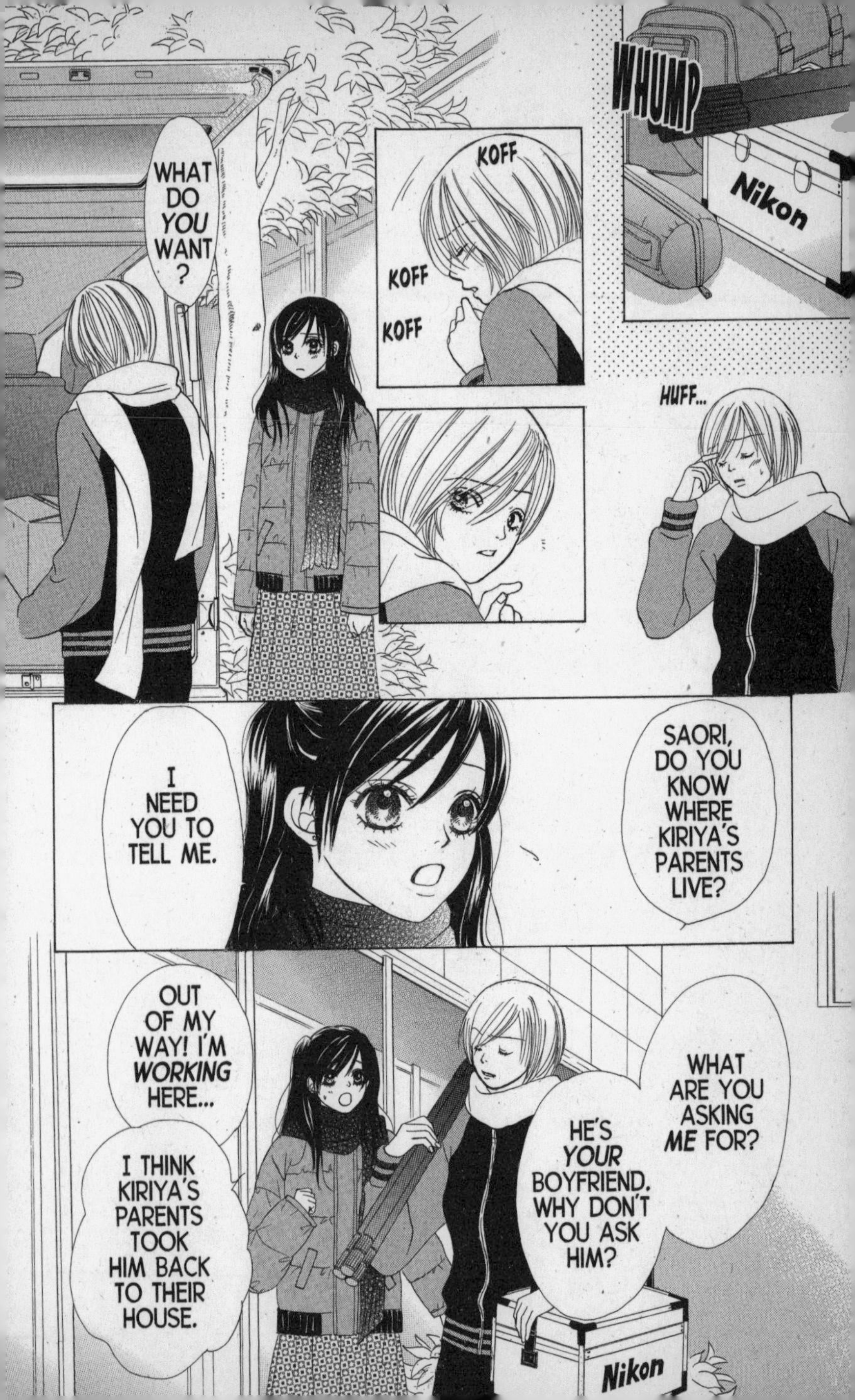
WHUMP
Nikon
HUFF...
KOFF
KOFF
KOFF
WHAT DO *YOU* WANT?
SAORI, DO YOU KNOW WHERE KIRIYA'S PARENTS LIVE?
I NEED YOU TO TELL ME.
WHAT ARE YOU ASKING *ME* FOR?
HE'S *YOUR* BOYFRIEND. WHY DON'T YOU ASK HIM?
OUT OF MY WAY! I'M *WORKING* HERE...
I THINK KIRIYA'S PARENTS TOOK HIM BACK TO THEIR HOUSE.
Nikon

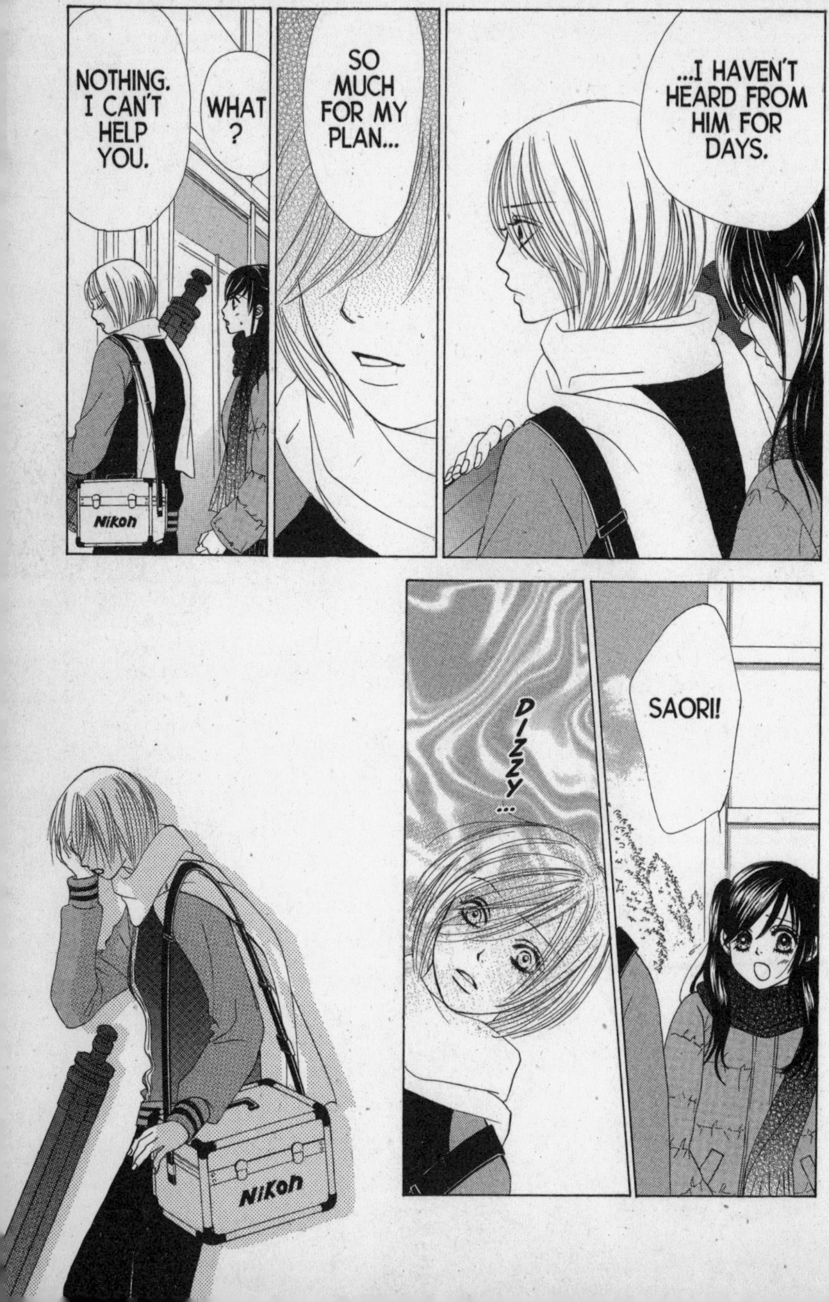
...I HAVEN'T HEARD FROM HIM FOR DAYS.
SO MUCH FOR MY PLAN...
WHAT?
NOTHING. I CAN'T HELP YOU.
Nikon
SAORI!
DIZZY...
Nikon

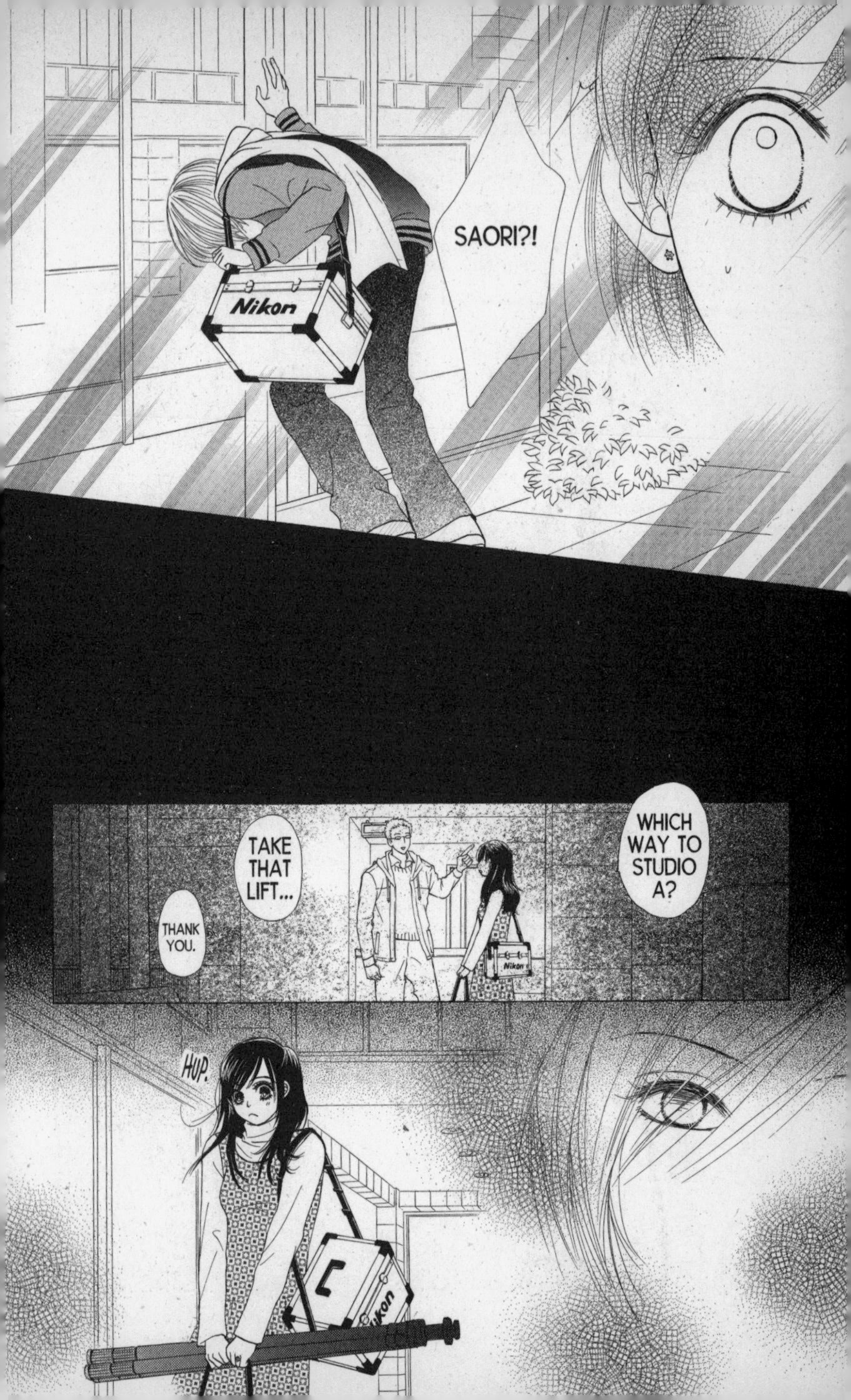
SAORI?!
WHICH WAY TO STUDIO A?
TAKE THAT LIFT...
THANK YOU.
HUP.
Nikon

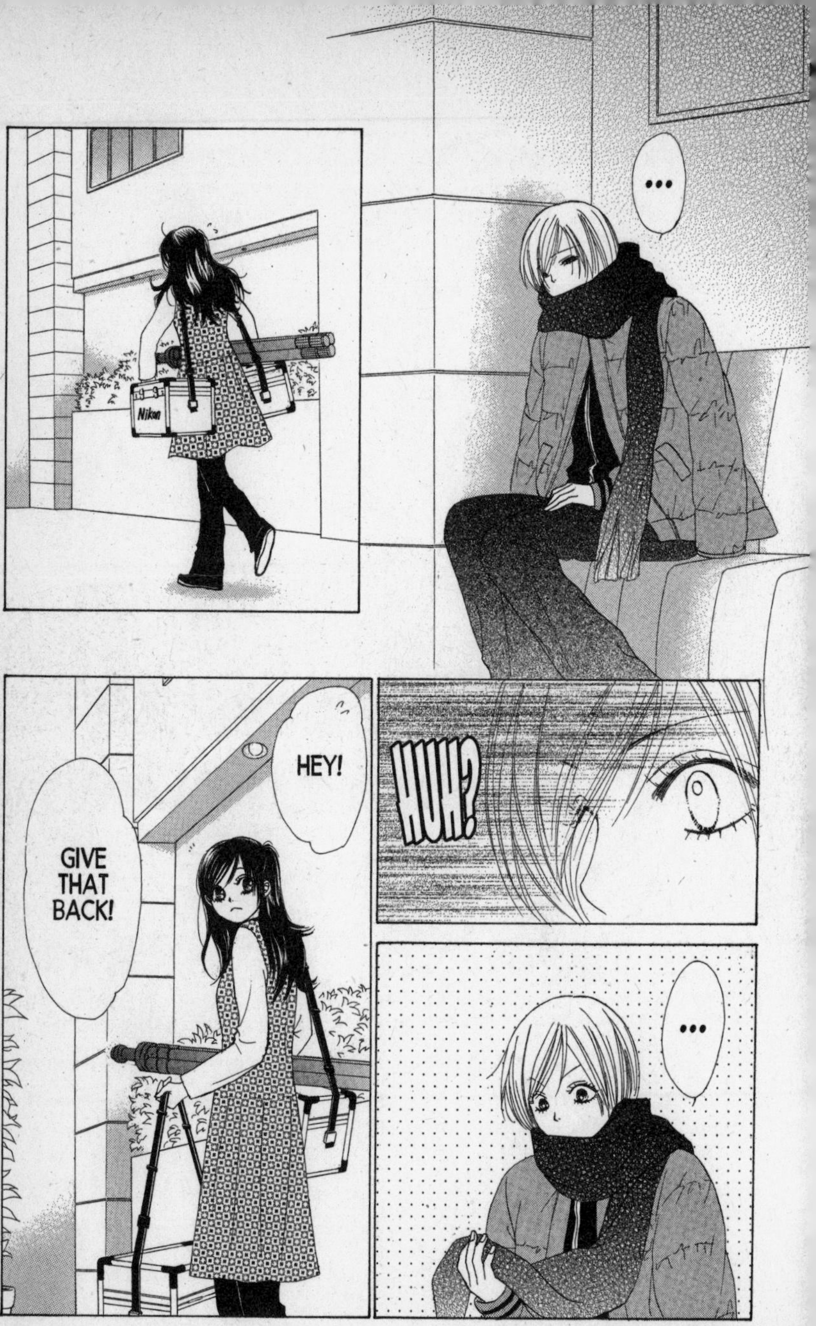
...
HUH?
...
HEY!
GIVE THAT BACK!

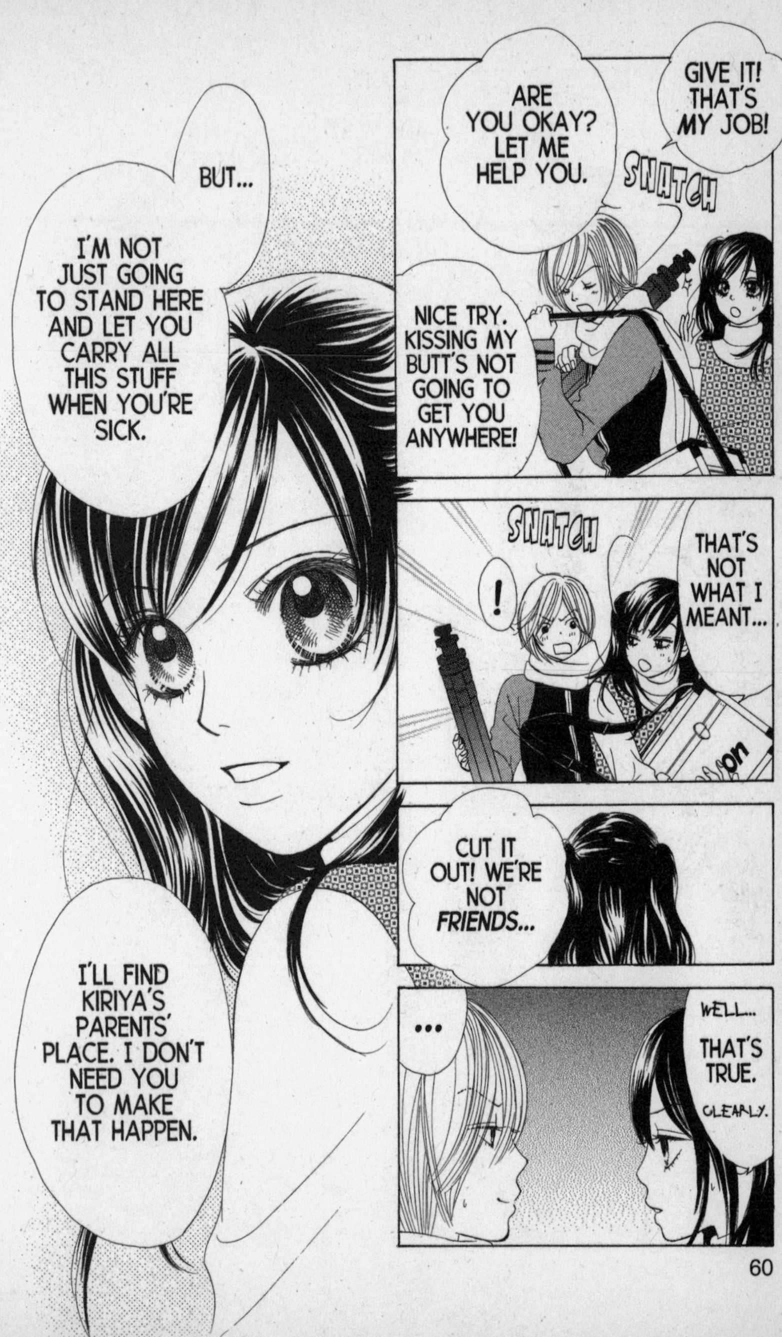
GIVE IT! THAT'S MY JOB!
ARE YOU OKAY? LET ME HELP YOU.
SNATCH
NICE TRY. KISSING MY BUTT'S NOT GOING TO GET YOU ANYWHERE!
THAT'S NOT WHAT I MEANT...
SNATCH
!
CUT IT OUT! WE'RE NOT *FRIENDS*...
WELL...
THAT'S TRUE.
CLEARLY.
...
BUT...
I'M NOT JUST GOING TO STAND HERE AND LET YOU CARRY ALL THIS STUFF WHEN YOU'RE SICK.
I'LL FIND KIRIYA'S PARENTS' PLACE. I DON'T NEED YOU TO MAKE THAT HAPPEN.

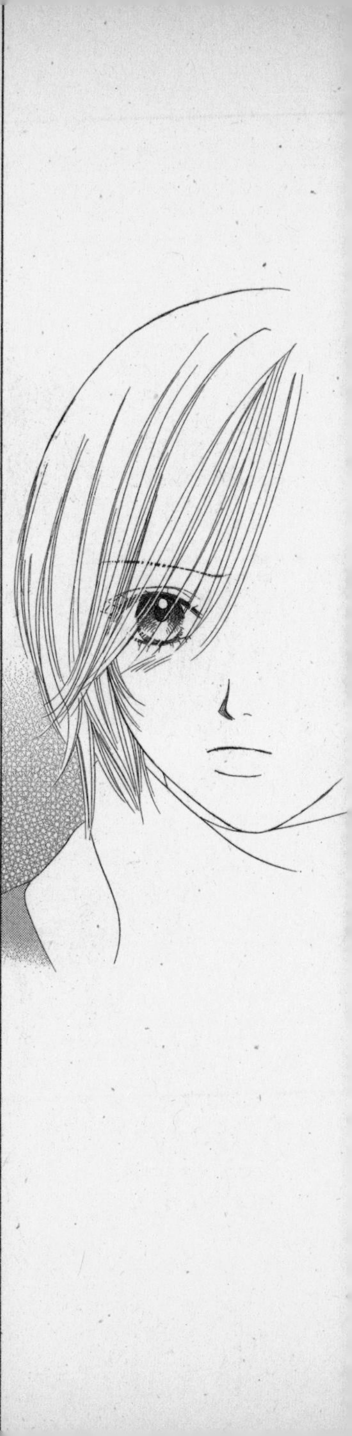
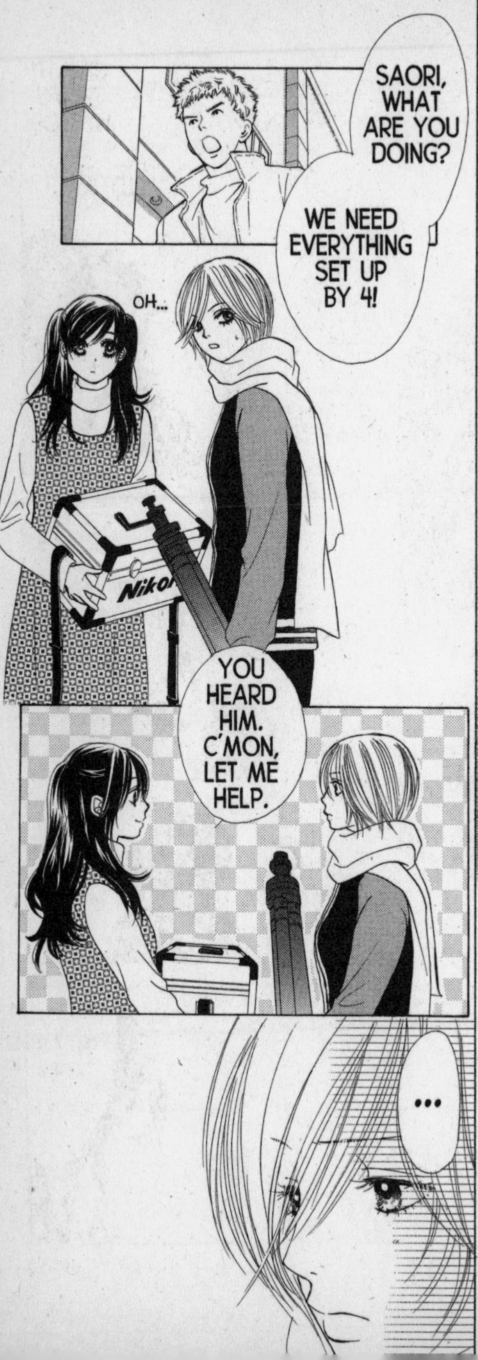
SAORI, WHAT ARE YOU DOING?
WE NEED EVERYTHING SET UP BY 4!
OH...
YOU HEARD HIM. C'MON, LET ME HELP.
...

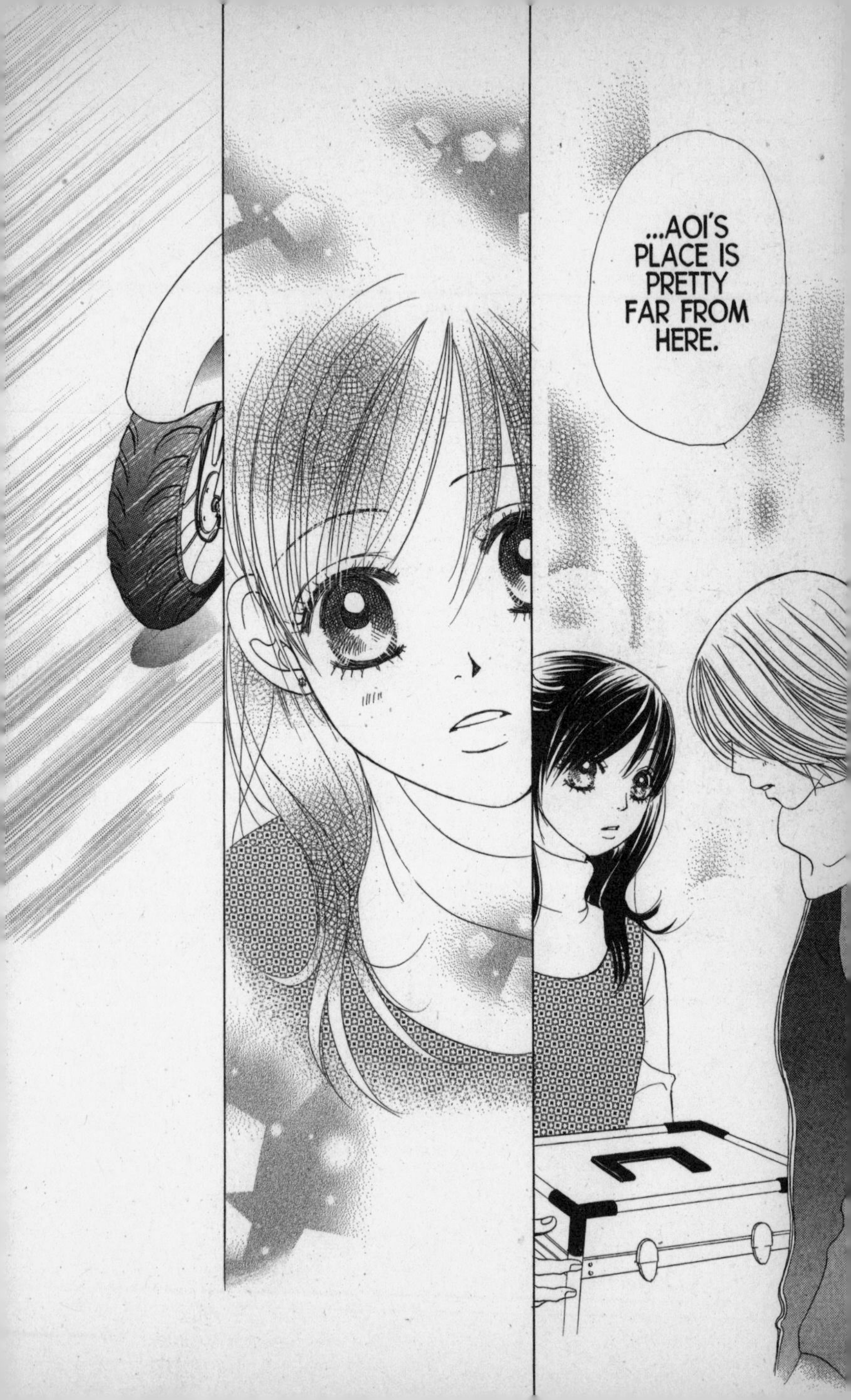
...AOI'S PLACE IS PRETTY FAR FROM HERE.

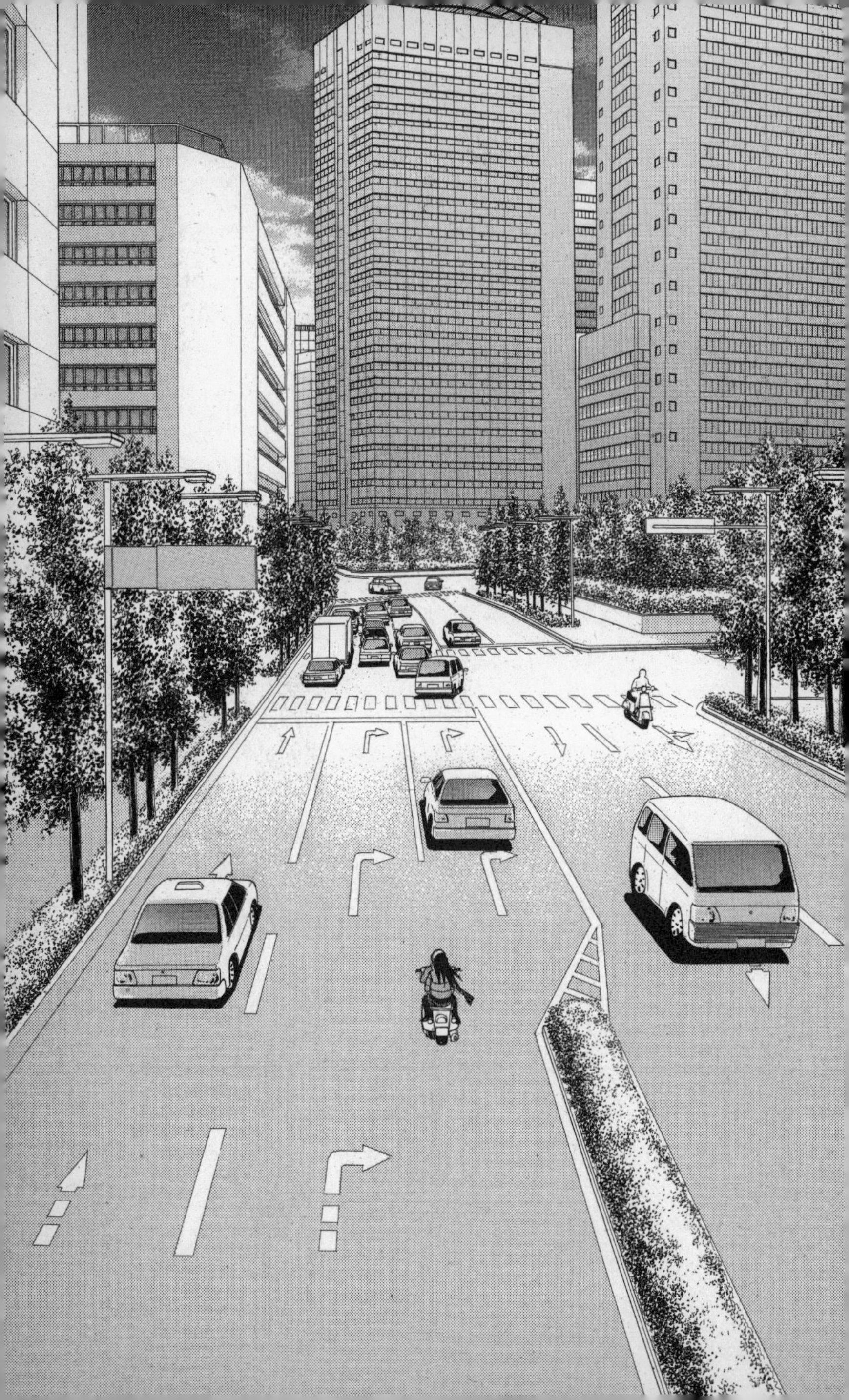

KARE

彼 First Love

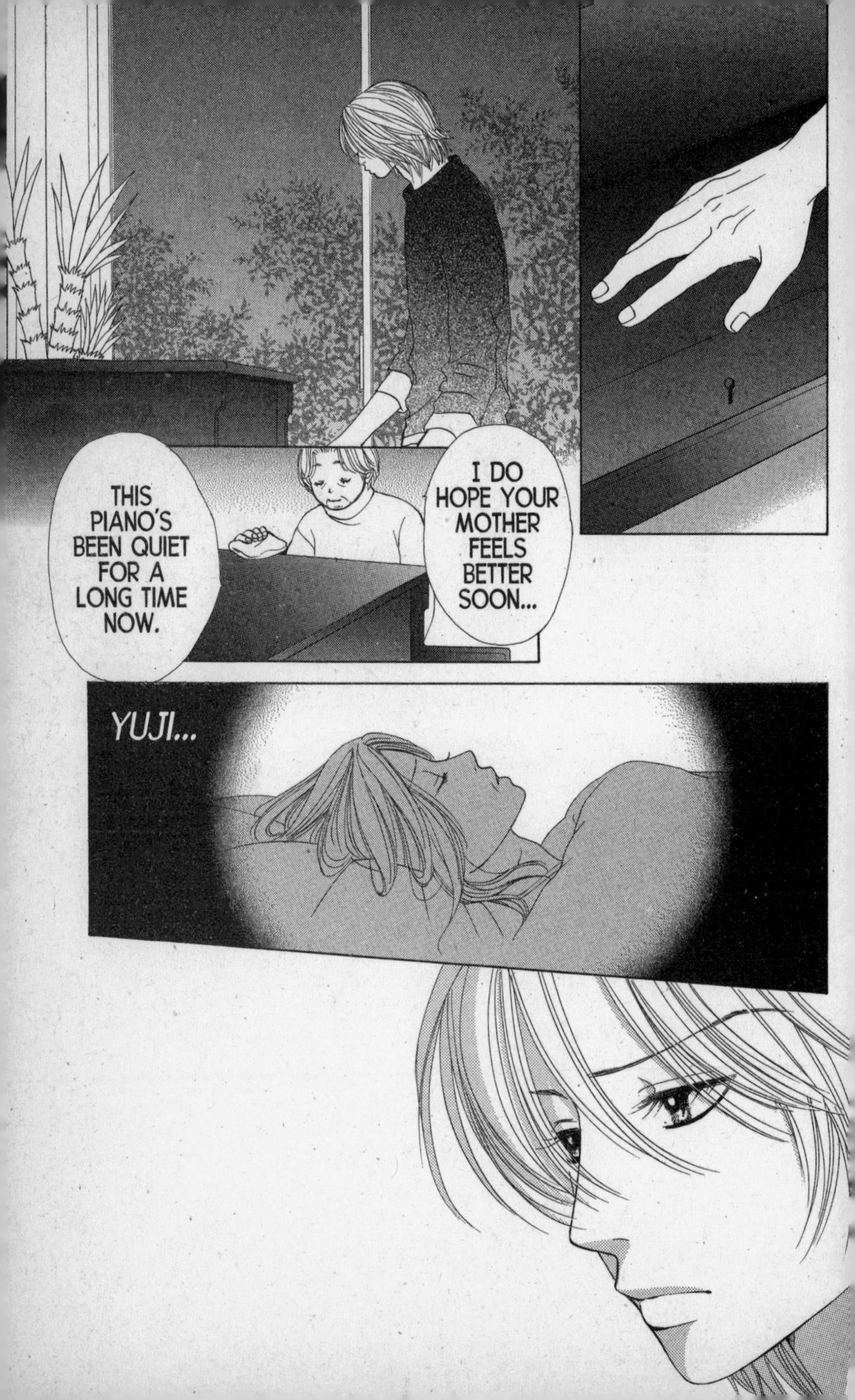
I DO HOPE YOUR MOTHER FEELS BETTER SOON...
THIS PIANO'S BEEN QUIET FOR A LONG TIME NOW.
YUJI...

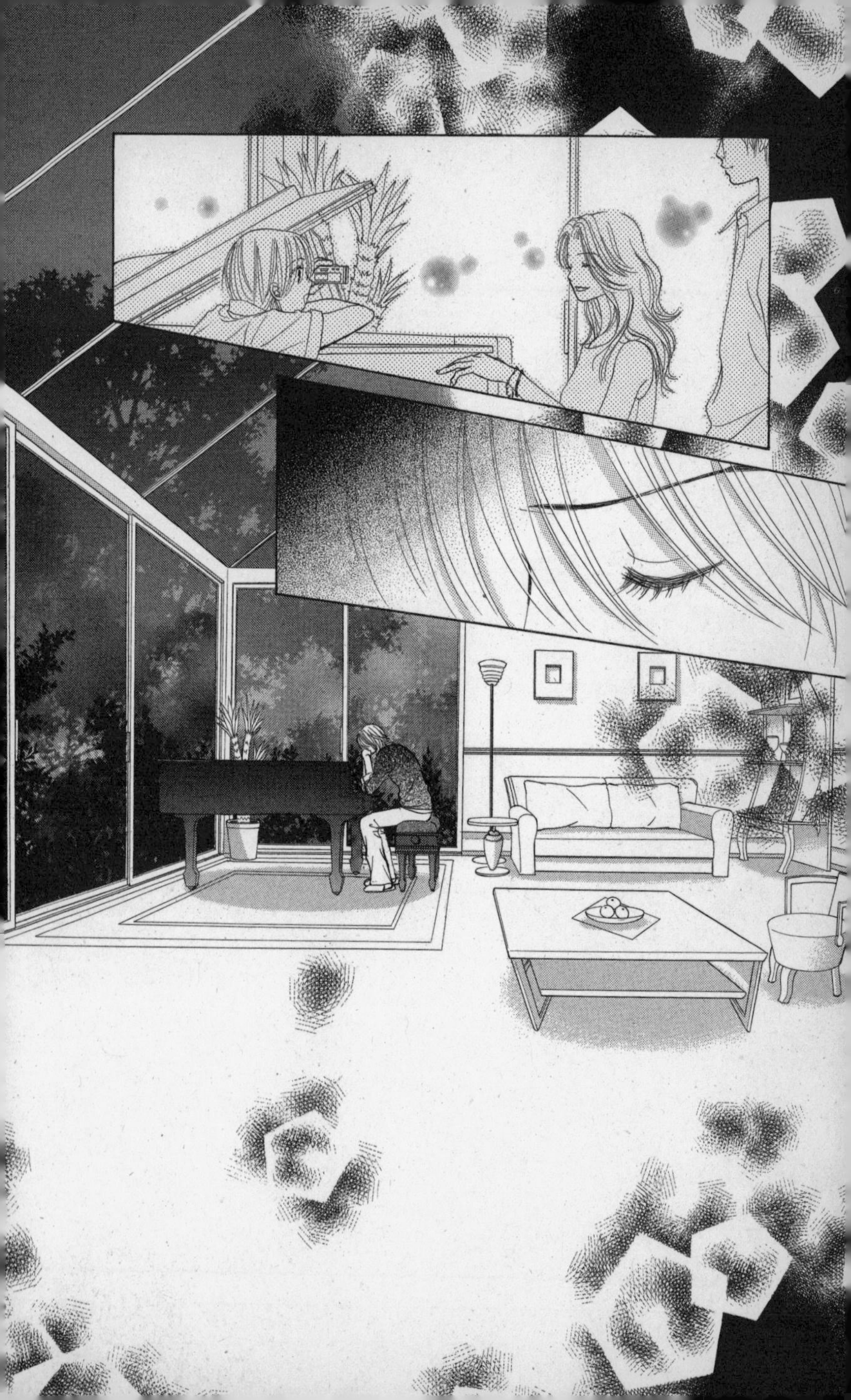

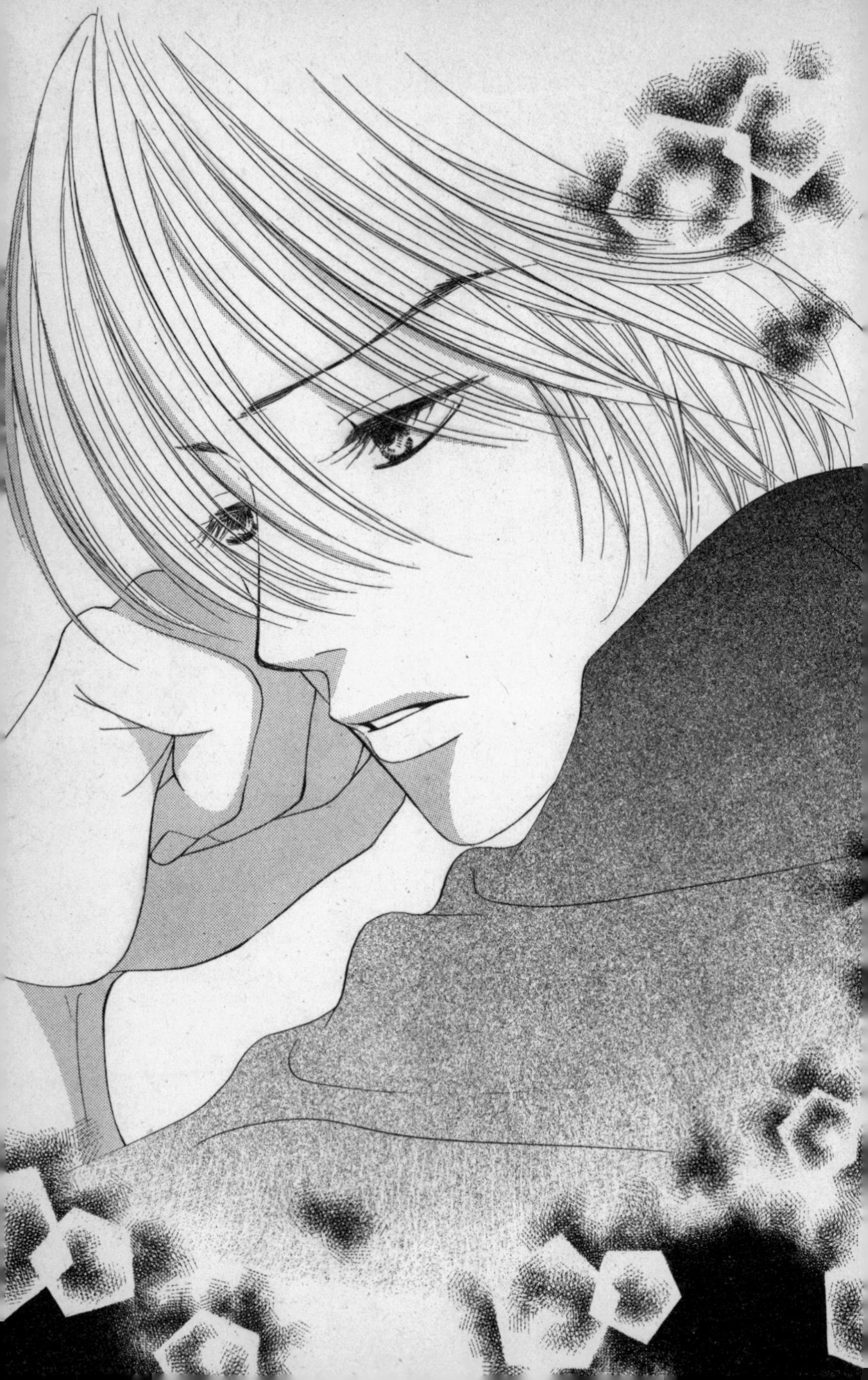

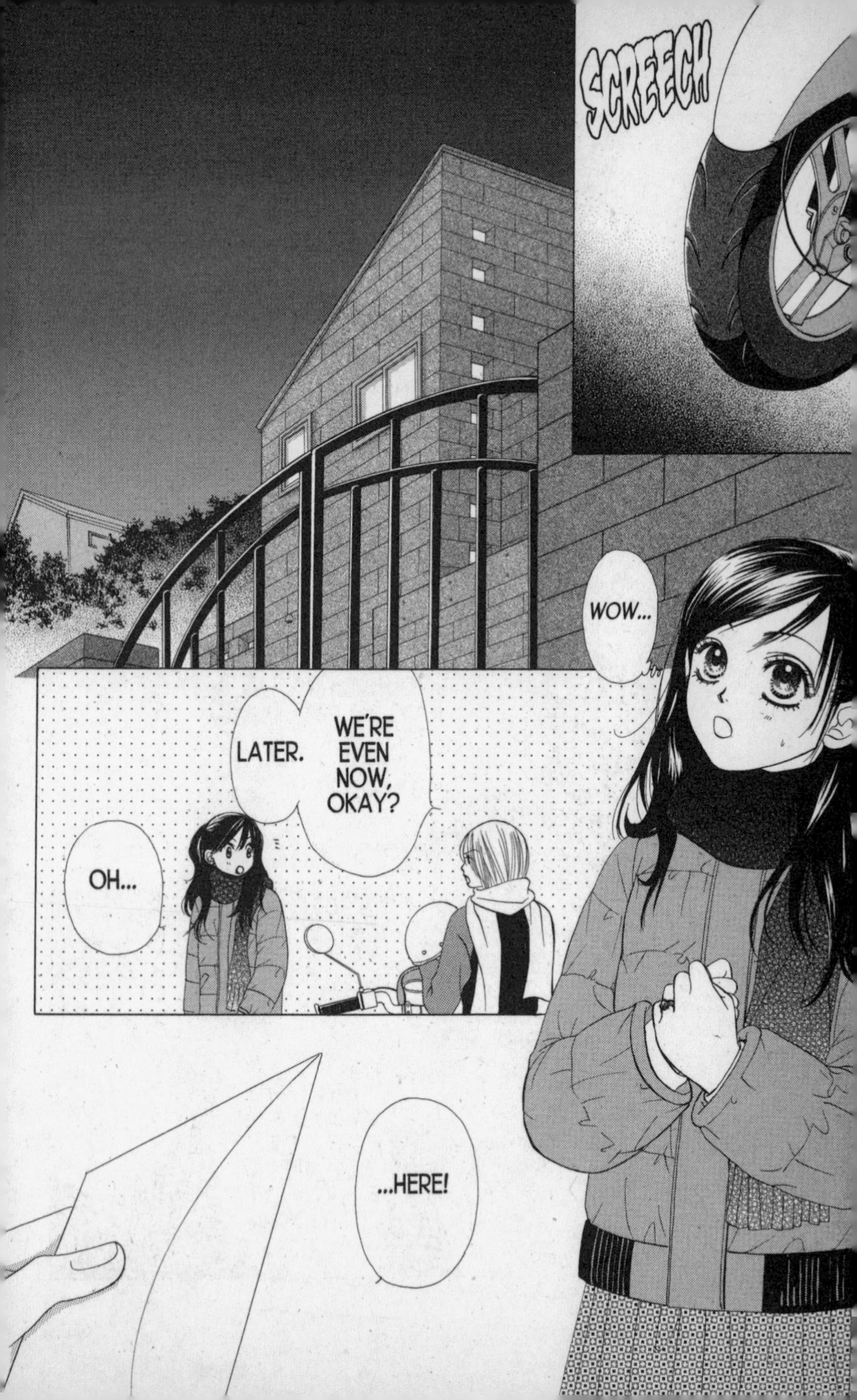
SCREECH
WOW...
WE'RE EVEN NOW, OKAY?
LATER.
OH...
...HERE!

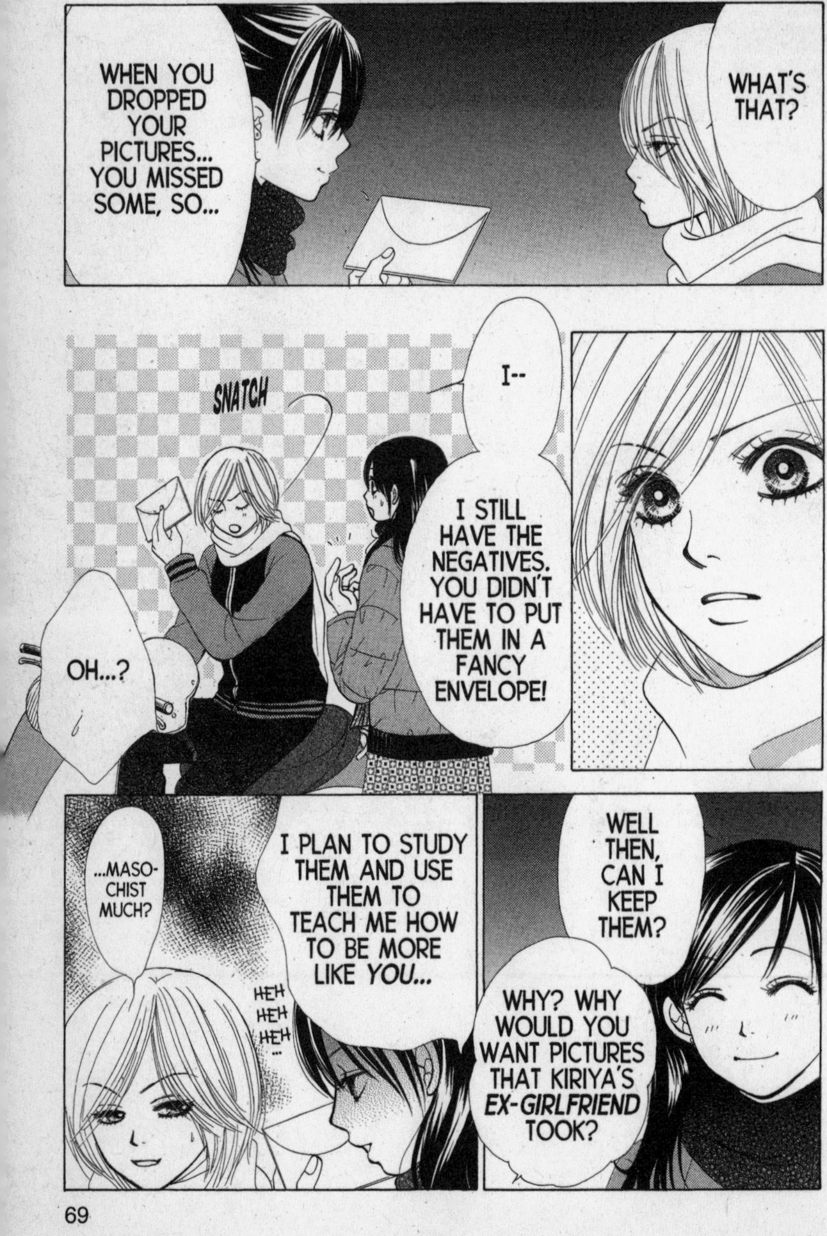
WHAT'S THAT?
WHEN YOU DROPPED YOUR PICTURES... YOU MISSED SOME, SO...
I--
I STILL HAVE THE NEGATIVES. YOU DIDN'T HAVE TO PUT THEM IN A FANCY ENVELOPE!
SNATCH
OH...?
WELL THEN, CAN I KEEP THEM?
WHY? WHY WOULD YOU WANT PICTURES THAT KIRIYA'S *EX-GIRLFRIEND* TOOK?
I PLAN TO STUDY THEM AND USE THEM TO TEACH ME HOW TO BE MORE LIKE *YOU...*
HEH HEH HEH...
...MASO-CHIST MUCH?

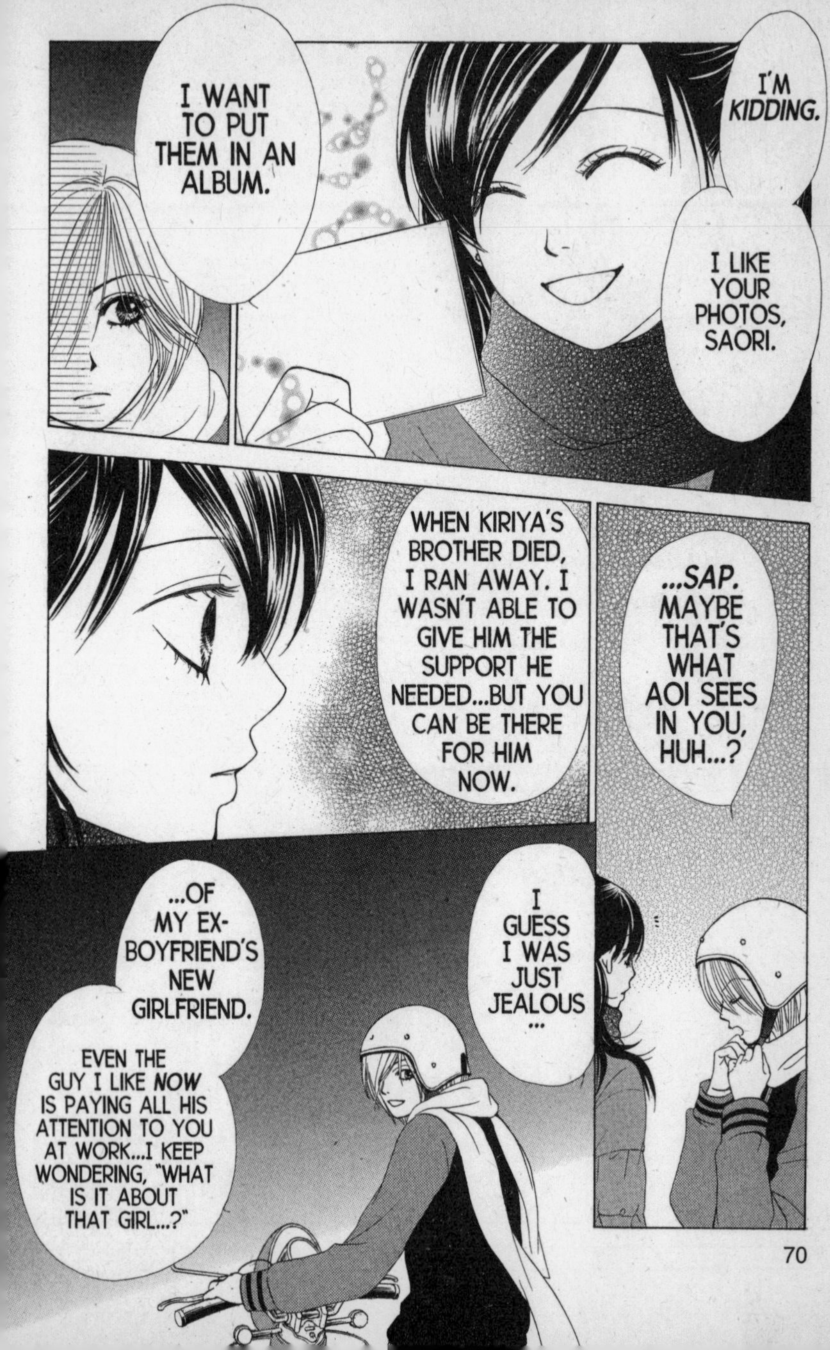
I'M *KIDDING.*
I LIKE YOUR PHOTOS, SAORI.
I WANT TO PUT THEM IN AN ALBUM.
...SAP. MAYBE THAT'S WHAT AOI SEES IN YOU, HUH...?
WHEN KIRIYA'S BROTHER DIED, I RAN AWAY. I WASN'T ABLE TO GIVE HIM THE SUPPORT HE NEEDED...BUT YOU CAN BE THERE FOR HIM NOW.
I GUESS I WAS JUST JEALOUS...
...OF MY EX-BOYFRIEND'S NEW GIRLFRIEND.
EVEN THE GUY I LIKE *NOW* IS PAYING ALL HIS ATTENTION TO YOU AT WORK...I KEEP WONDERING, "WHAT IS IT ABOUT THAT GIRL...?"

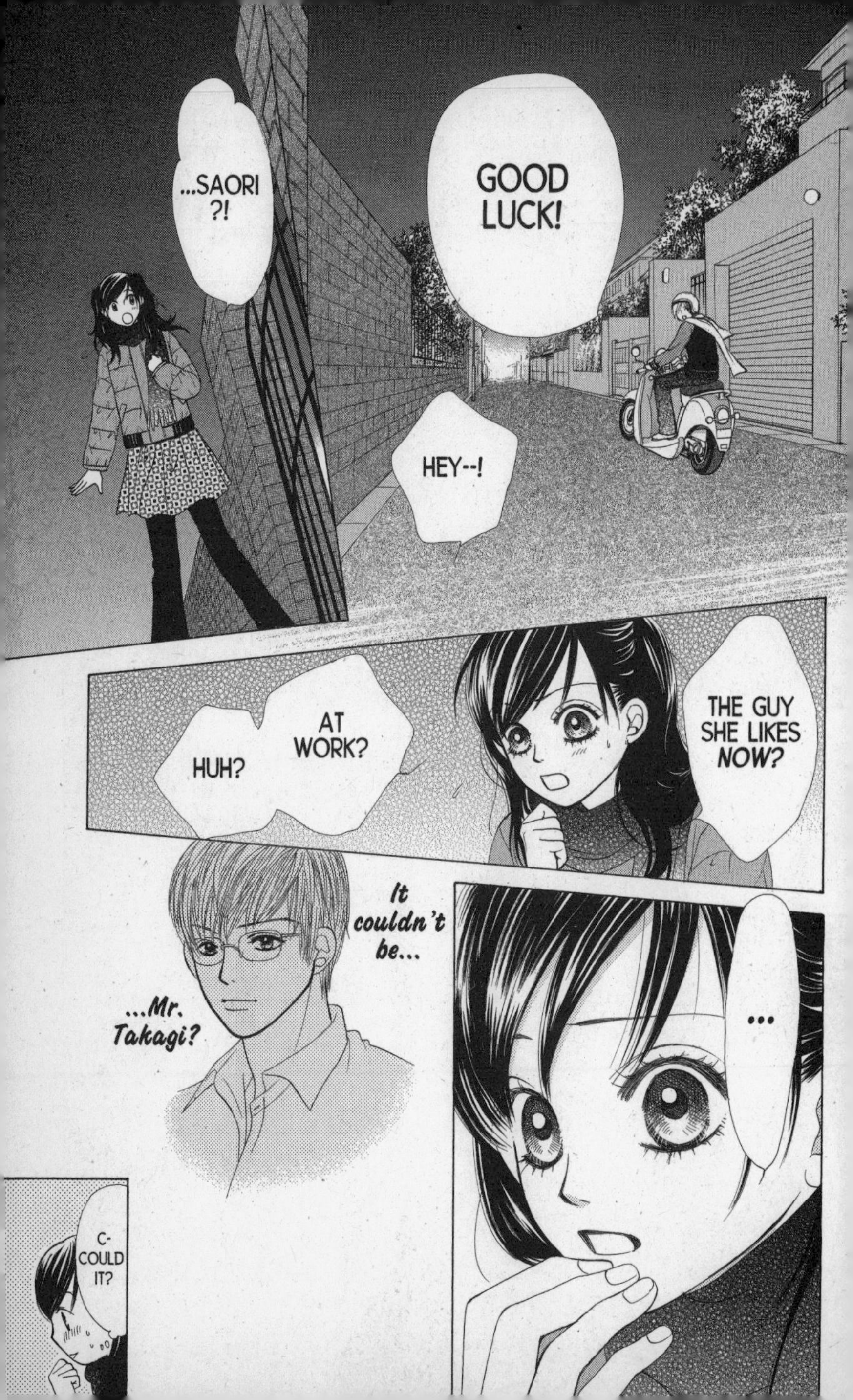
GOOD LUCK!
...SAORI ?!
HEY--!
THE GUY SHE LIKES *NOW?*
AT WORK?
HUH?
...
It couldn't be...
...Mr. Takagi?
C-COULD IT?

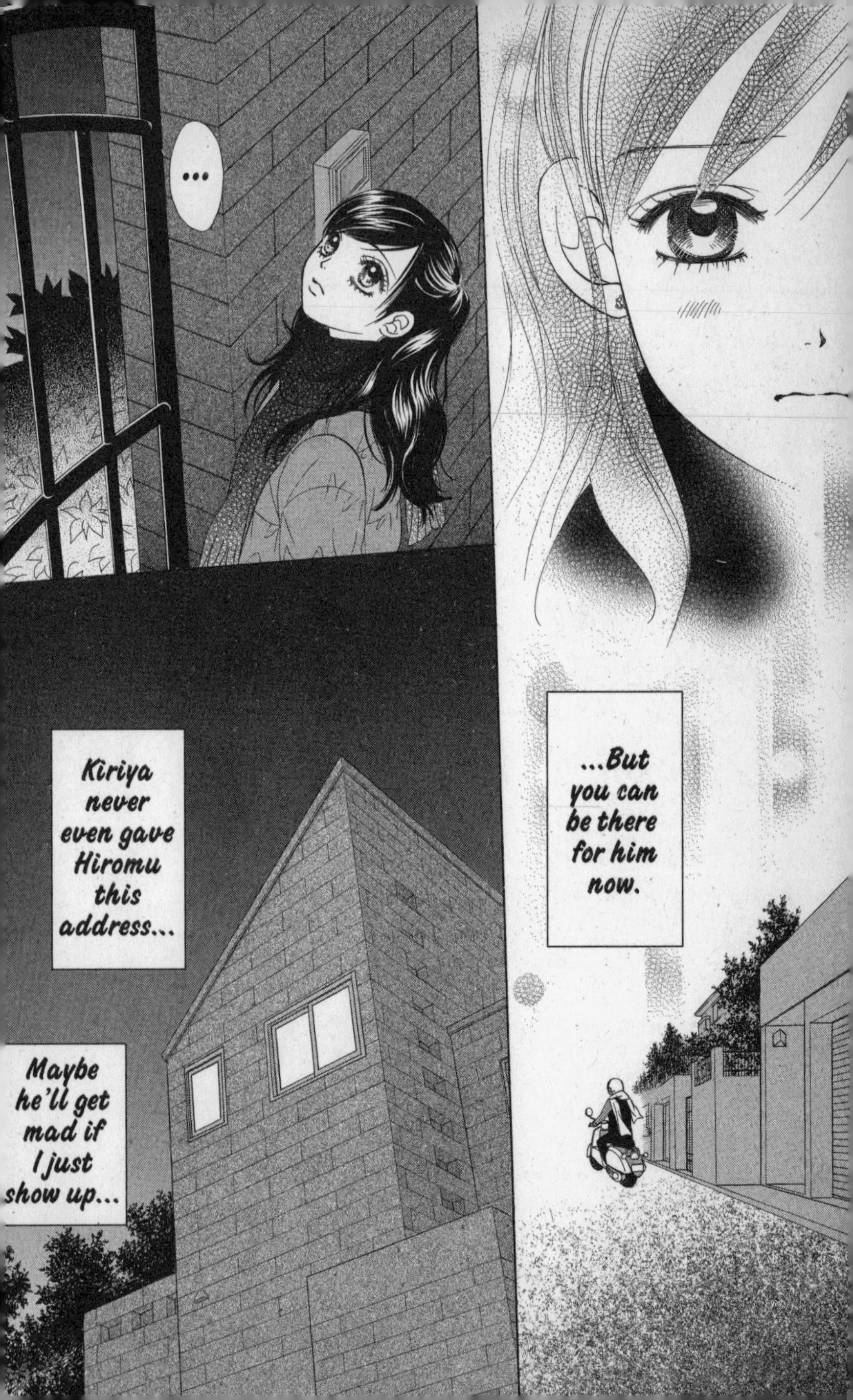
...But you can be there for him now.
...
Kiriya never even gave Hiromu this address...
Maybe he'll get mad if I just show up...

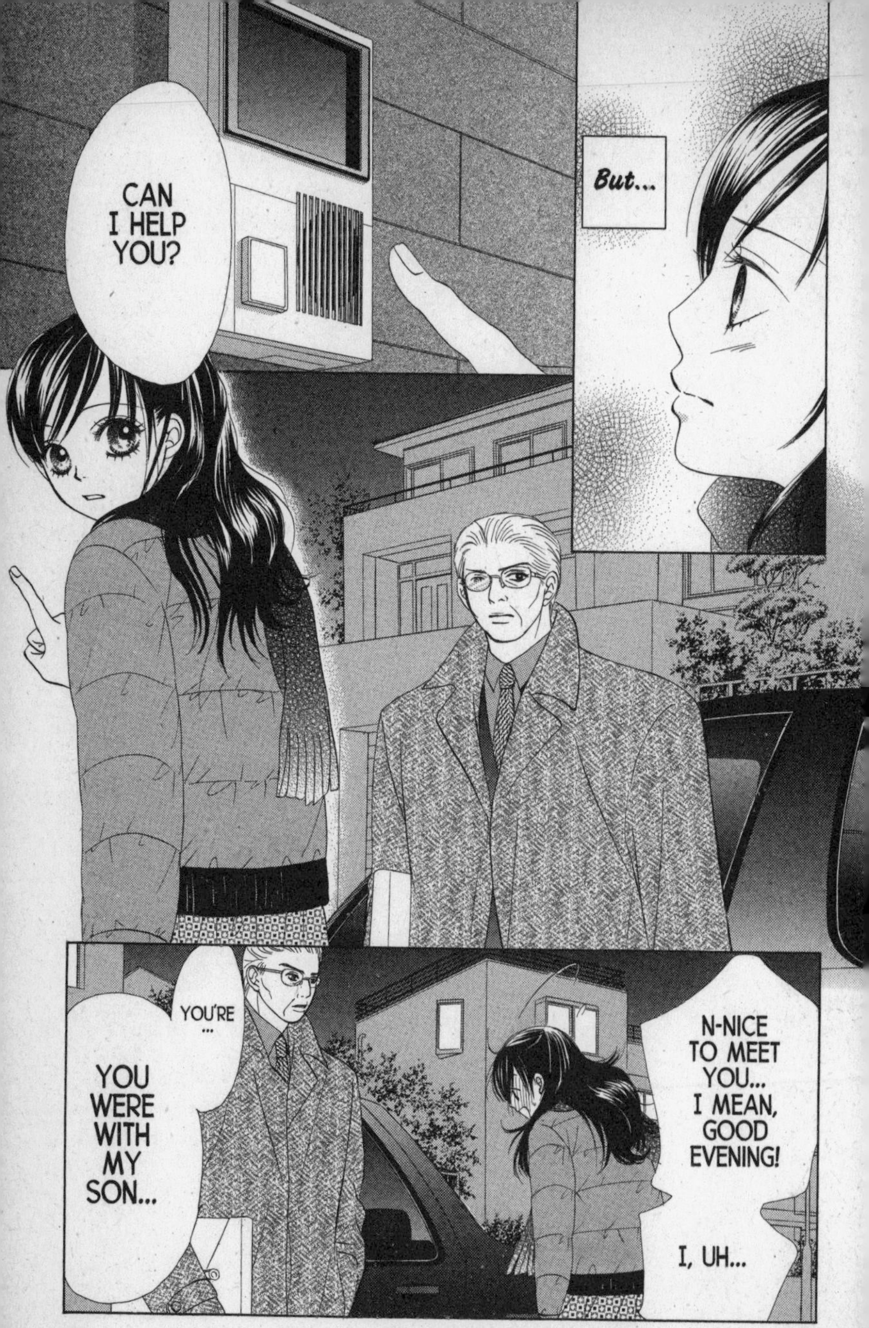
But...
CAN I HELP YOU?
N-NICE TO MEET YOU... I MEAN, GOOD EVENING!
I, UH...
YOU'RE ...
YOU WERE WITH MY SON...

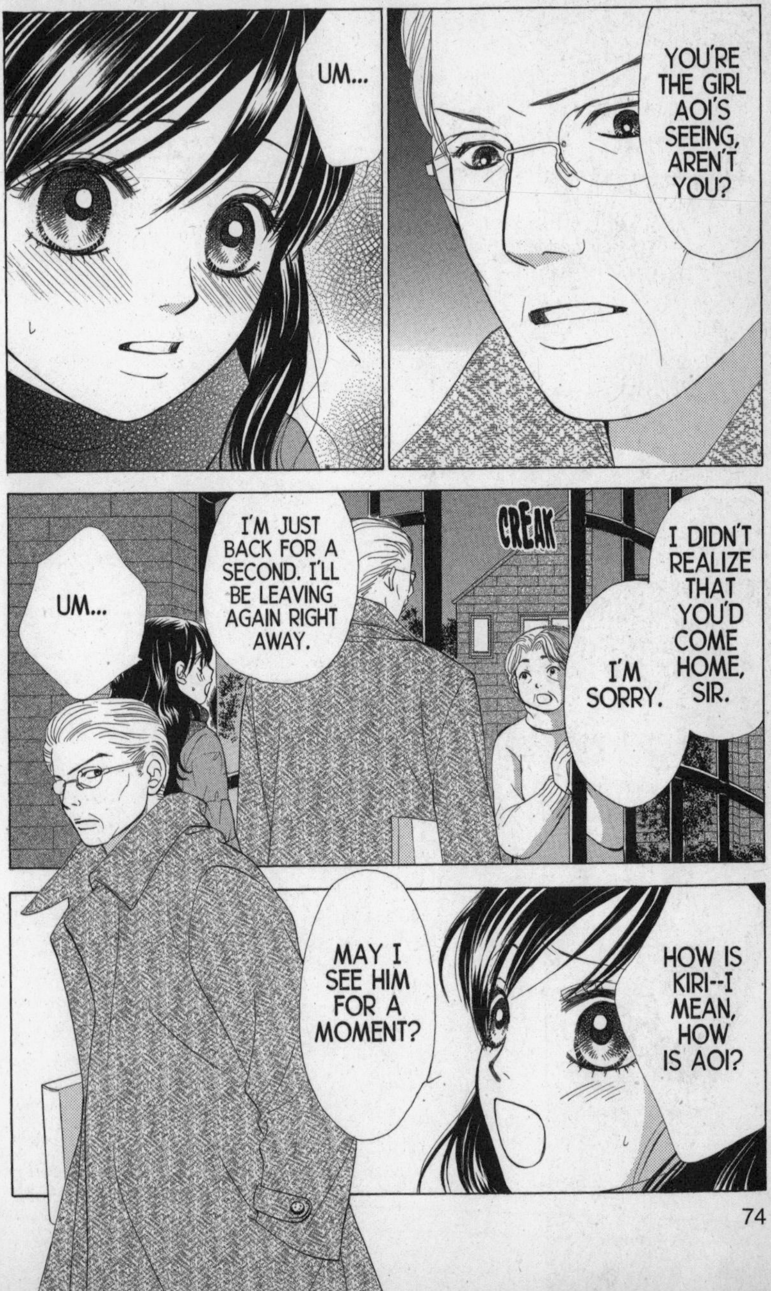
YOU'RE THE GIRL AOI'S SEEING, AREN'T YOU?
UM...
CREAK
I DIDN'T REALIZE THAT YOU'D COME HOME, SIR.
I'M SORRY.
I'M JUST BACK FOR A SECOND. I'LL BE LEAVING AGAIN RIGHT AWAY.
UM...
HOW IS KIRI--I MEAN, HOW IS AOI?
MAY I SEE HIM FOR A MOMENT?

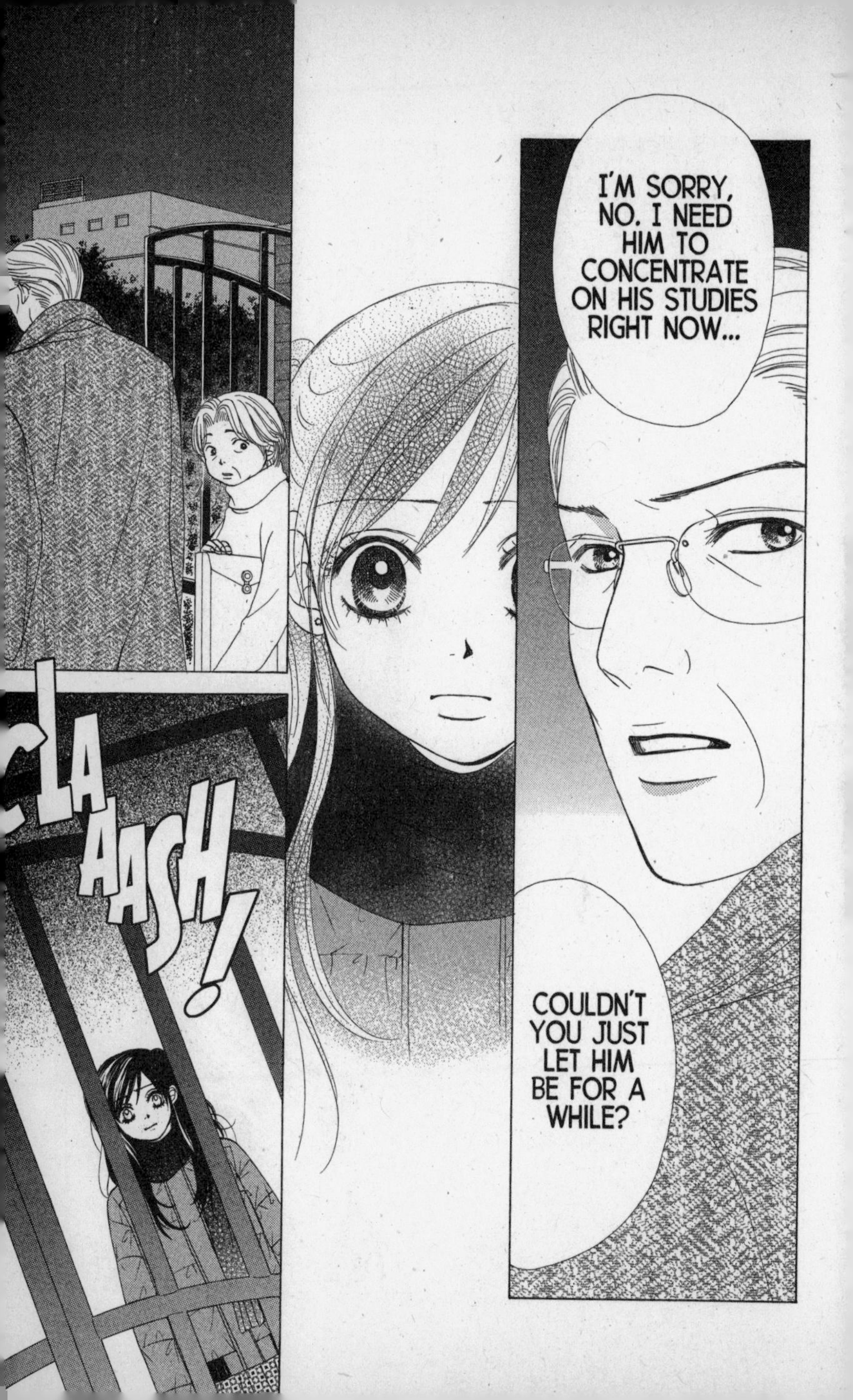
I'M SORRY, NO. I NEED HIM TO CONCENTRATE ON HIS STUDIES RIGHT NOW...
COULDN'T YOU JUST LET HIM BE FOR A WHILE?
CLAAASH!

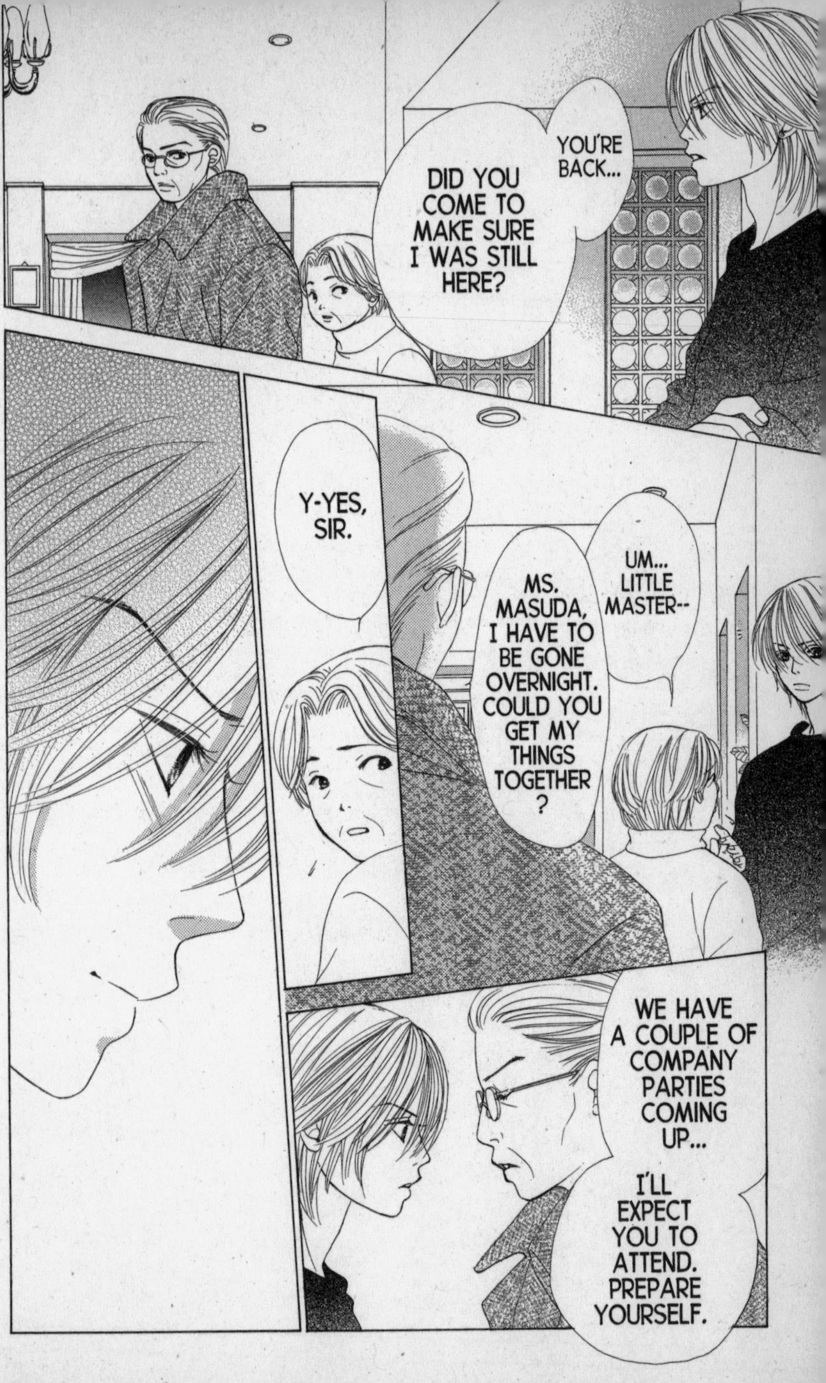
YOU'RE BACK...
DID YOU COME TO MAKE SURE I WAS STILL HERE?
UM... LITTLE MASTER--
MS. MASUDA, I HAVE TO BE GONE OVERNIGHT. COULD YOU GET MY THINGS TOGETHER?
Y-YES, SIR.
WE HAVE A COUPLE OF COMPANY PARTIES COMING UP...
I'LL EXPECT YOU TO ATTEND. PREPARE YOURSELF.

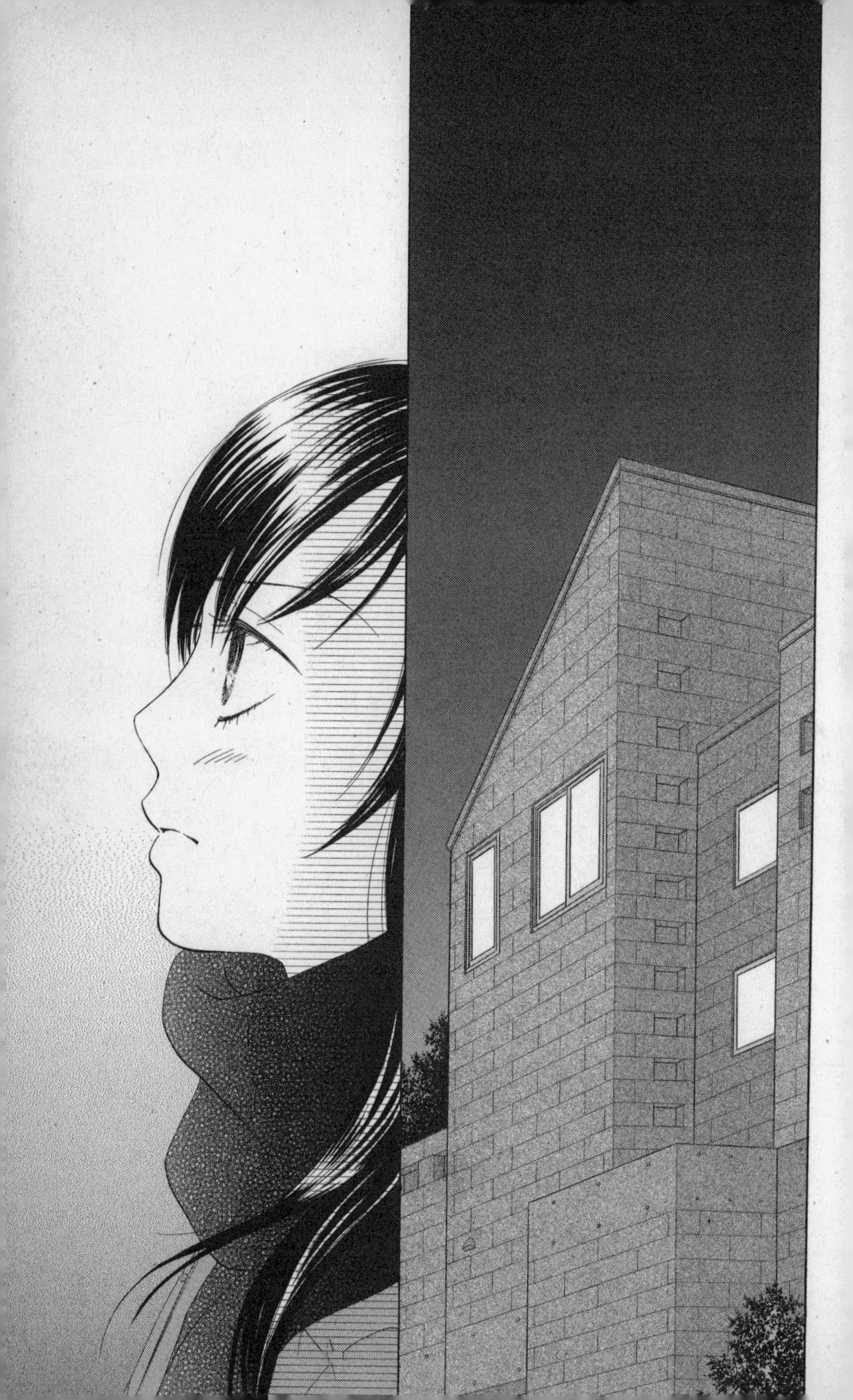

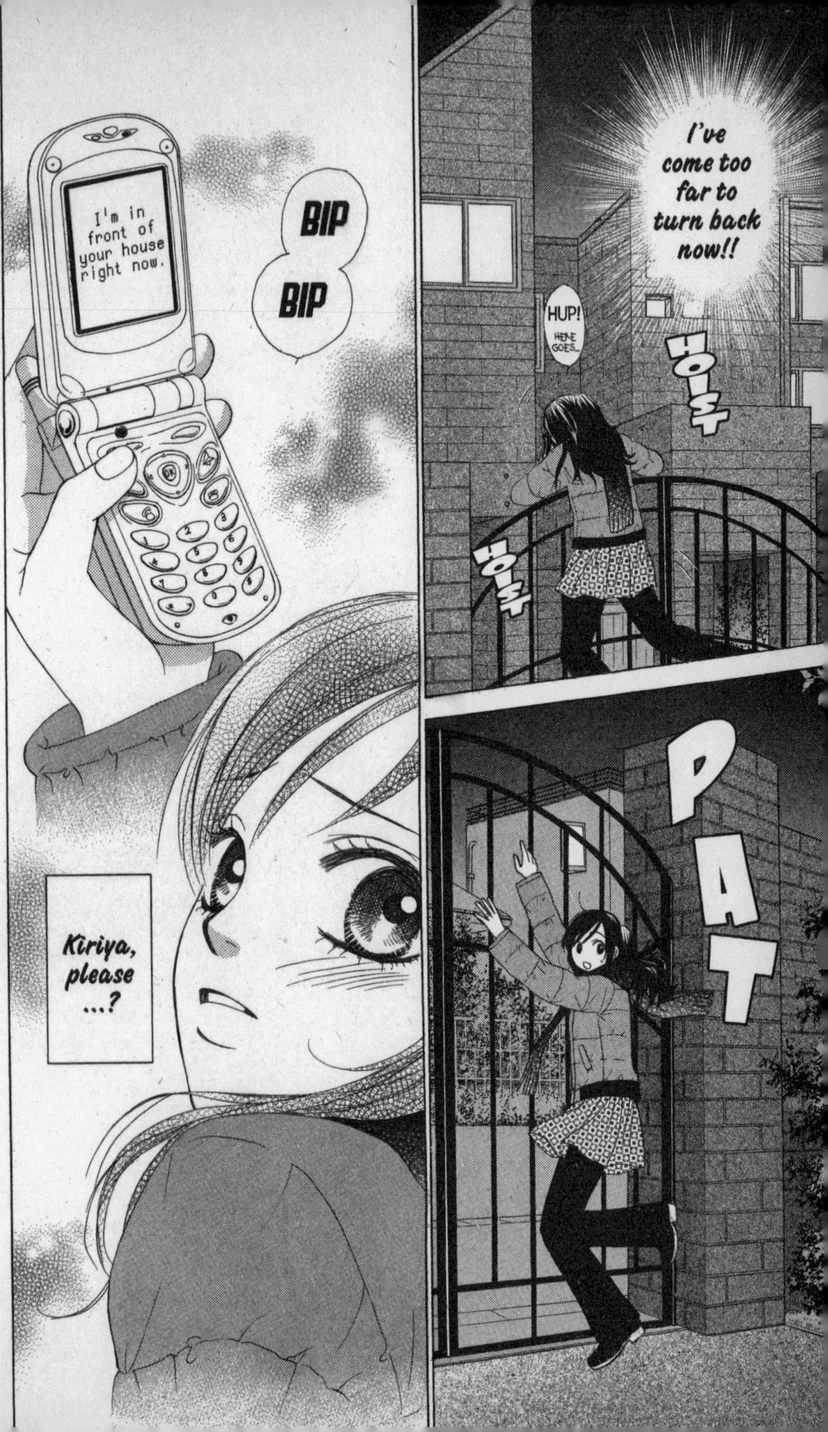
I've come too far to turn back now!!
HUP! HERE GOES...
HOIST
HOIST
PAT
I'm in front of your house right now.
BIP
BIP
Kiriya, please ...?

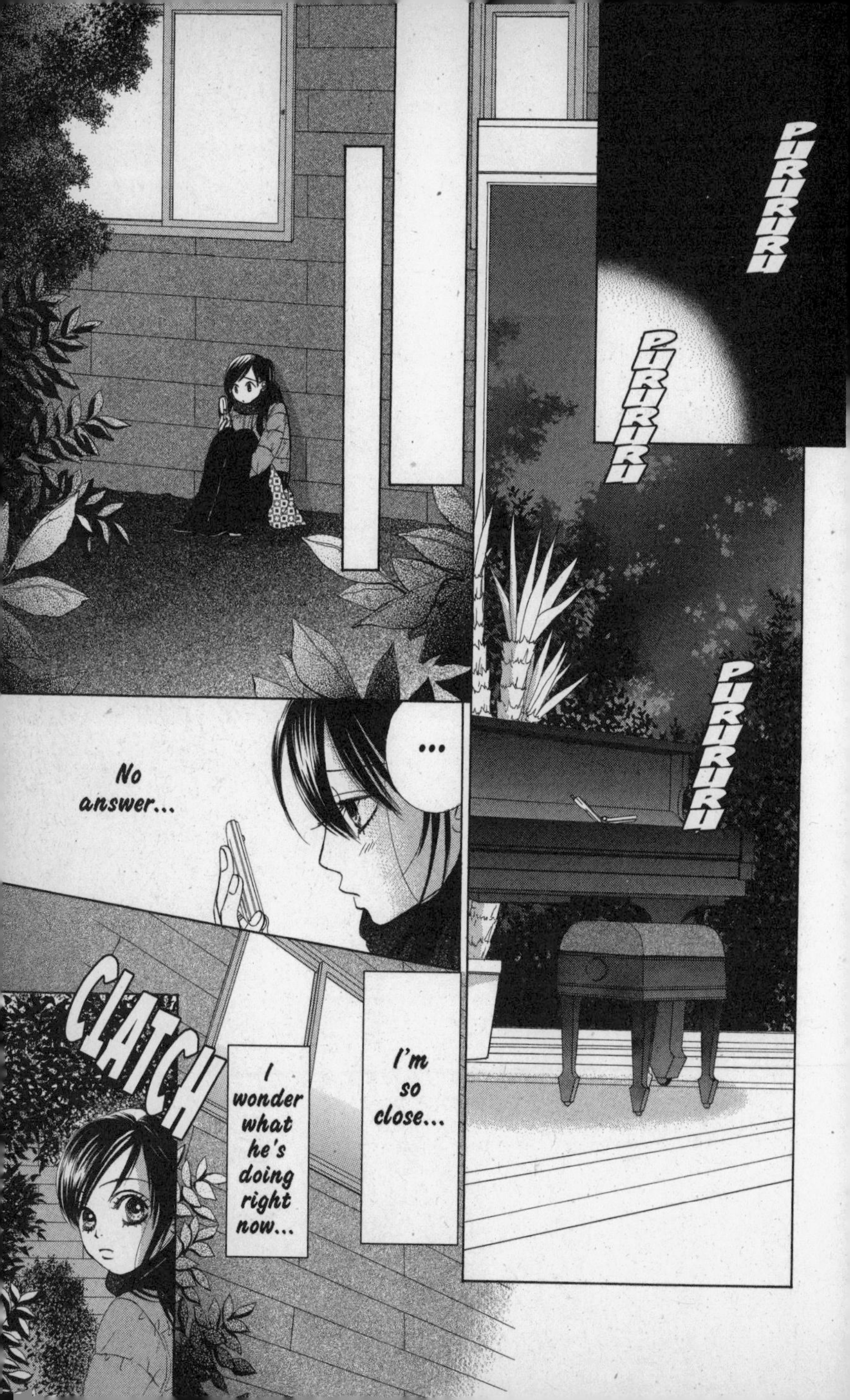
PURURURU
PURURURU
PURURURU
...
No answer...
CLATCH
I'm so close...
I wonder what he's doing right now...

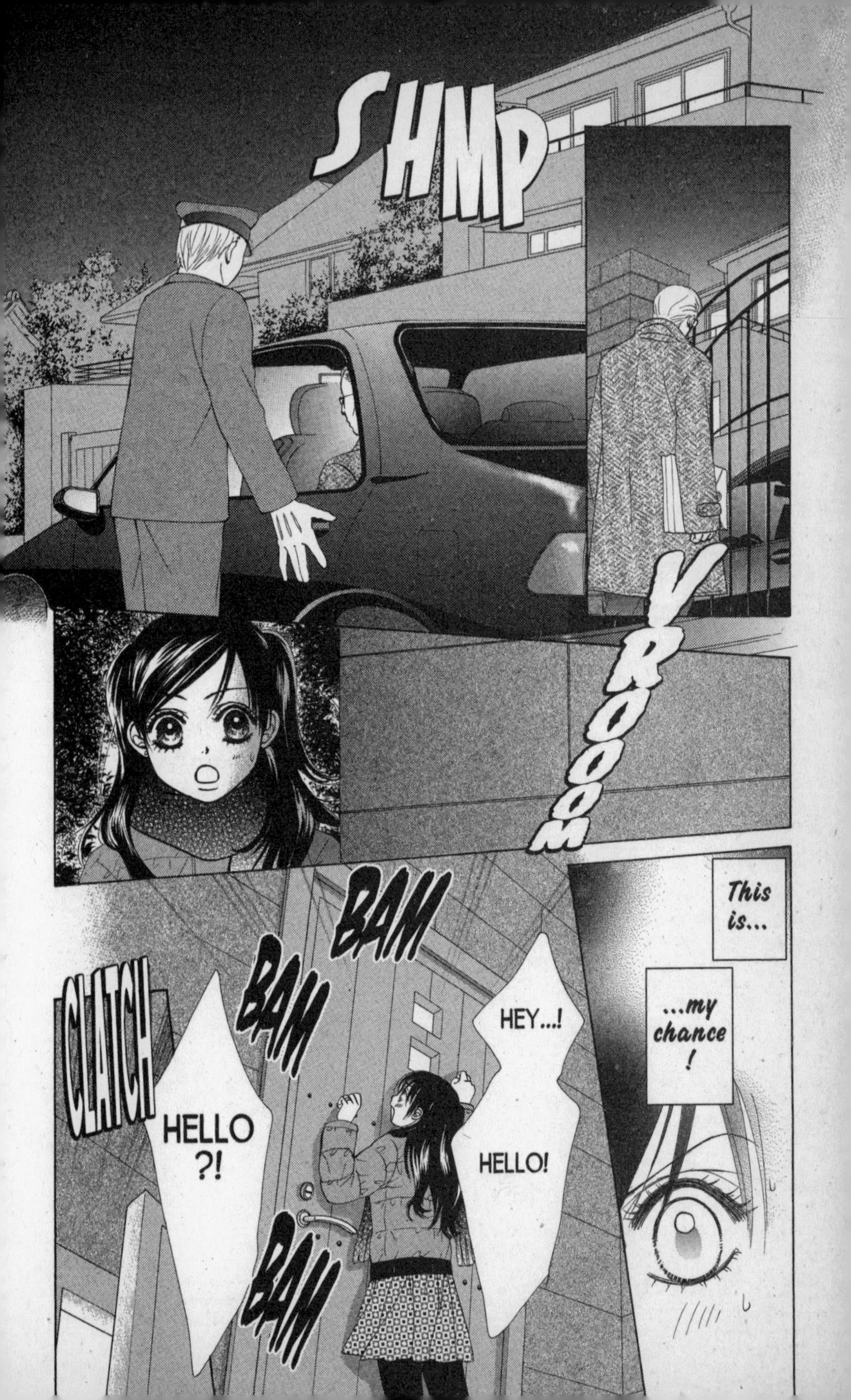
SHMP
VROOOM
This is...
...my chance!
HEY...!
BAM
BAM
HELLO!
CLATCH
HELLO ?!
BAM

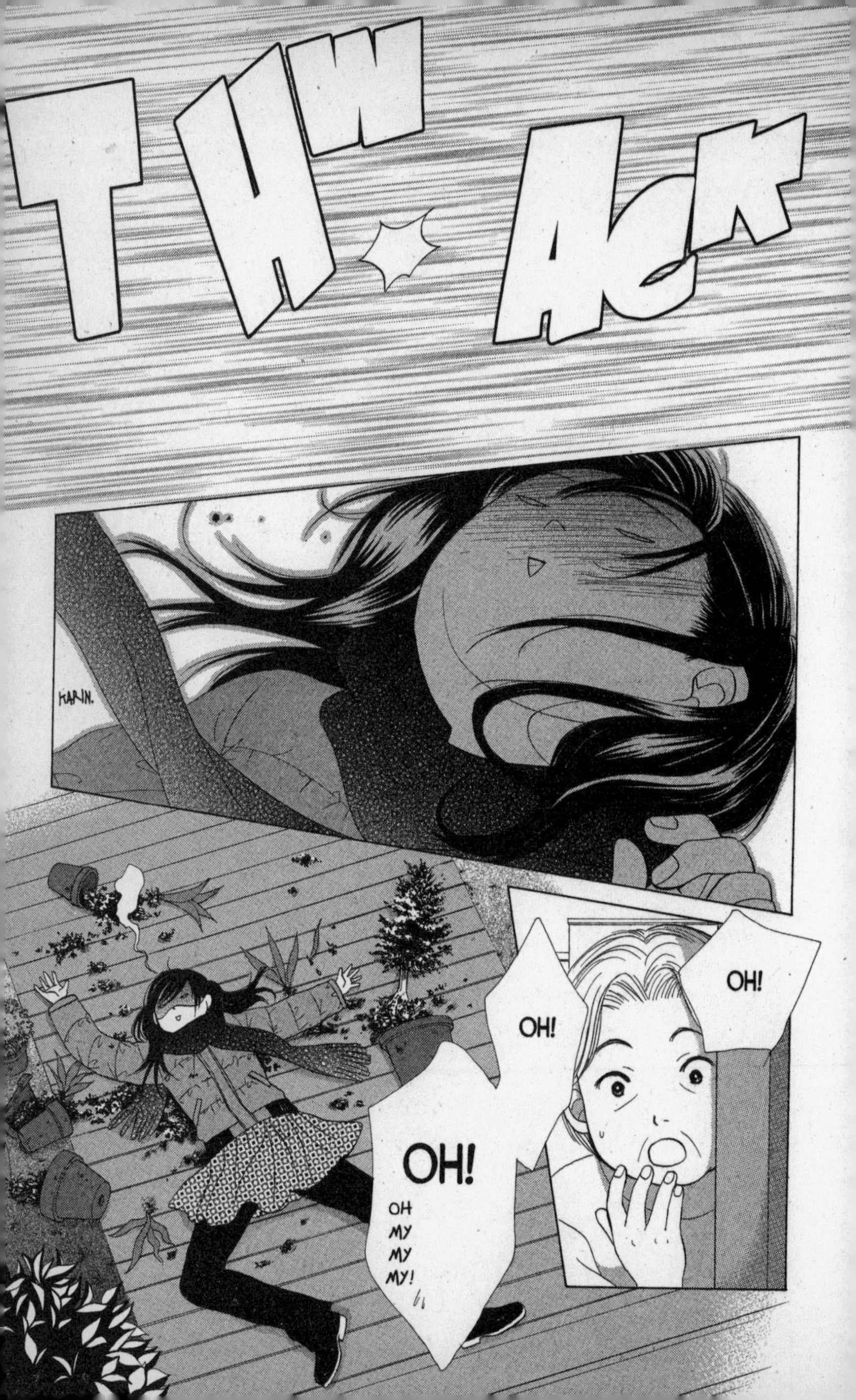
THWACK
KARIN.
OH!
OH!
OH!
OH MY MY MY!

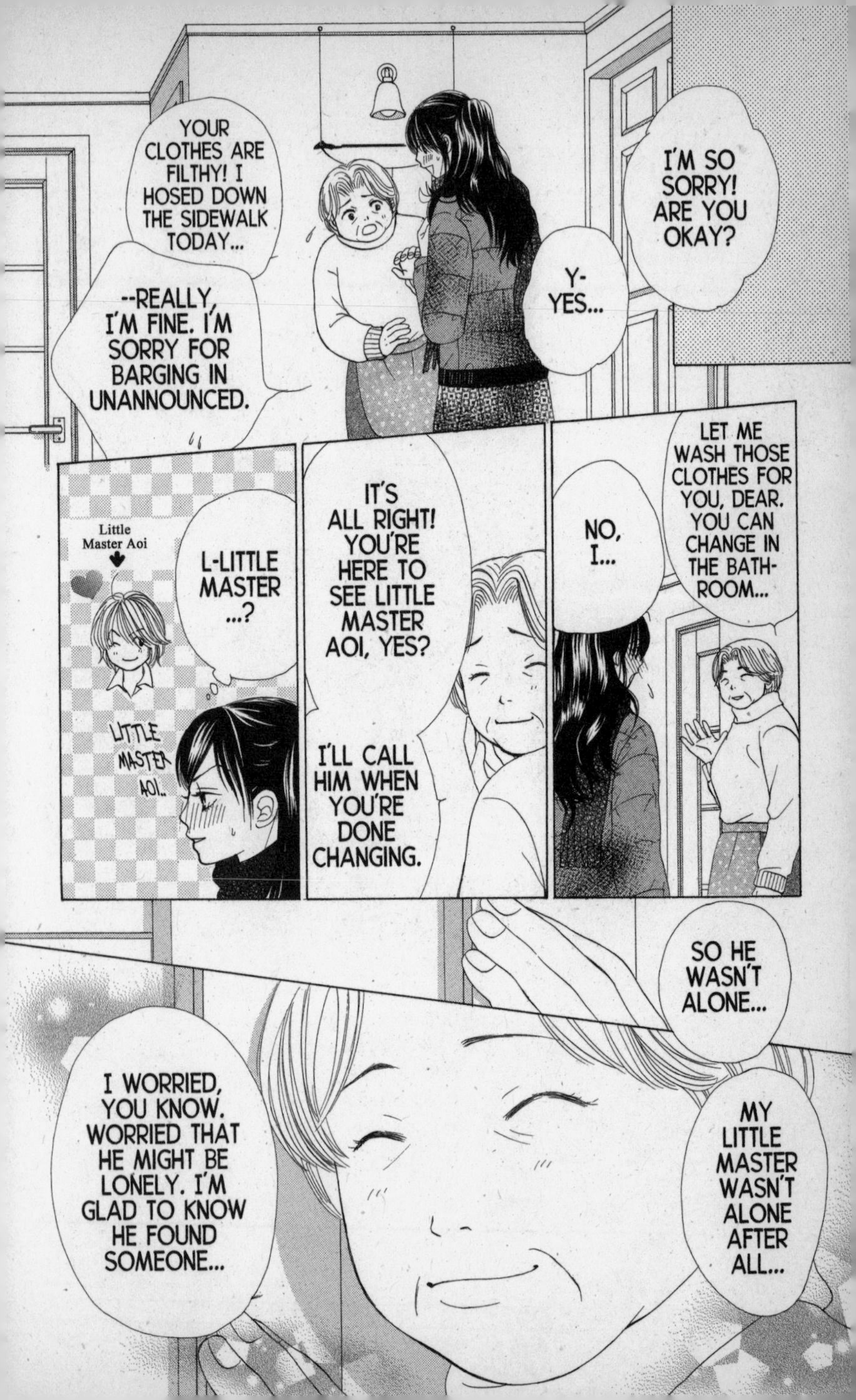
I'M SO SORRY! ARE YOU OKAY?
Y-YES...
YOUR CLOTHES ARE FILTHY! I HOSED DOWN THE SIDEWALK TODAY...
--REALLY, I'M FINE. I'M SORRY FOR BARGING IN UNANNOUNCED.
LET ME WASH THOSE CLOTHES FOR YOU, DEAR. YOU CAN CHANGE IN THE BATH-ROOM...
NO, I...
IT'S ALL RIGHT! YOU'RE HERE TO SEE LITTLE MASTER AOI, YES?
I'LL CALL HIM WHEN YOU'RE DONE CHANGING.
L-LITTLE MASTER ...?
Little Master Aoi
LITTLE MASTER AOI..
SO HE WASN'T ALONE...
MY LITTLE MASTER WASN'T ALONE AFTER ALL...
I WORRIED, YOU KNOW. WORRIED THAT HE MIGHT BE LONELY. I'M GLAD TO KNOW HE FOUND SOMEONE...

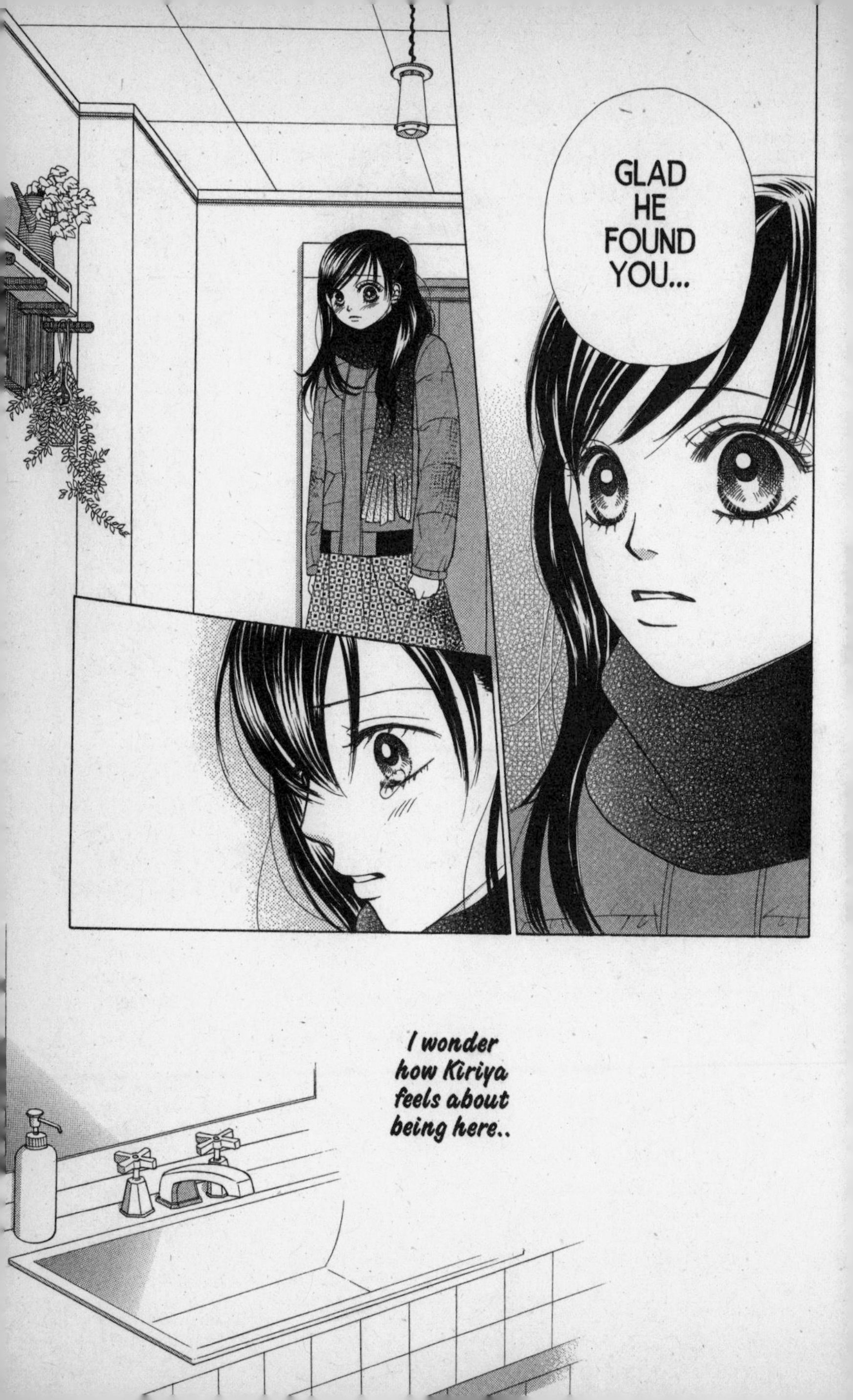
GLAD HE FOUND YOU...
I wonder how Kiriya feels about being here..

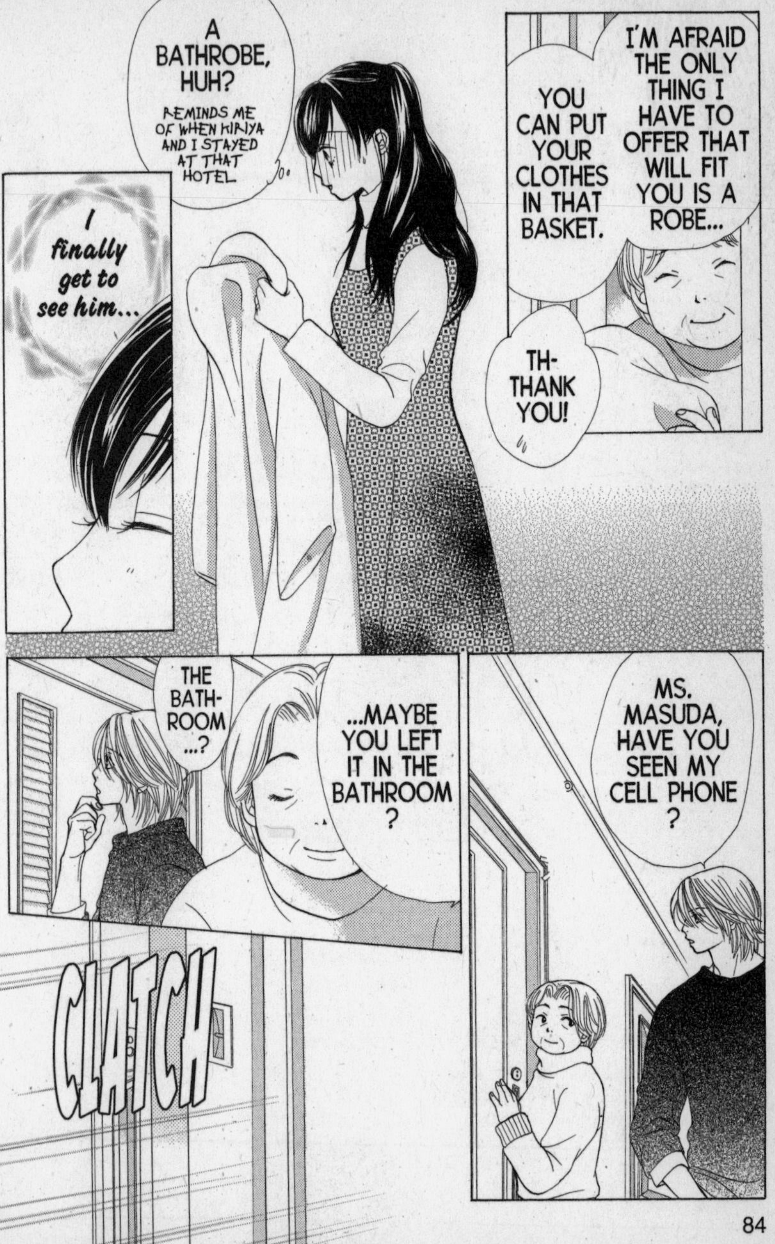
I'M AFRAID THE ONLY THING I HAVE TO OFFER THAT WILL FIT YOU IS A ROBE...
YOU CAN PUT YOUR CLOTHES IN THAT BASKET.
TH- THANK YOU!
A BATHROBE, HUH?
REMINDS ME OF WHEN KIRIYA AND I STAYED AT THAT HOTEL
I finally get to see him...
MS. MASUDA, HAVE YOU SEEN MY CELL PHONE?
...MAYBE YOU LEFT IT IN THE BATHROOM?
THE BATH-ROOM...?
CLATCH

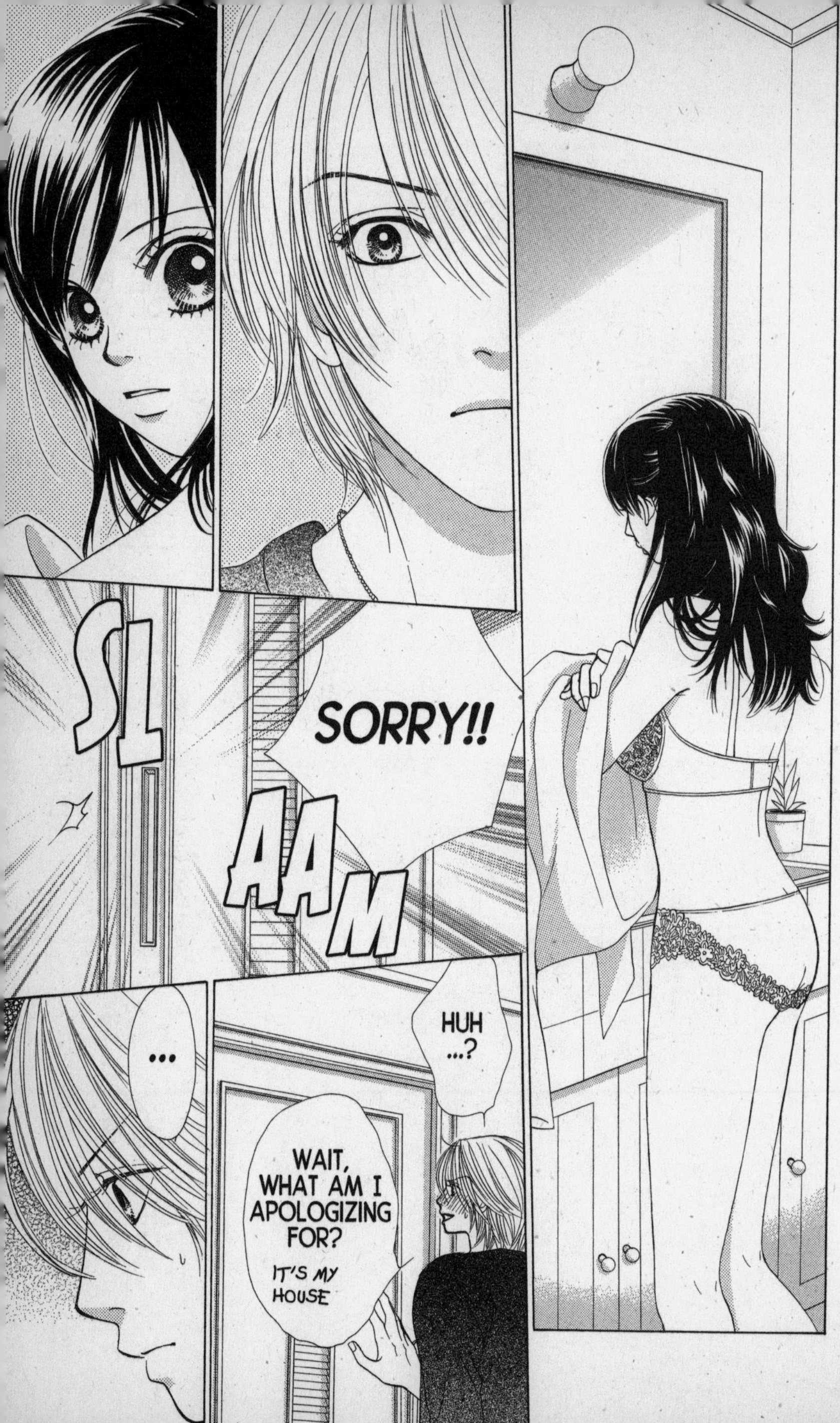
SORRY!!
SLAAM
HUH ...?
WAIT, WHAT AM I APOLOGIZING FOR?
IT'S MY HOUSE
...

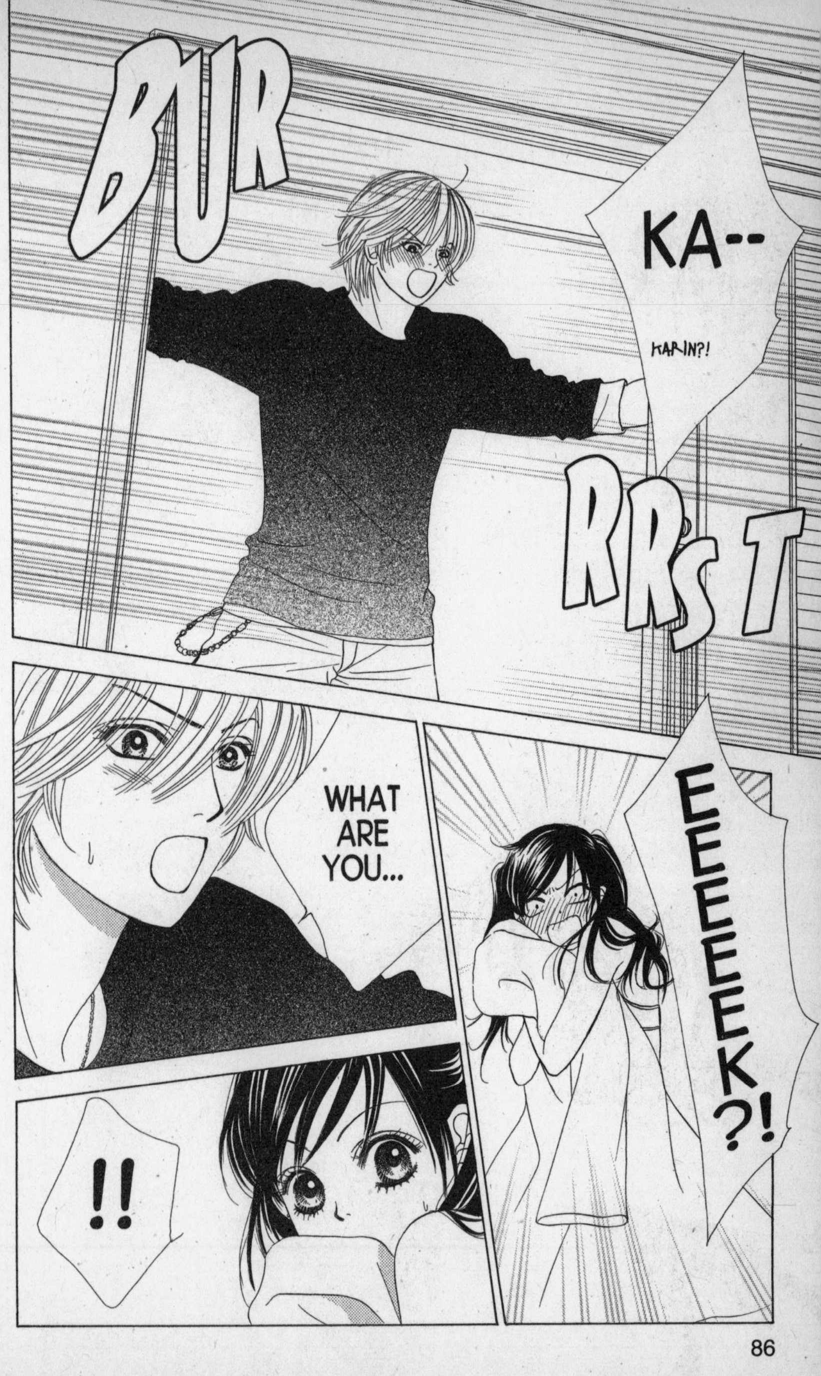
KA--
KARIN?!
BUR
RRST
EEEEEEK?!
WHAT ARE YOU...
!!

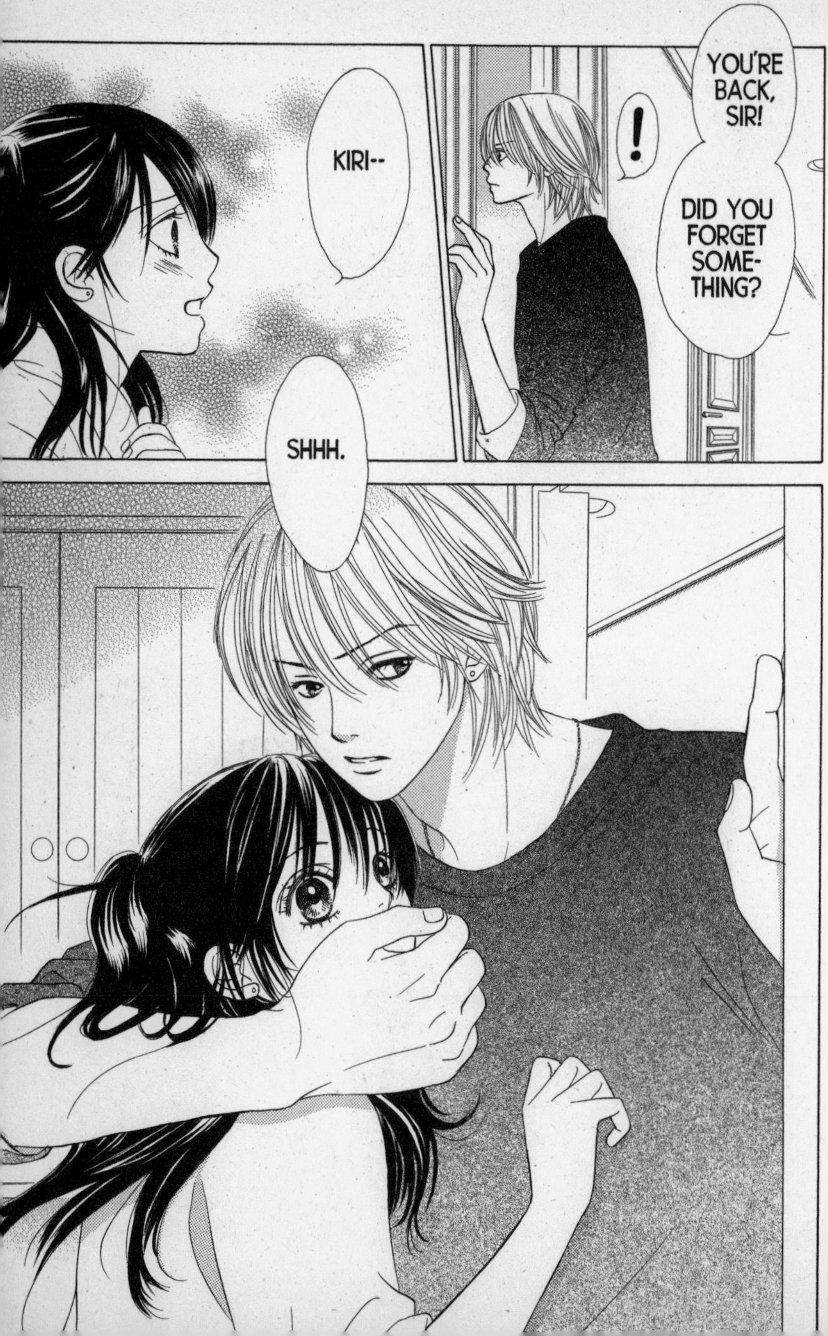
YOU'RE BACK, SIR!
!
DID YOU FORGET SOME-THING?
KIRI--
SHHH.

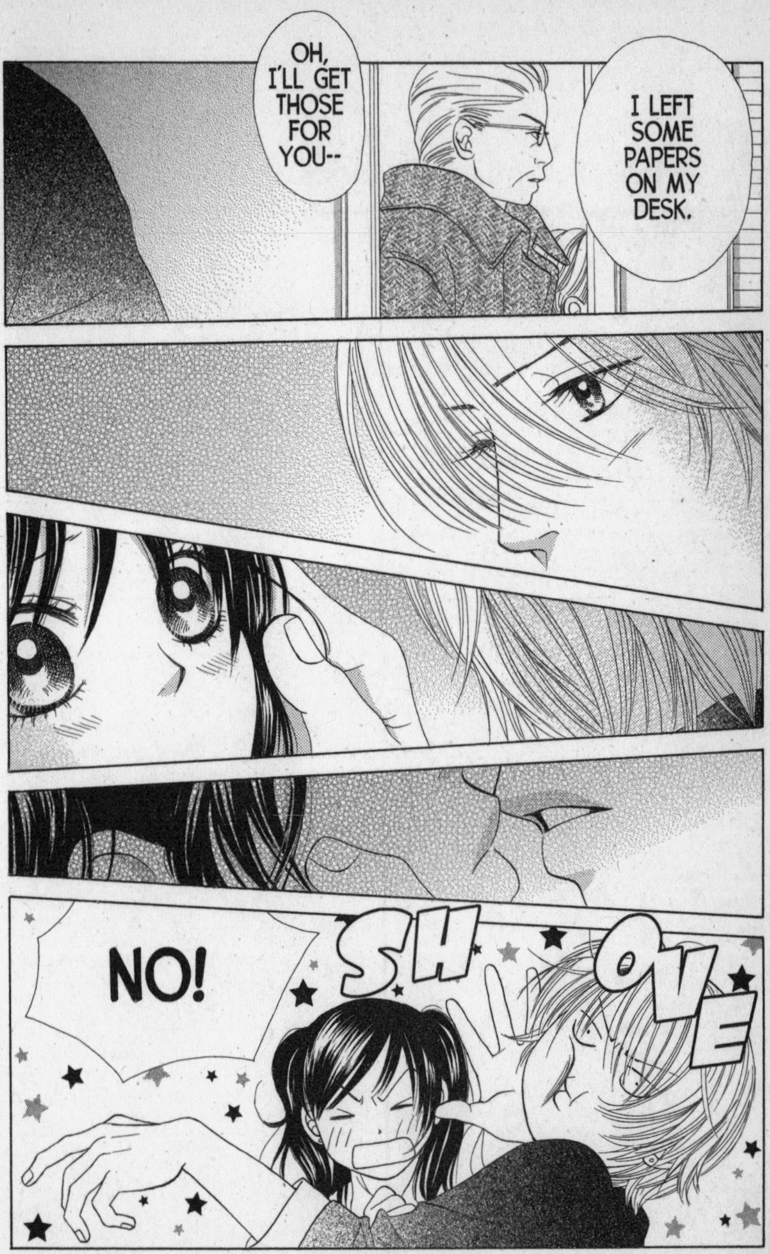
I LEFT SOME PAPERS ON MY DESK.
OH, I'LL GET THOSE FOR YOU--
NO!
SHOVE

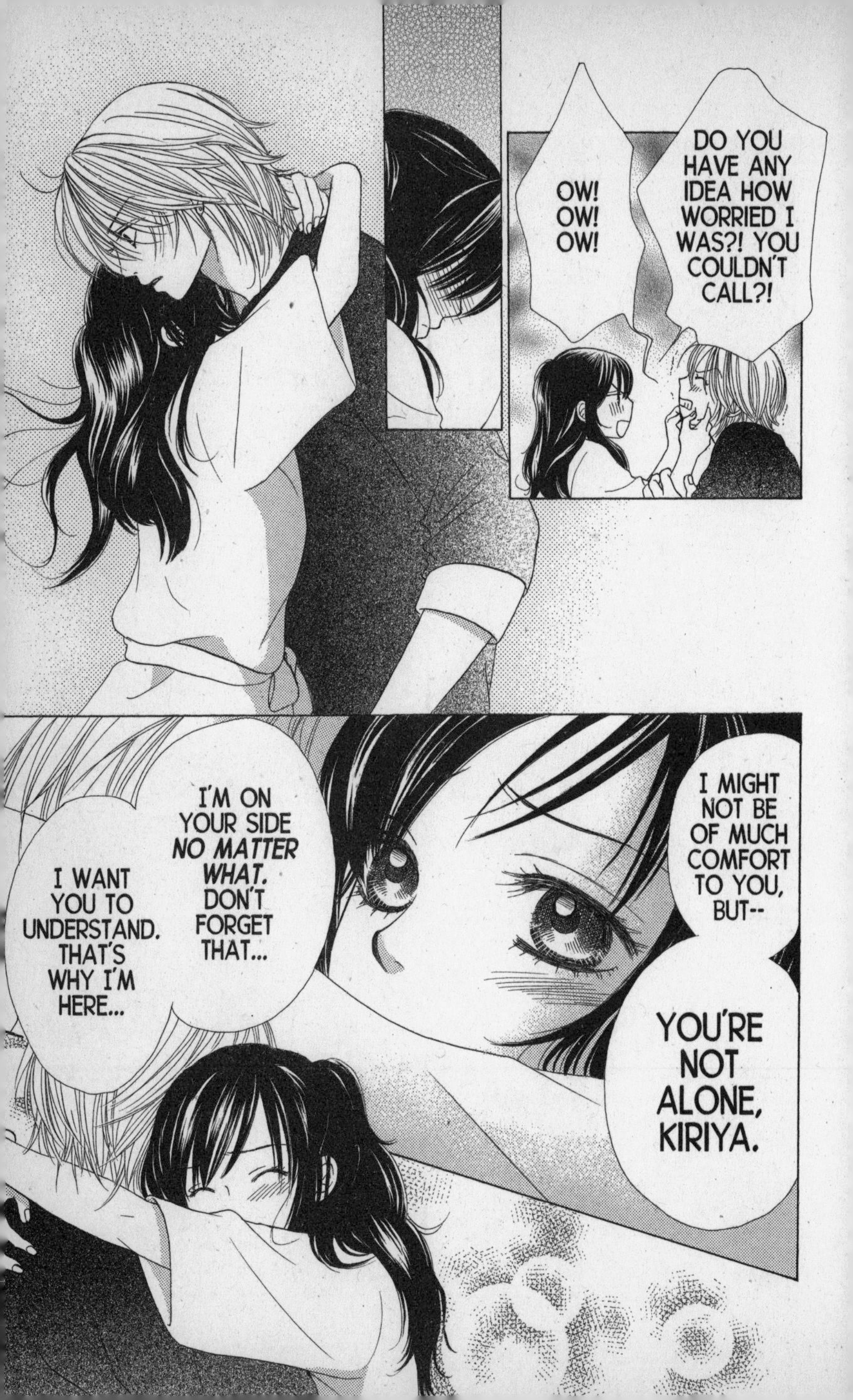
DO YOU HAVE ANY IDEA HOW WORRIED I WAS?! YOU COULDN'T CALL?!
OW! OW! OW!
I MIGHT NOT BE OF MUCH COMFORT TO YOU, BUT--
YOU'RE NOT ALONE, KIRIYA.
I'M ON YOUR SIDE *NO MATTER WHAT.* DON'T FORGET THAT...
I WANT YOU TO UNDERSTAND. THAT'S WHY I'M HERE...

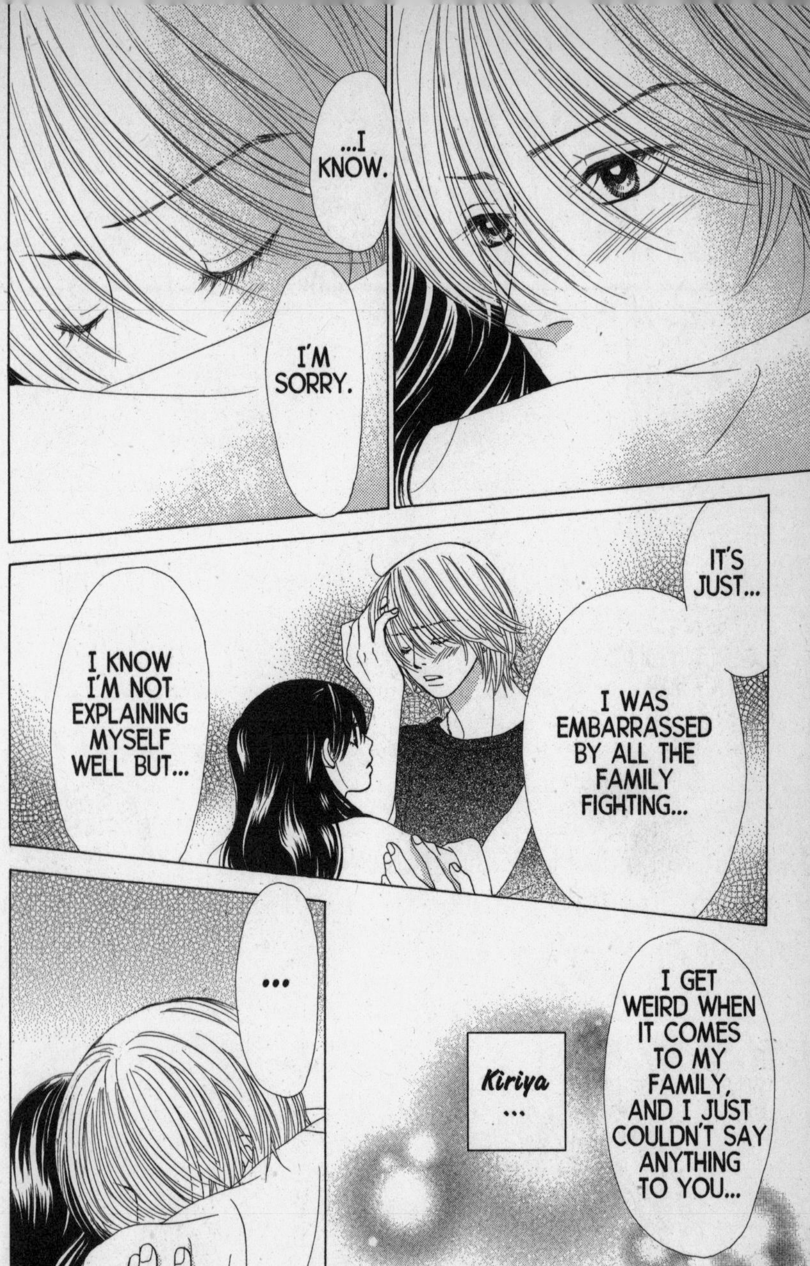
...I KNOW.
I'M SORRY.
IT'S JUST...
I WAS EMBARRASSED BY ALL THE FAMILY FIGHTING...
I KNOW I'M NOT EXPLAINING MYSELF WELL BUT...
I GET WEIRD WHEN IT COMES TO MY FAMILY, AND I JUST COULDN'T SAY ANYTHING TO YOU...
Kiriya ...
...

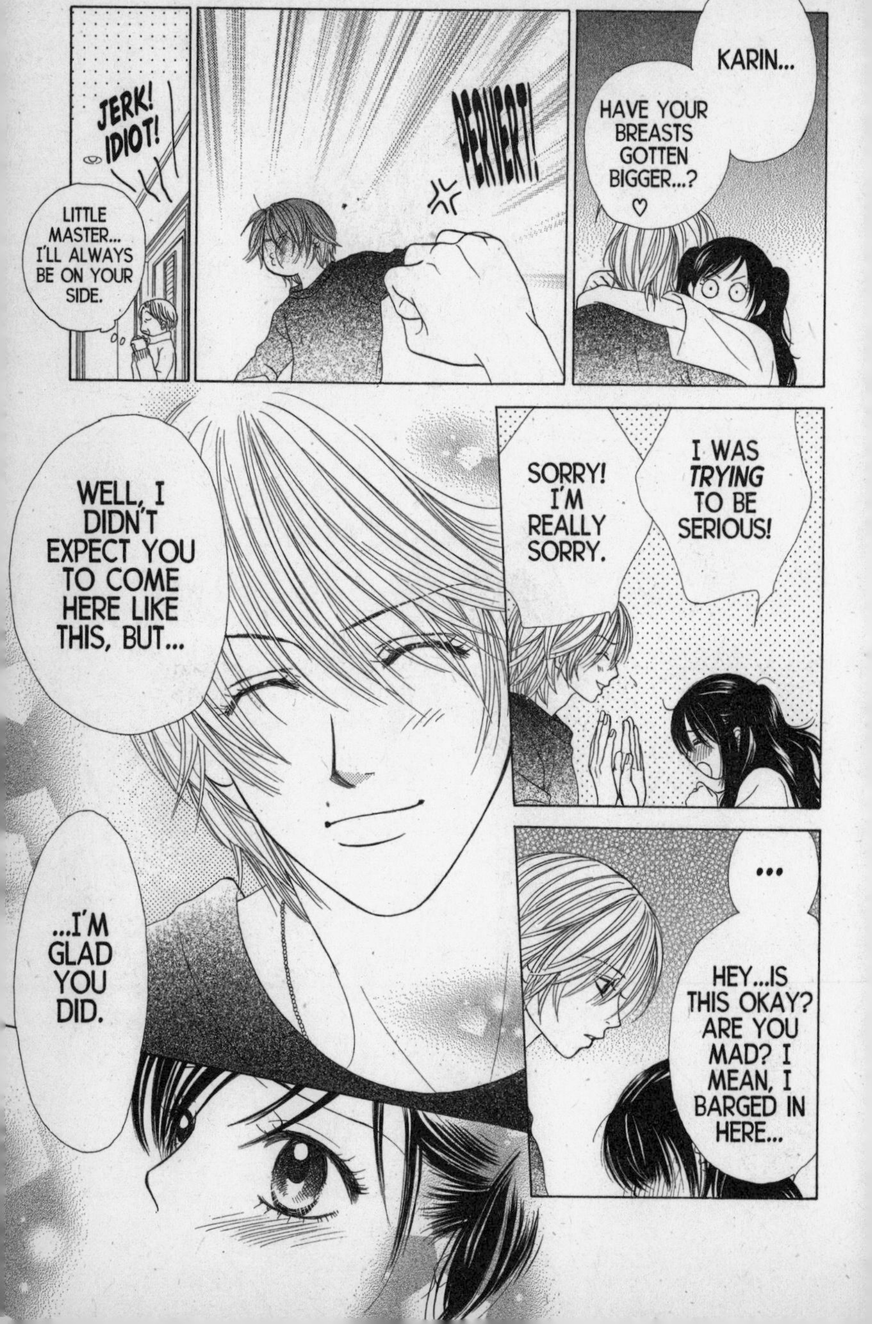
KARIN...
HAVE YOUR BREASTS GOTTEN BIGGER...? ♡
PERVERT!
JERK! IDIOT!
LITTLE MASTER... I'LL ALWAYS BE ON YOUR SIDE.
I WAS *TRYING* TO BE SERIOUS!
SORRY! I'M REALLY SORRY.
...
HEY...IS THIS OKAY? ARE YOU MAD? I MEAN, I BARGED IN HERE...
WELL, I DIDN'T EXPECT YOU TO COME HERE LIKE THIS, BUT...
...I'M GLAD YOU DID.

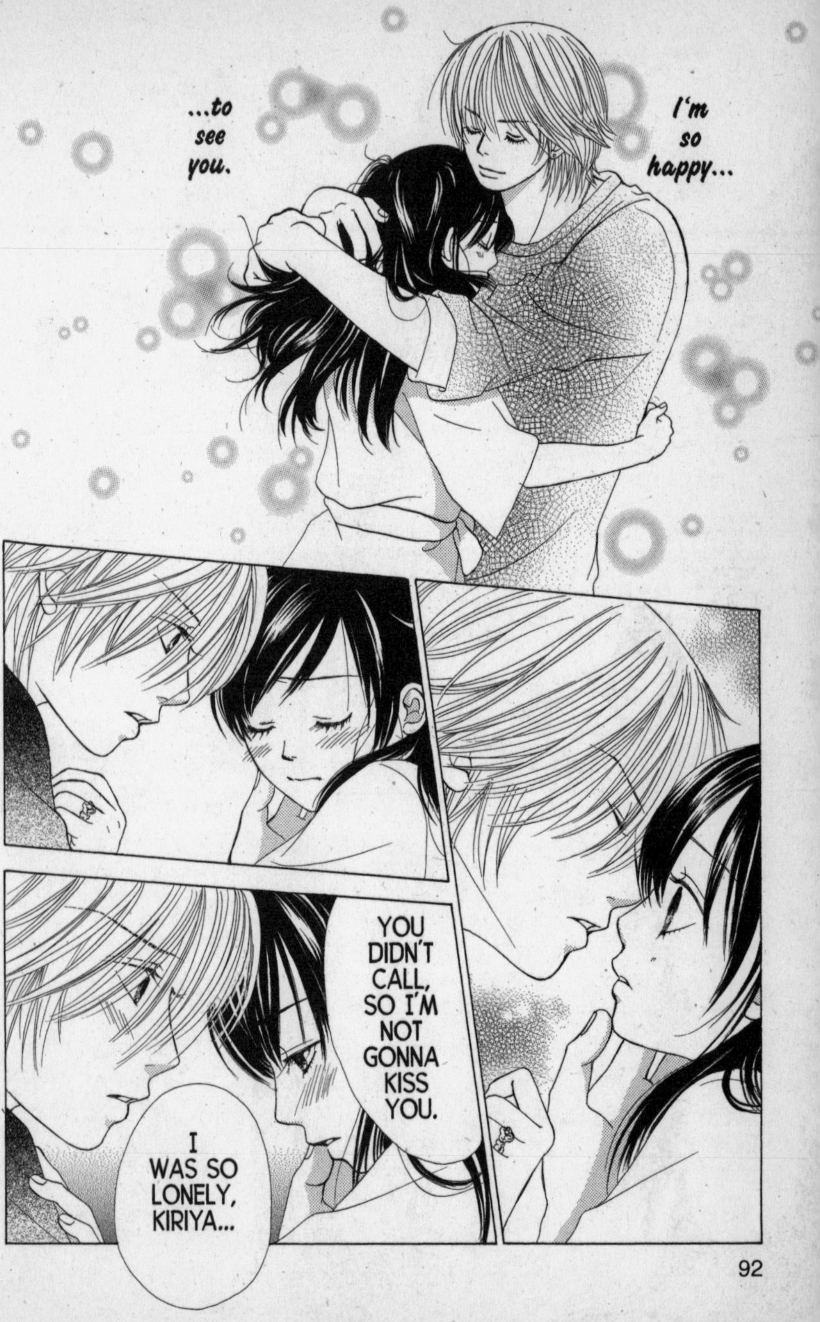
I'm so happy...
...to see you.
YOU DIDN'T CALL, SO I'M NOT GONNA KISS YOU.
I WAS SO LONELY, KIRIYA...

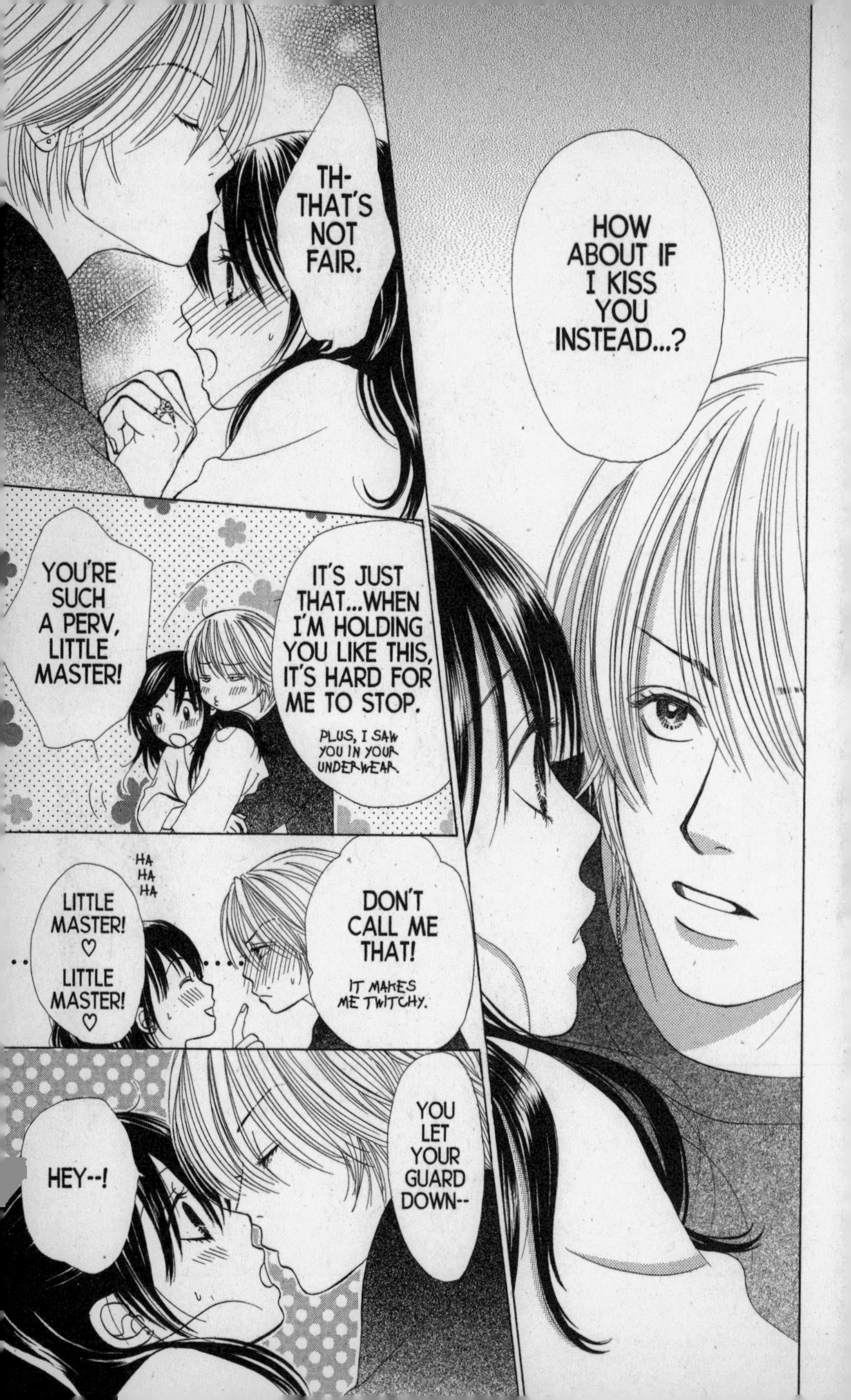
HOW ABOUT IF I KISS YOU INSTEAD...?
TH-THAT'S NOT FAIR.
IT'S JUST THAT...WHEN I'M HOLDING YOU LIKE THIS, IT'S HARD FOR ME TO STOP.
PLUS, I SAW YOU IN YOUR UNDERWEAR.
YOU'RE SUCH A PERV, LITTLE MASTER!
DON'T CALL ME THAT!
IT MAKES ME TWITCHY.
HA HA HA
LITTLE MASTER! ♡ LITTLE MASTER! ♡
YOU LET YOUR GUARD DOWN--
HEY--!

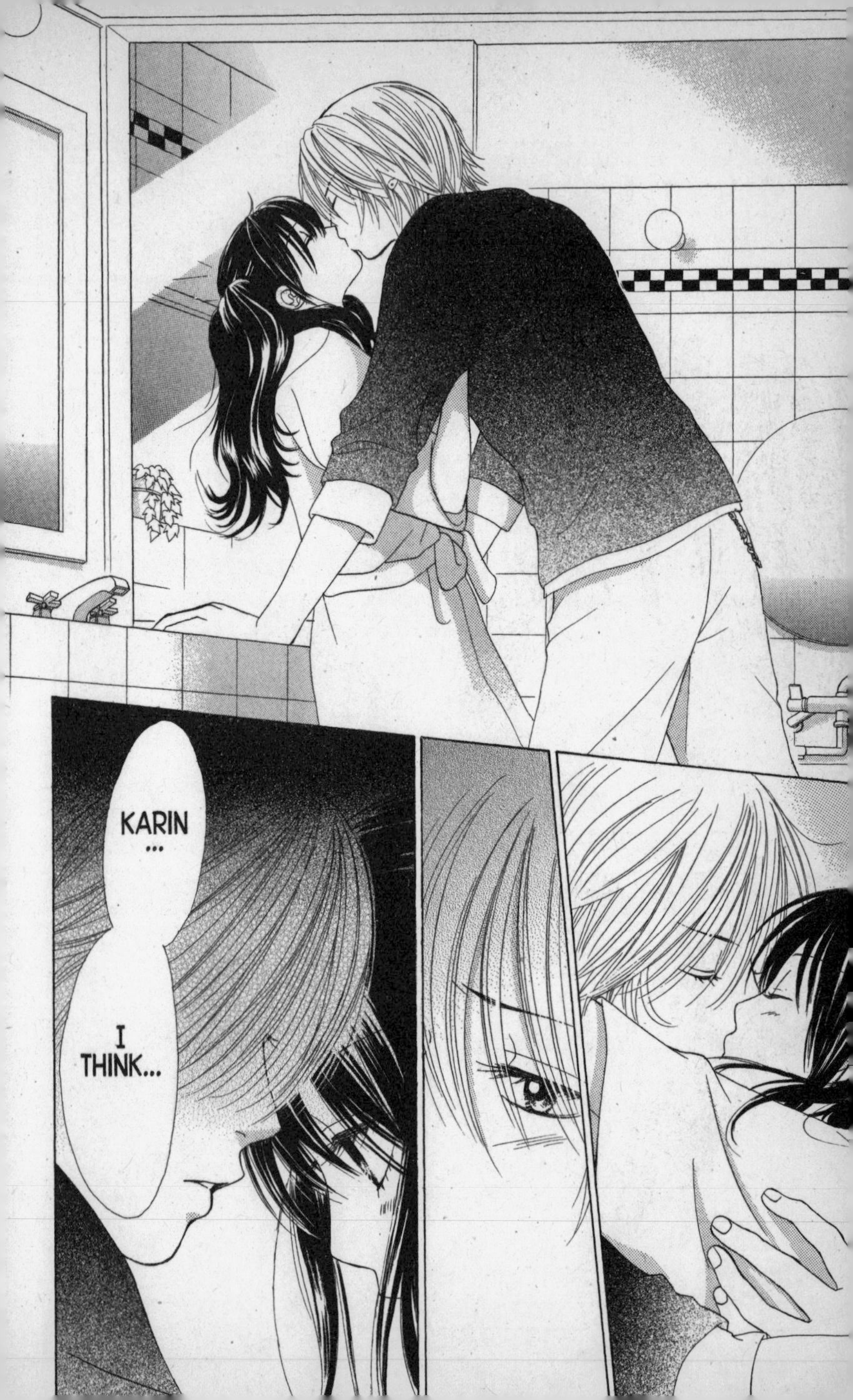
KARIN ...
I THINK...

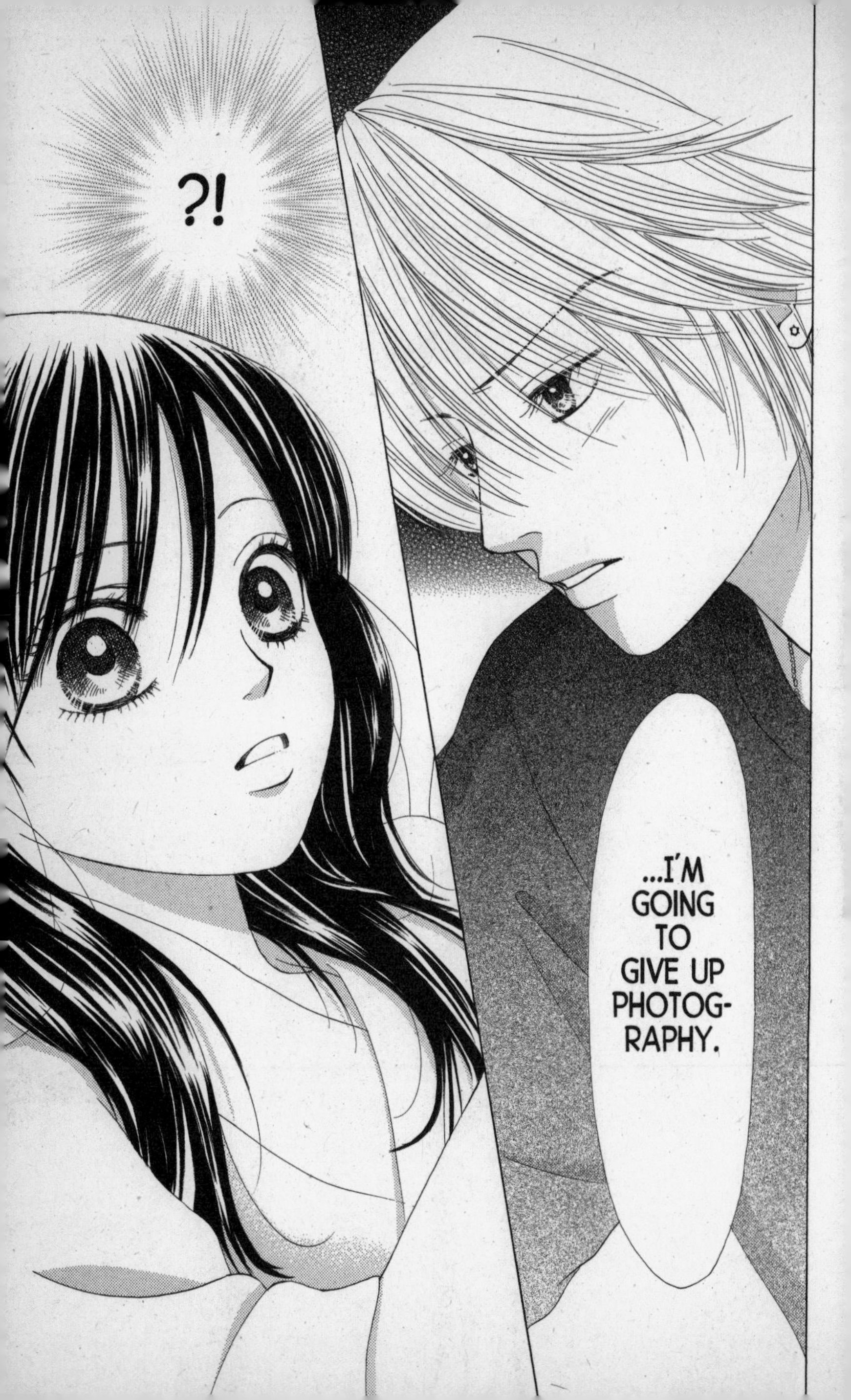
...I'M GOING TO GIVE UP PHOTOG-RAPHY.
?!

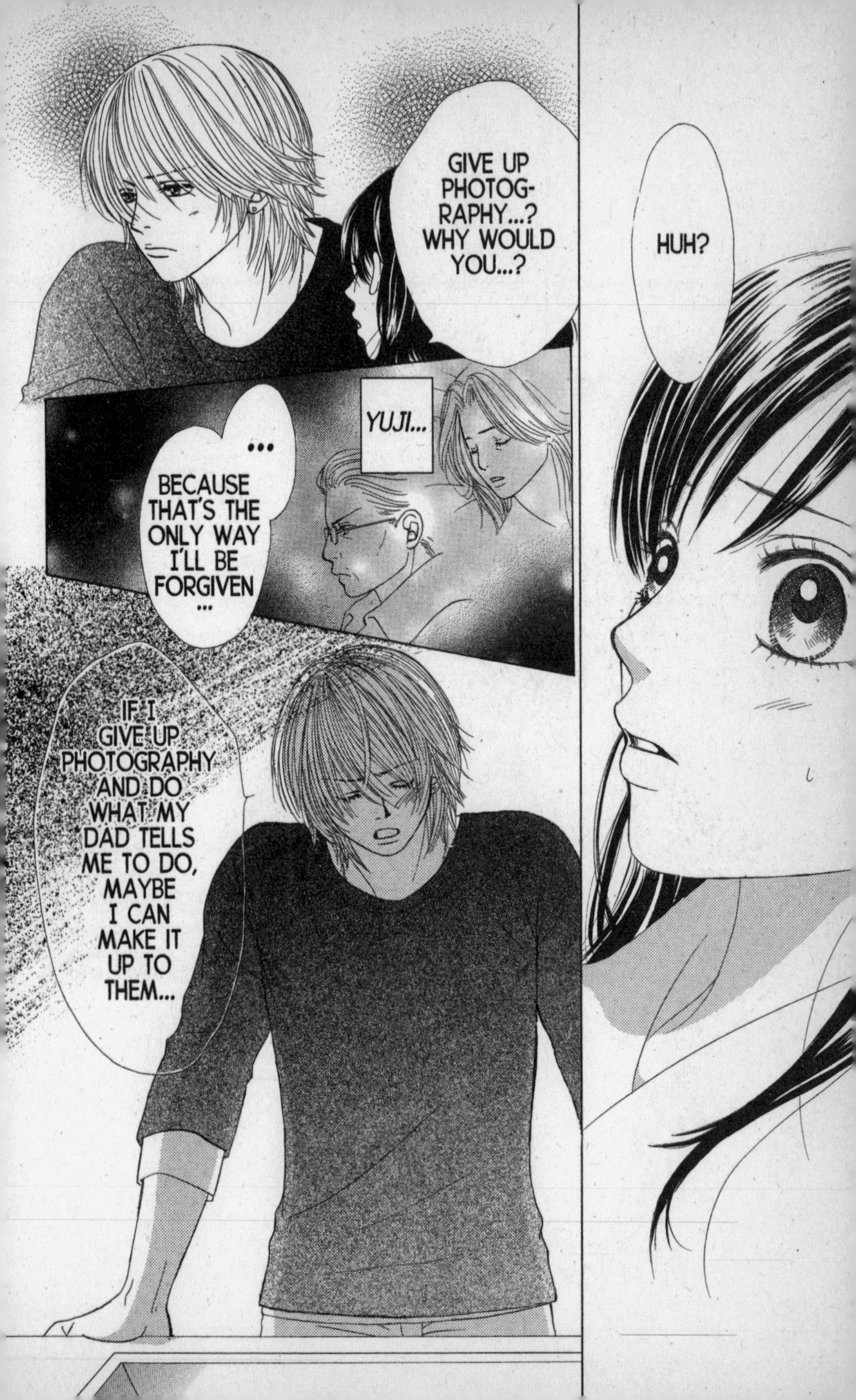
HUH?
GIVE UP PHOTOG-RAPHY...? WHY WOULD YOU...?
YUJI...
... BECAUSE THAT'S THE ONLY WAY I'LL BE FORGIVEN ...
IF I GIVE UP PHOTOGRAPHY AND DO WHAT MY DAD TELLS ME TO DO, MAYBE I CAN MAKE IT UP TO THEM...

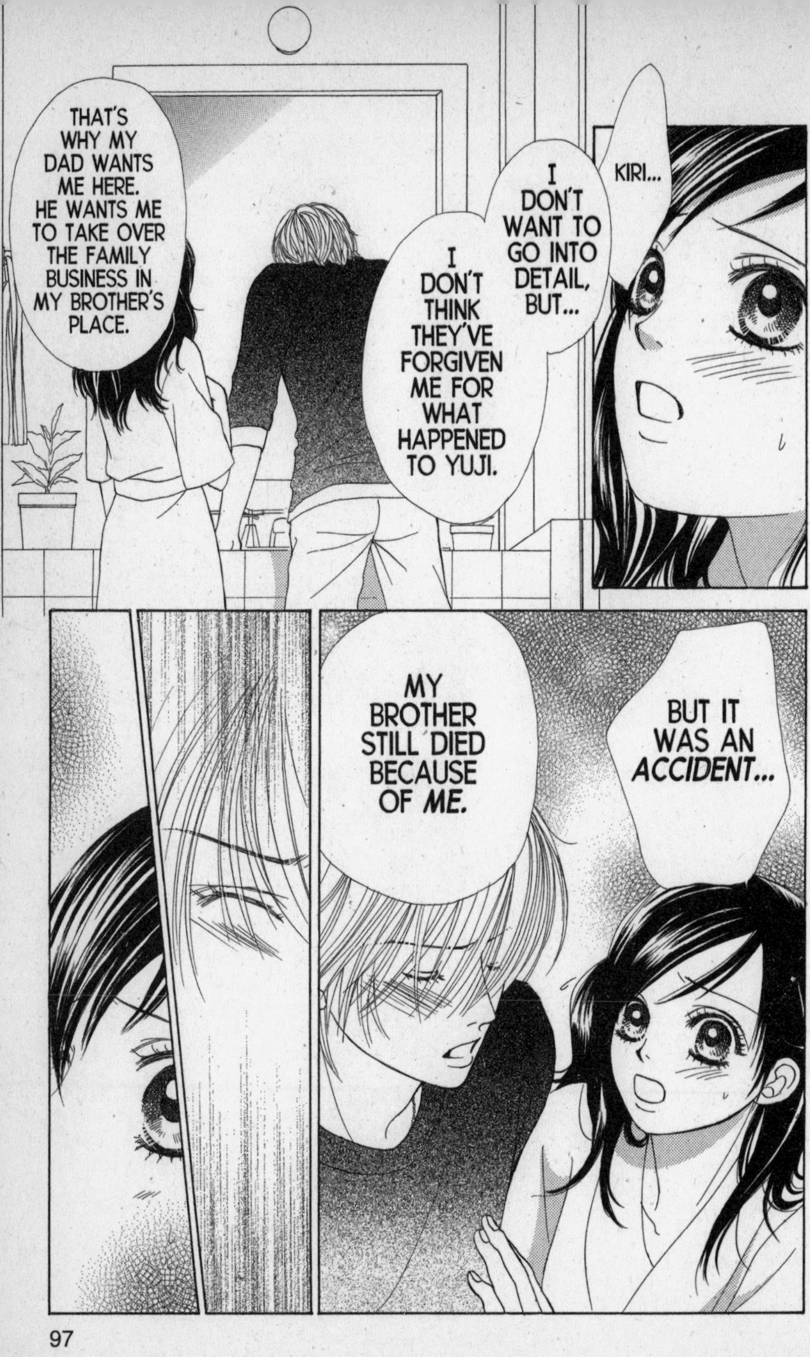
KIRI...
I DON'T WANT TO GO INTO DETAIL, BUT...
I DON'T THINK THEY'VE FORGIVEN ME FOR WHAT HAPPENED TO YUJI.
THAT'S WHY MY DAD WANTS ME HERE. HE WANTS ME TO TAKE OVER THE FAMILY BUSINESS IN MY BROTHER'S PLACE.
BUT IT WAS AN *ACCIDENT*...
MY BROTHER STILL DIED BECAUSE OF *ME*.

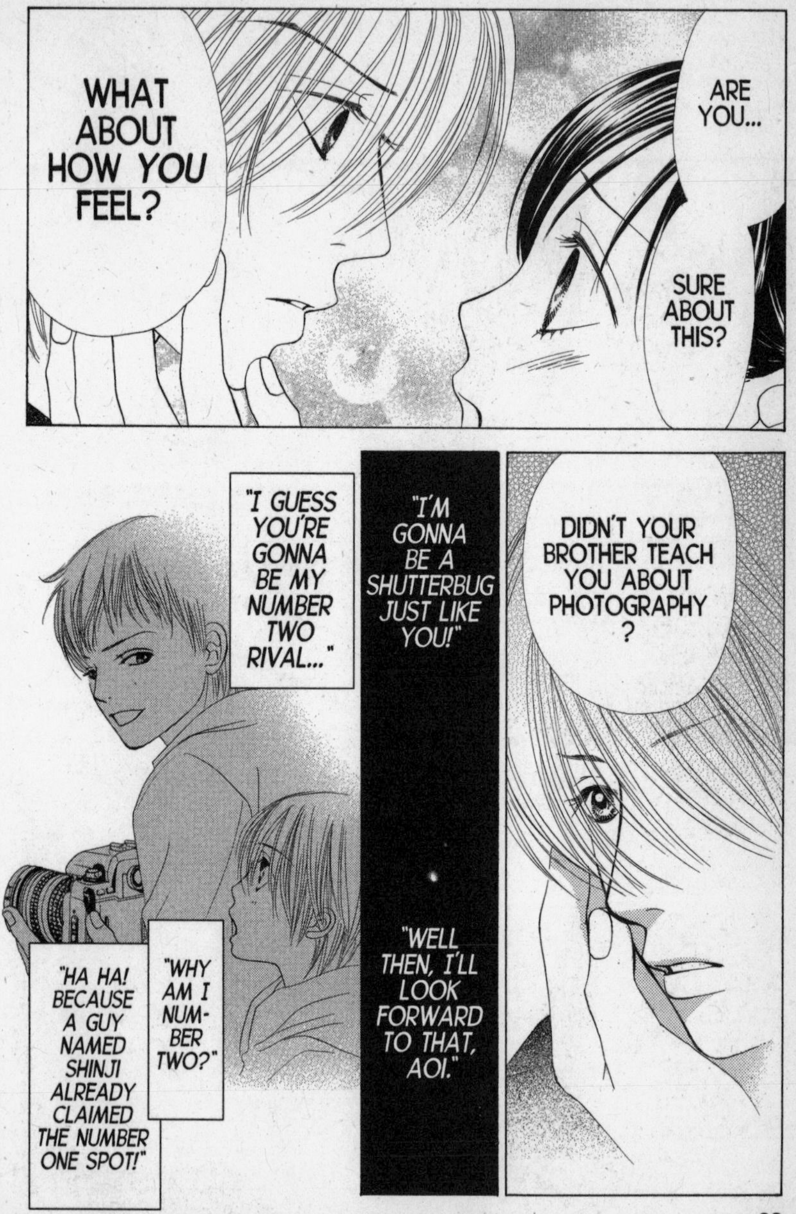
ARE YOU...
SURE ABOUT THIS?
WHAT ABOUT HOW *YOU* FEEL?
DIDN'T YOUR BROTHER TEACH YOU ABOUT PHOTOGRAPHY?
"I'M GONNA BE A SHUTTERBUG JUST LIKE YOU!"
"WELL THEN, I'LL LOOK FORWARD TO THAT, AOI."
"I GUESS YOU'RE GONNA BE MY NUMBER TWO RIVAL..."
"WHY AM I NUM-BER TWO?"
"HA HA! BECAUSE A GUY NAMED SHINJI ALREADY CLAIMED THE NUMBER ONE SPOT!"

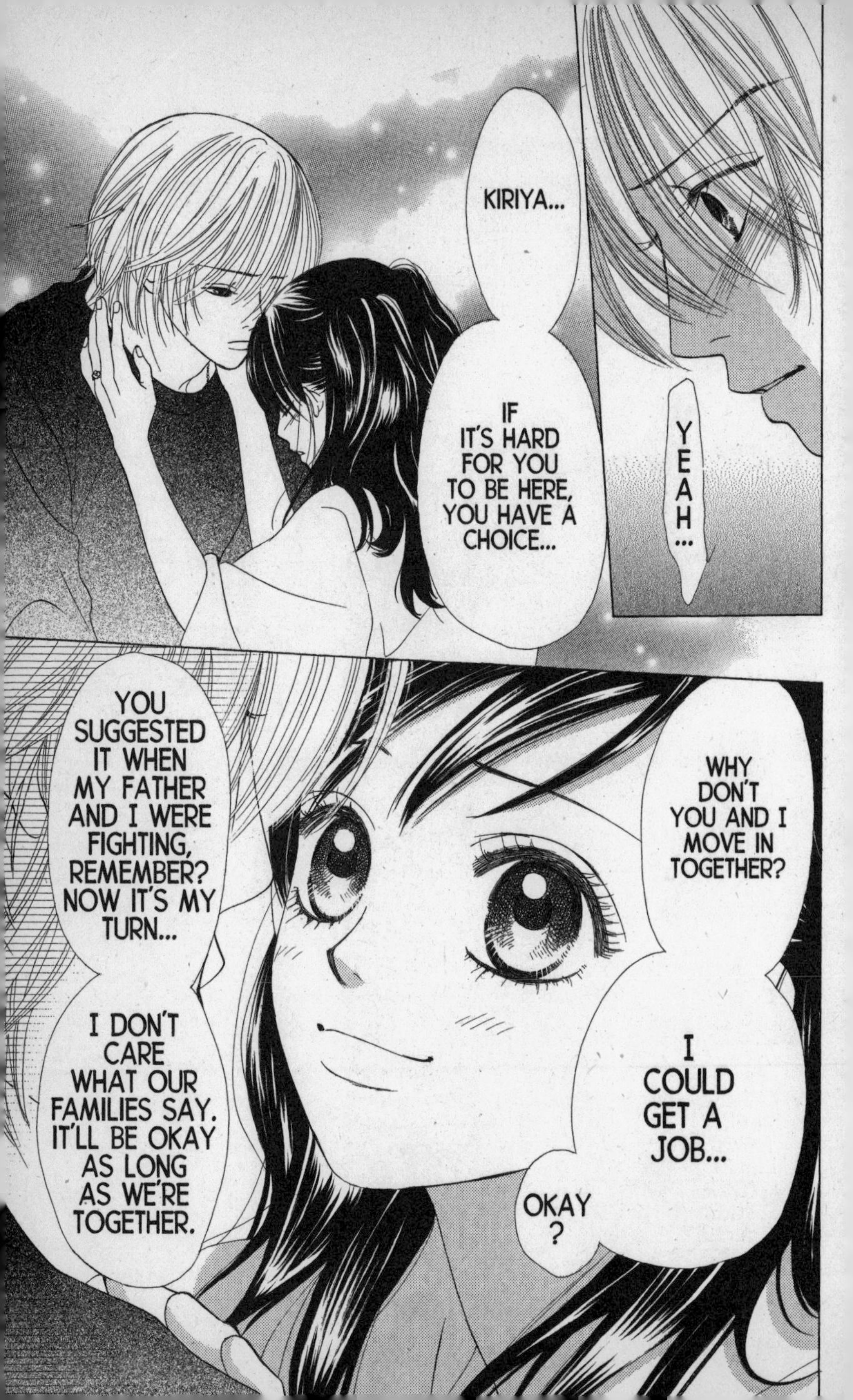
KIRIYA...
IF IT'S HARD FOR YOU TO BE HERE, YOU HAVE A CHOICE...
YEAH...
WHY DON'T YOU AND I MOVE IN TOGETHER?
I COULD GET A JOB...
OKAY?
YOU SUGGESTED IT WHEN MY FATHER AND I WERE FIGHTING, REMEMBER? NOW IT'S MY TURN...
I DON'T CARE WHAT OUR FAMILIES SAY. IT'LL BE OKAY AS LONG AS WE'RE TOGETHER.

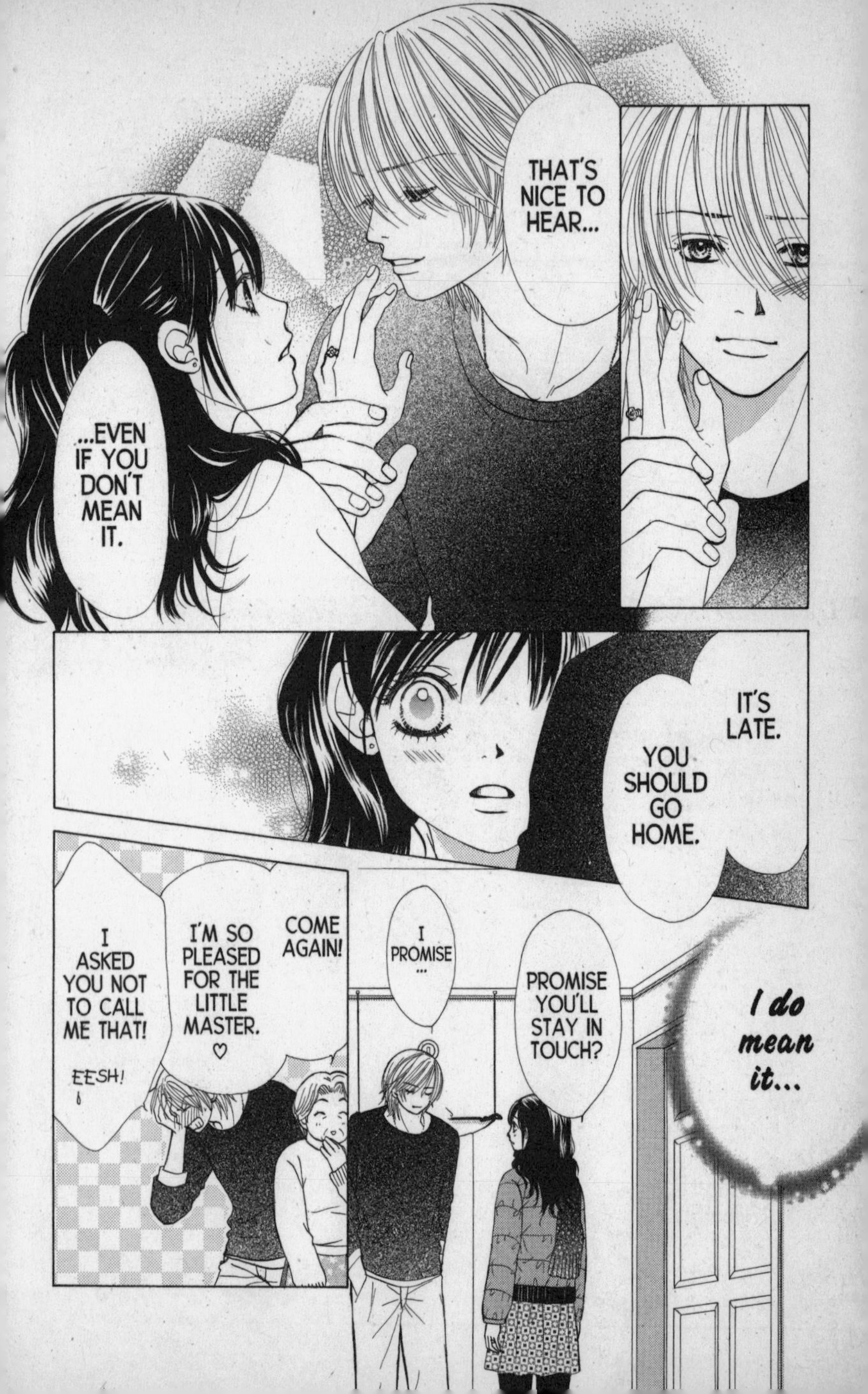
THAT'S NICE TO HEAR...
...EVEN IF YOU DON'T MEAN IT.
IT'S LATE. YOU SHOULD GO HOME.
I do mean it...
PROMISE YOU'LL STAY IN TOUCH?
I PROMISE...
COME AGAIN!
I'M SO PLEASED FOR THE LITTLE MASTER. ♡
I ASKED YOU NOT TO CALL ME THAT!
EESH!

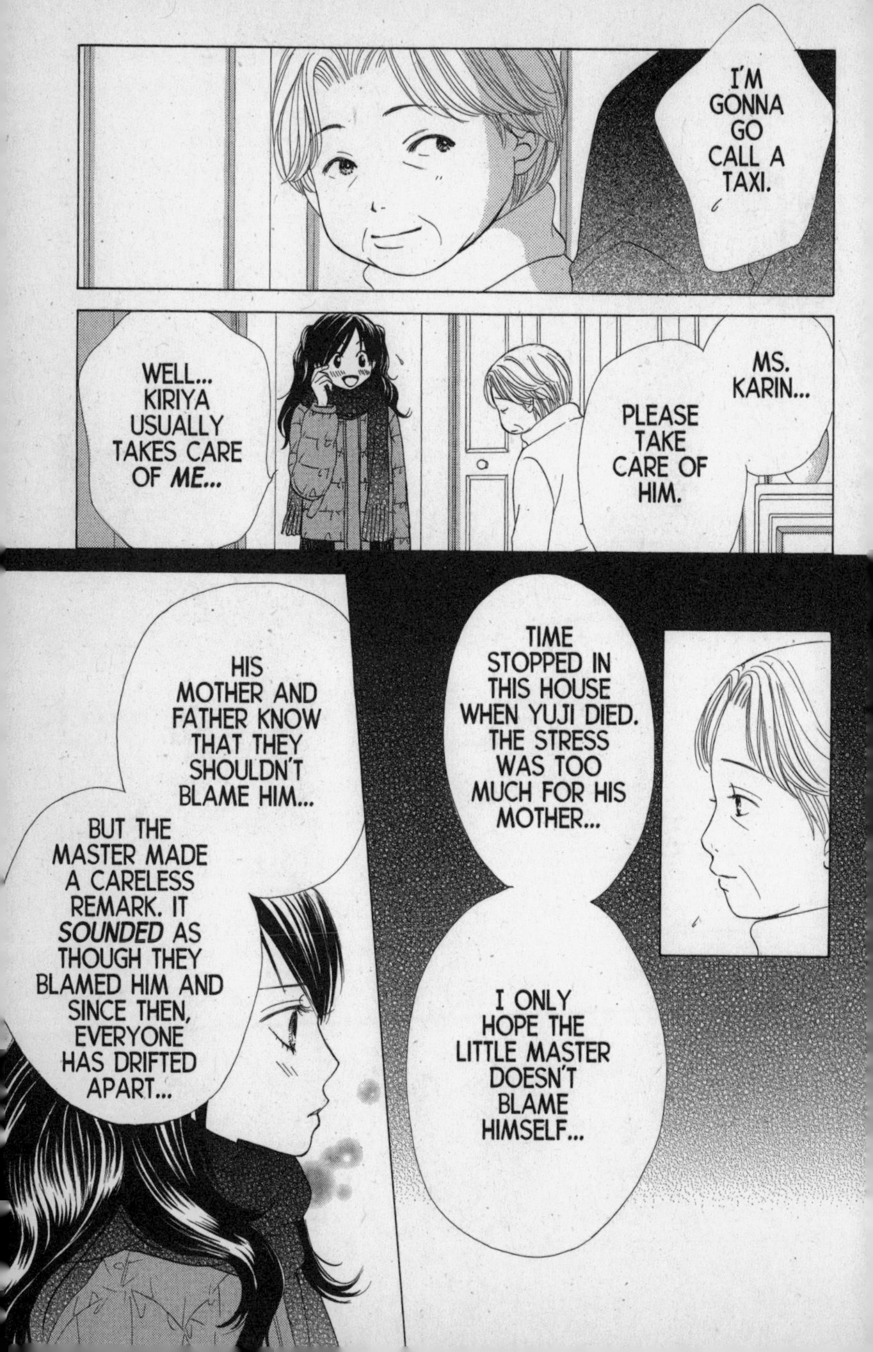
I'M GONNA GO CALL A TAXI.
MS. KARIN... PLEASE TAKE CARE OF HIM.
WELL... KIRIYA USUALLY TAKES CARE OF *ME*...
TIME STOPPED IN THIS HOUSE WHEN YUJI DIED. THE STRESS WAS TOO MUCH FOR HIS MOTHER...
HIS MOTHER AND FATHER KNOW THAT THEY SHOULDN'T BLAME HIM...
BUT THE MASTER MADE A CARELESS REMARK. IT *SOUNDED* AS THOUGH THEY BLAMED HIM AND SINCE THEN, EVERYONE HAS DRIFTED APART...
I ONLY HOPE THE LITTLE MASTER DOESN'T BLAME HIMSELF...

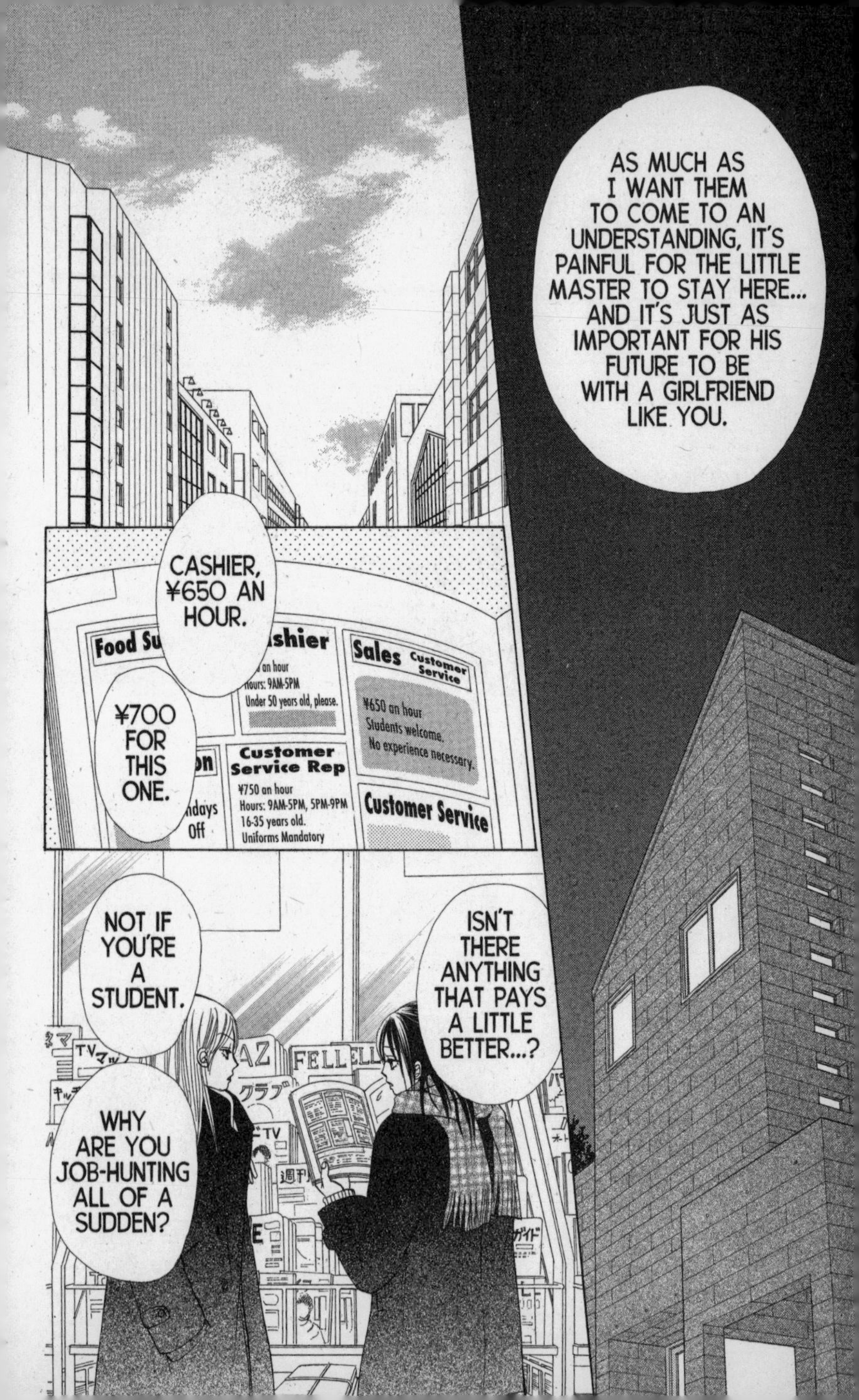
AS MUCH AS I WANT THEM TO COME TO AN UNDERSTANDING, IT'S PAINFUL FOR THE LITTLE MASTER TO STAY HERE... AND IT'S JUST AS IMPORTANT FOR HIS FUTURE TO BE WITH A GIRLFRIEND LIKE YOU.
CASHIER, ¥650 AN HOUR.
¥700 FOR THIS ONE.
Sales Customer Service
¥650 an hour
Students welcome.
No experience necessary.
ashier
an hour
Hours: 9AM-5PM
Under 50 years old, please.
Food Su
Customer Service
Customer Service Rep
¥750 an hour
Hours: 9AM-5PM, 5PM-9PM
16-35 years old.
Uniforms Mandatory
ndays Off
ISN'T THERE ANYTHING THAT PAYS A LITTLE BETTER...?
NOT IF YOU'RE A STUDENT.
WHY ARE YOU JOB-HUNTING ALL OF A SUDDEN?

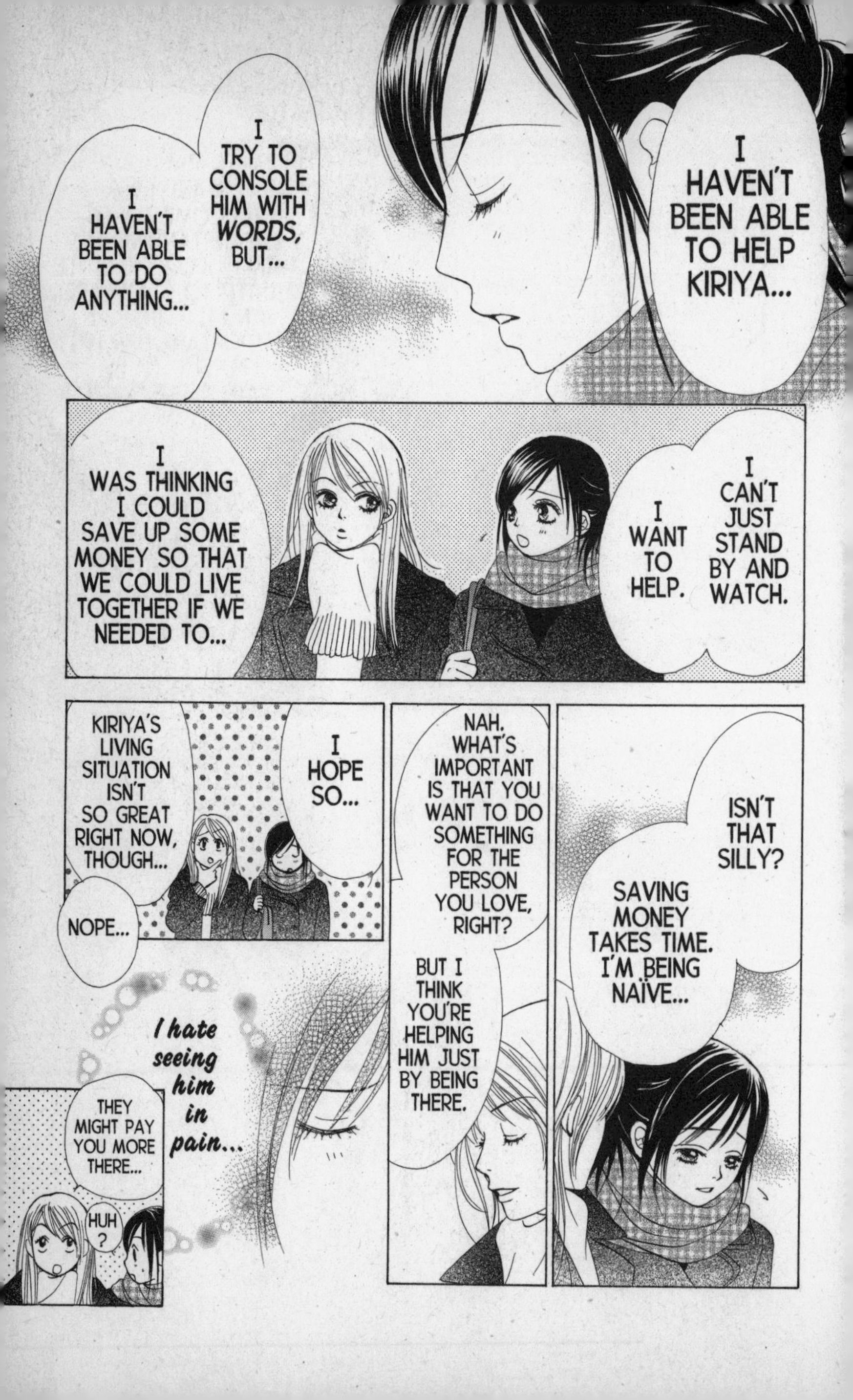
I HAVEN'T BEEN ABLE TO HELP KIRIYA...
I TRY TO CONSOLE HIM WITH *WORDS,* BUT...
I HAVEN'T BEEN ABLE TO DO ANYTHING...
I CAN'T JUST STAND BY AND WATCH.
I WANT TO HELP.
I WAS THINKING I COULD SAVE UP SOME MONEY SO THAT WE COULD LIVE TOGETHER IF WE NEEDED TO...
ISN'T THAT SILLY?
SAVING MONEY TAKES TIME. I'M BEING NAÏVE...
NAH. WHAT'S IMPORTANT IS THAT YOU WANT TO DO SOMETHING FOR THE PERSON YOU LOVE, RIGHT?
BUT I THINK YOU'RE HELPING HIM JUST BY BEING THERE.
I HOPE SO...
KIRIYA'S LIVING SITUATION ISN'T SO GREAT RIGHT NOW, THOUGH...
NOPE...
I hate seeing him in pain...
THEY MIGHT PAY YOU MORE THERE...
HUH?

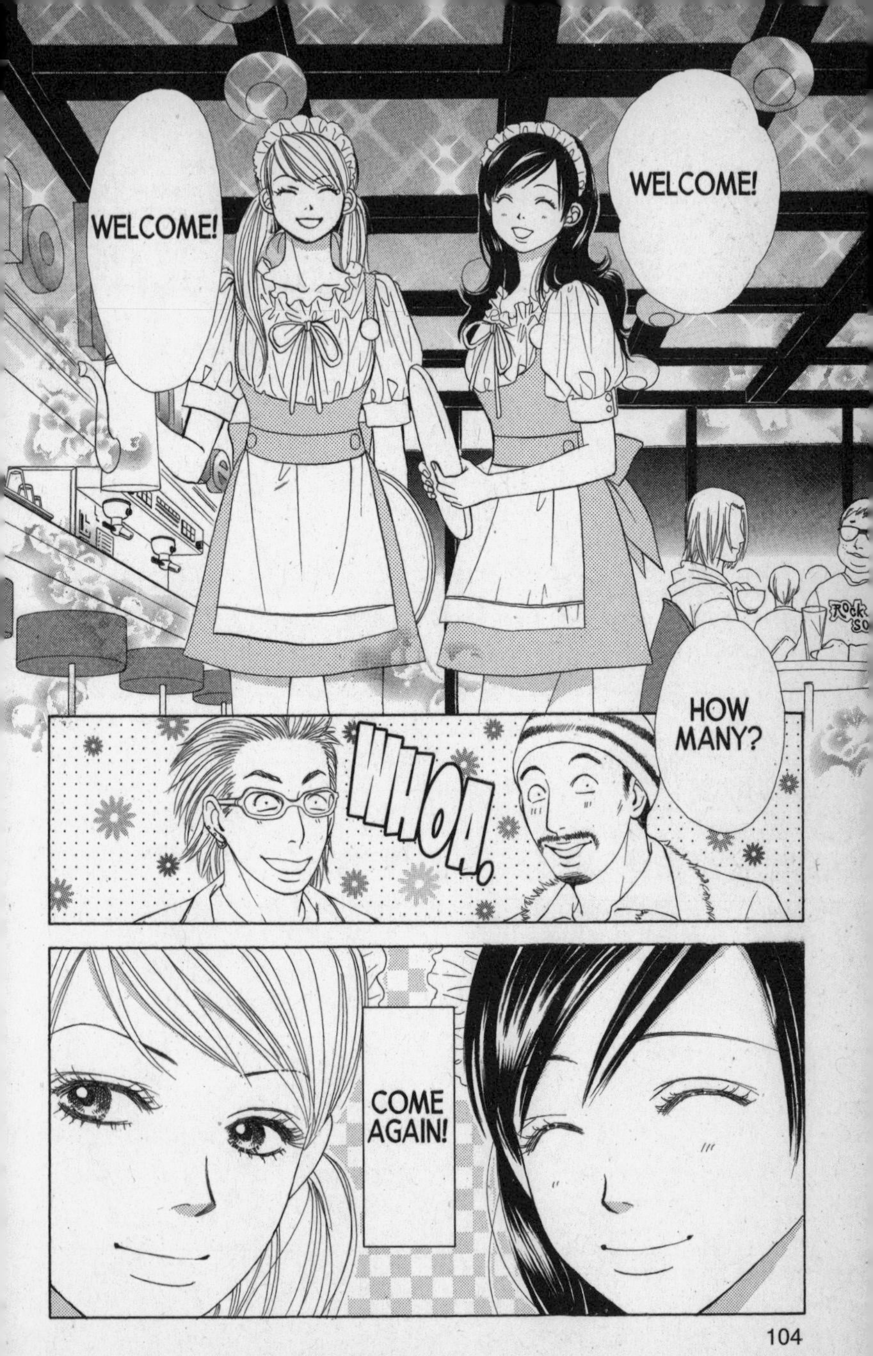
WELCOME!
WELCOME!
HOW MANY?
WHOA.
COME AGAIN!

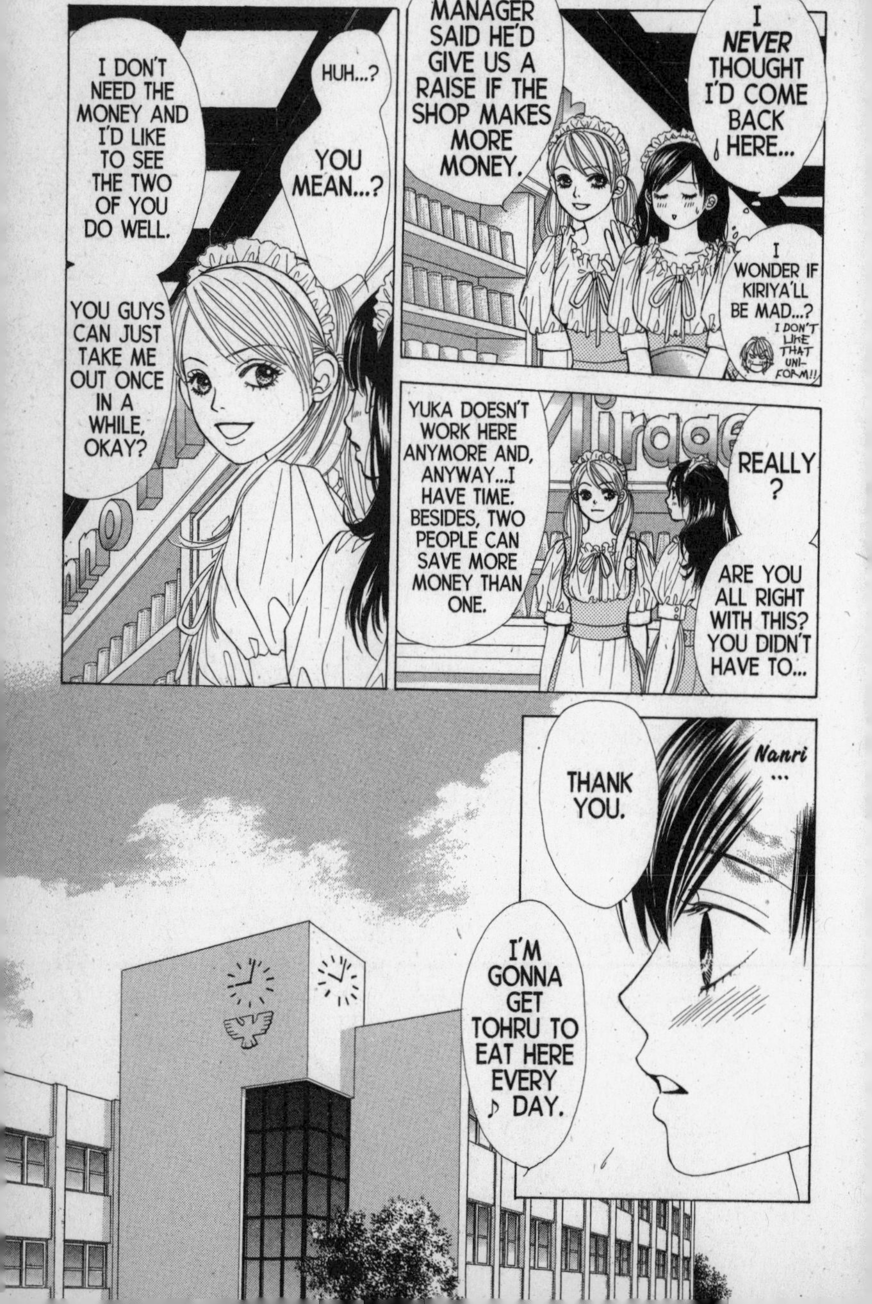
I *NEVER* THOUGHT I'D COME BACK HERE...
THE MANAGER SAID HE'D GIVE US A RAISE IF THE SHOP MAKES MORE MONEY.
I WONDER IF KIRIYA'LL BE MAD...?
I DON'T LIKE THAT UNI-FORM!!
REALLY?
ARE YOU ALL RIGHT WITH THIS? YOU DIDN'T HAVE TO...
YUKA DOESN'T WORK HERE ANYMORE AND, ANYWAY...I HAVE TIME. BESIDES, TWO PEOPLE CAN SAVE MORE MONEY THAN ONE.
HUH...?
YOU MEAN...?
I DON'T NEED THE MONEY AND I'D LIKE TO SEE THE TWO OF YOU DO WELL.
YOU GUYS CAN JUST TAKE ME OUT ONCE IN A WHILE, OKAY?
Nanri...
THANK YOU.
I'M GONNA GET TOHRU TO EAT HERE EVERY ♪ DAY.

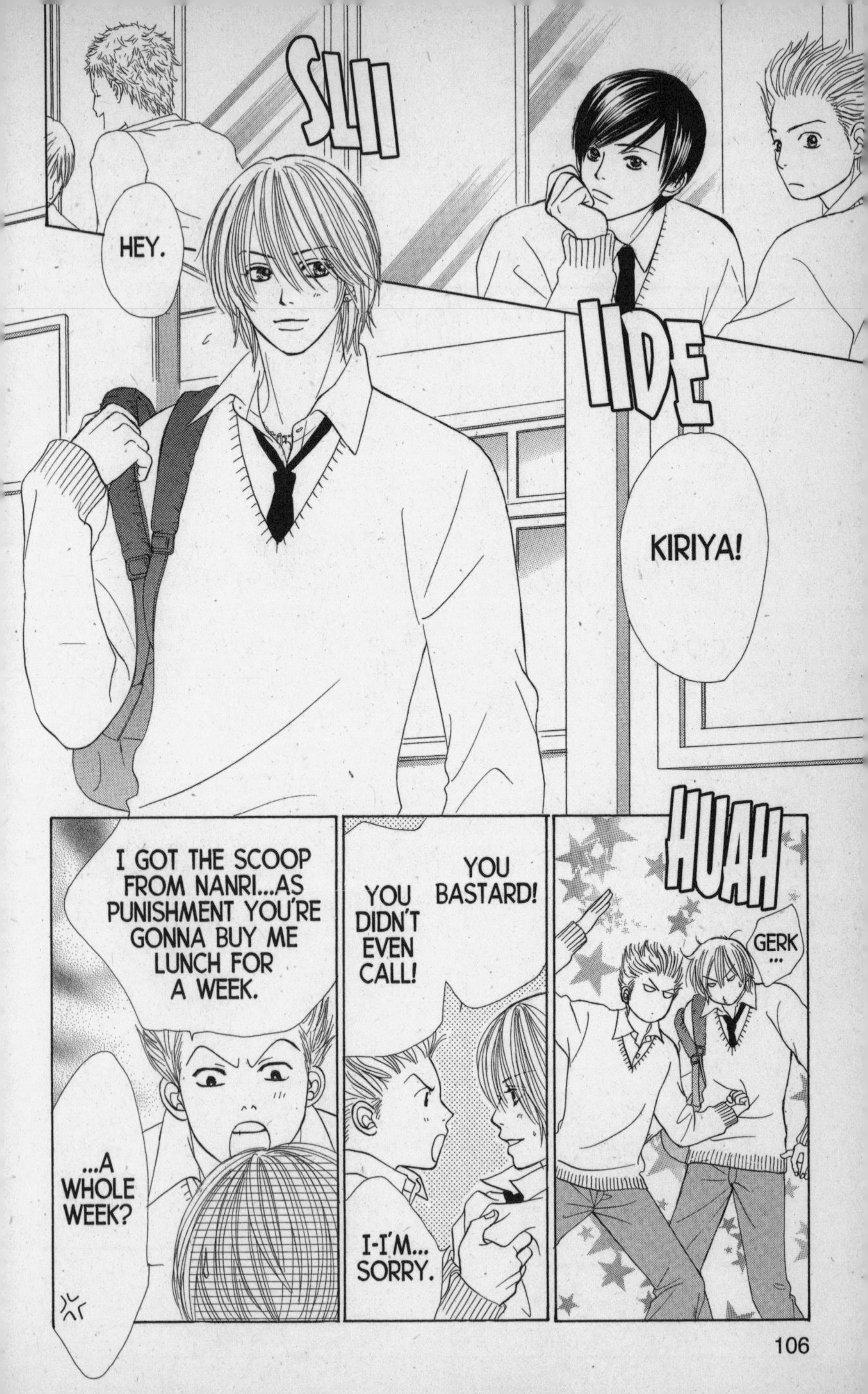
SLII
IIDE
HEY.
KIRIYA!
HUAH
GERK...
YOU BASTARD!
YOU DIDN'T EVEN CALL!
I-I'M... SORRY.
I GOT THE SCOOP FROM NANRI...AS PUNISHMENT YOU'RE GONNA BUY ME LUNCH FOR A WEEK.
...A WHOLE WEEK?

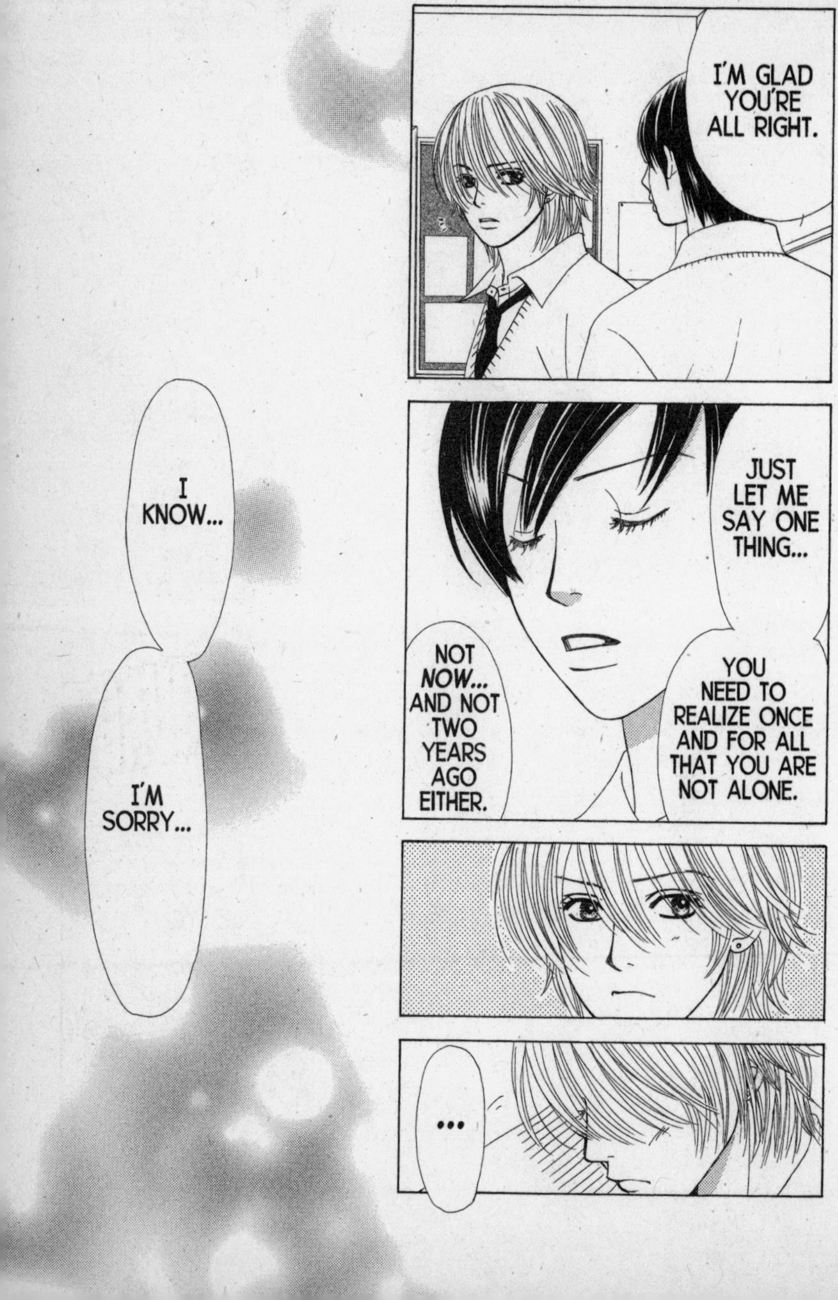
I'M GLAD YOU'RE ALL RIGHT.
JUST LET ME SAY ONE THING...
YOU NEED TO REALIZE ONCE AND FOR ALL THAT YOU ARE NOT ALONE.
NOT *NOW*... AND NOT TWO YEARS AGO EITHER.
...
I KNOW...
I'M SORRY...

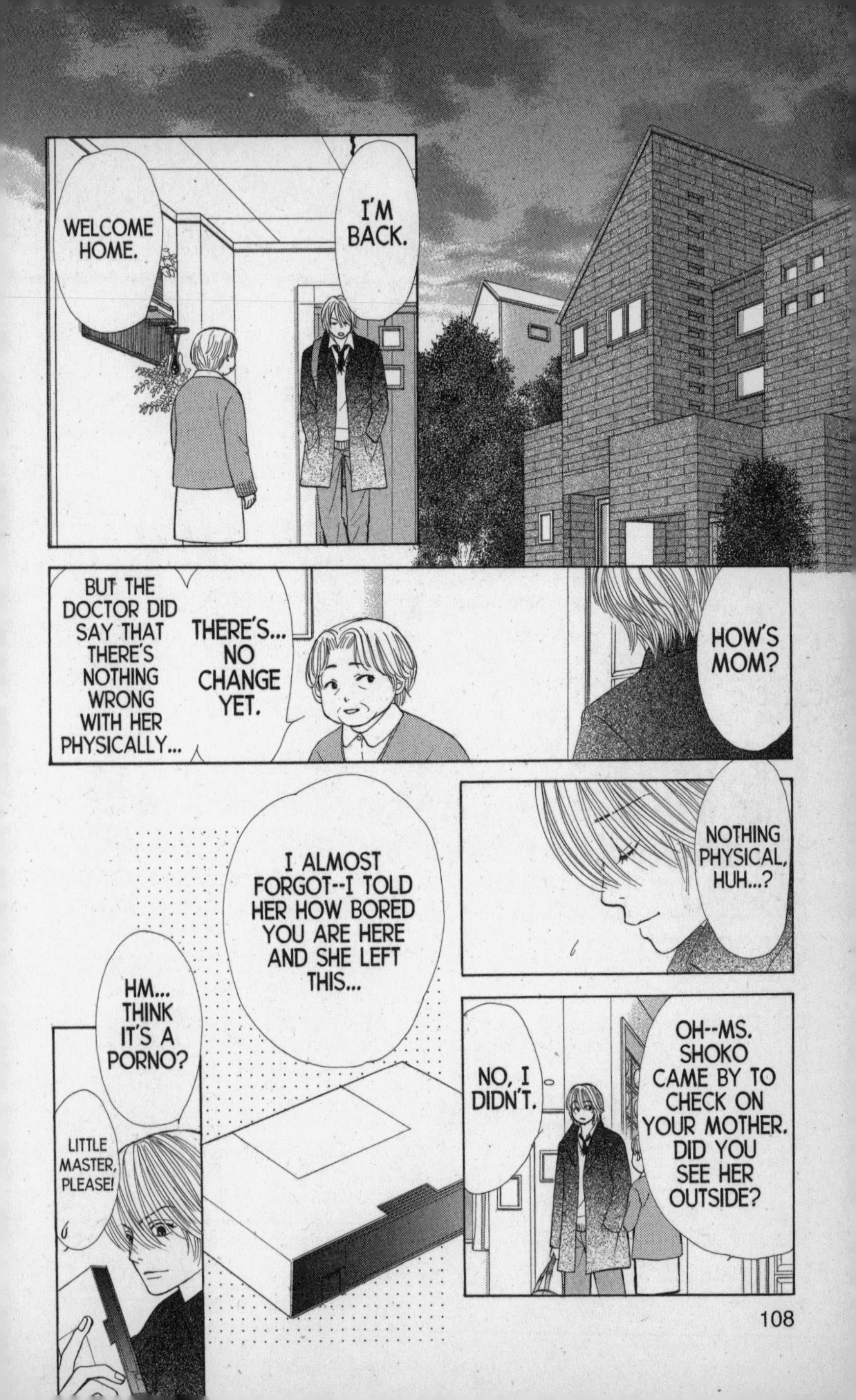
I'M BACK.
WELCOME HOME.
HOW'S MOM?
THERE'S... NO CHANGE YET.
BUT THE DOCTOR DID SAY THAT THERE'S NOTHING WRONG WITH HER PHYSICALLY...
NOTHING PHYSICAL, HUH...?
OH--MS. SHOKO CAME BY TO CHECK ON YOUR MOTHER. DID YOU SEE HER OUTSIDE?
NO, I DIDN'T.
I ALMOST FORGOT--I TOLD HER HOW BORED YOU ARE HERE AND SHE LEFT THIS...
HM... THINK IT'S A PORNO?
LITTLE MASTER, PLEASE!

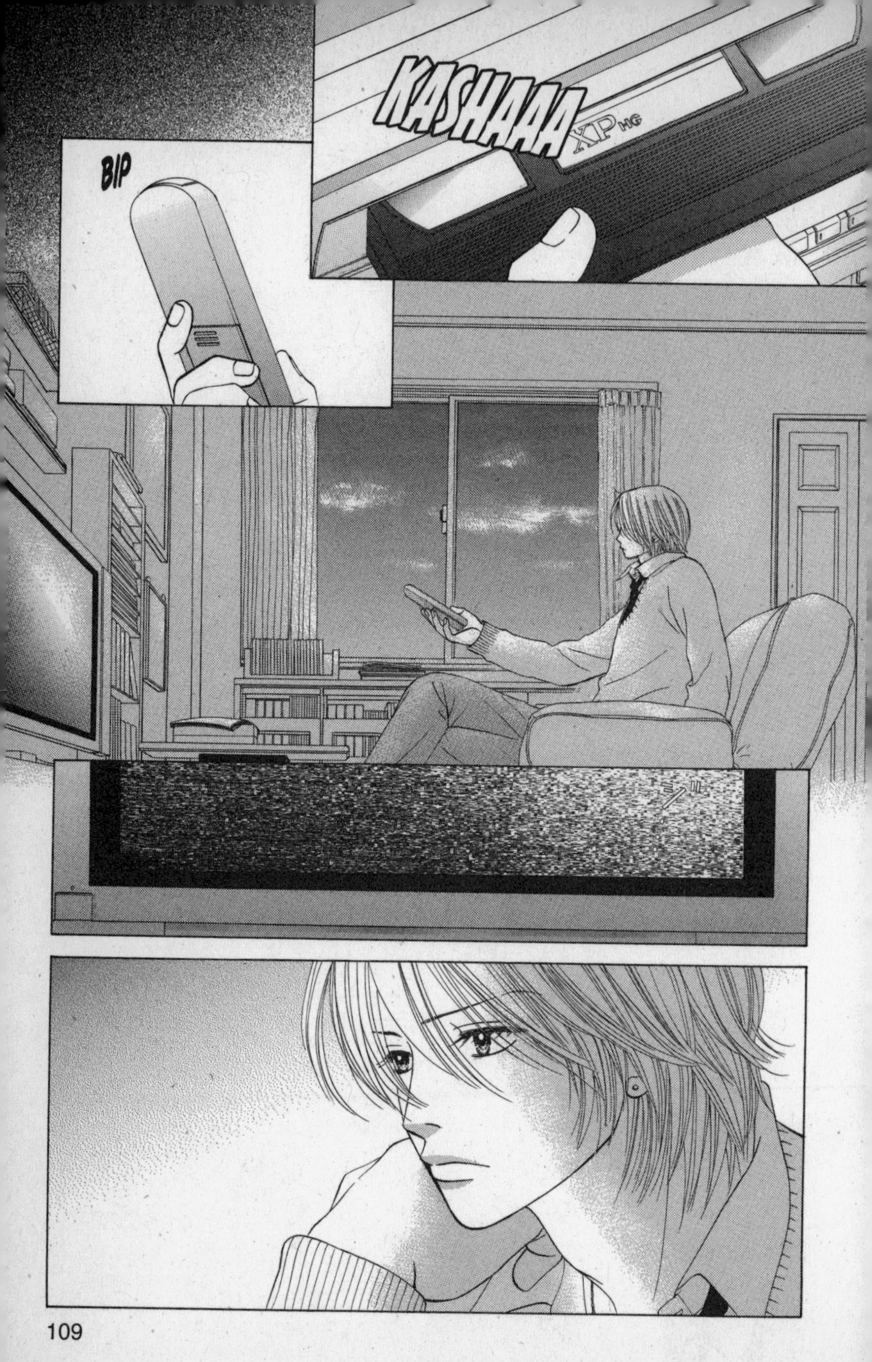
KASHAAA
XP HG
BIP

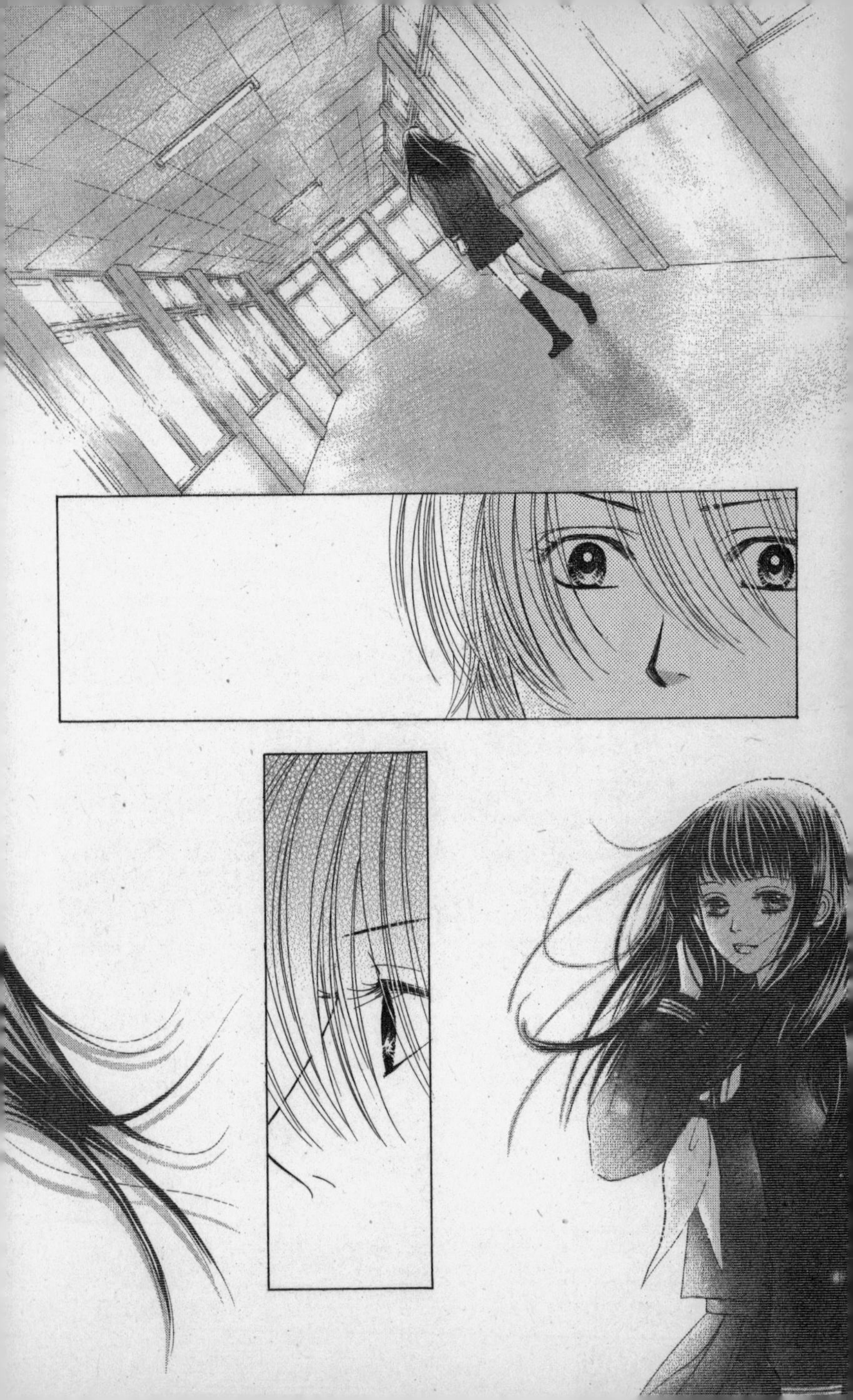

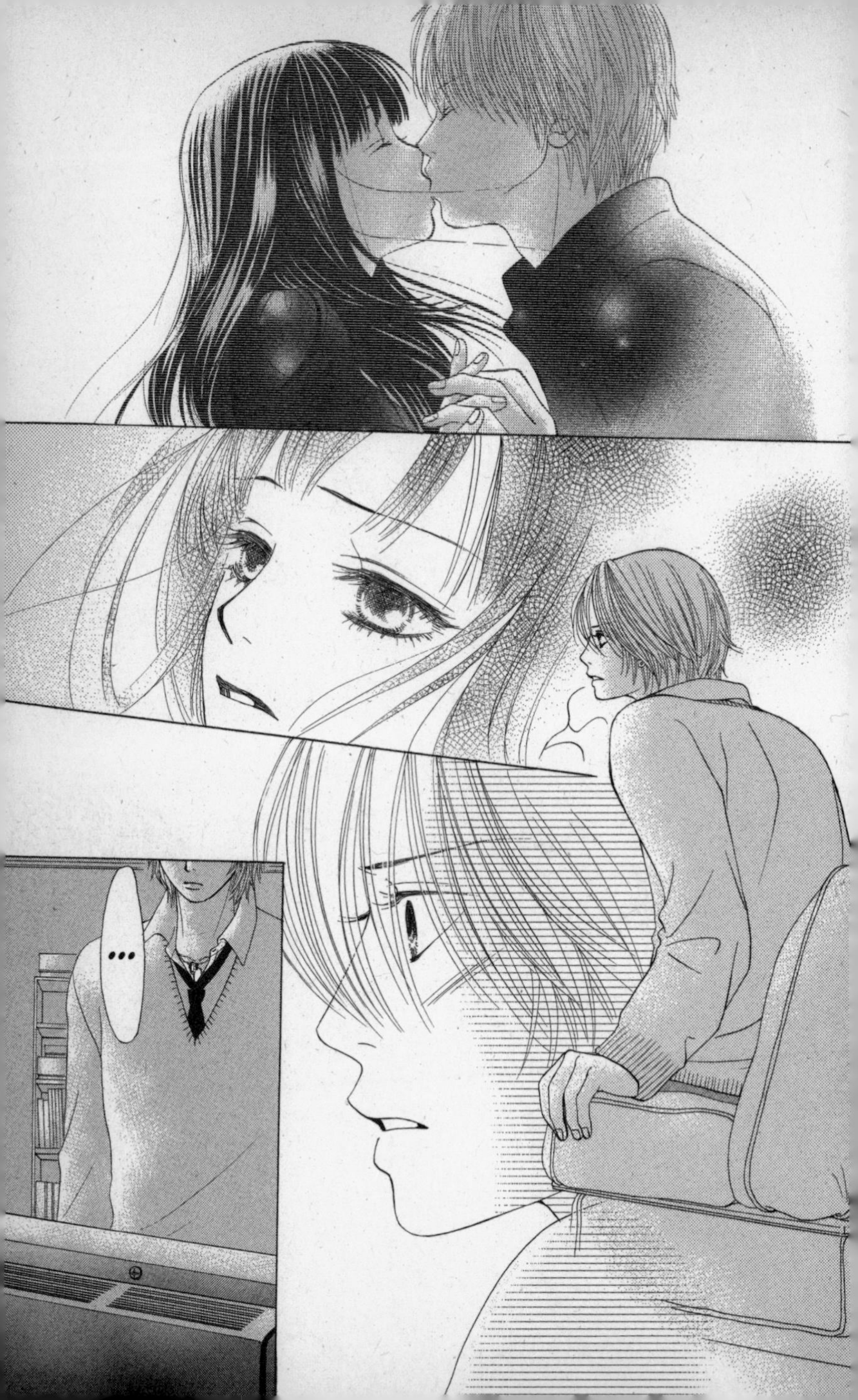
...

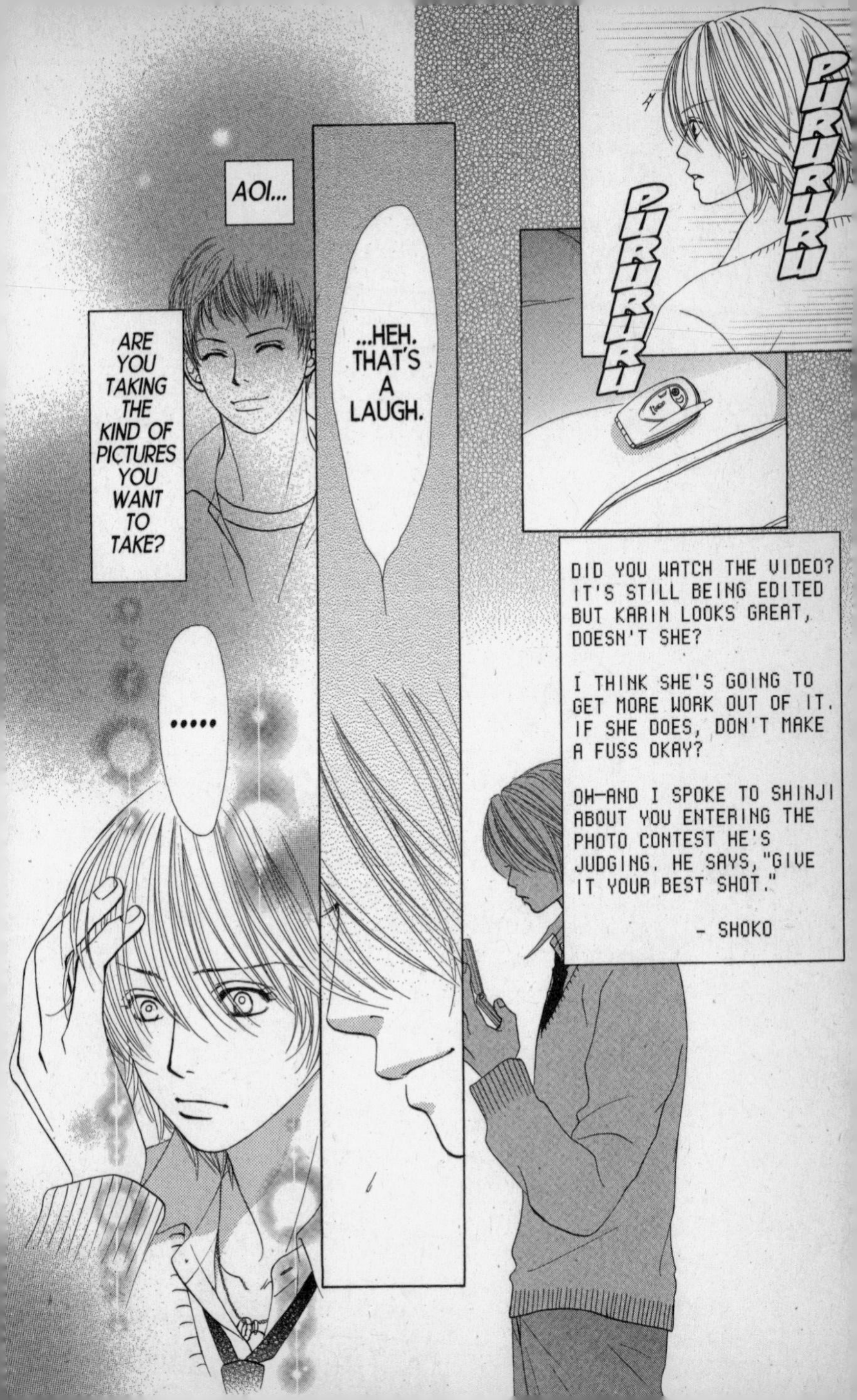
PURURURU
PURURURU
DID YOU WATCH THE VIDEO? IT'S STILL BEING EDITED BUT KARIN LOOKS GREAT, DOESN'T SHE?
I THINK SHE'S GOING TO GET MORE WORK OUT OF IT. IF SHE DOES, DON'T MAKE A FUSS OKAY?
OH—AND I SPOKE TO SHINJI ABOUT YOU ENTERING THE PHOTO CONTEST HE'S JUDGING. HE SAYS, "GIVE IT YOUR BEST SHOT."
- SHOKO
...HEH. THAT'S A LAUGH.
AOI...
ARE YOU TAKING THE KIND OF PICTURES YOU WANT TO TAKE?
.....

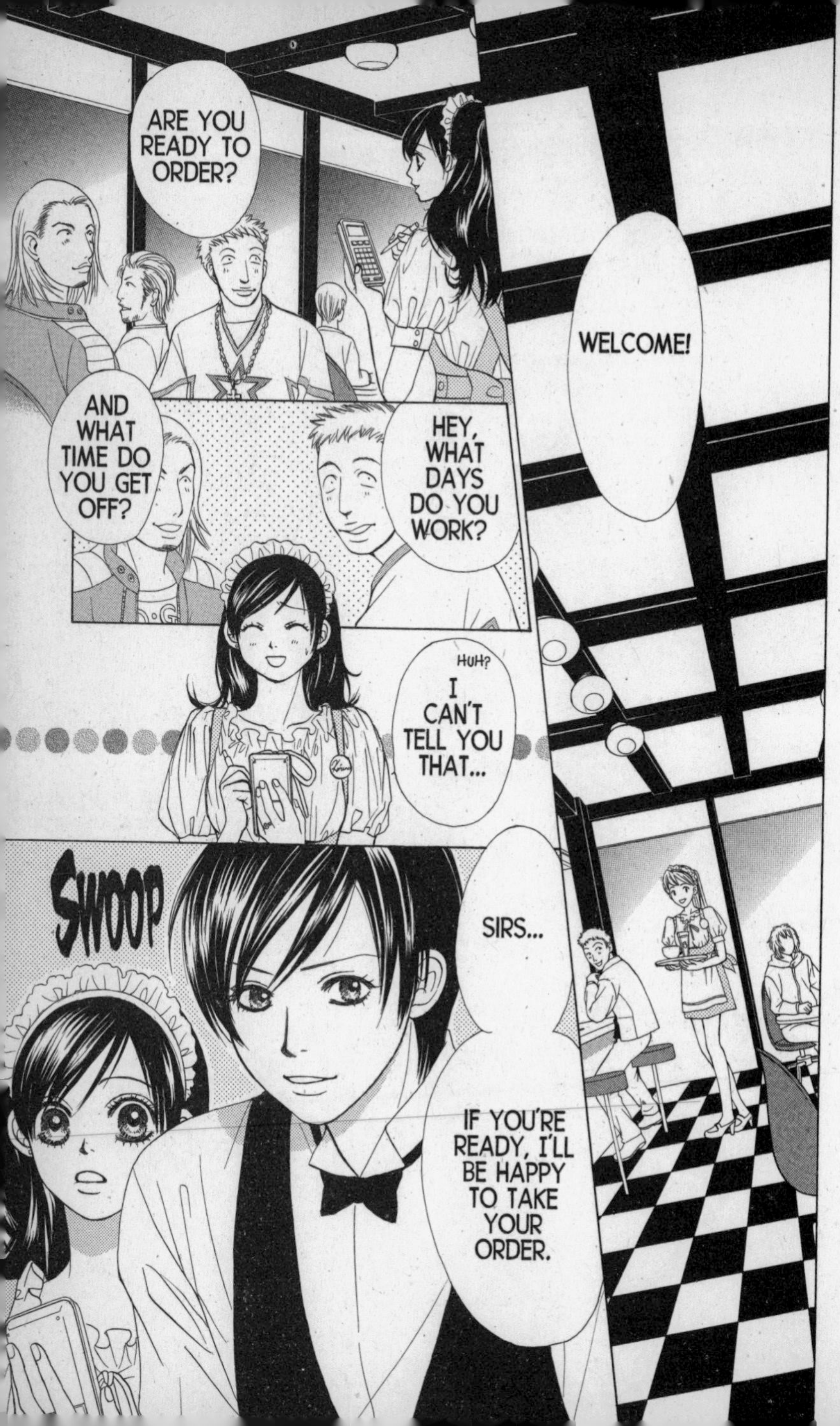
WELCOME!
ARE YOU READY TO ORDER?
HEY, WHAT DAYS DO YOU WORK?
AND WHAT TIME DO YOU GET OFF?
HUH?
I CAN'T TELL YOU THAT...
SWOOP
SIRS...
IF YOU'RE READY, I'LL BE HAPPY TO TAKE YOUR ORDER.

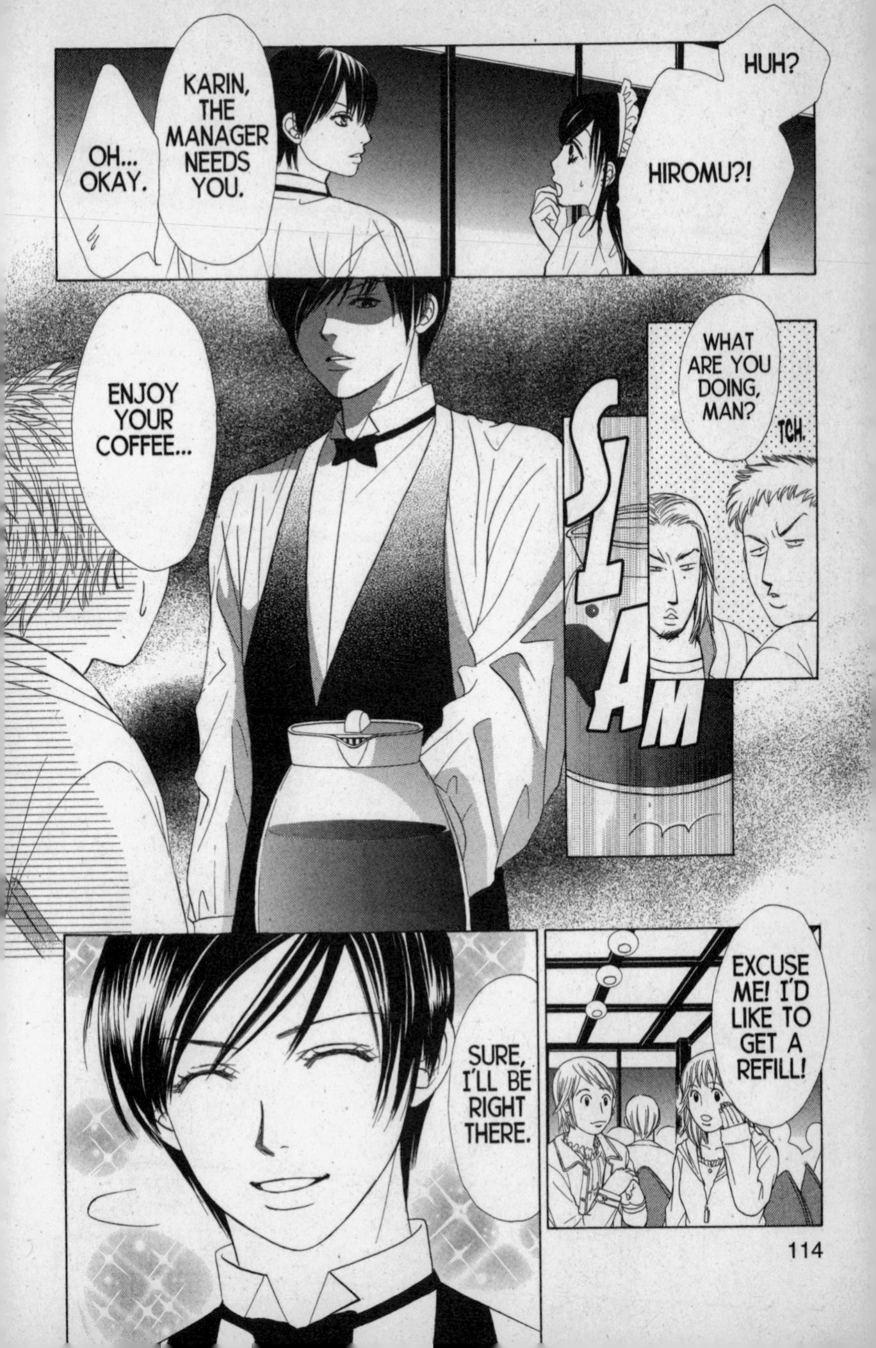
HUH?
HIROMU?!
KARIN, THE MANAGER NEEDS YOU.
OH... OKAY.
WHAT ARE YOU DOING, MAN?
TCH.
SLAM
ENJOY YOUR COFFEE...
EXCUSE ME! I'D LIKE TO GET A REFILL!
SURE, I'LL BE RIGHT THERE.

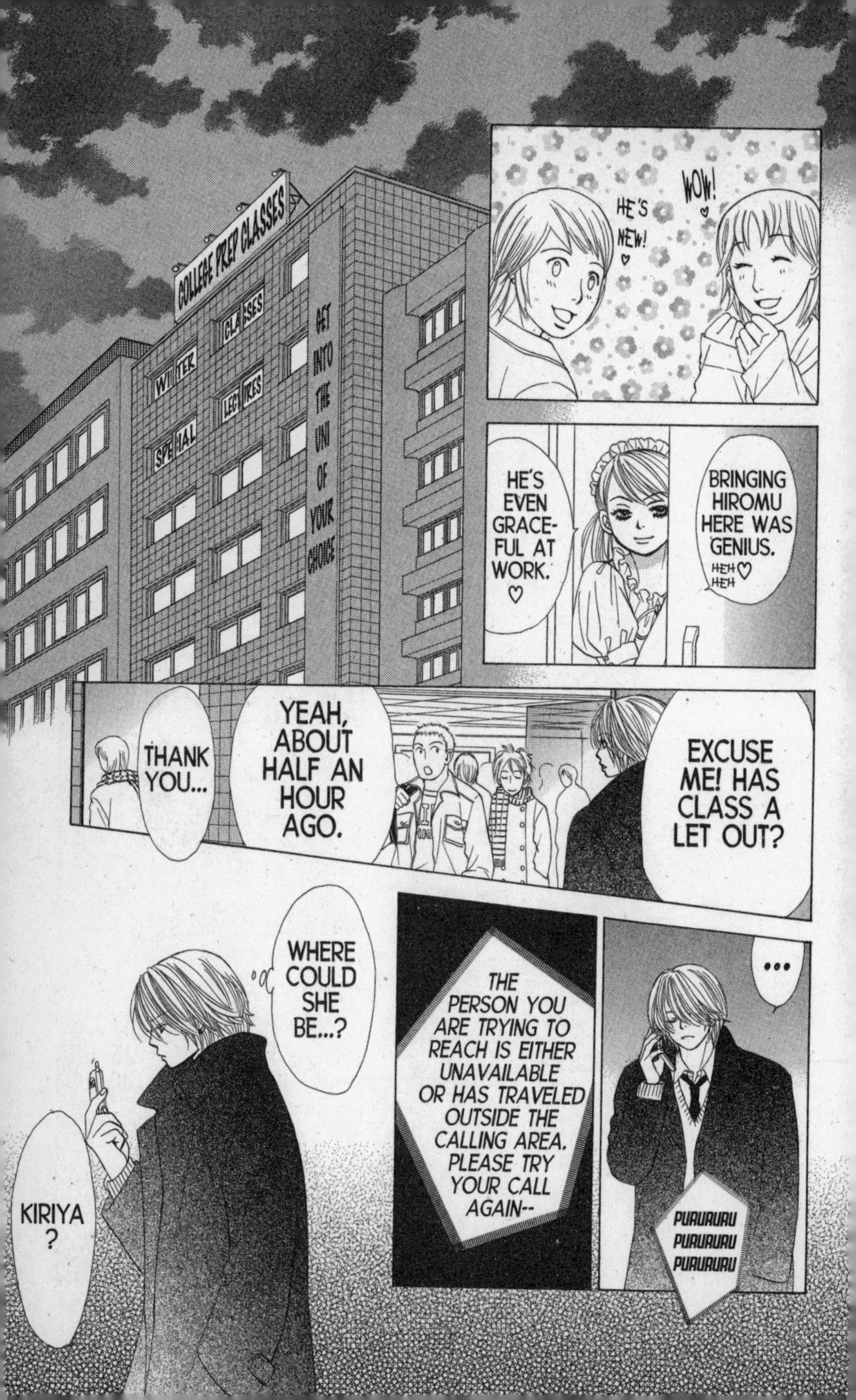
WOW! ♡
HE'S NEW! ♡
BRINGING HIROMU HERE WAS GENIUS. HEH HEH ♡
HE'S EVEN GRACEFUL AT WORK. ♡
COLLEGE PREP CLASSES
GET INTO THE UNI OF YOUR CHOICE
EXCUSE ME! HAS CLASS A LET OUT?
YEAH, ABOUT HALF AN HOUR AGO.
THANK YOU...
PURURURU PURURURU PURURURU
...
THE PERSON YOU ARE TRYING TO REACH IS EITHER UNAVAILABLE OR HAS TRAVELED OUTSIDE THE CALLING AREA. PLEASE TRY YOUR CALL AGAIN--
WHERE COULD SHE BE...?
KIRIYA ?

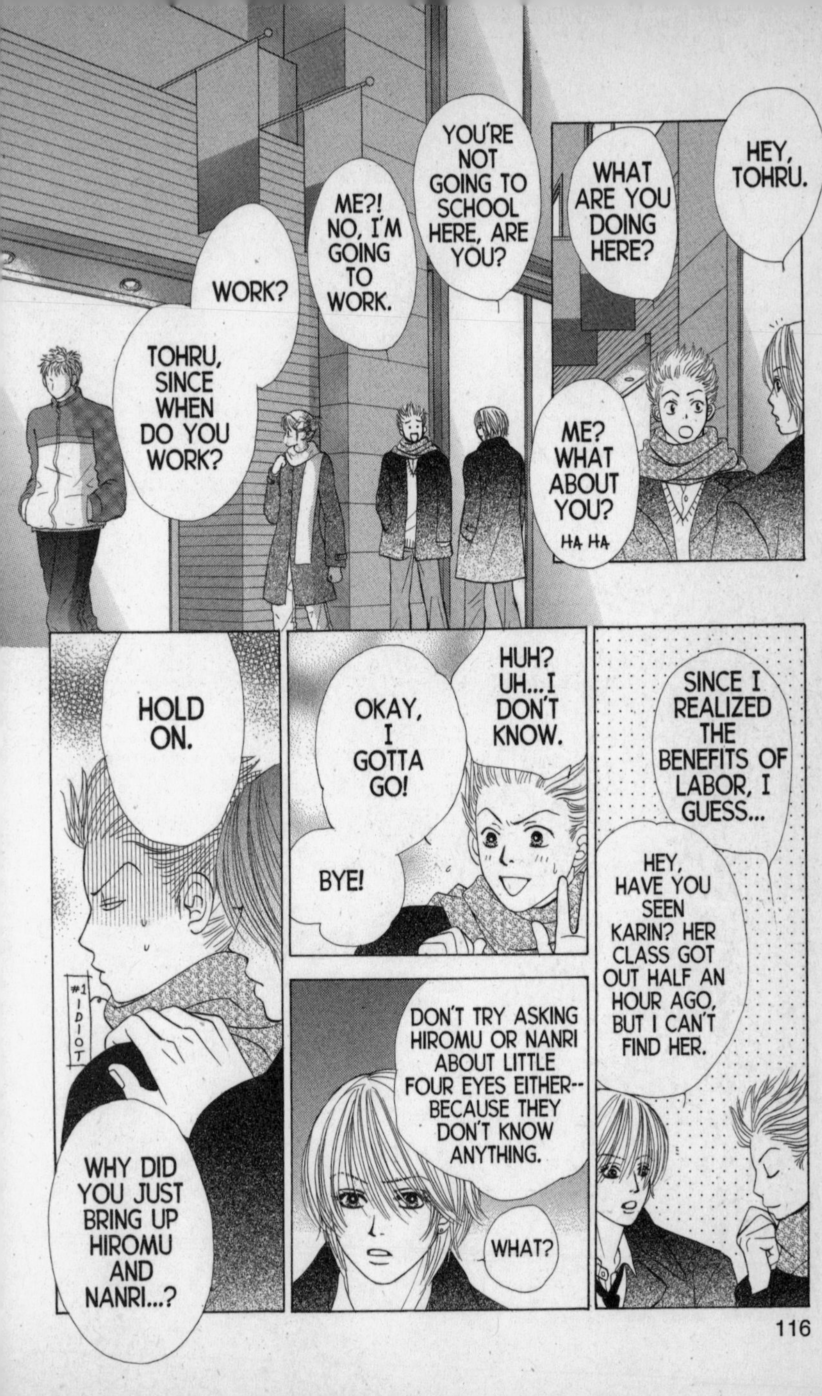
HEY, TOHRU.
WHAT ARE YOU DOING HERE?
ME? WHAT ABOUT YOU?
HA HA
YOU'RE NOT GOING TO SCHOOL HERE, ARE YOU?
ME?! NO, I'M GOING TO WORK.
WORK?
TOHRU, SINCE WHEN DO YOU WORK?
SINCE I REALIZED THE BENEFITS OF LABOR, I GUESS...
HEY, HAVE YOU SEEN KARIN? HER CLASS GOT OUT HALF AN HOUR AGO, BUT I CAN'T FIND HER.
HUH? UH...I DON'T KNOW.
OKAY, I GOTTA GO!
BYE!
DON'T TRY ASKING HIROMU OR NANRI ABOUT LITTLE FOUR EYES EITHER--BECAUSE THEY DON'T KNOW ANYTHING.
WHAT?
HOLD ON.
#1 IDIOT
WHY DID YOU JUST BRING UP HIROMU AND NANRI...?

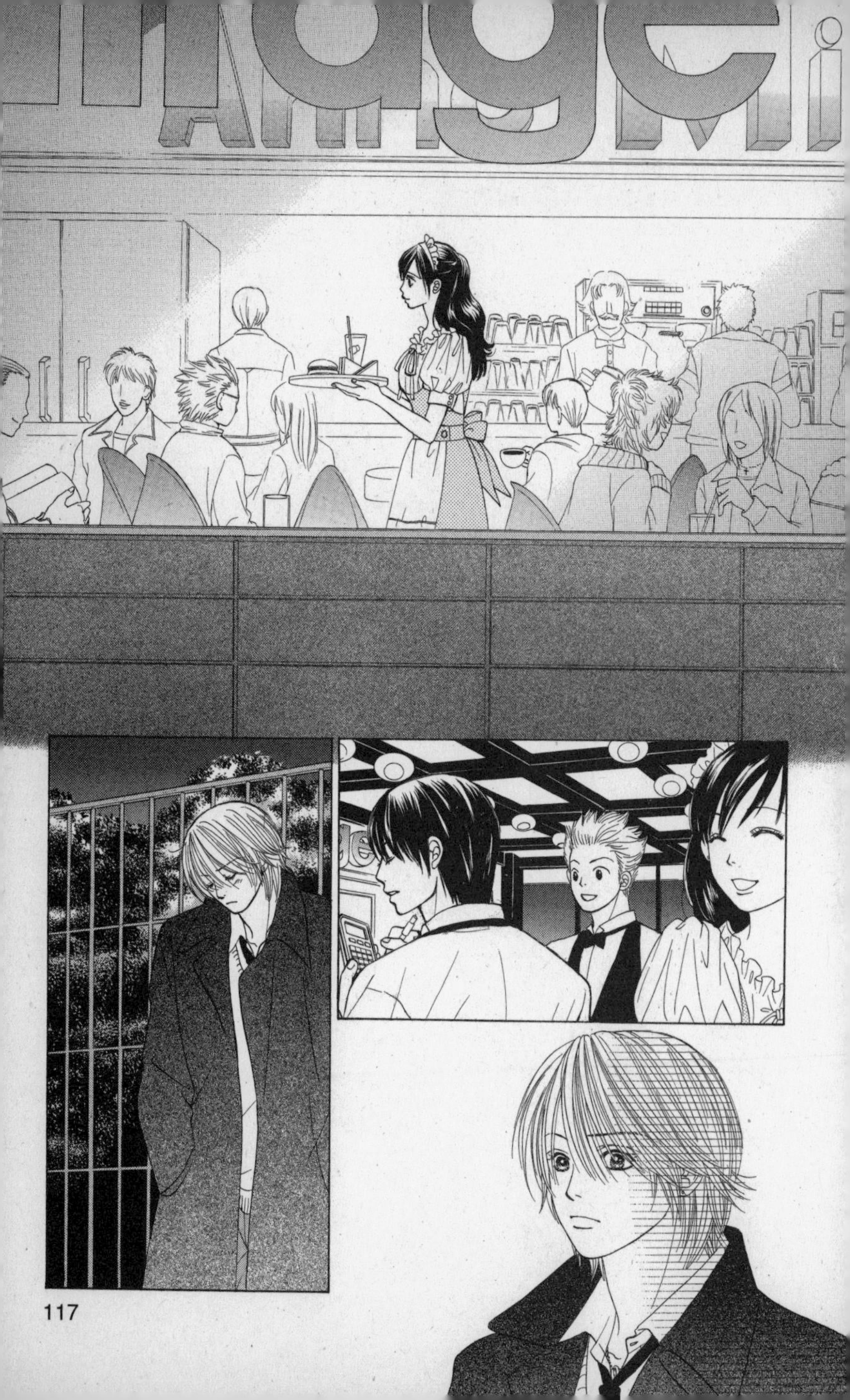

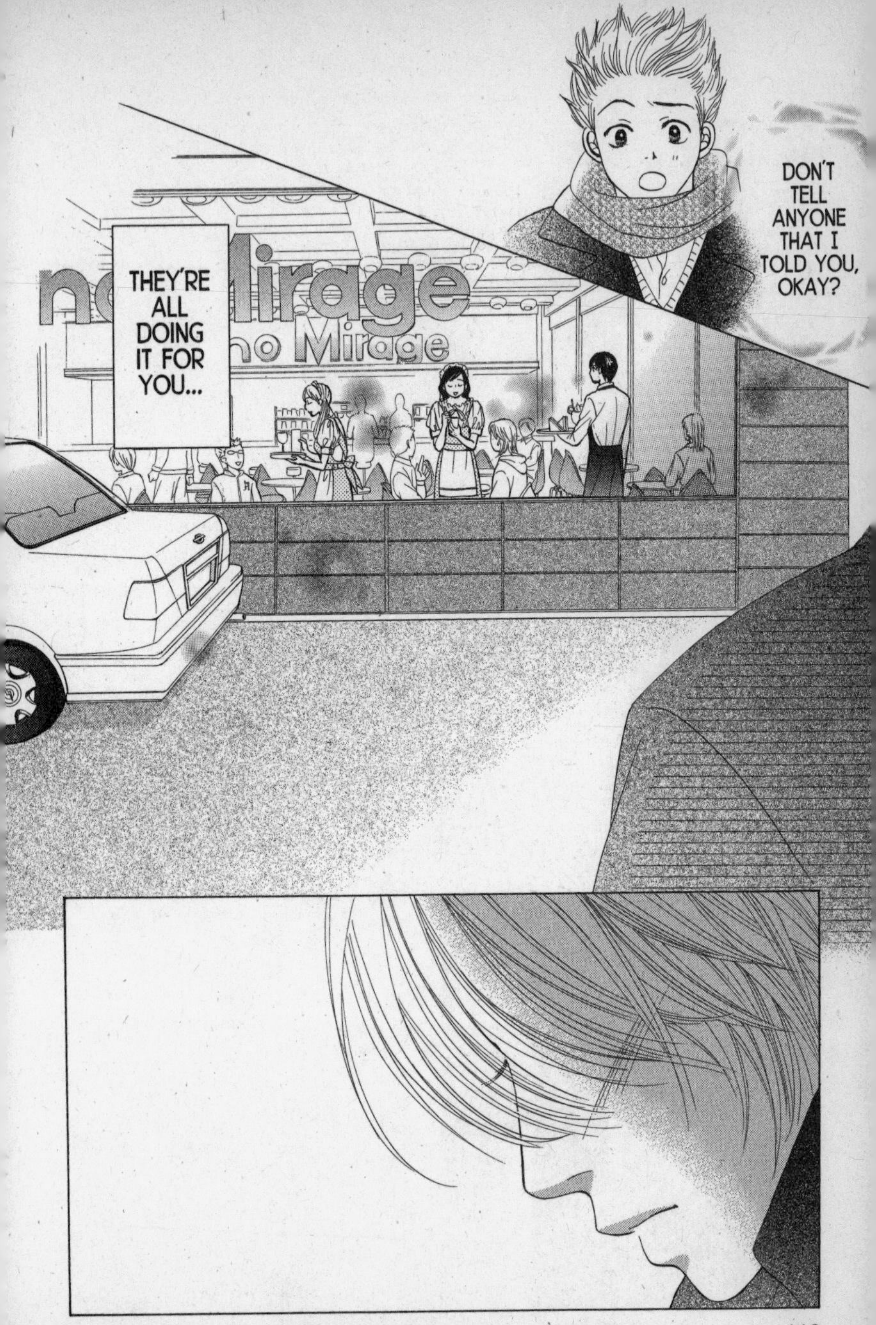
DON'T TELL ANYONE THAT I TOLD YOU, OKAY?
THEY'RE ALL DOING IT FOR YOU...

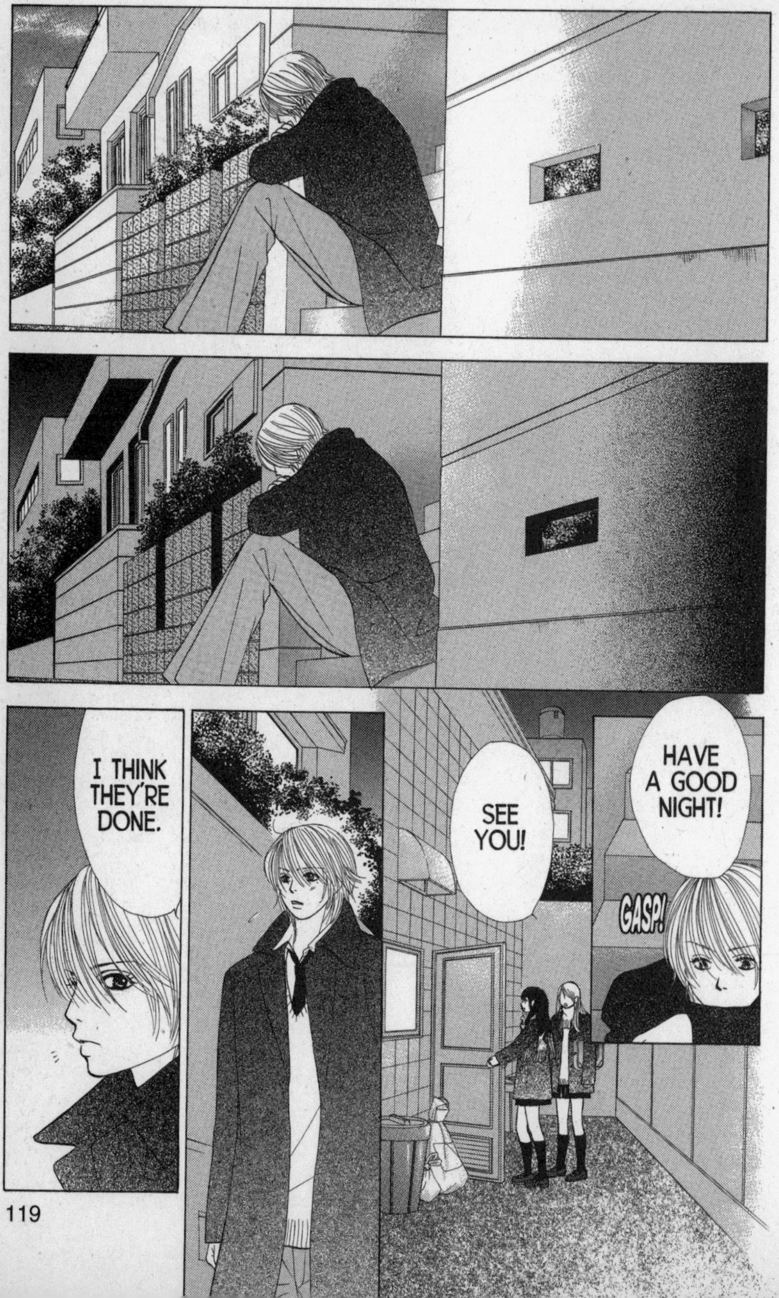
HAVE A GOOD NIGHT!
GASP!
SEE YOU!
I THINK THEY'RE DONE.

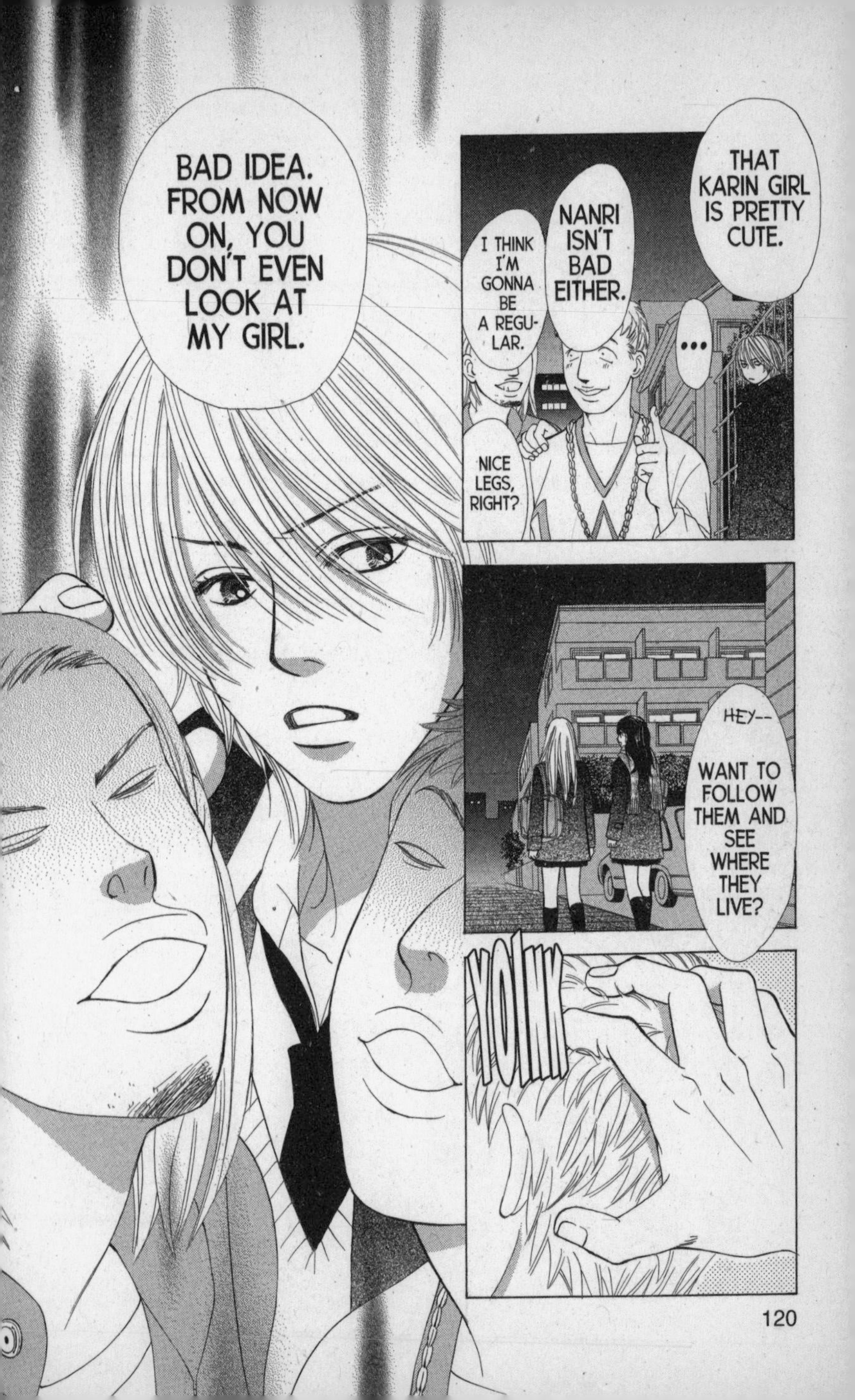
THAT KARIN GIRL IS PRETTY CUTE.
...
NANRI ISN'T BAD EITHER.
I THINK I'M GONNA BE A REGU-LAR.
NICE LEGS, RIGHT?
HEY--
WANT TO FOLLOW THEM AND SEE WHERE THEY LIVE?
YOINK
BAD IDEA. FROM NOW ON, YOU DON'T EVEN LOOK AT MY GIRL.

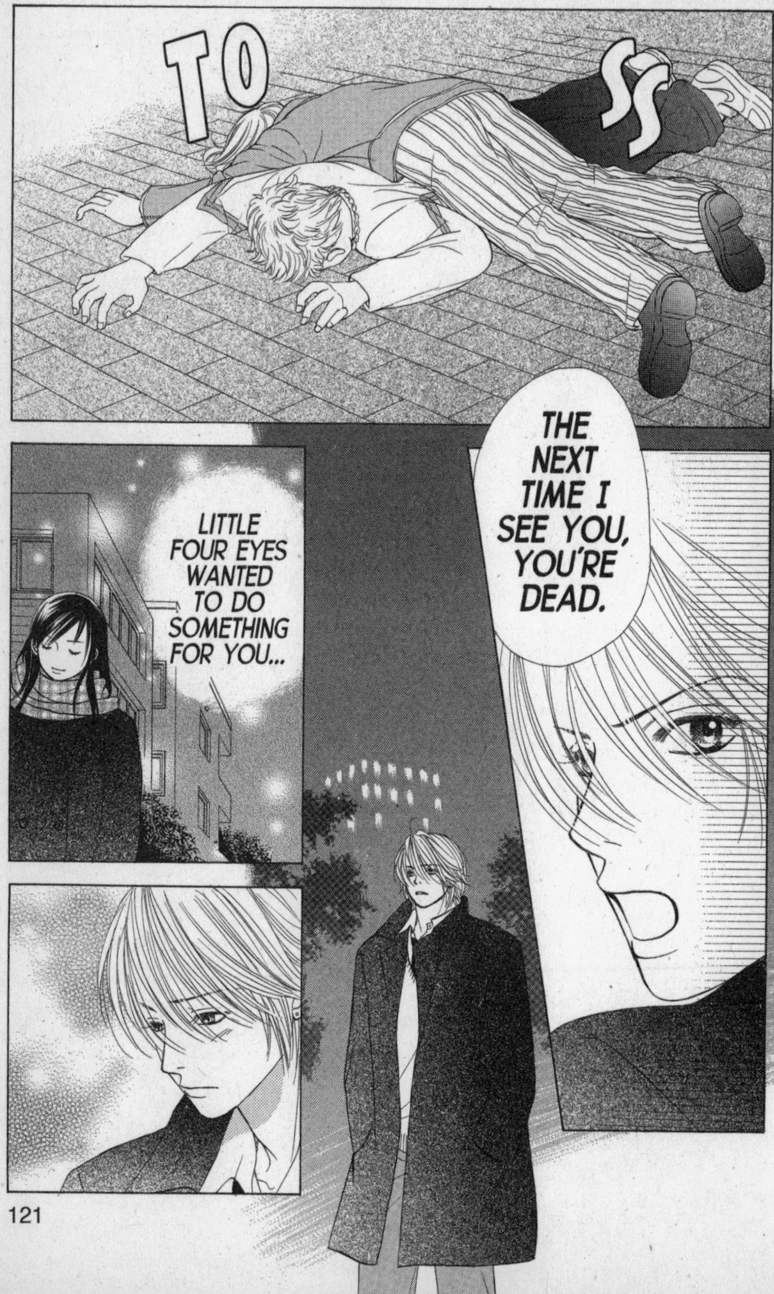
TO SS
THE NEXT TIME I SEE YOU, YOU'RE DEAD.
LITTLE FOUR EYES WANTED TO DO SOMETHING FOR YOU...

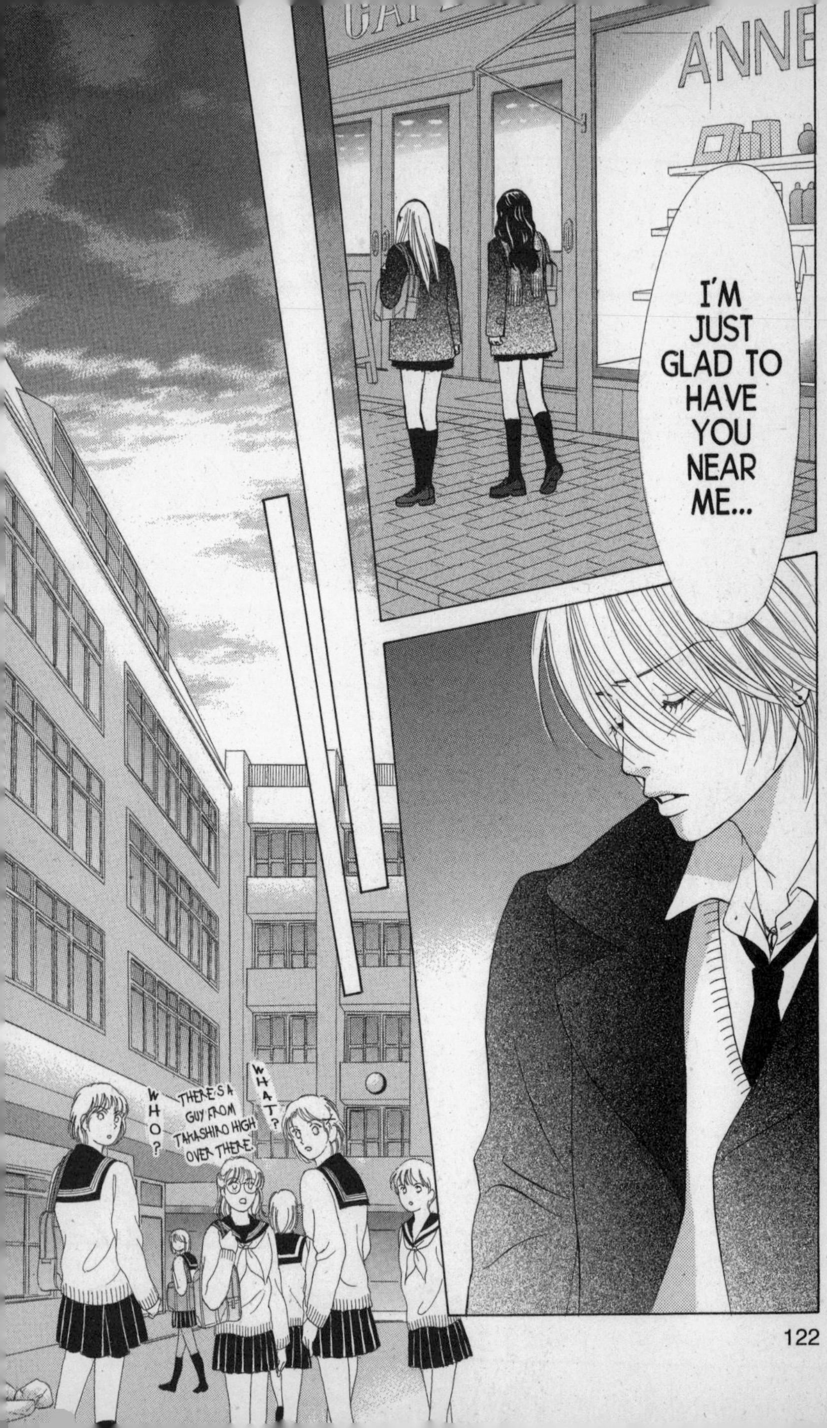
I'M JUST GLAD TO HAVE YOU NEAR ME...
WHAT?
THERE'S A GUY FROM TAKASHIRO HIGH OVER THERE.
WHO?

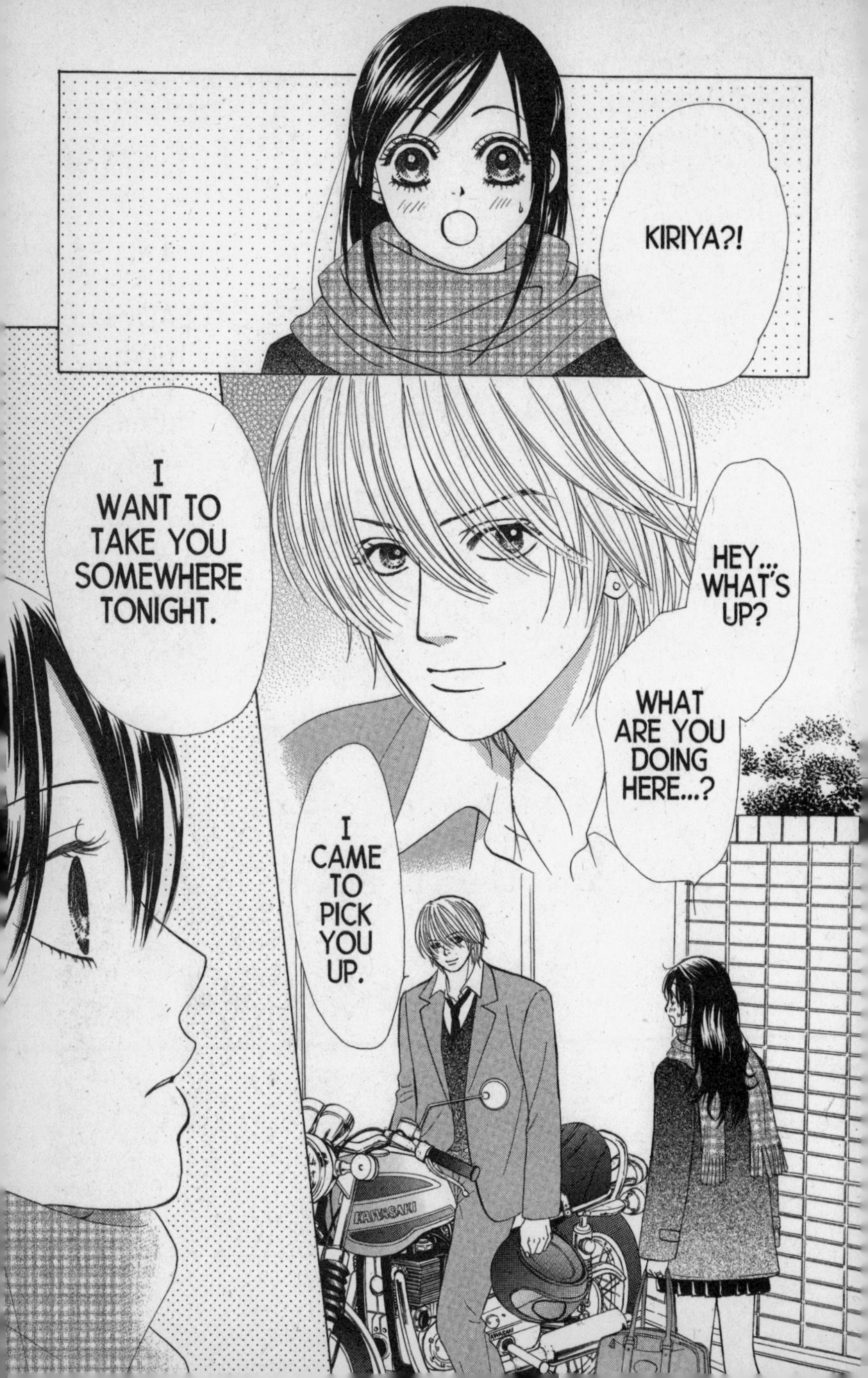
KIRIYA?!
HEY... WHAT'S UP?
WHAT ARE YOU DOING HERE...?
I CAME TO PICK YOU UP.
I WANT TO TAKE YOU SOMEWHERE TONIGHT.
KAWASAKI

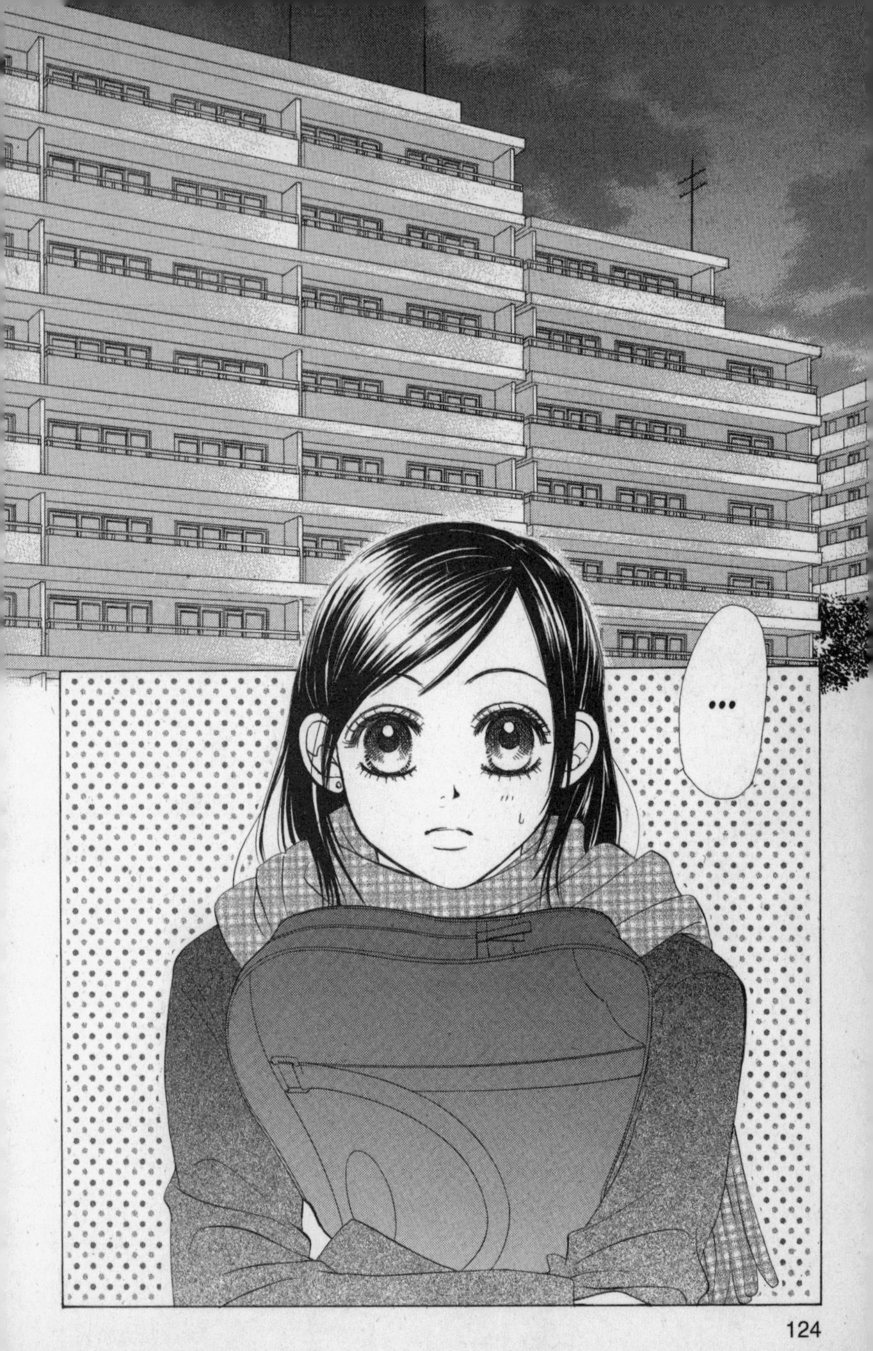
...

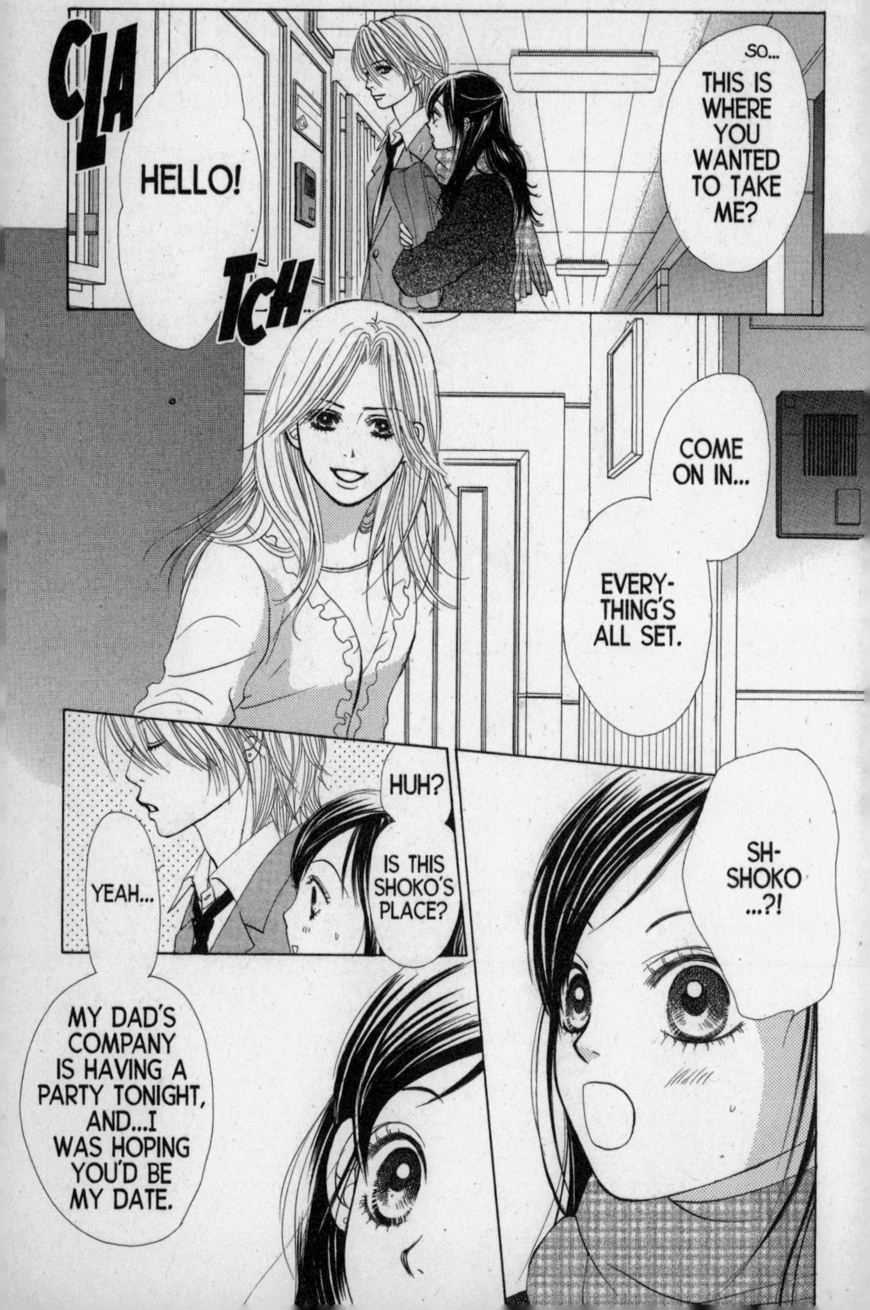
SO... THIS IS WHERE YOU WANTED TO TAKE ME?
CLATCH...
HELLO!
COME ON IN...
EVERYTHING'S ALL SET.
SH-SHOKO...?!
HUH?
IS THIS SHOKO'S PLACE?
YEAH...
MY DAD'S COMPANY IS HAVING A PARTY TONIGHT, AND...I WAS HOPING YOU'D BE MY DATE.

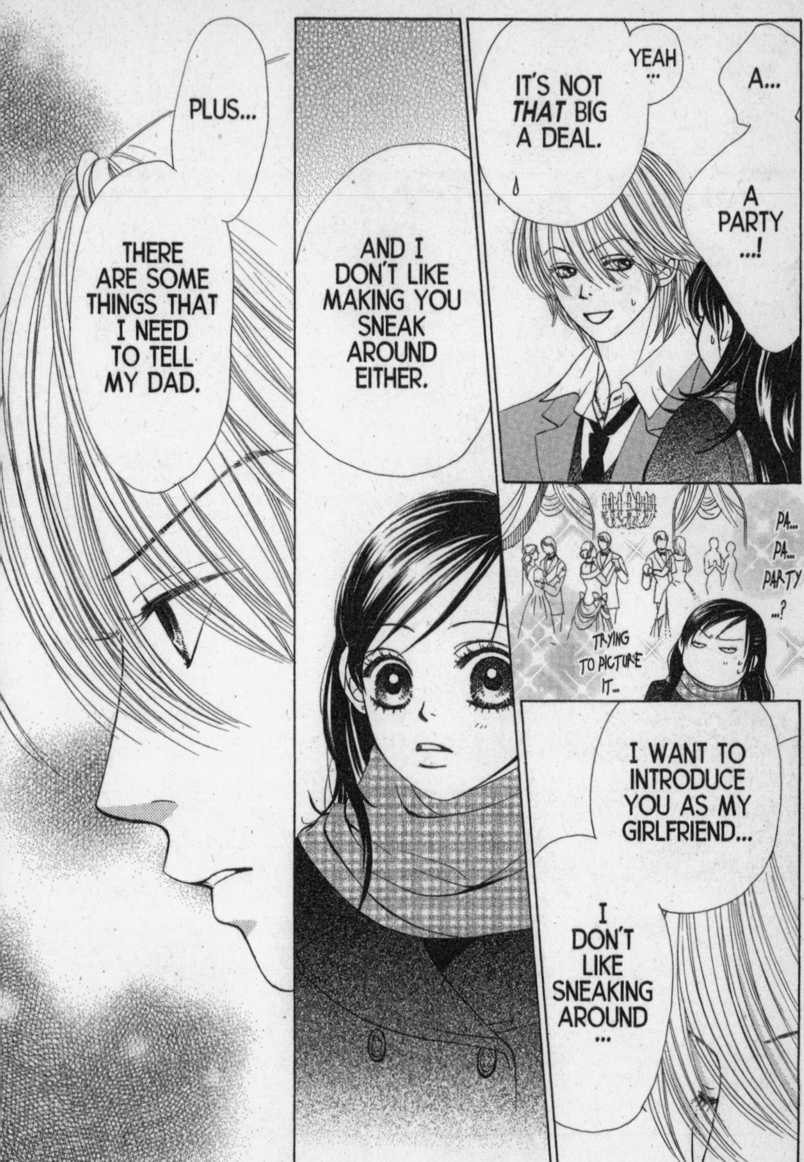
A...
A PARTY ...!
YEAH ...
IT'S NOT *THAT* BIG A DEAL.
PA... PA... PARTY ...?
TRYING TO PICTURE IT...
I WANT TO INTRODUCE YOU AS MY GIRLFRIEND...
I DON'T LIKE SNEAKING AROUND ...
AND I DON'T LIKE MAKING YOU SNEAK AROUND EITHER.
PLUS...
THERE ARE SOME THINGS THAT I NEED TO TELL MY DAD.

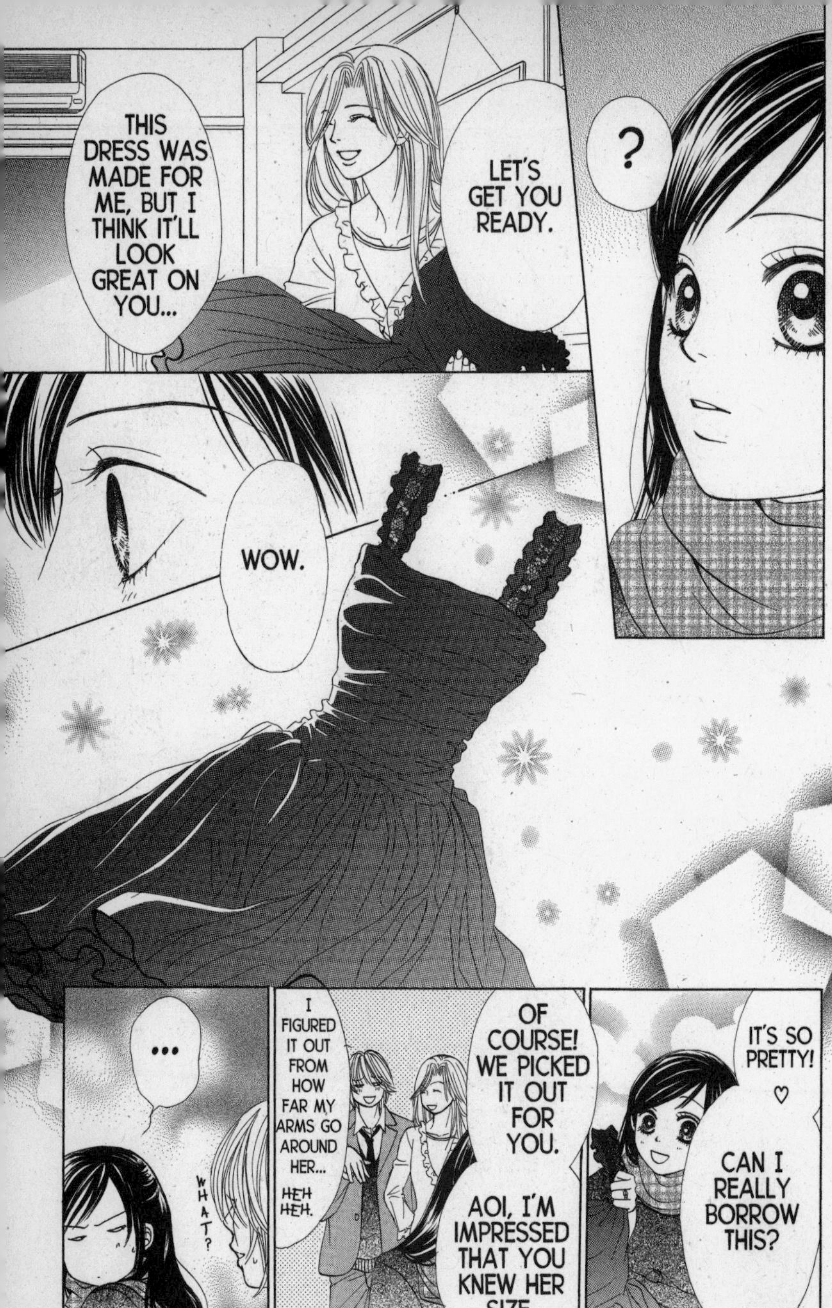
?
LET'S GET YOU READY.
THIS DRESS WAS MADE FOR ME, BUT I THINK IT'LL LOOK GREAT ON YOU...
WOW.
IT'S SO PRETTY! ♡
CAN I REALLY BORROW THIS?
OF COURSE! WE PICKED IT OUT FOR YOU.
AOI, I'M IMPRESSED THAT YOU KNEW HER SIZE.
I FIGURED IT OUT FROM HOW FAR MY ARMS GO AROUND HER...
HEH HEH.
...
WHAT?

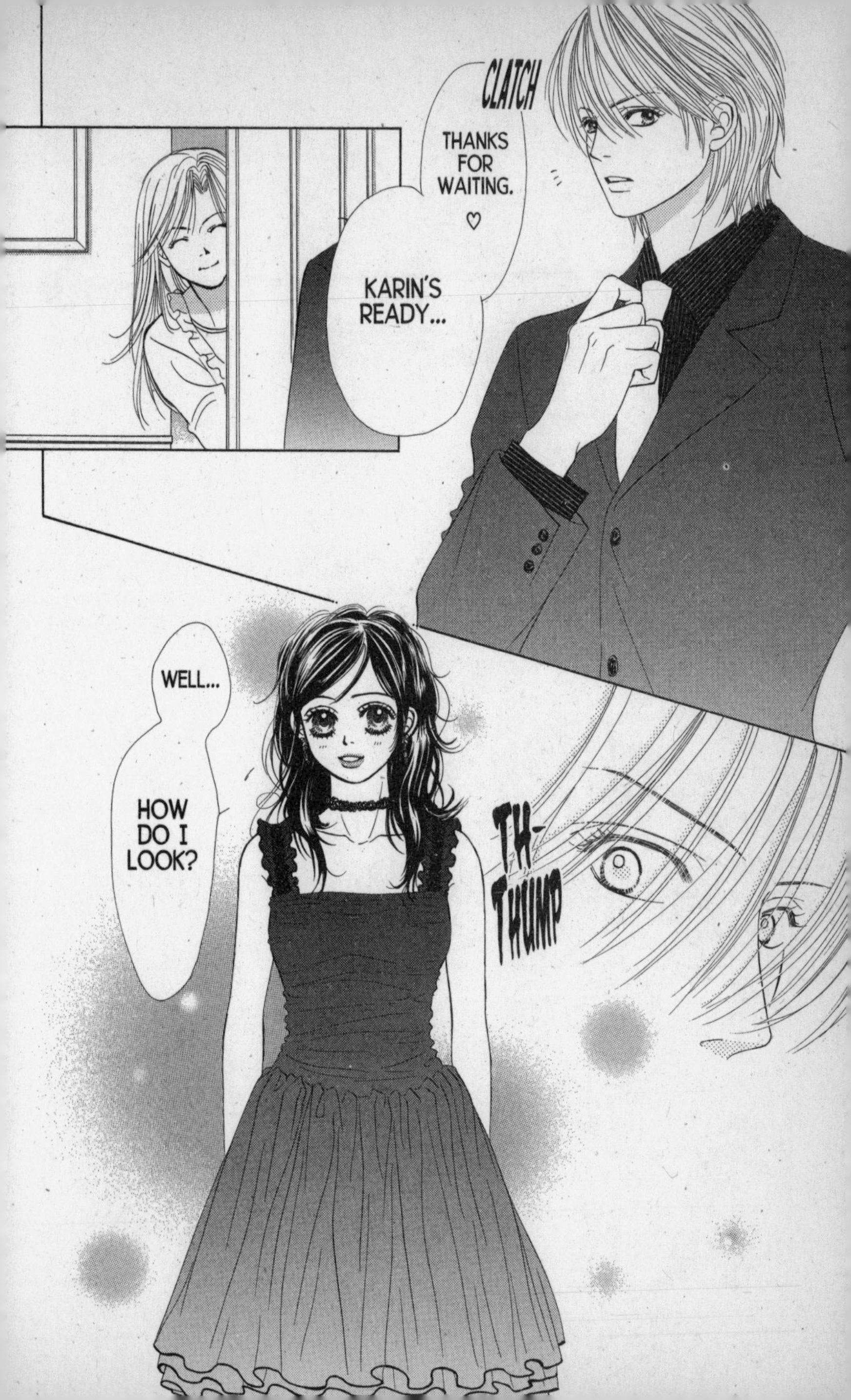
CLATCH
THANKS FOR WAITING. ♡
KARIN'S READY...
TH-THUMP
WELL...
HOW DO I LOOK?

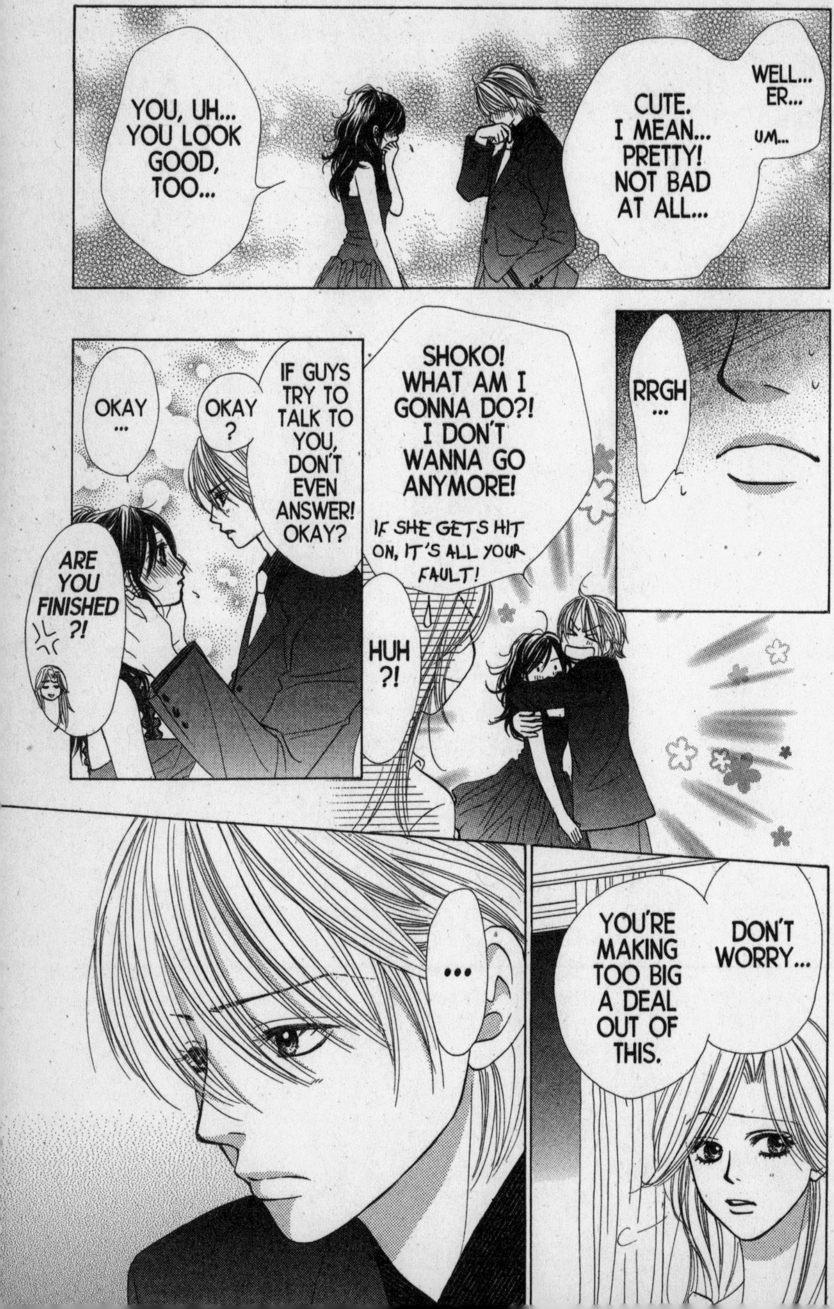
WELL... ER... UM...
CUTE. I MEAN... PRETTY! NOT BAD AT ALL...
YOU, UH... YOU LOOK GOOD, TOO...
RRGH...
SHOKO! WHAT AM I GONNA DO?! I DON'T WANNA GO ANYMORE!
IF SHE GETS HIT ON, IT'S ALL YOUR FAULT!
HUH?!
IF GUYS TRY TO TALK TO YOU, DON'T EVEN ANSWER! OKAY?
OKAY?
OKAY...
ARE YOU FINISHED?!
DON'T WORRY...
YOU'RE MAKING TOO BIG A DEAL OUT OF THIS.
...

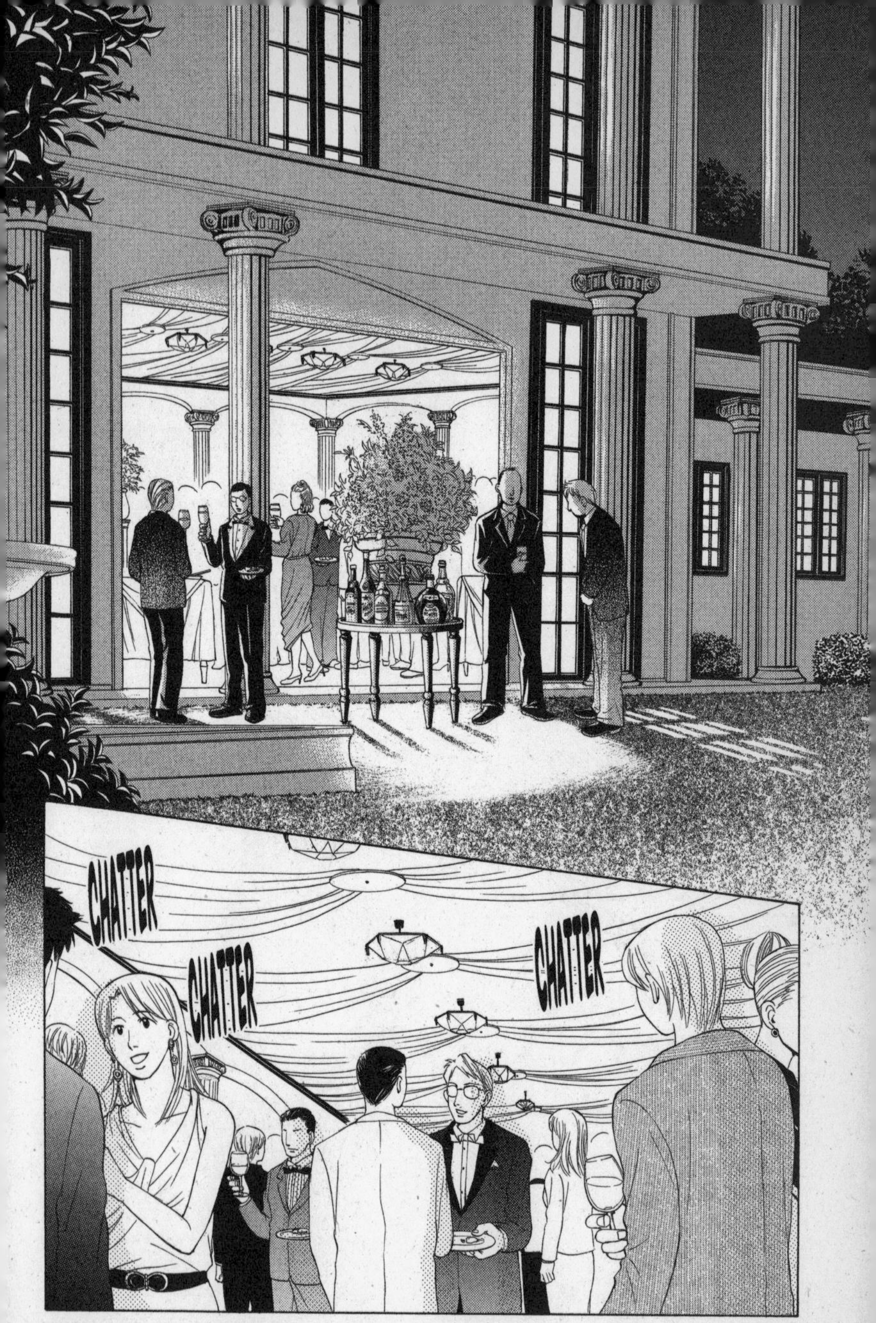
CHATTER
CHATTER
CHATTER

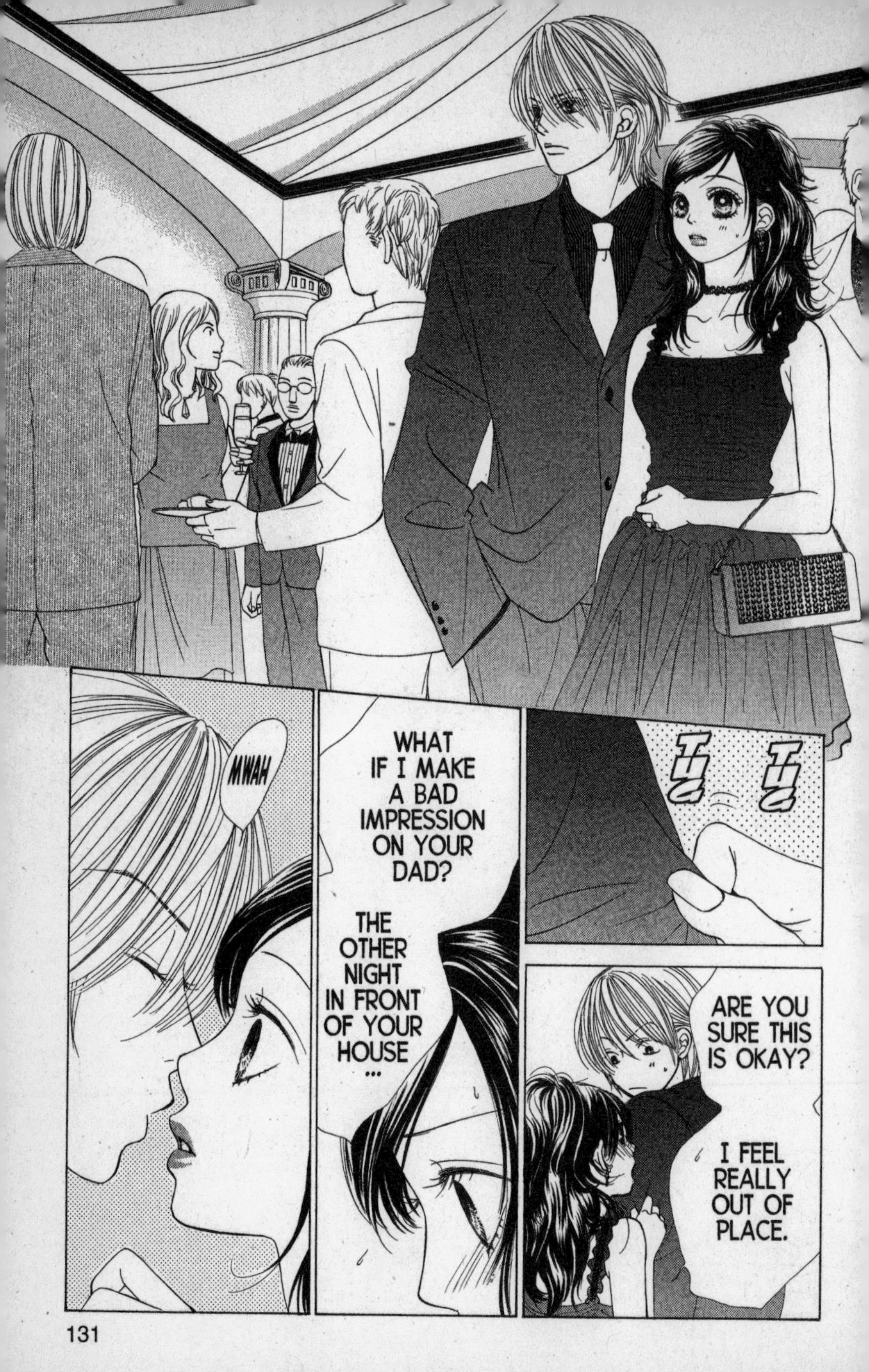
TUG TUG
ARE YOU SURE THIS IS OKAY?
I FEEL REALLY OUT OF PLACE.
WHAT IF I MAKE A BAD IMPRESSION ON YOUR DAD?
THE OTHER NIGHT IN FRONT OF YOUR HOUSE...
MWAH

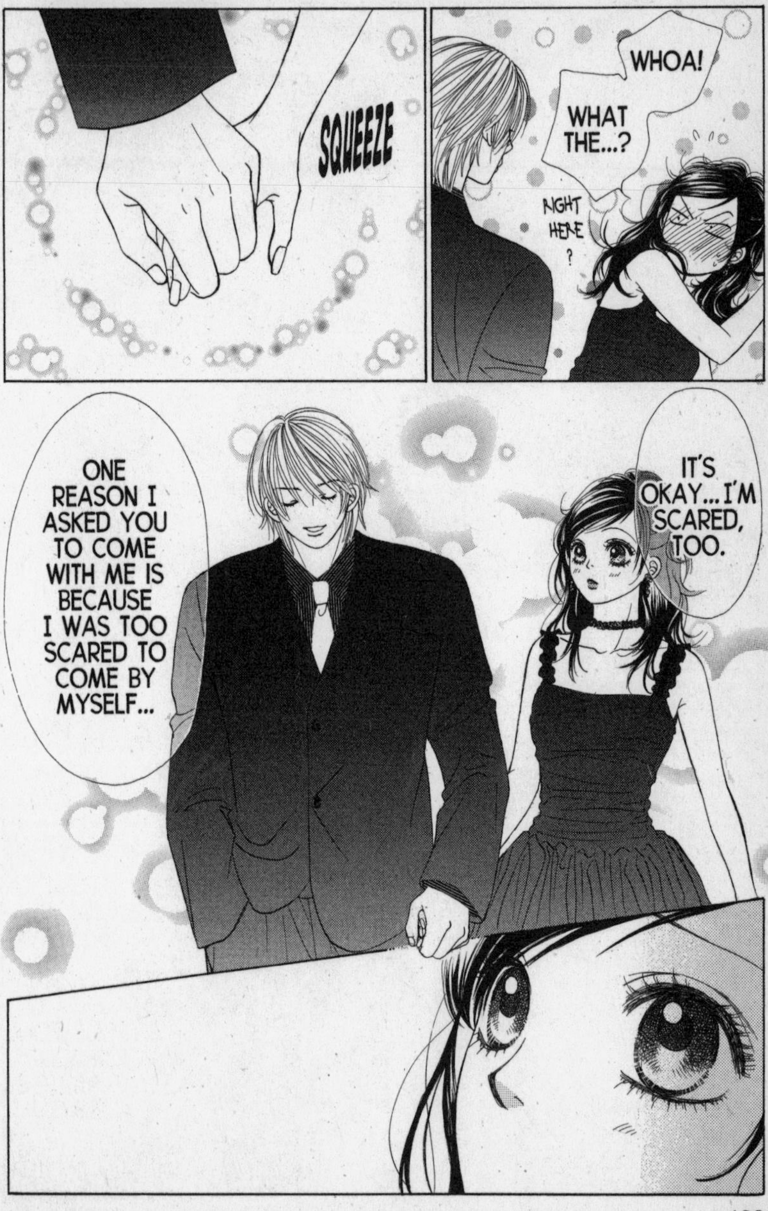
WHOA!
WHAT THE...?
RIGHT HERE ?
SQUEEZE
ONE REASON I ASKED YOU TO COME WITH ME IS BECAUSE I WAS TOO SCARED TO COME BY MYSELF...
IT'S OKAY...I'M SCARED, TOO.

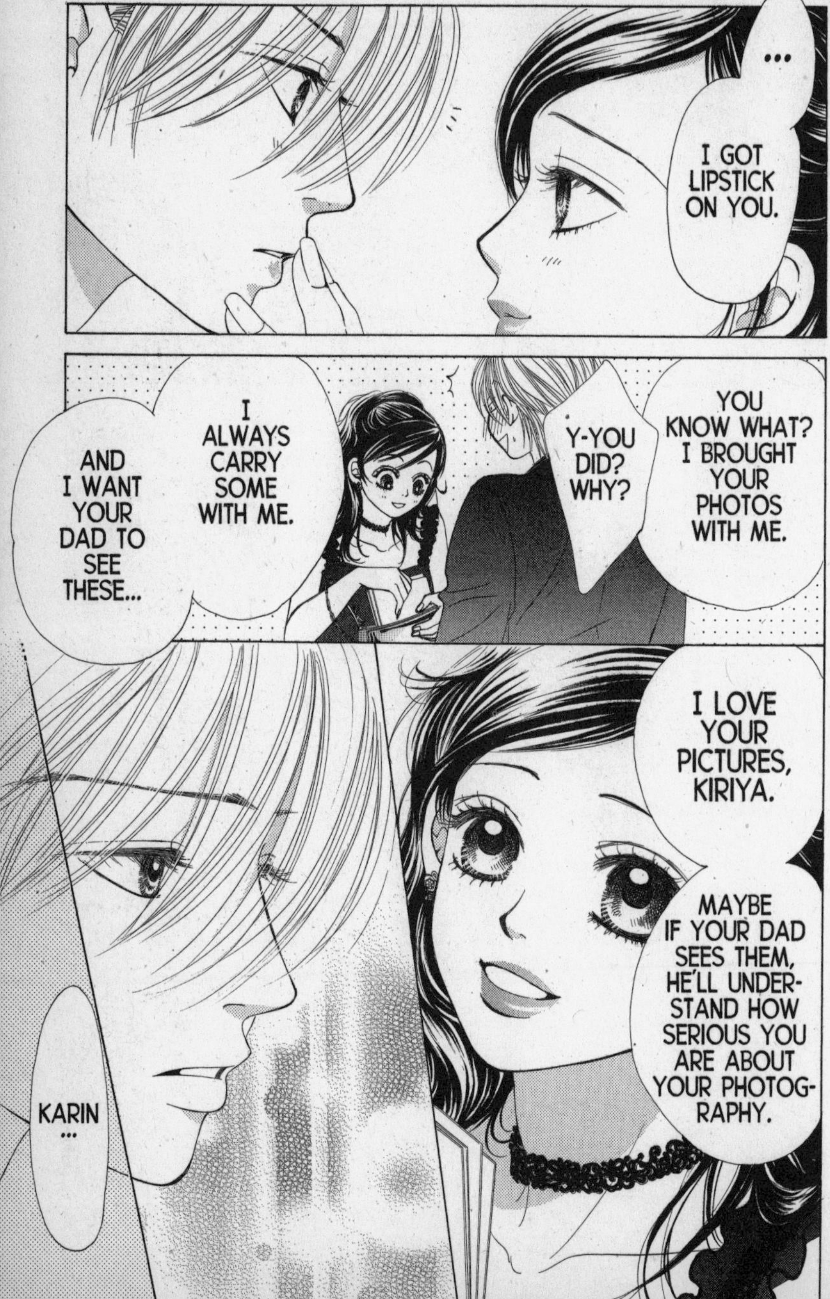
...
I GOT LIPSTICK ON YOU.
YOU KNOW WHAT? I BROUGHT YOUR PHOTOS WITH ME.
Y-YOU DID? WHY?
I ALWAYS CARRY SOME WITH ME.
AND I WANT YOUR DAD TO SEE THESE...
I LOVE YOUR PICTURES, KIRIYA.
MAYBE IF YOUR DAD SEES THEM, HE'LL UNDER-STAND HOW SERIOUS YOU ARE ABOUT YOUR PHOTOG-RAPHY.
KARIN ...

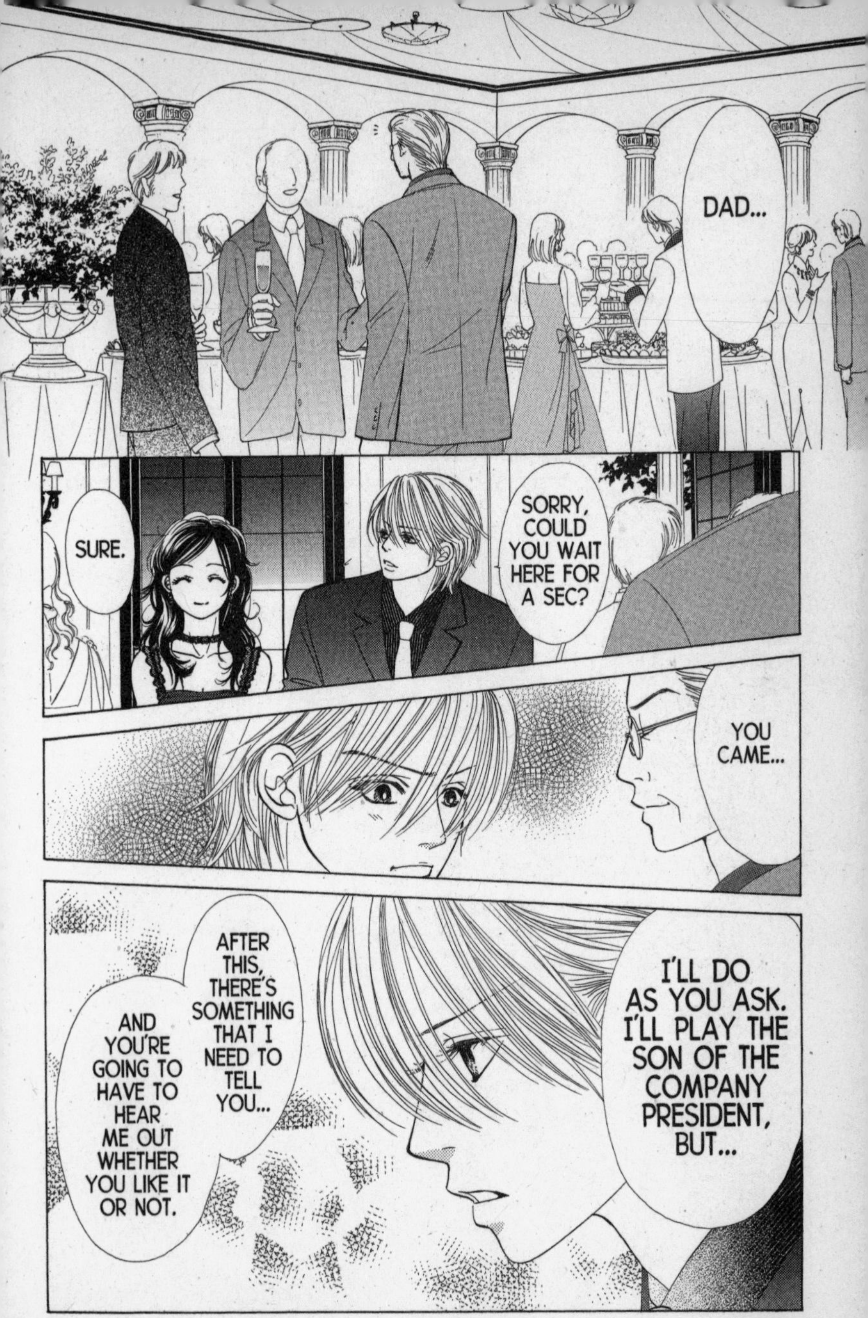
DAD...
SORRY, COULD YOU WAIT HERE FOR A SEC?
SURE.
YOU CAME...
I'LL DO AS YOU ASK. I'LL PLAY THE SON OF THE COMPANY PRESIDENT, BUT...
AFTER THIS, THERE'S SOMETHING THAT I NEED TO TELL YOU...
AND YOU'RE GOING TO HAVE TO HEAR ME OUT WHETHER YOU LIKE IT OR NOT.

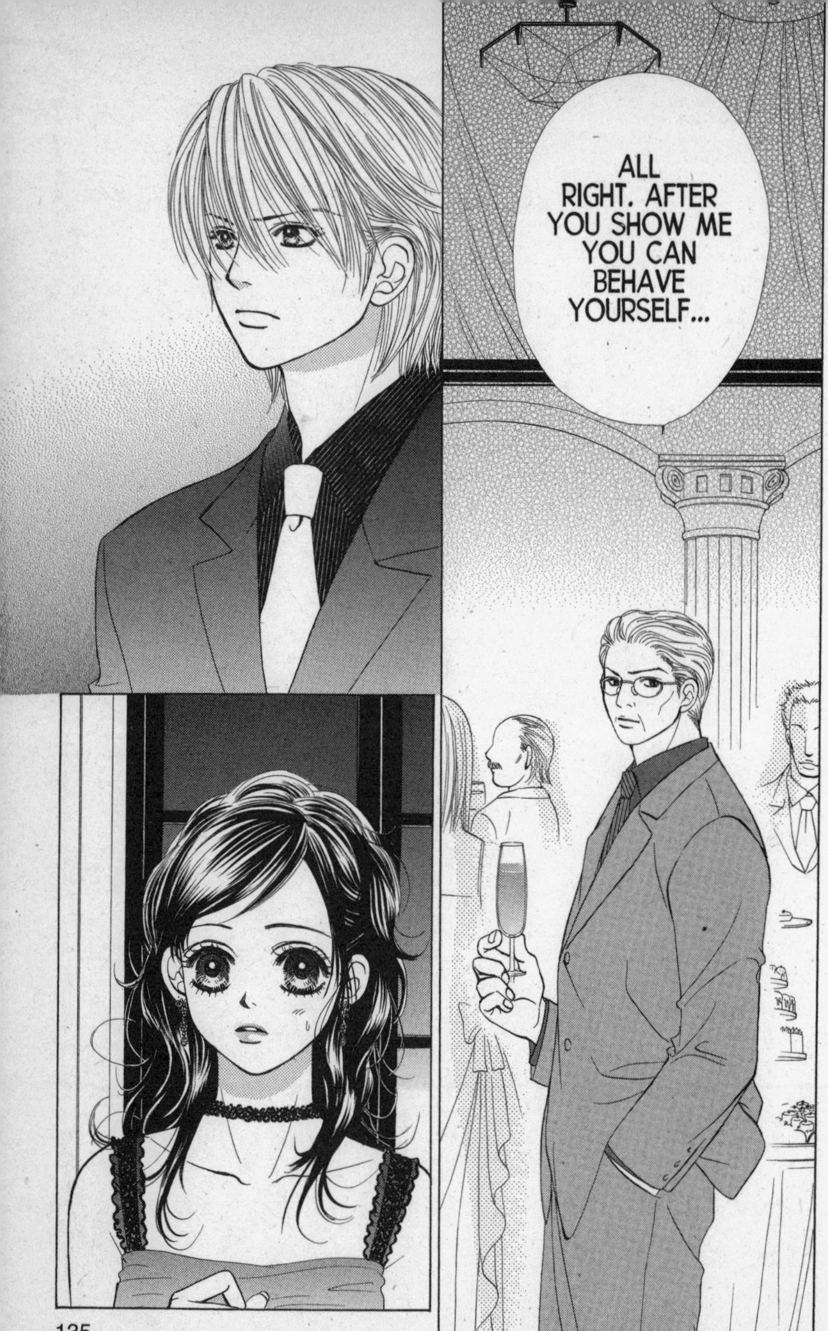
ALL RIGHT. AFTER YOU SHOW ME YOU CAN BEHAVE YOURSELF...

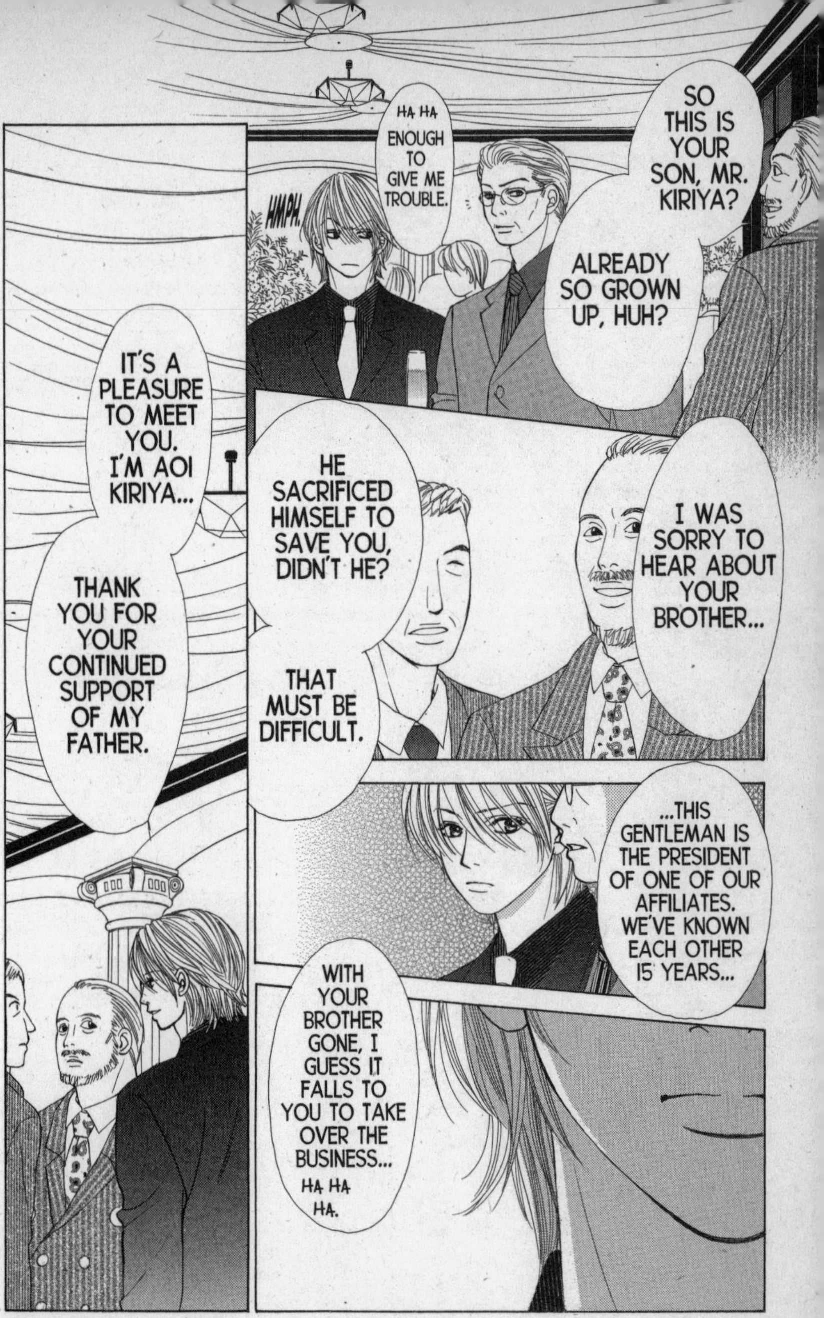
SO THIS IS YOUR SON, MR. KIRIYA?
ALREADY SO GROWN UP, HUH?
HA HA ENOUGH TO GIVE ME TROUBLE.
HMPH.
I WAS SORRY TO HEAR ABOUT YOUR BROTHER...
HE SACRIFICED HIMSELF TO SAVE YOU, DIDN'T HE?
THAT MUST BE DIFFICULT.
...THIS GENTLEMAN IS THE PRESIDENT OF ONE OF OUR AFFILIATES. WE'VE KNOWN EACH OTHER 15 YEARS...
WITH YOUR BROTHER GONE, I GUESS IT FALLS TO YOU TO TAKE OVER THE BUSINESS...
HA HA HA.
IT'S A PLEASURE TO MEET YOU. I'M AOI KIRIYA...
THANK YOU FOR YOUR CONTINUED SUPPORT OF MY FATHER.

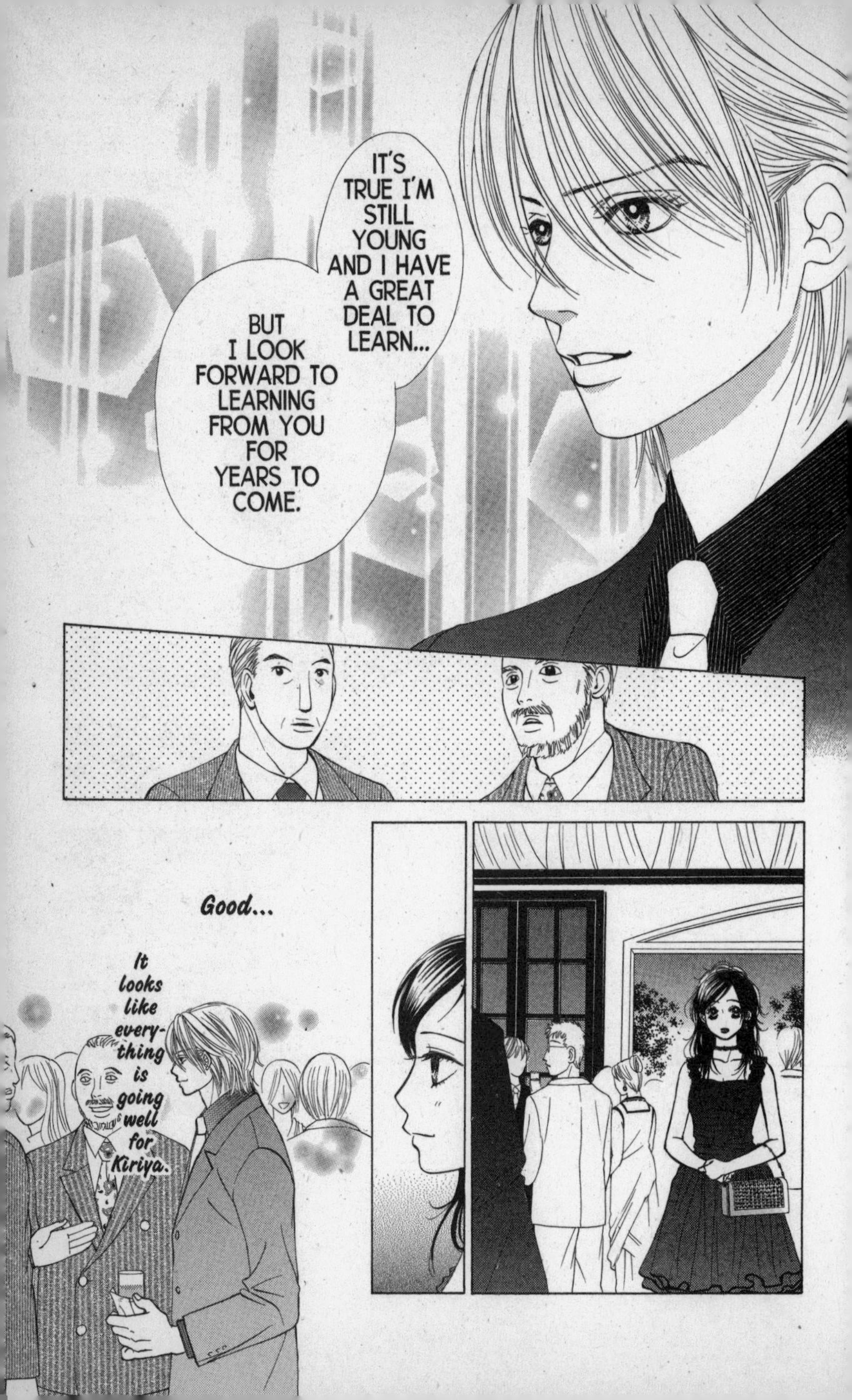
IT'S TRUE I'M STILL YOUNG AND I HAVE A GREAT DEAL TO LEARN...
BUT I LOOK FORWARD TO LEARNING FROM YOU FOR YEARS TO COME.
Good...
It looks like every-thing is going well for Kiriya.

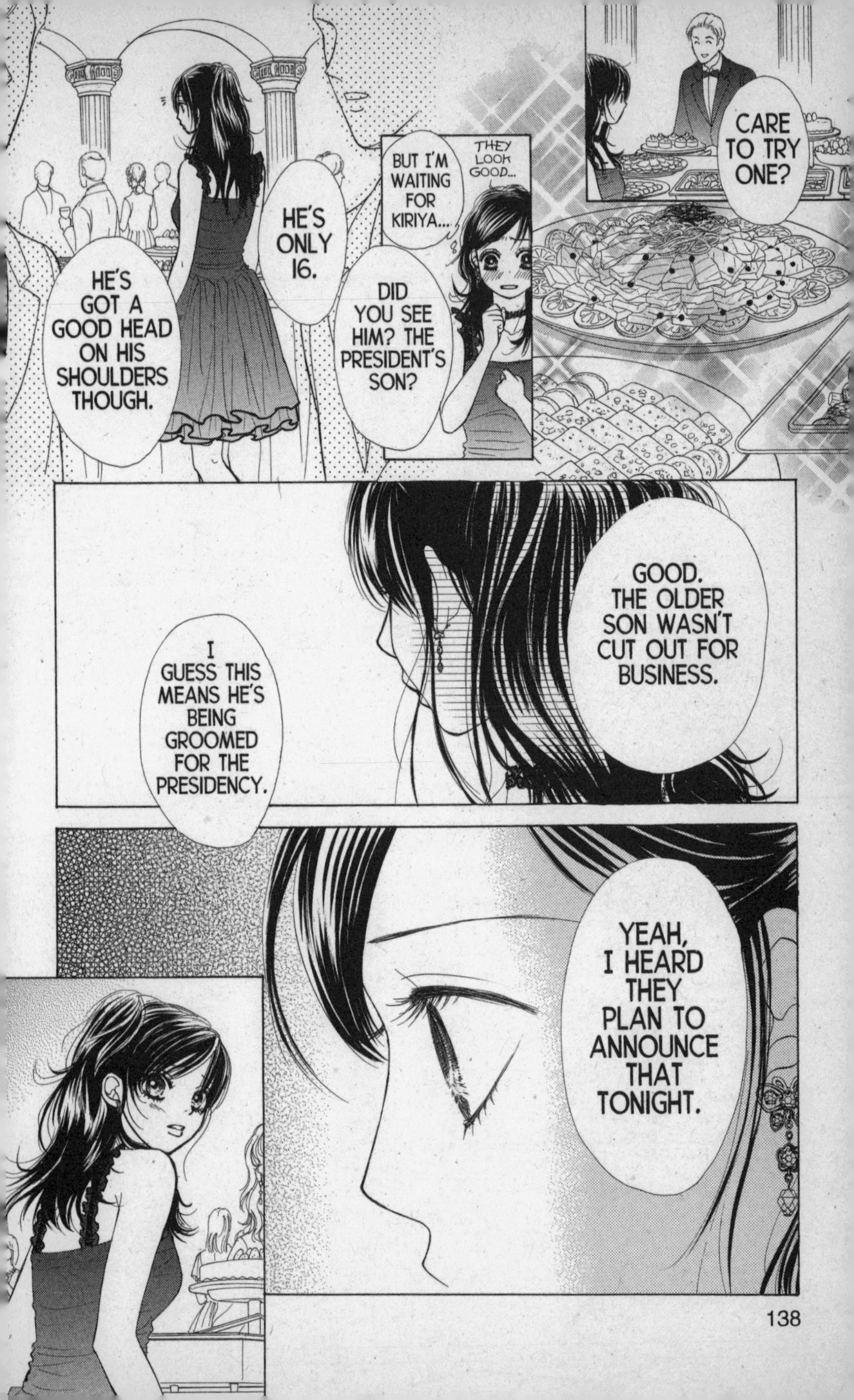
CARE TO TRY ONE?
THEY LOOK GOOD...
BUT I'M WAITING FOR KIRIYA...
DID YOU SEE HIM? THE PRESIDENT'S SON?
HE'S ONLY 16.
HE'S GOT A GOOD HEAD ON HIS SHOULDERS THOUGH.
GOOD. THE OLDER SON WASN'T CUT OUT FOR BUSINESS.
I GUESS THIS MEANS HE'S BEING GROOMED FOR THE PRESIDENCY.
YEAH, I HEARD THEY PLAN TO ANNOUNCE THAT TONIGHT.

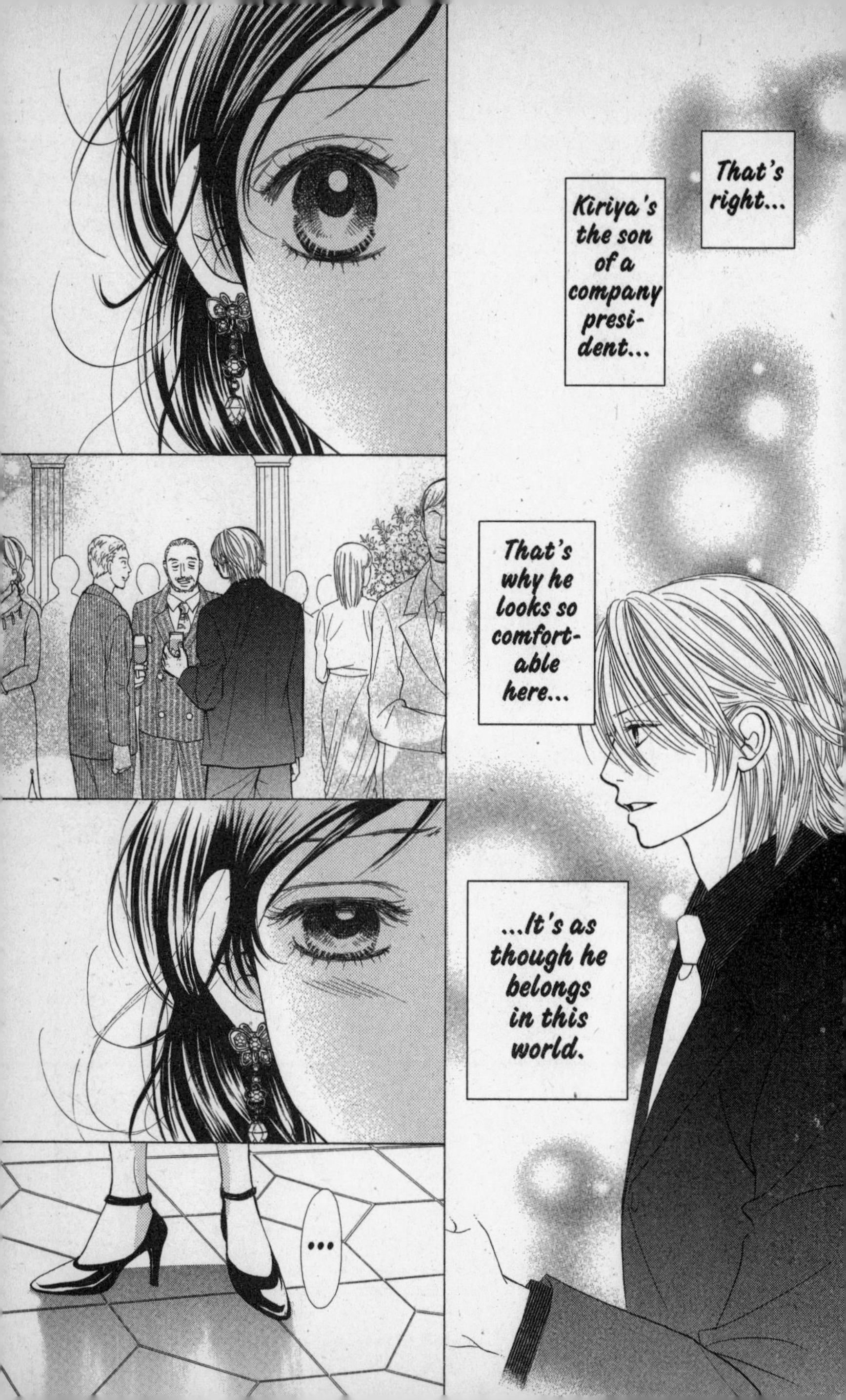
That's right...
Kiriya's the son of a company presi-dent...
That's why he looks so comfort-able here...
...It's as though he belongs in this world.
...

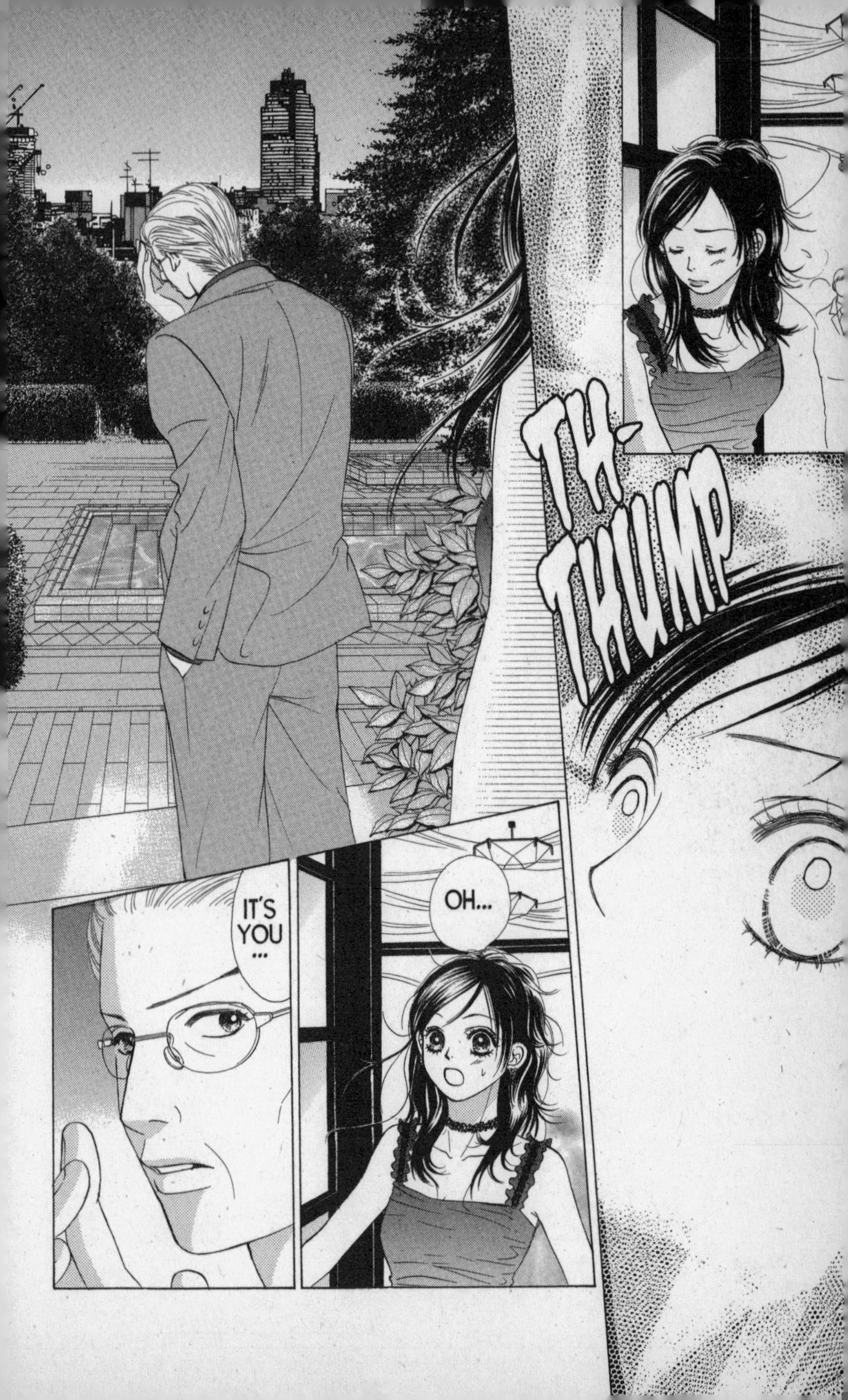
TH-THUMP
OH...
IT'S YOU ...

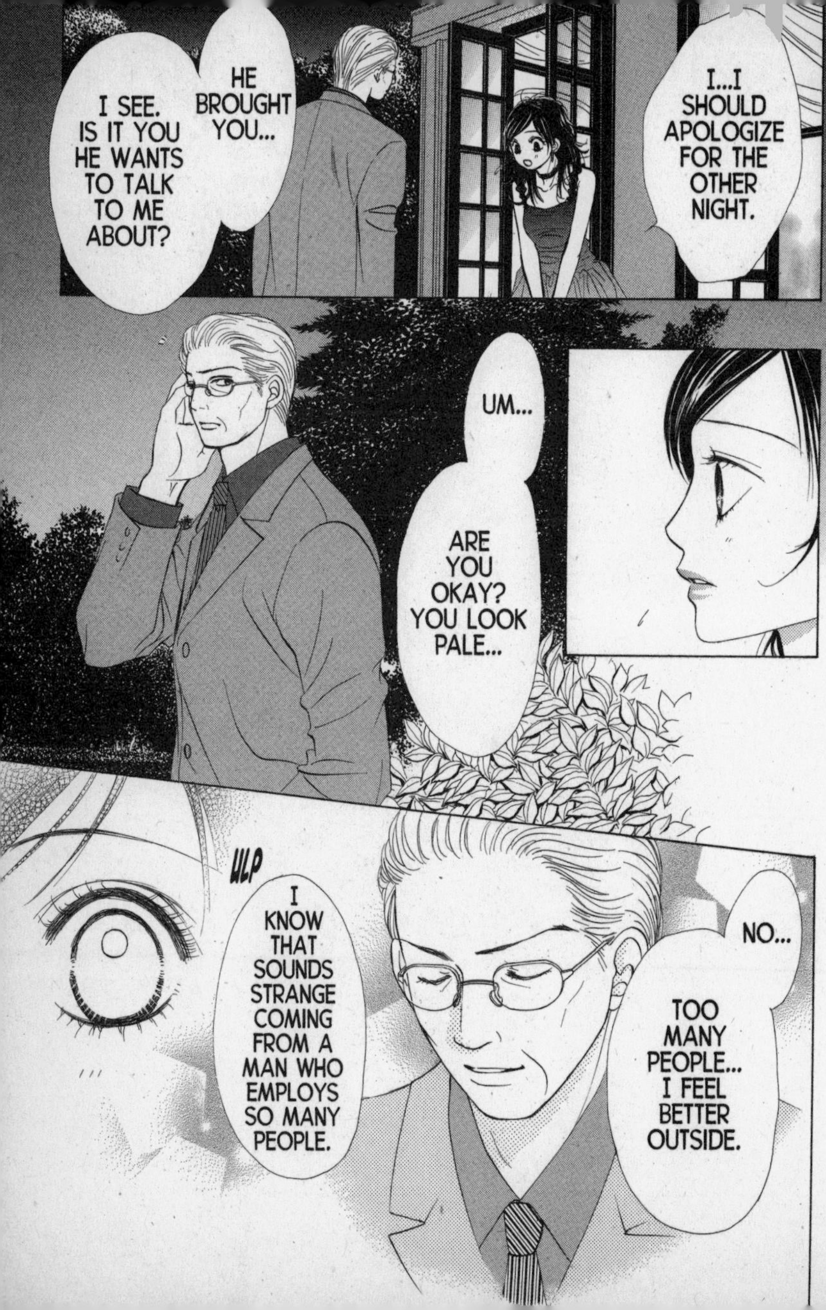
I...I SHOULD APOLOGIZE FOR THE OTHER NIGHT.
HE BROUGHT YOU...
I SEE. IS IT YOU HE WANTS TO TALK TO ME ABOUT?
UM...
ARE YOU OKAY? YOU LOOK PALE...
NO...
TOO MANY PEOPLE... I FEEL BETTER OUTSIDE.
ULP
I KNOW THAT SOUNDS STRANGE COMING FROM A MAN WHO EMPLOYS SO MANY PEOPLE.

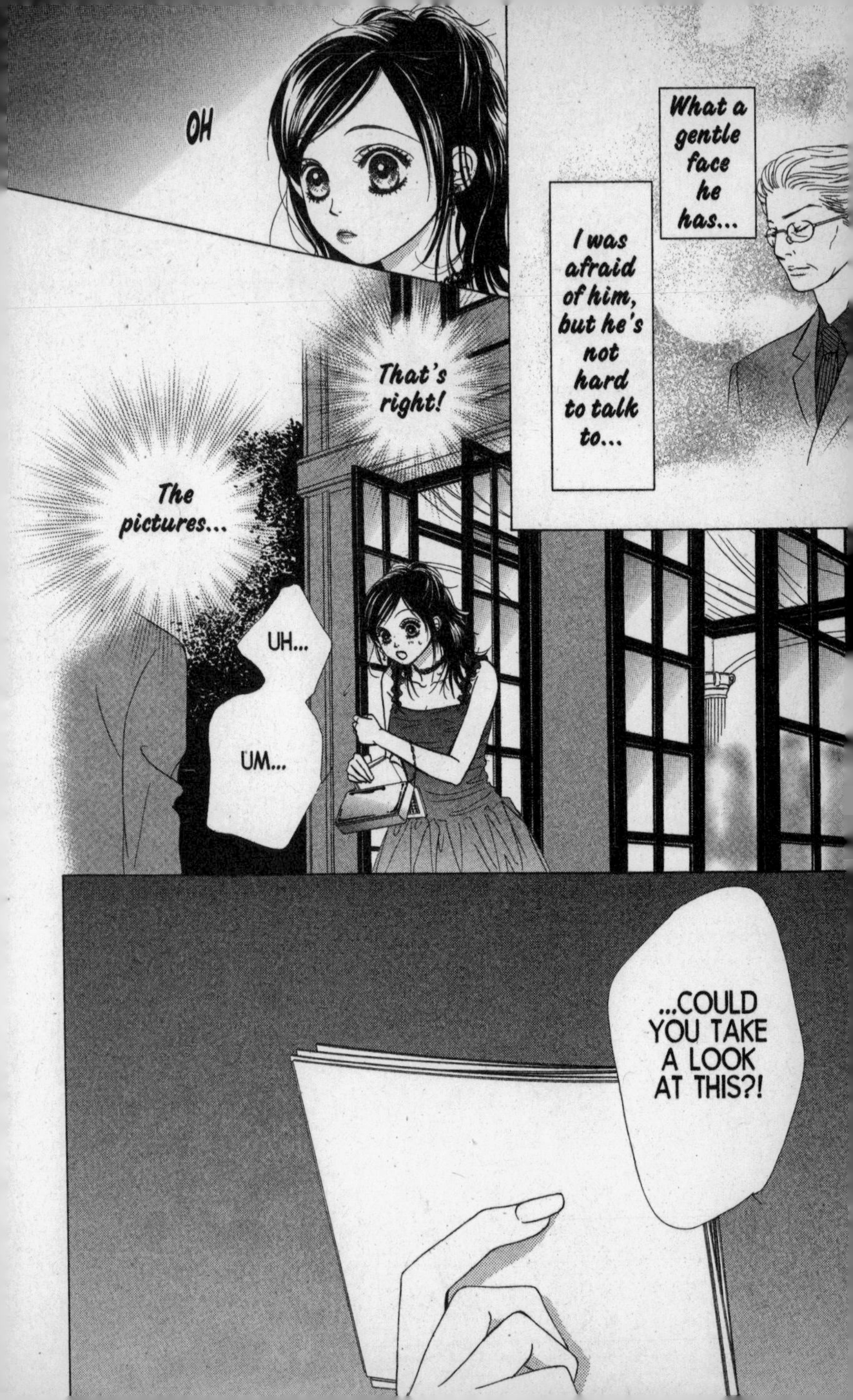
What a gentle face he has...
I was afraid of him, but he's not hard to talk to...
OH
That's right!
The pictures...
UH...
UM...
...COULD YOU TAKE A LOOK AT THIS?!

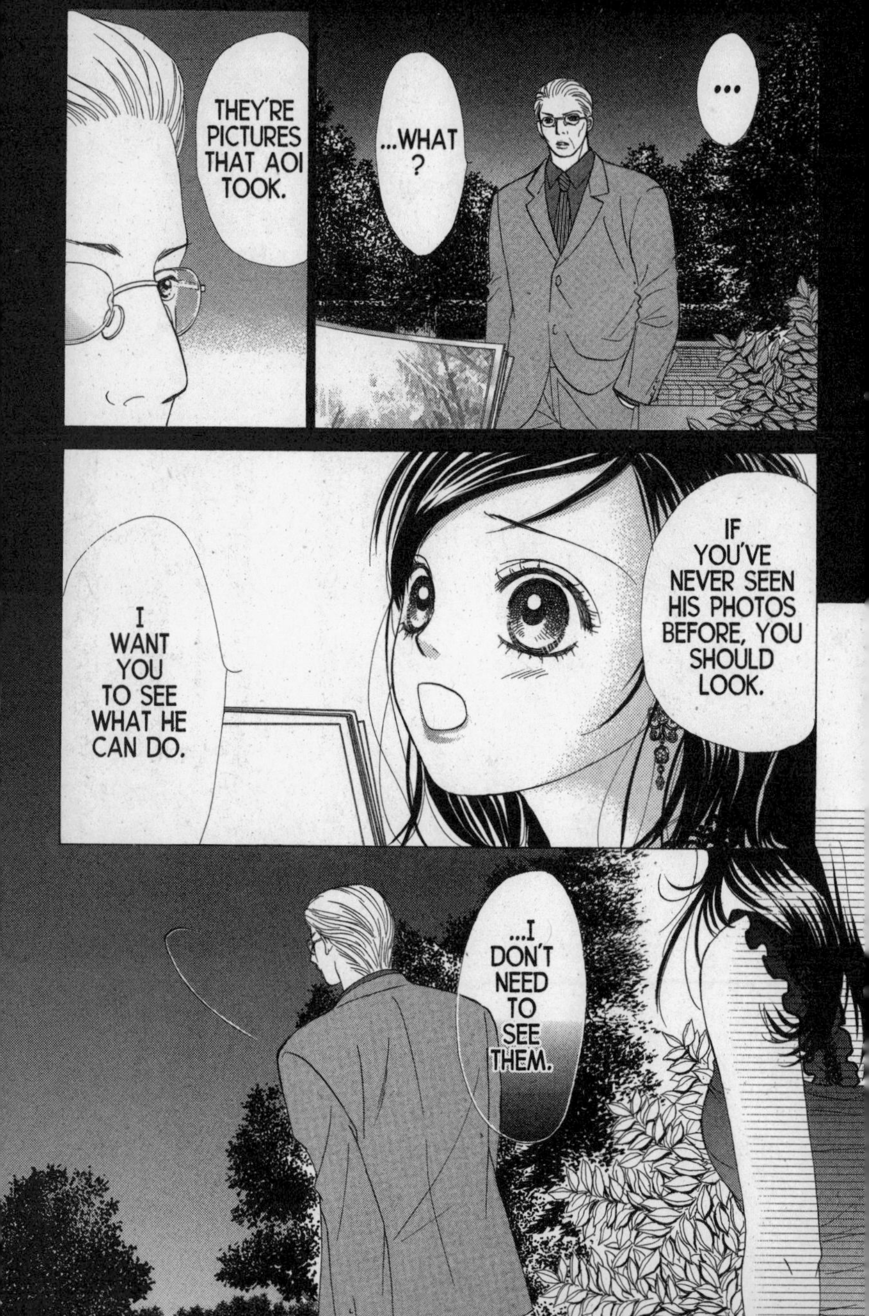
...
...WHAT ?
THEY'RE PICTURES THAT AOI TOOK.
IF YOU'VE NEVER SEEN HIS PHOTOS BEFORE, YOU SHOULD LOOK.
I WANT YOU TO SEE WHAT HE CAN DO.
...I DON'T NEED TO SEE THEM.

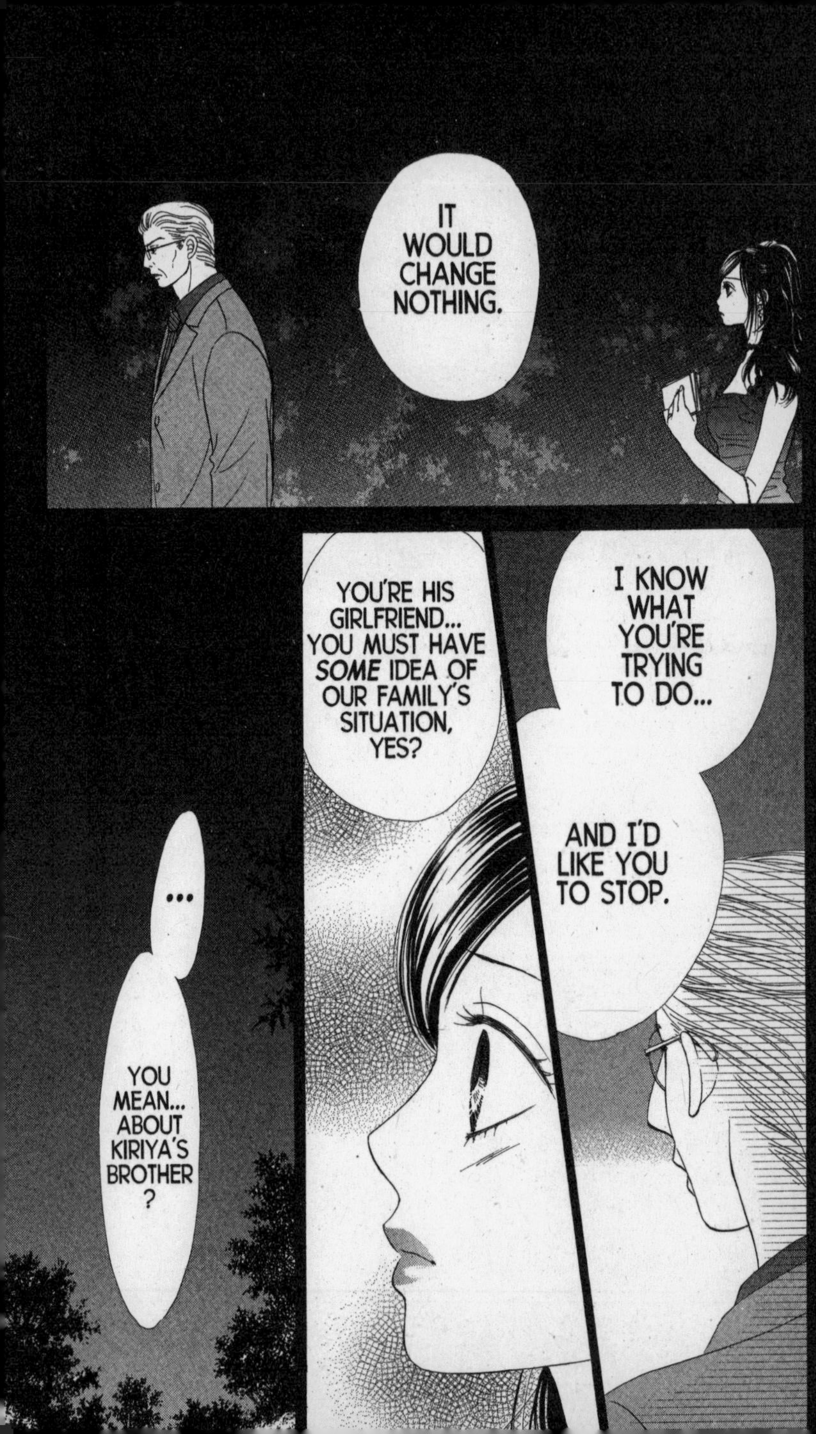
IT WOULD CHANGE NOTHING.
I KNOW WHAT YOU'RE TRYING TO DO...
AND I'D LIKE YOU TO STOP.
YOU'RE HIS GIRLFRIEND... YOU MUST HAVE *SOME* IDEA OF OUR FAMILY'S SITUATION, YES?
...
YOU MEAN... ABOUT KIRIYA'S BROTHER?

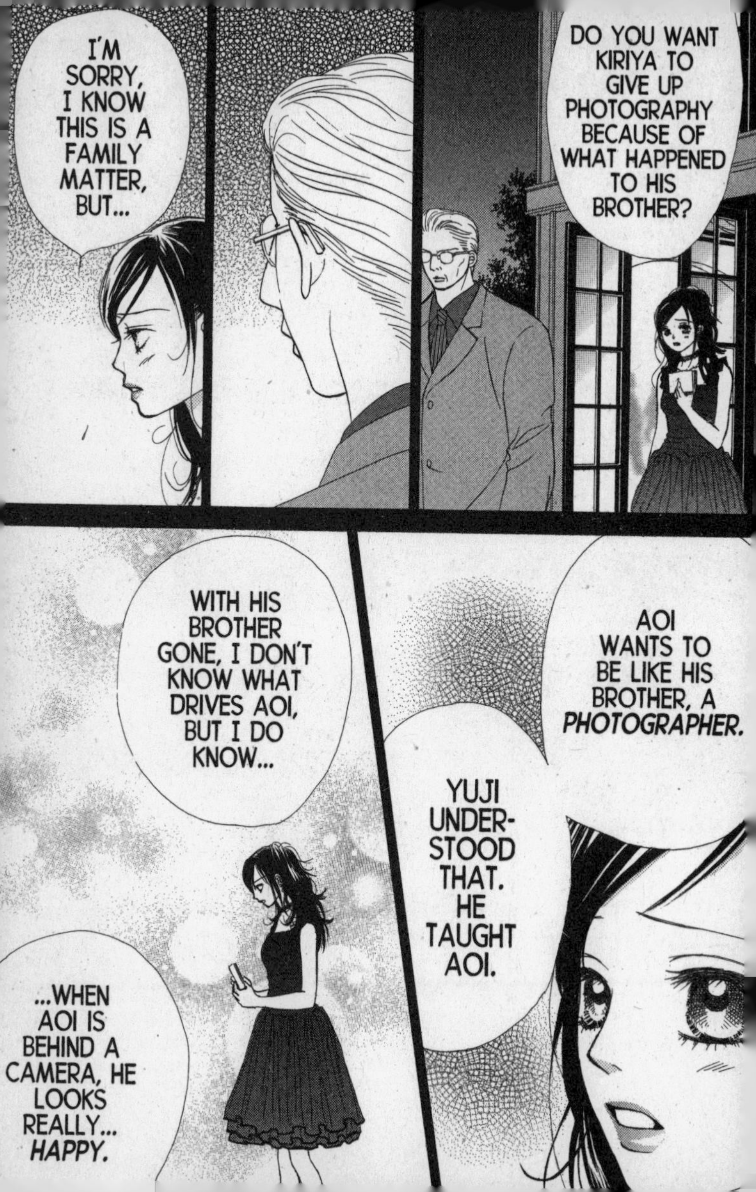
DO YOU WANT KIRIYA TO GIVE UP PHOTOGRAPHY BECAUSE OF WHAT HAPPENED TO HIS BROTHER?
I'M SORRY, I KNOW THIS IS A FAMILY MATTER, BUT...
AOI WANTS TO BE LIKE HIS BROTHER, A *PHOTOGRAPHER.*
YUJI UNDER-STOOD THAT. HE TAUGHT AOI.
WITH HIS BROTHER GONE, I DON'T KNOW WHAT DRIVES AOI, BUT I DO KNOW...
...WHEN AOI IS BEHIND A CAMERA, HE LOOKS REALLY... *HAPPY.*

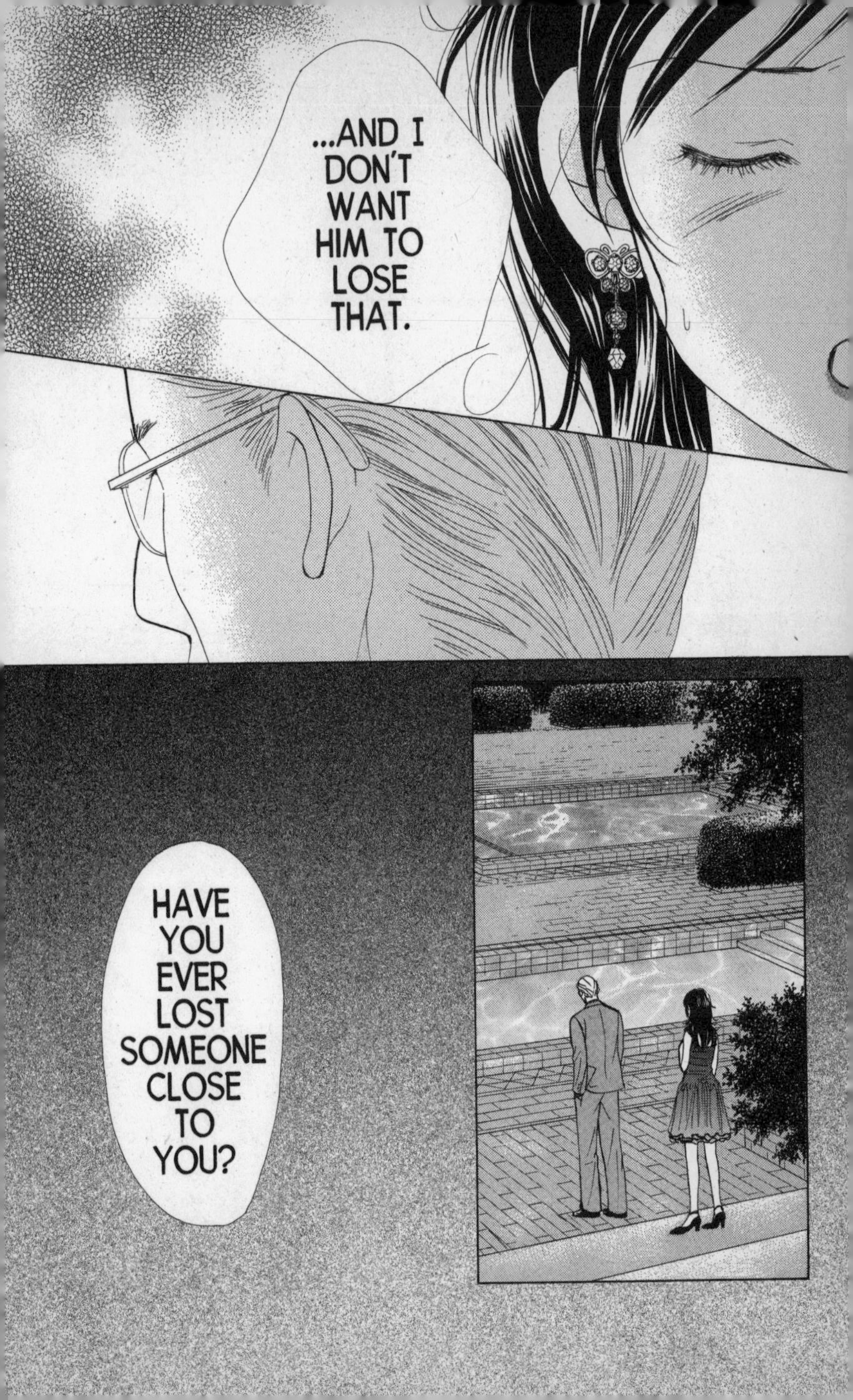
...AND I DON'T WANT HIM TO LOSE THAT.
HAVE YOU EVER LOST SOMEONE CLOSE TO YOU?

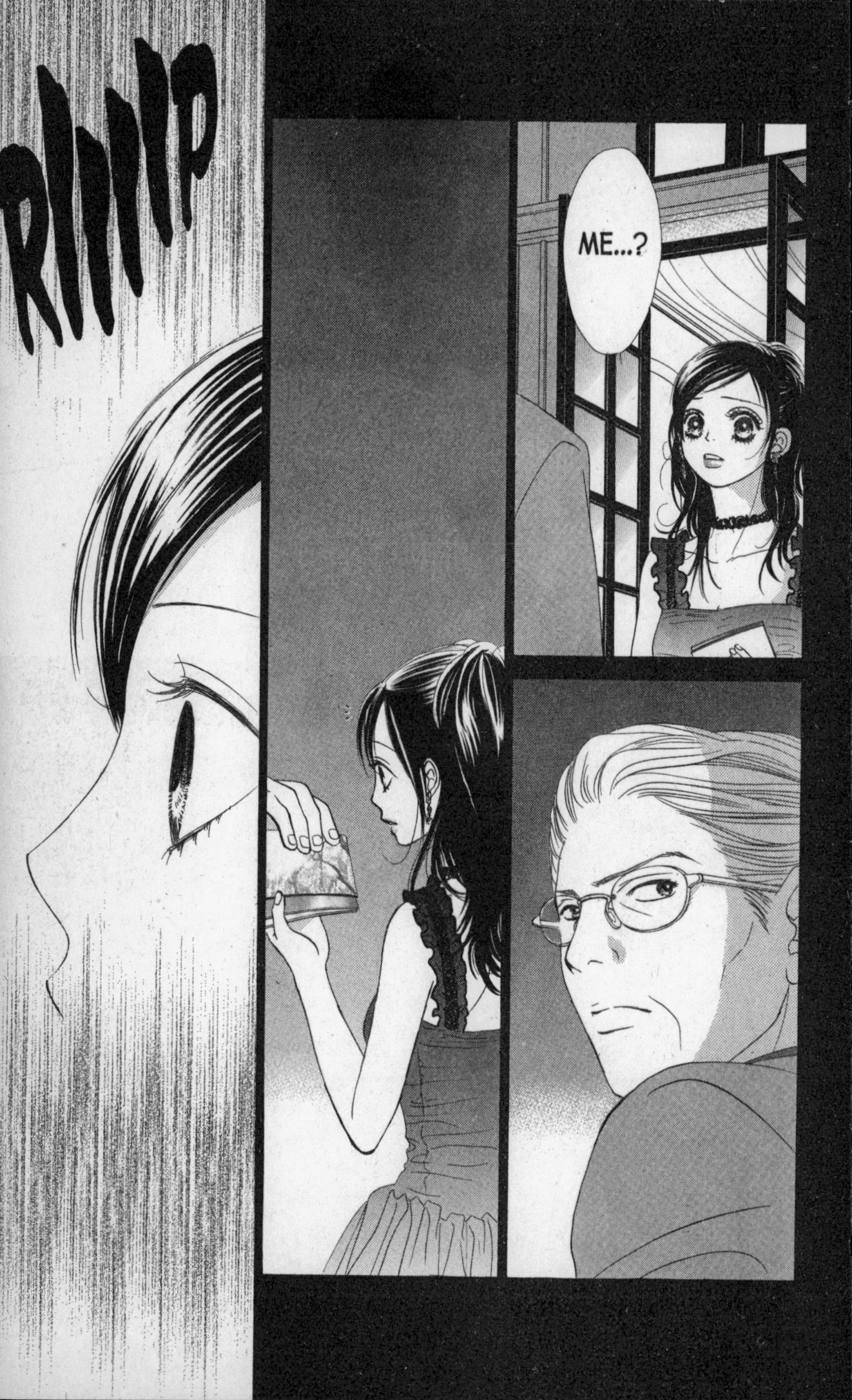

ME...?
RIIIIP

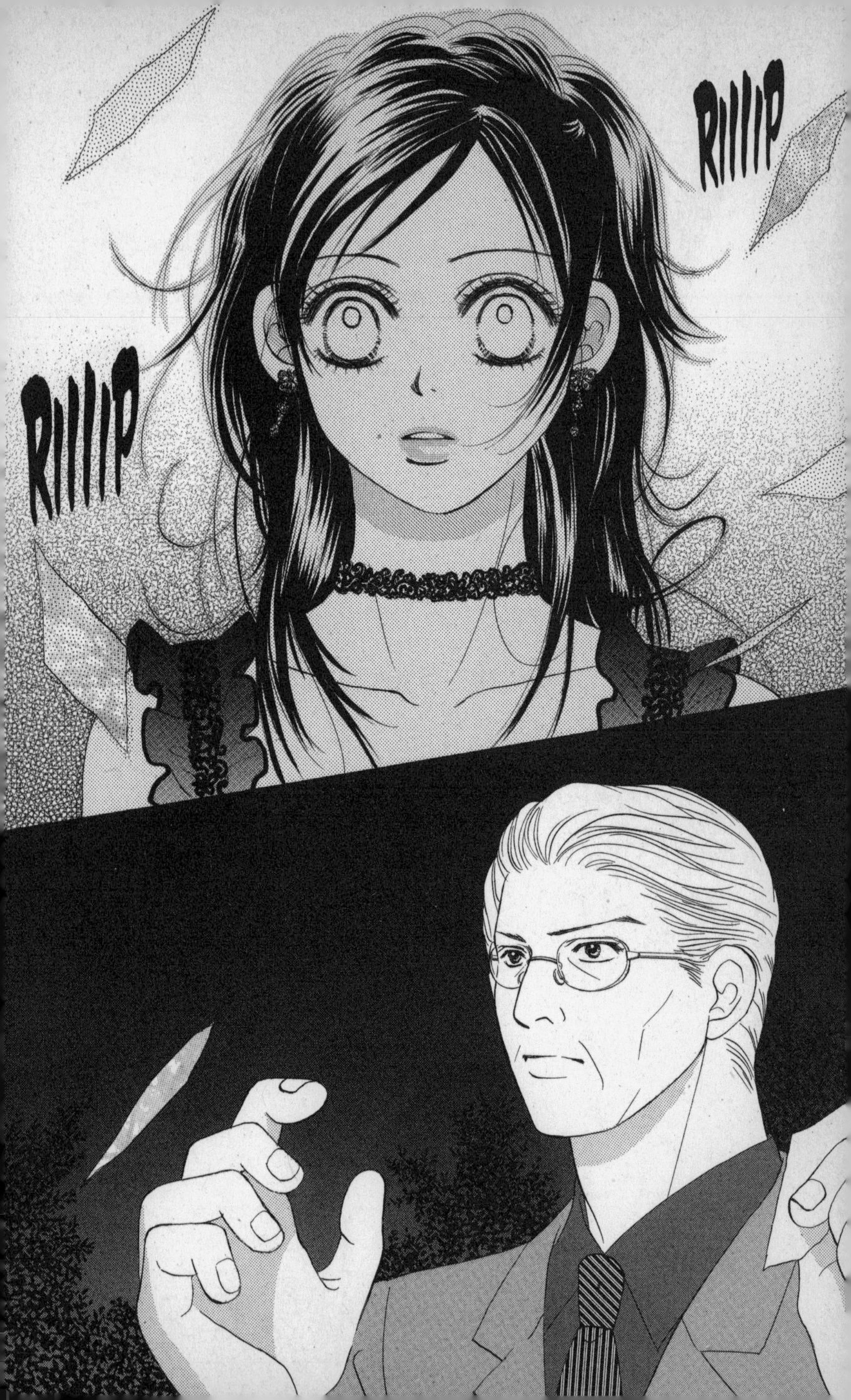
RIIIIP
RIIIIP

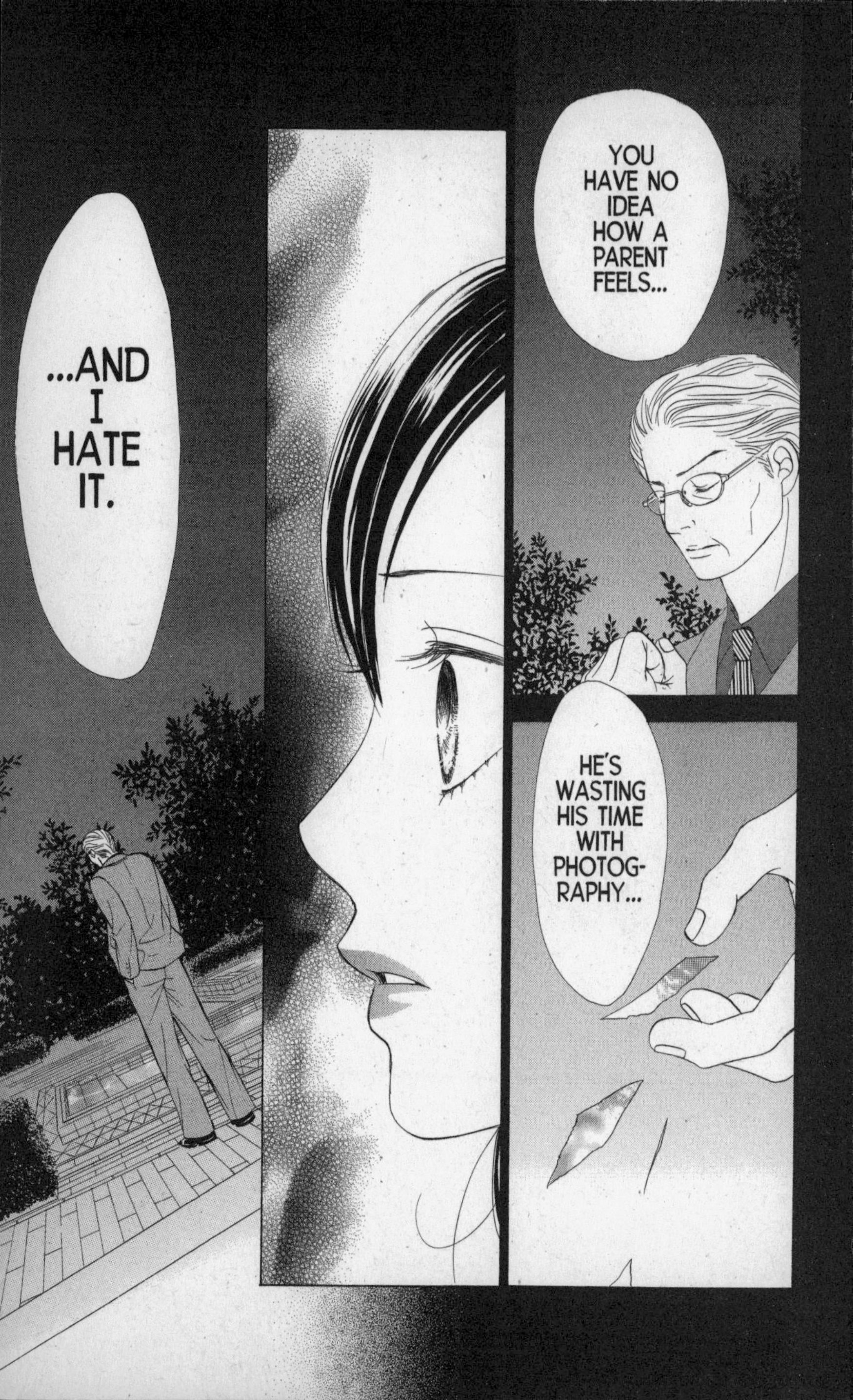
YOU HAVE NO IDEA HOW A PARENT FEELS...
HE'S WASTING HIS TIME WITH PHOTOG-RAPHY...
...AND I HATE IT.

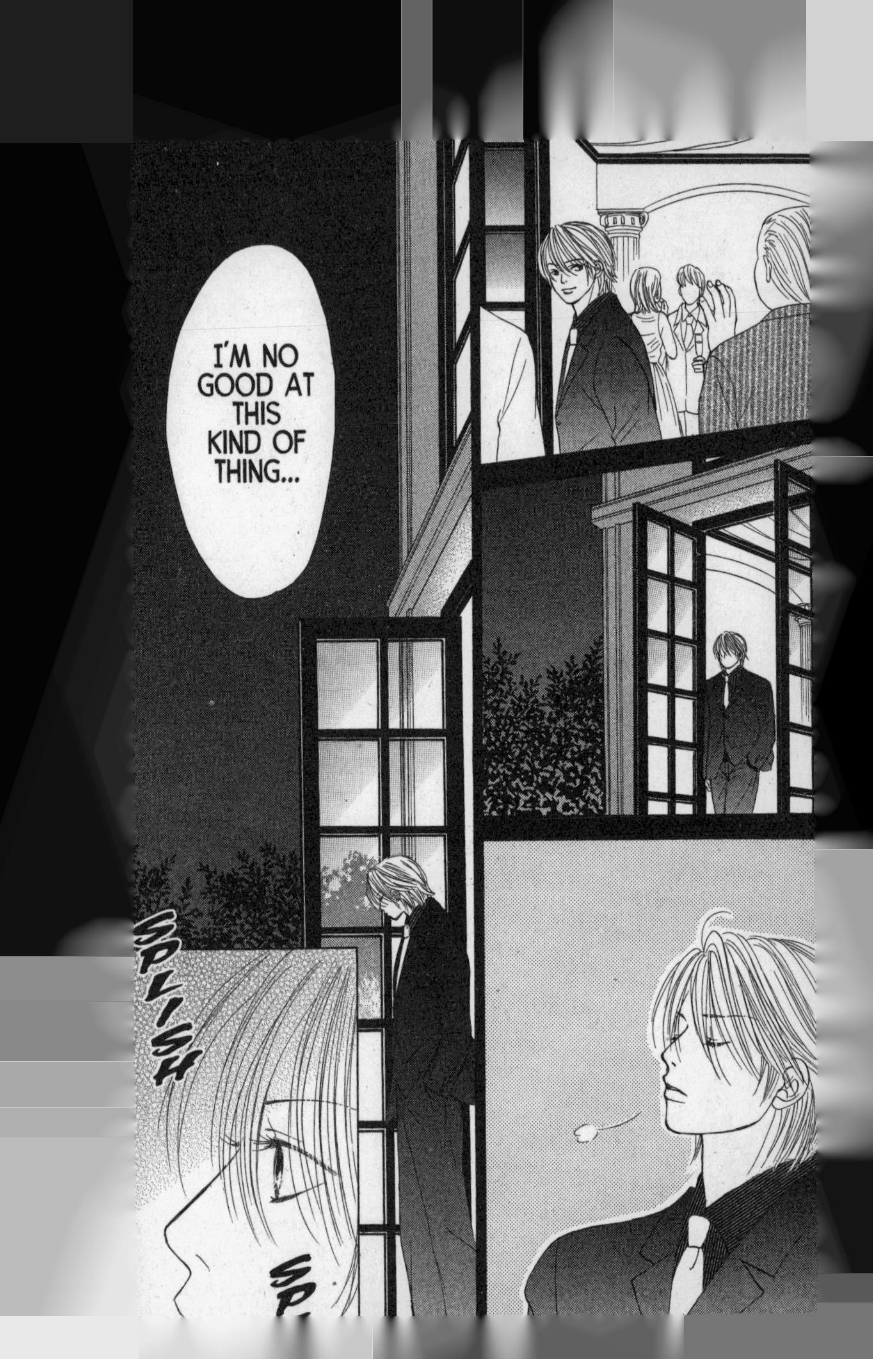
I'M NO GOOD AT THIS KIND OF THING...
SPLISH

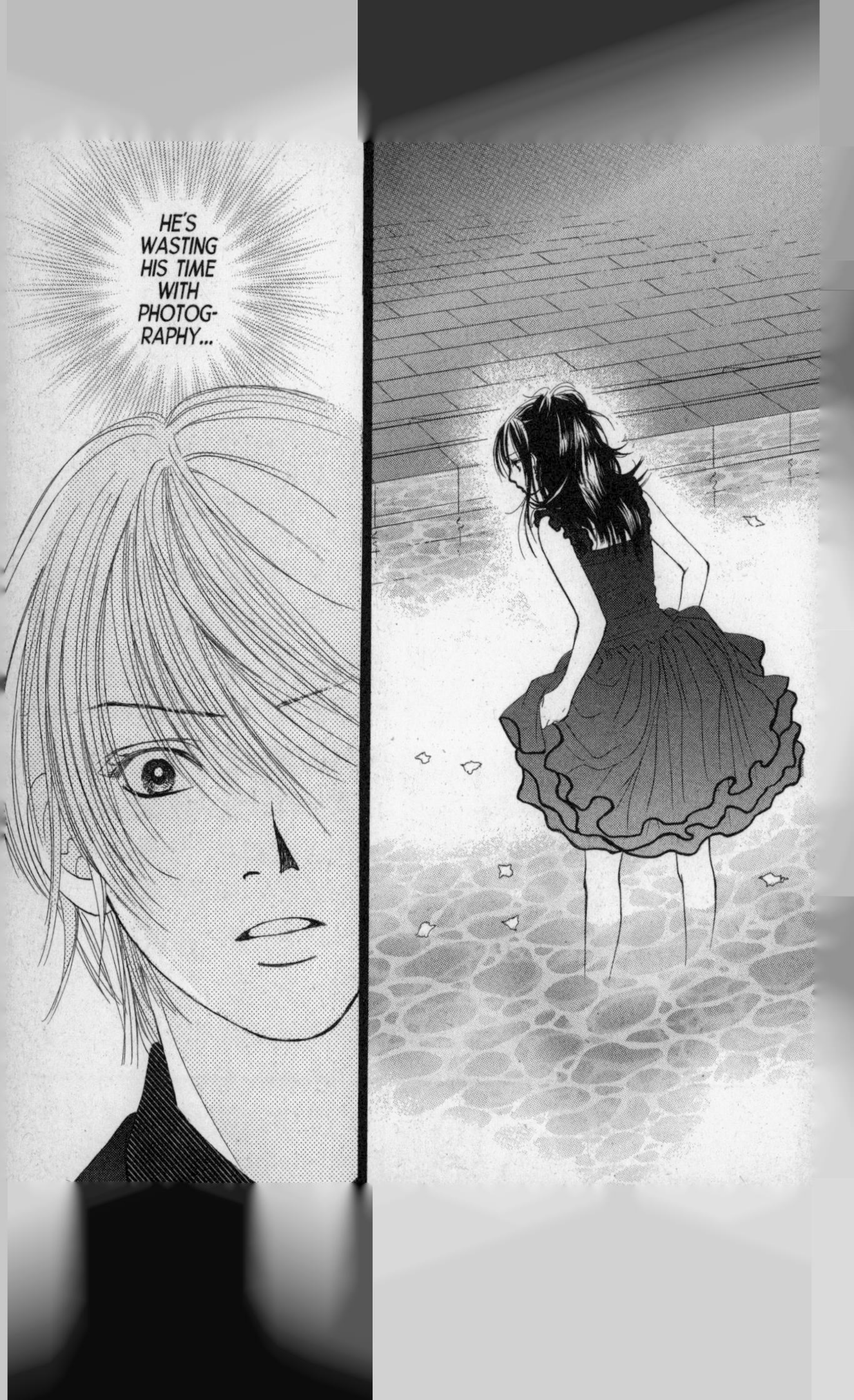
HE'S WASTING HIS TIME WITH PHOTOG-RAPHY...

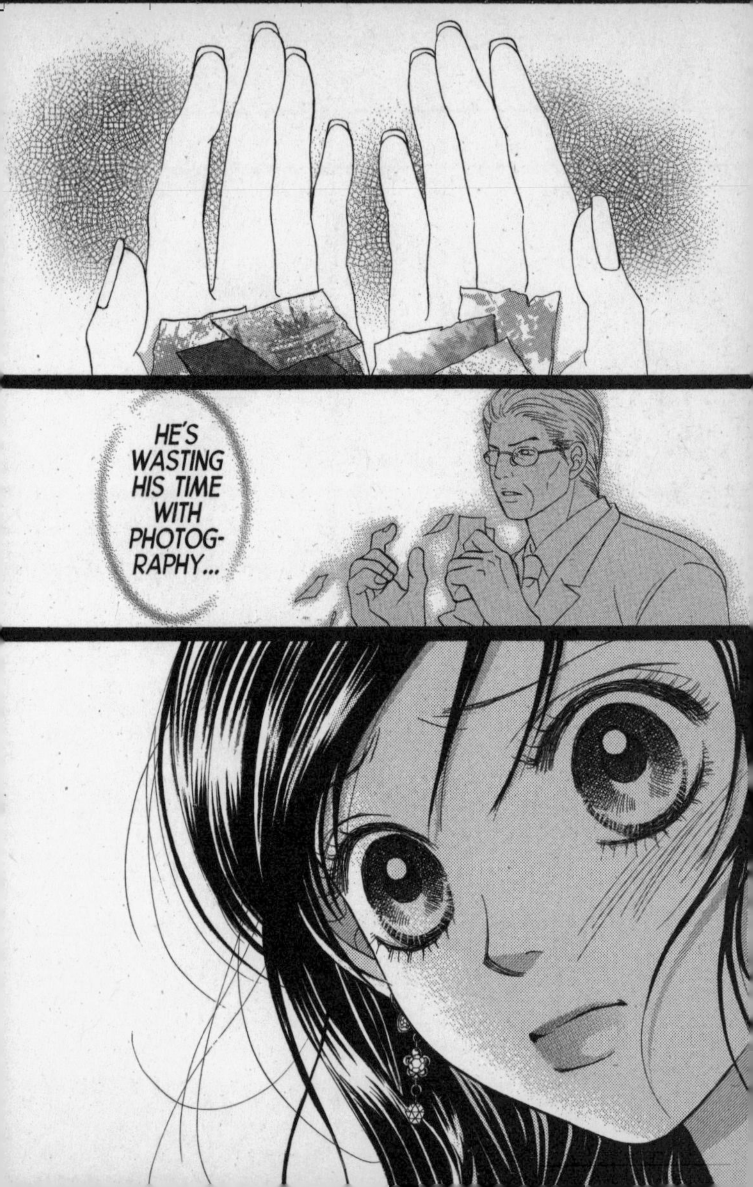
HE'S WASTING HIS TIME WITH PHOTOG-RAPHY...

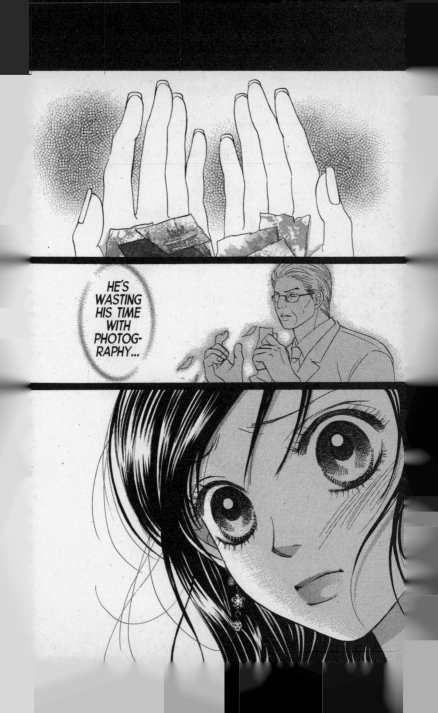

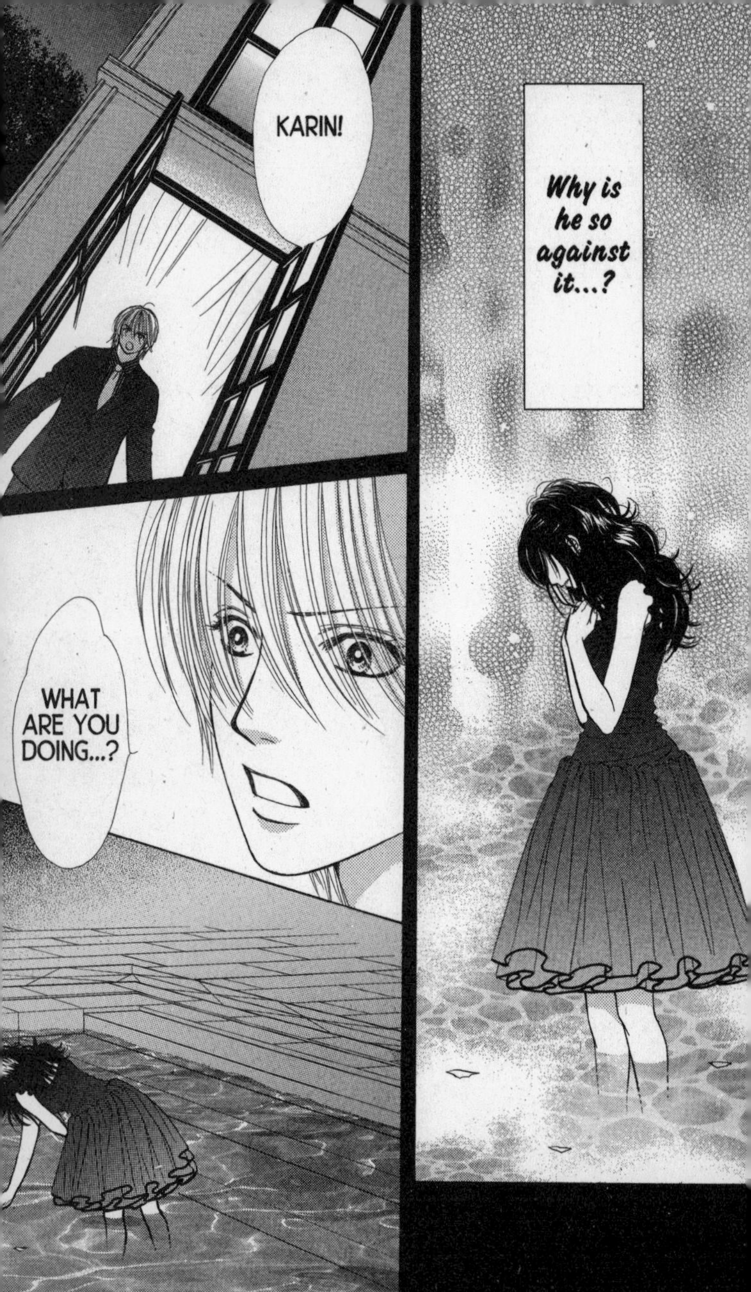
Why is he so against it...?
KARIN!
WHAT ARE YOU DOING...?

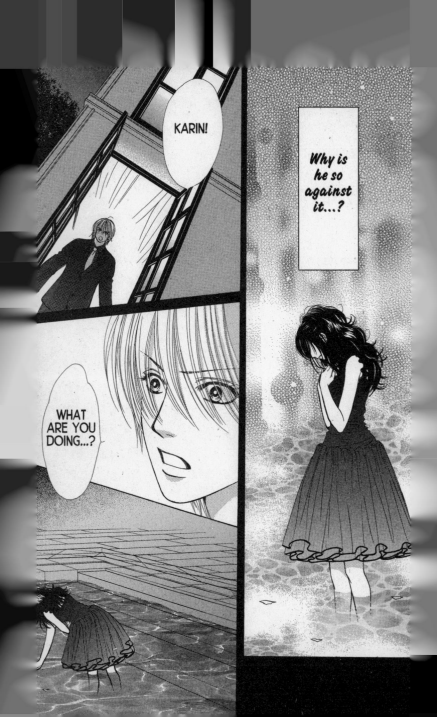

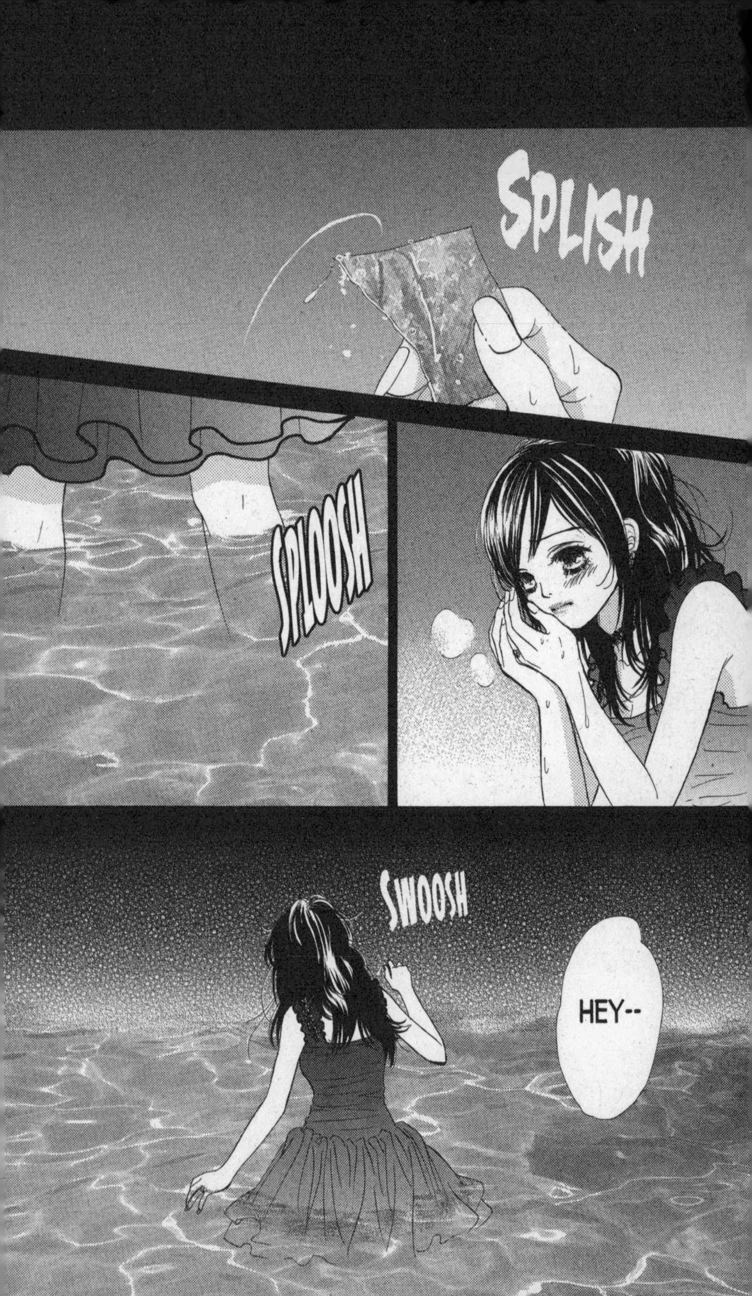
SPLISH
SPLOOSH
SWOOSH
HEY--

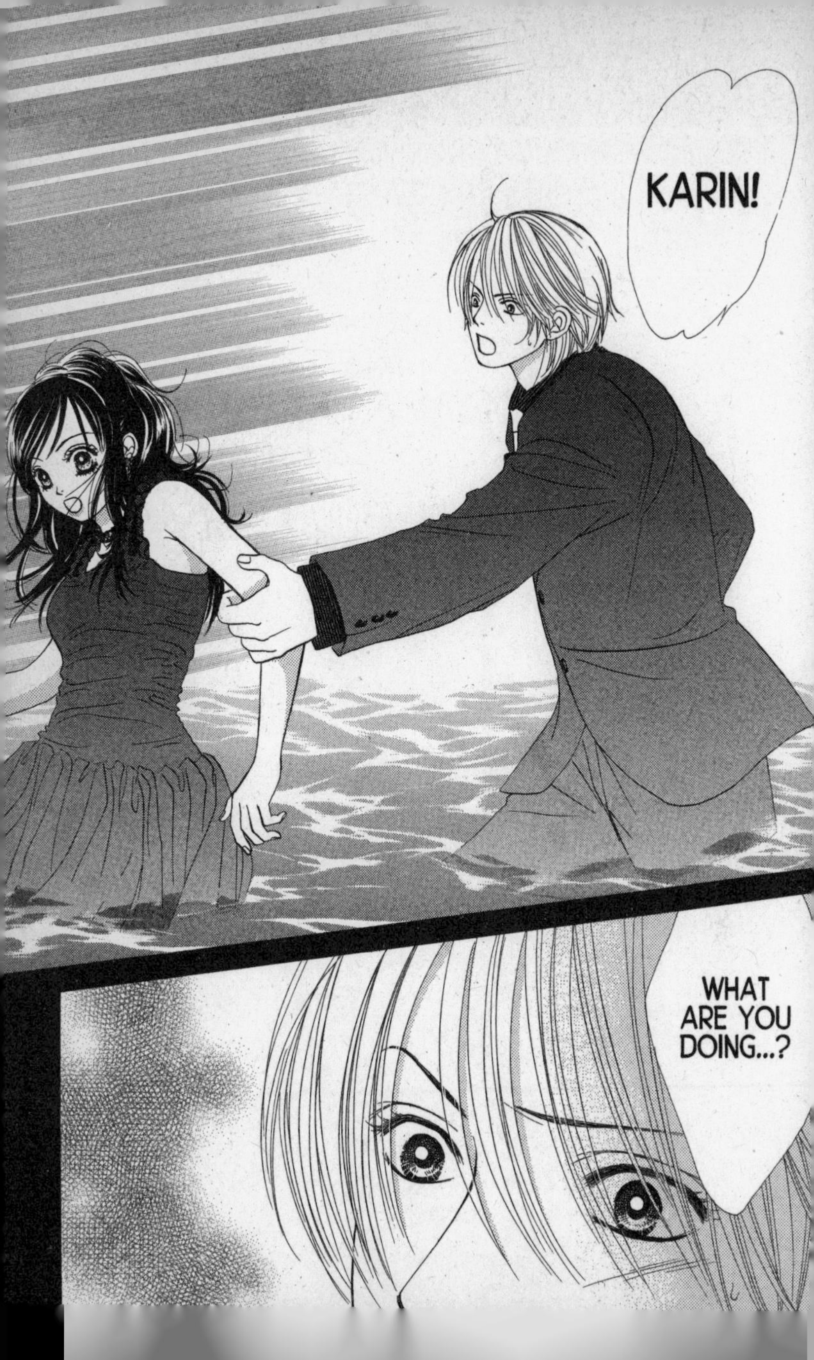
KARIN!
WHAT ARE YOU DOING...?

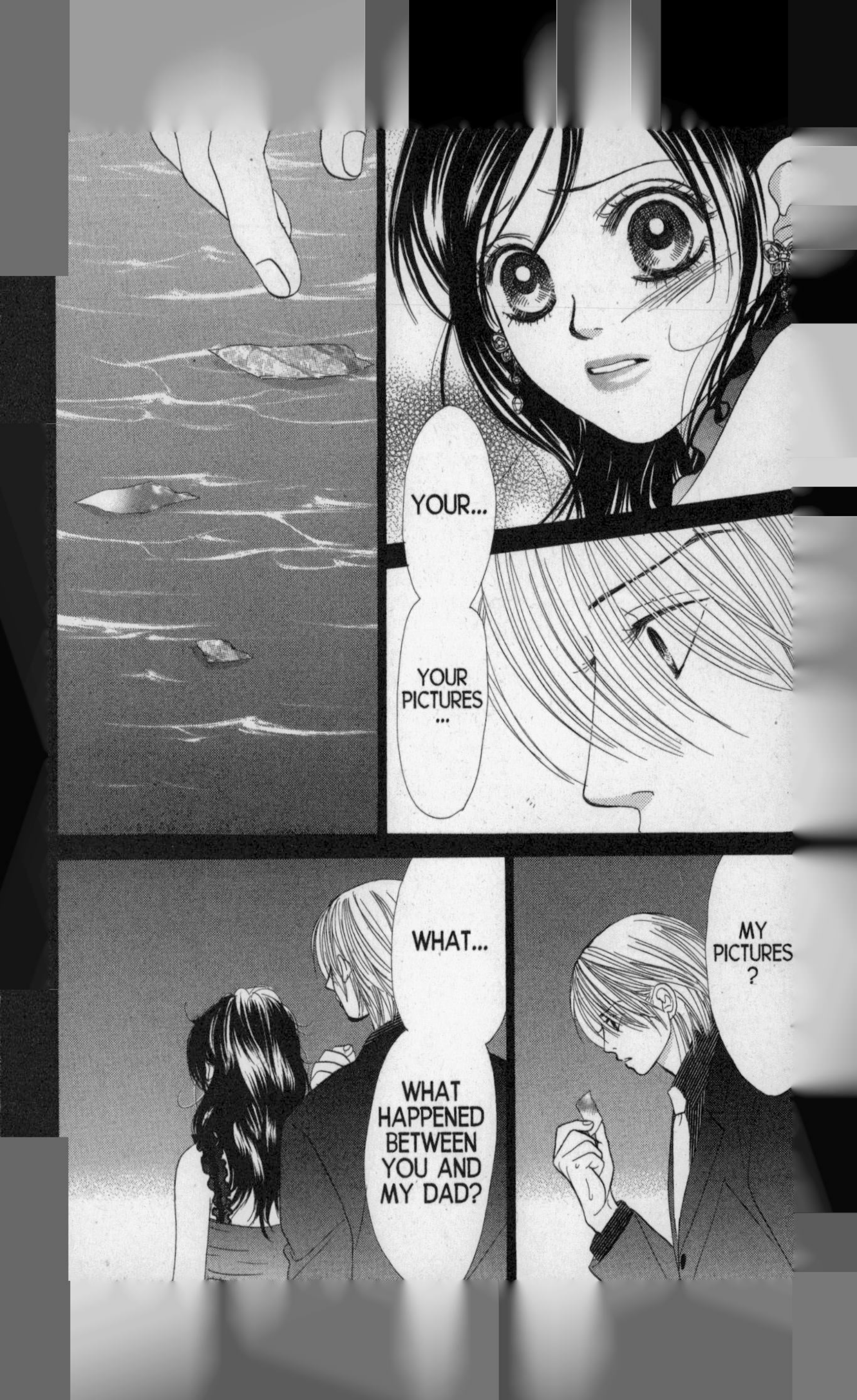
YOUR...
YOUR PICTURES ...
MY PICTURES ?
WHAT...
WHAT HAPPENED BETWEEN YOU AND MY DAD?

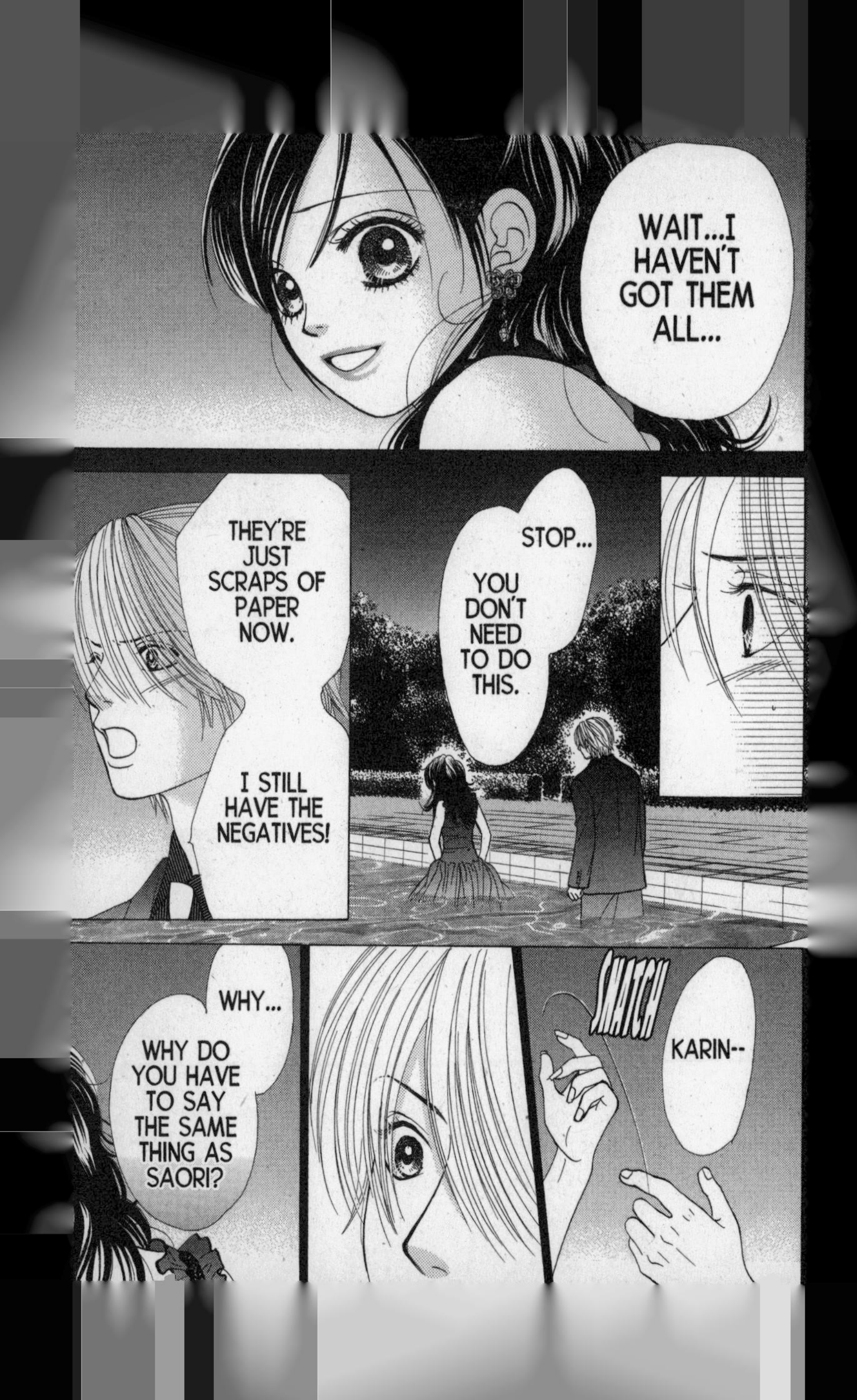
WAIT...I HAVEN'T GOT THEM ALL...
STOP...
YOU DON'T NEED TO DO THIS.
THEY'RE JUST SCRAPS OF PAPER NOW.
I STILL HAVE THE NEGATIVES!
SNATCH
KARIN--
WHY...
WHY DO YOU HAVE TO SAY THE SAME THING AS SAORI?

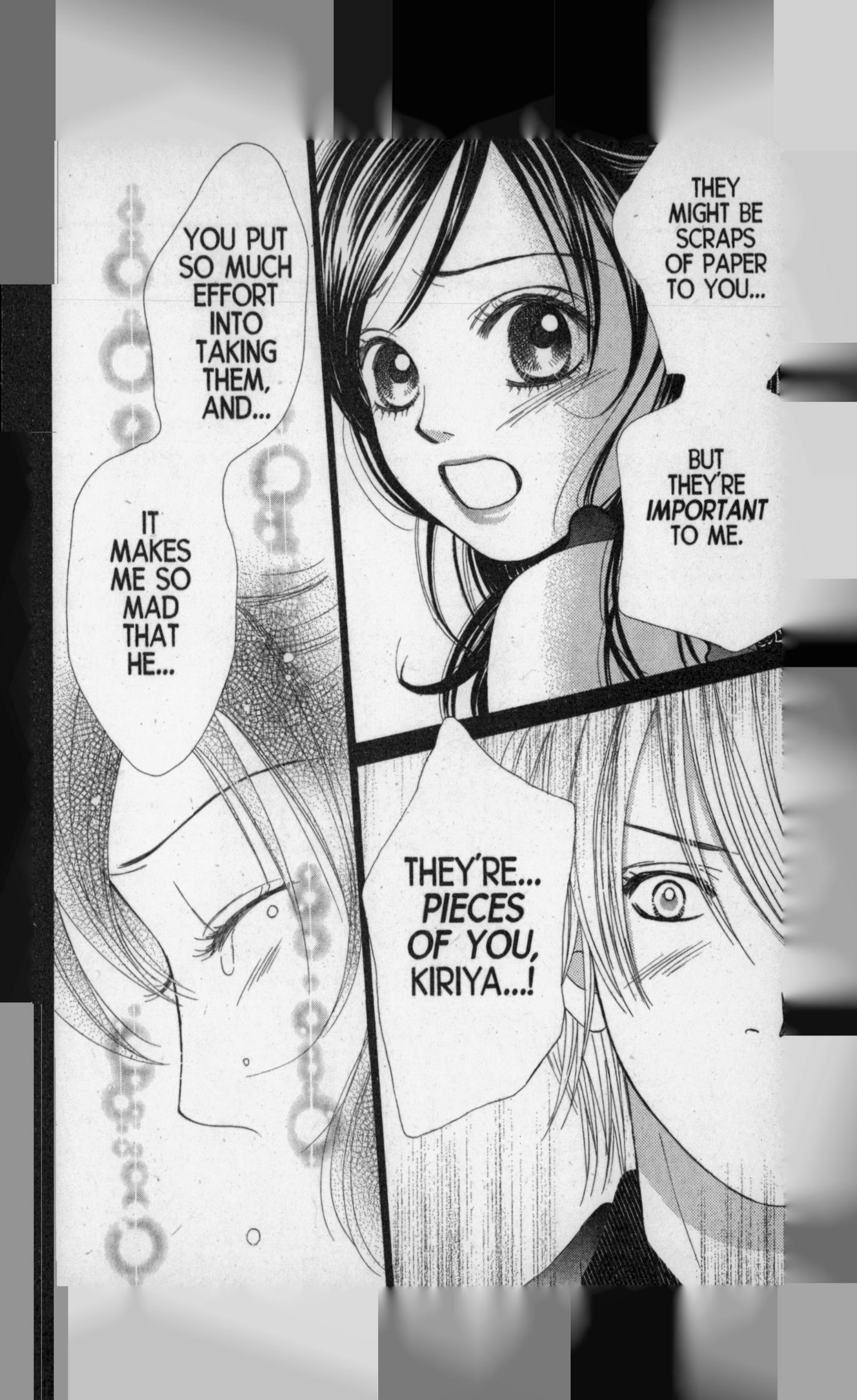
THEY MIGHT BE SCRAPS OF PAPER TO YOU...
BUT THEY'RE *IMPORTANT* TO ME.
THEY'RE... *PIECES OF YOU,* KIRIYA...!
YOU PUT SO MUCH EFFORT INTO TAKING THEM, AND...
IT MAKES ME SO MAD THAT HE...

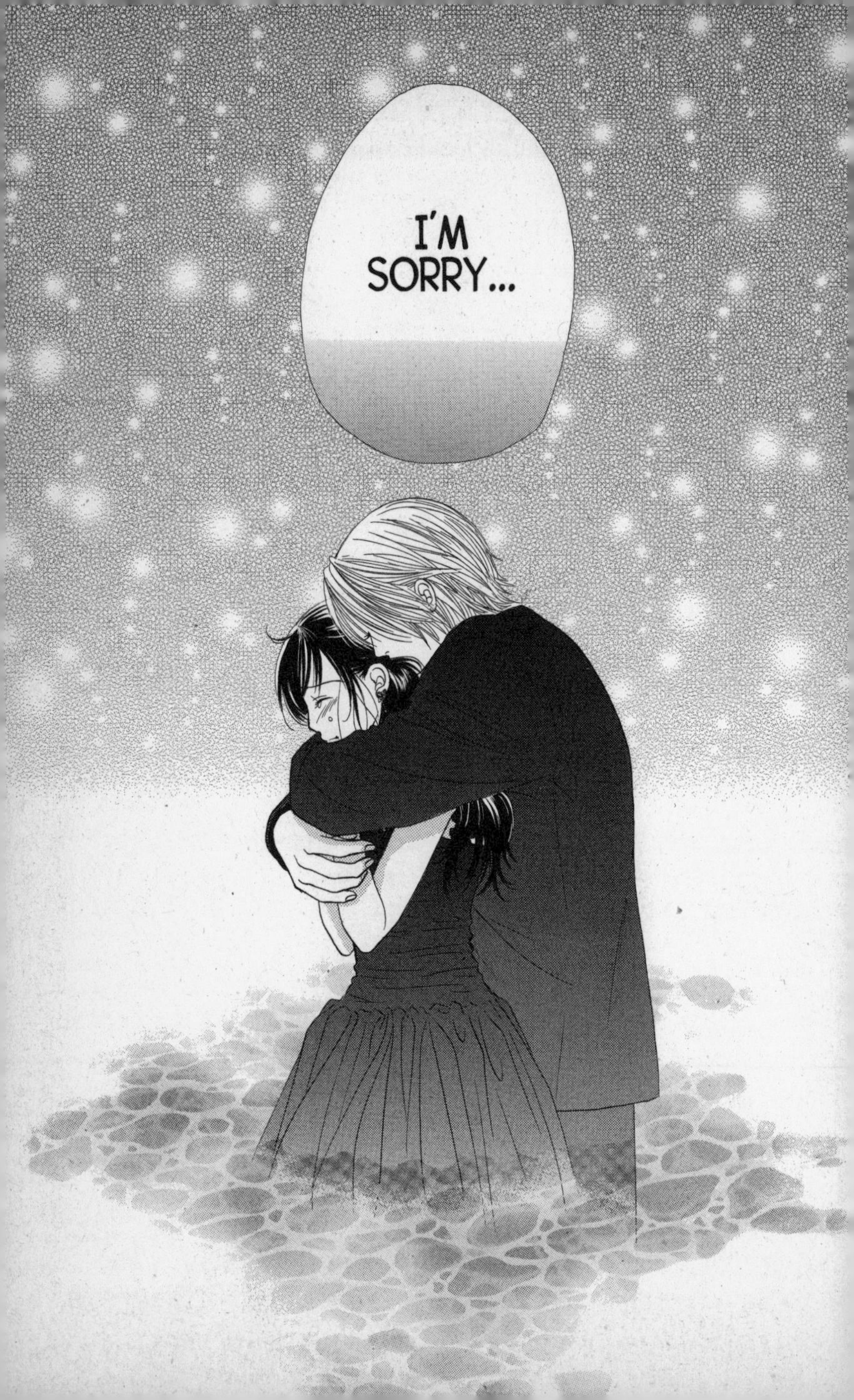
I'M SORRY...

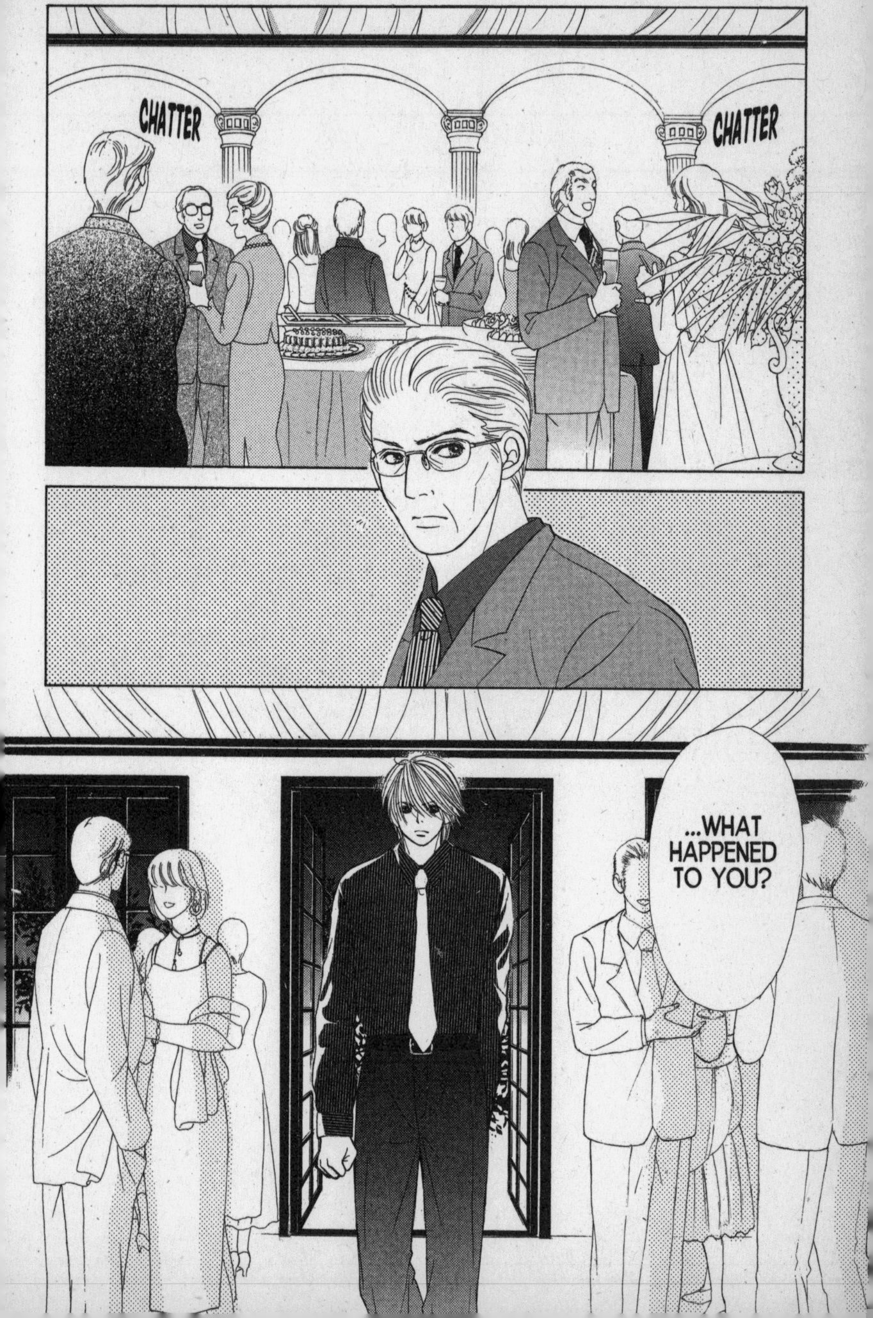
CHATTER
CHATTER
...WHAT HAPPENED TO YOU?

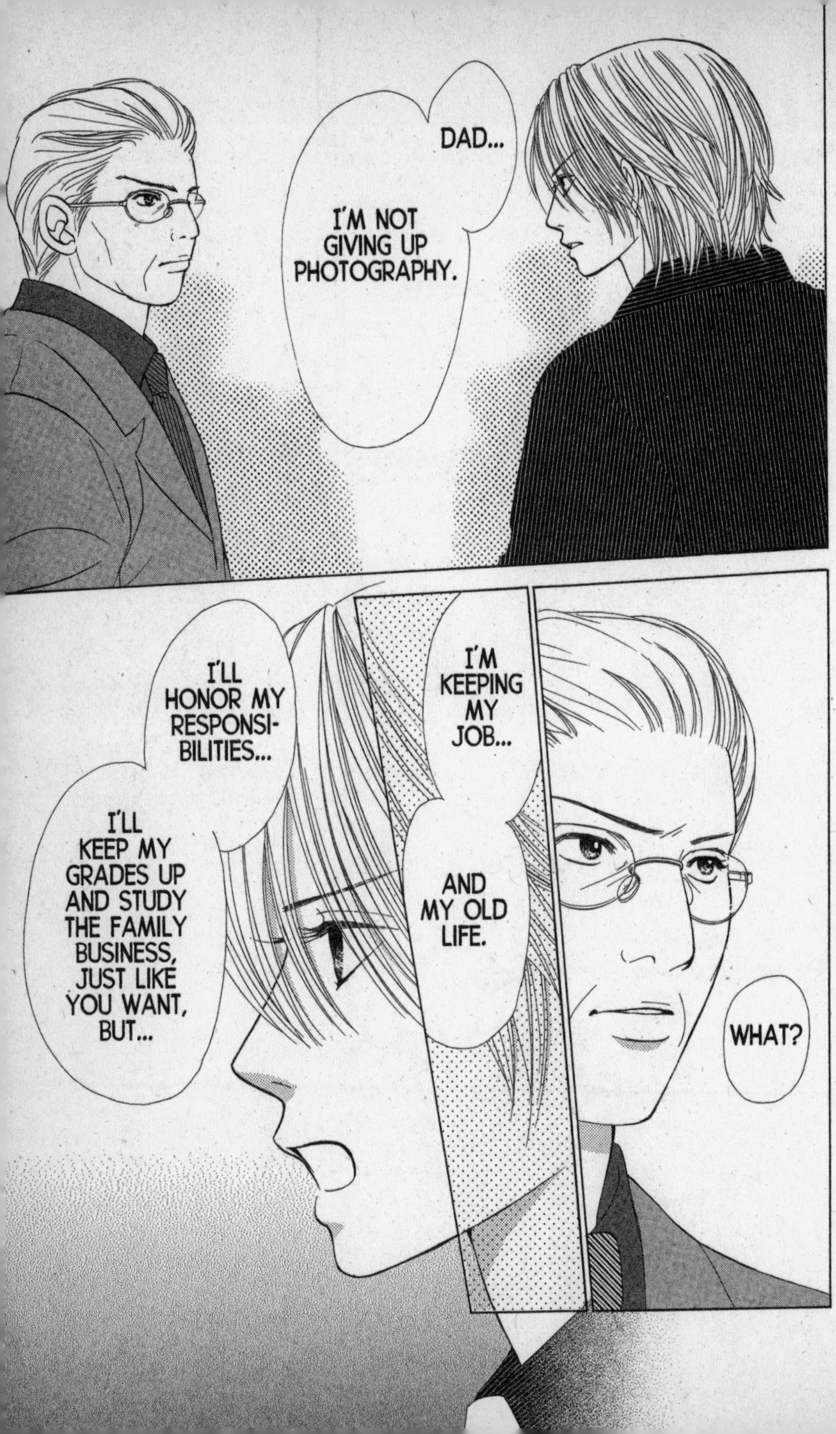
DAD...
I'M NOT GIVING UP PHOTOGRAPHY.
I'LL HONOR MY RESPONSI-BILITIES...
I'LL KEEP MY GRADES UP AND STUDY THE FAMILY BUSINESS, JUST LIKE YOU WANT, BUT...
I'M KEEPING MY JOB...
AND MY OLD LIFE.
WHAT?

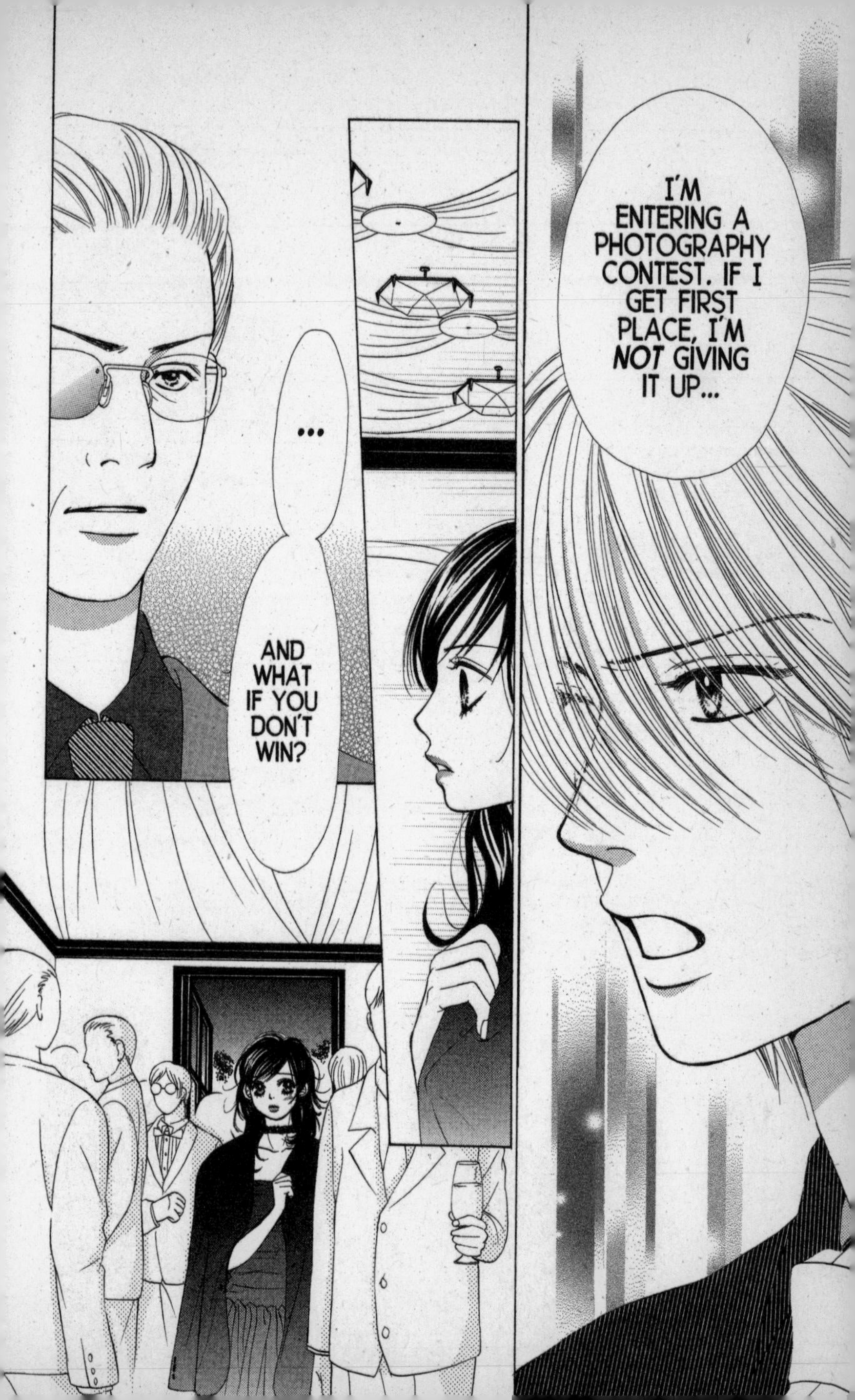
I'M ENTERING A PHOTOGRAPHY CONTEST. IF I GET FIRST PLACE, I'M *NOT* GIVING IT UP...
...
AND WHAT IF YOU DON'T WIN?

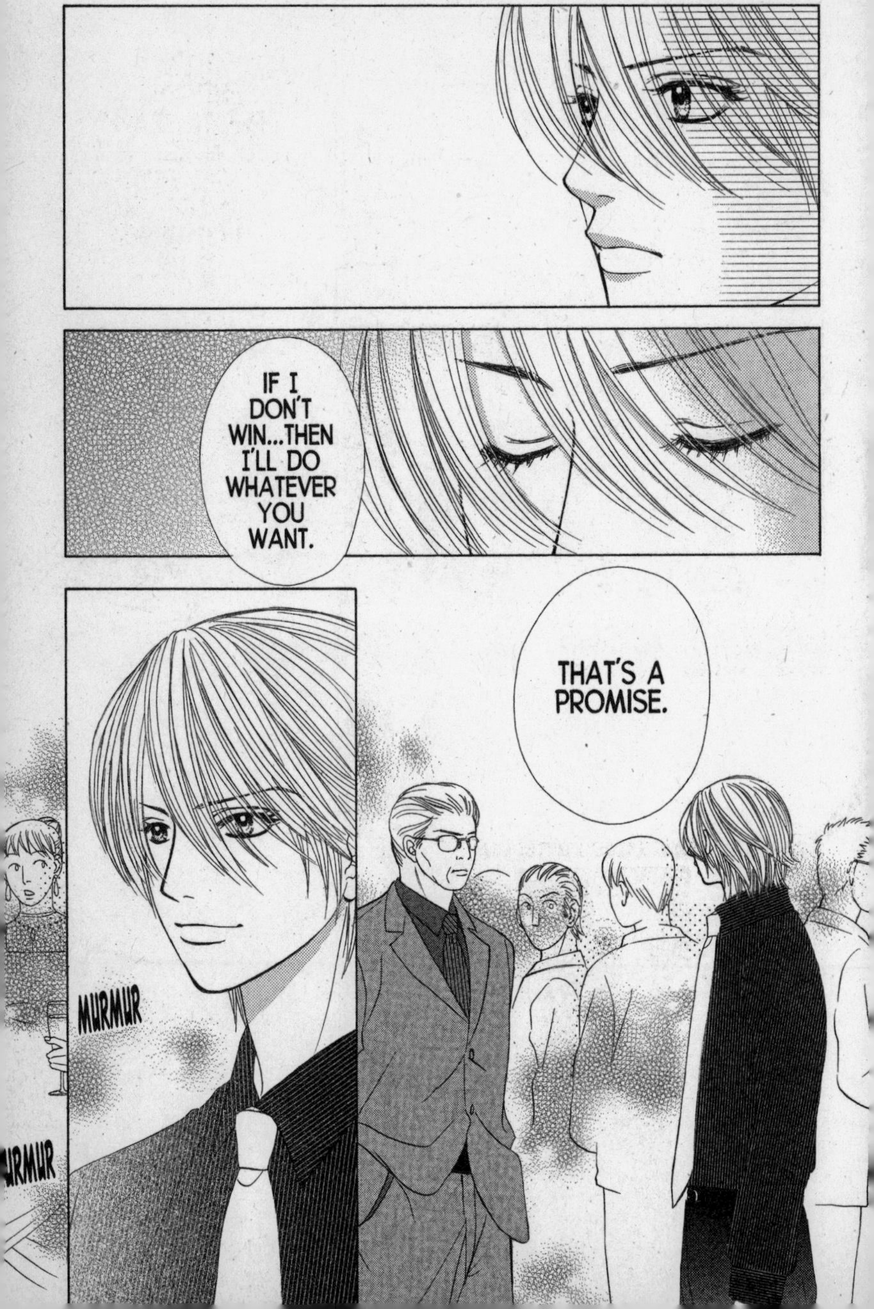
IF I DON'T WIN...THEN I'LL DO WHATEVER YOU WANT.
THAT'S A PROMISE.
MURMUR

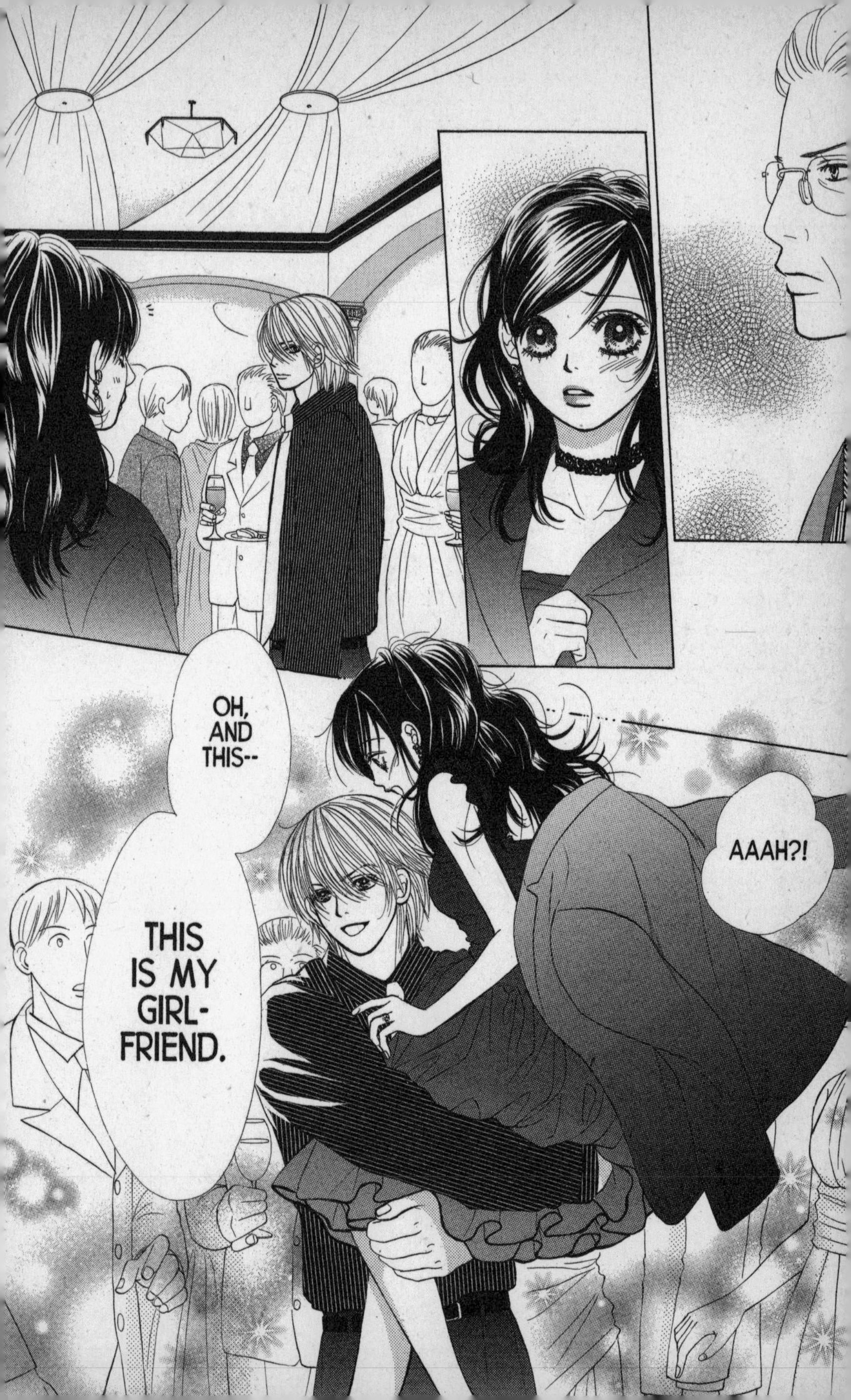
OH, AND THIS--
AAAH?!
THIS IS MY GIRL-FRIEND.

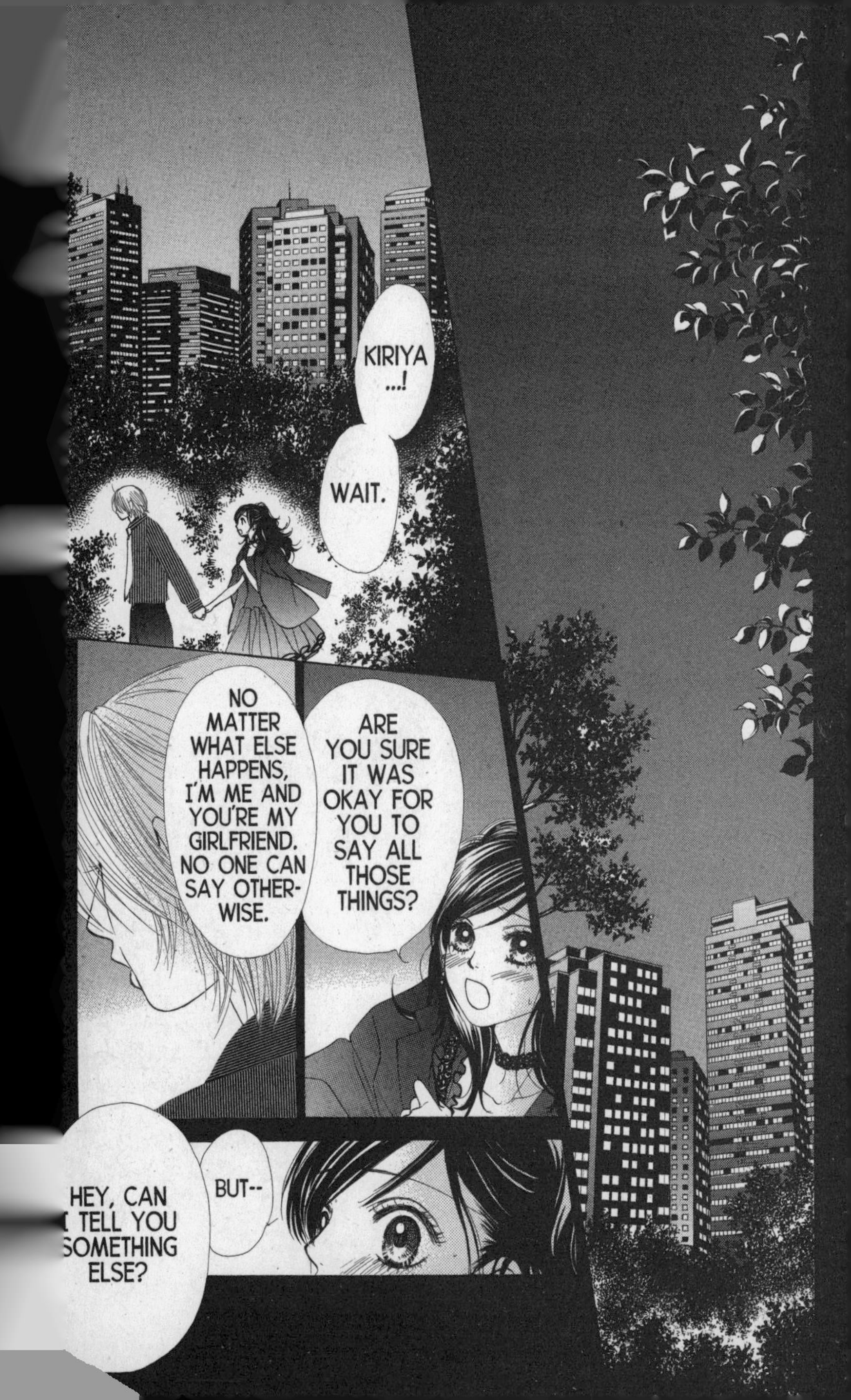
KIRIYA ...!
WAIT.
ARE YOU SURE IT WAS OKAY FOR YOU TO SAY ALL THOSE THINGS?
NO MATTER WHAT ELSE HAPPENS, I'M ME AND YOU'RE MY GIRLFRIEND. NO ONE CAN SAY OTHER-WISE.
BUT--
HEY, CAN I TELL YOU SOMETHING ELSE?

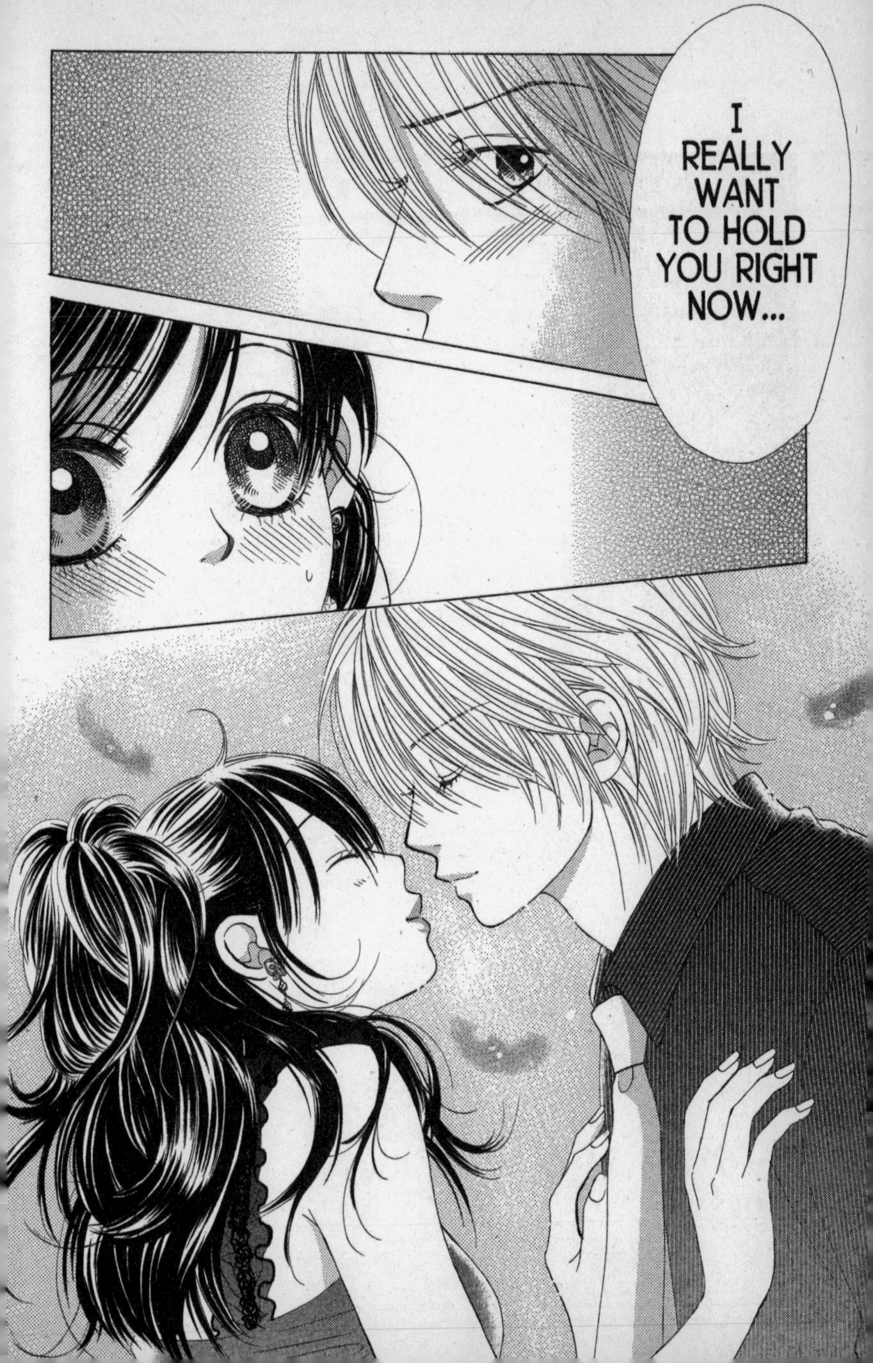
I REALLY WANT TO HOLD YOU RIGHT NOW...

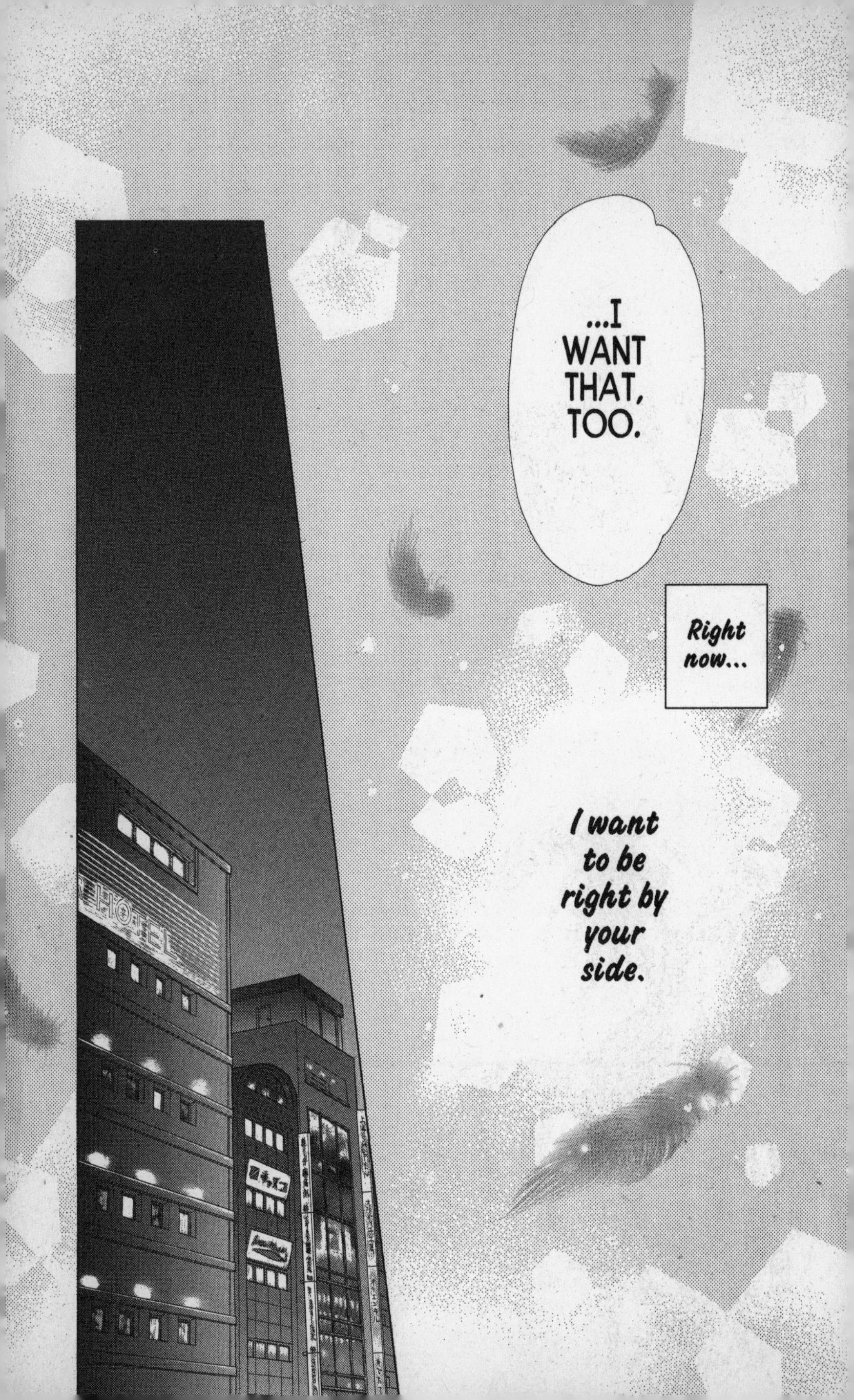
...I WANT THAT, TOO.
Right now...
I want to be right by your side.
HOTEL

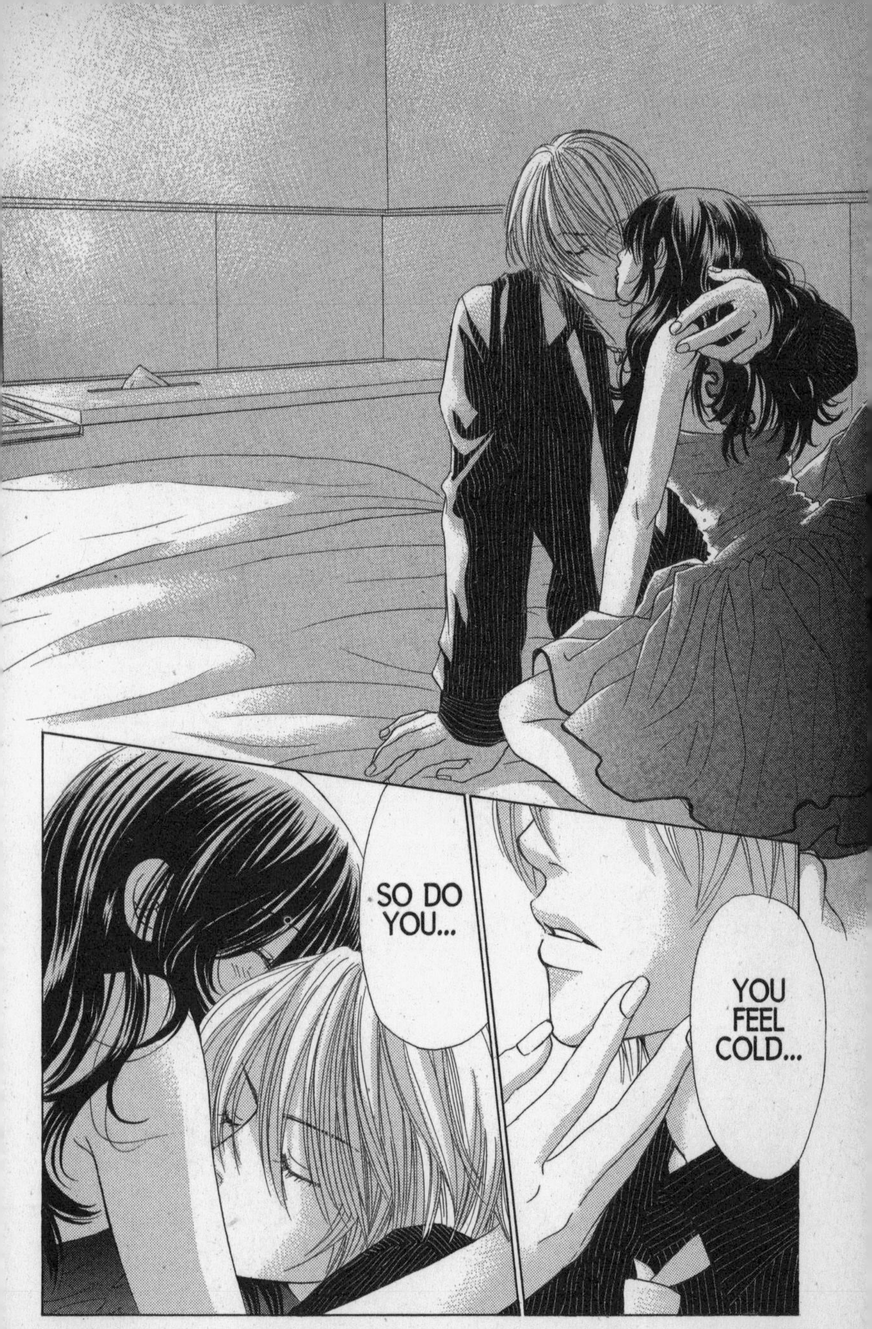
YOU FEEL COLD...
SO DO YOU...

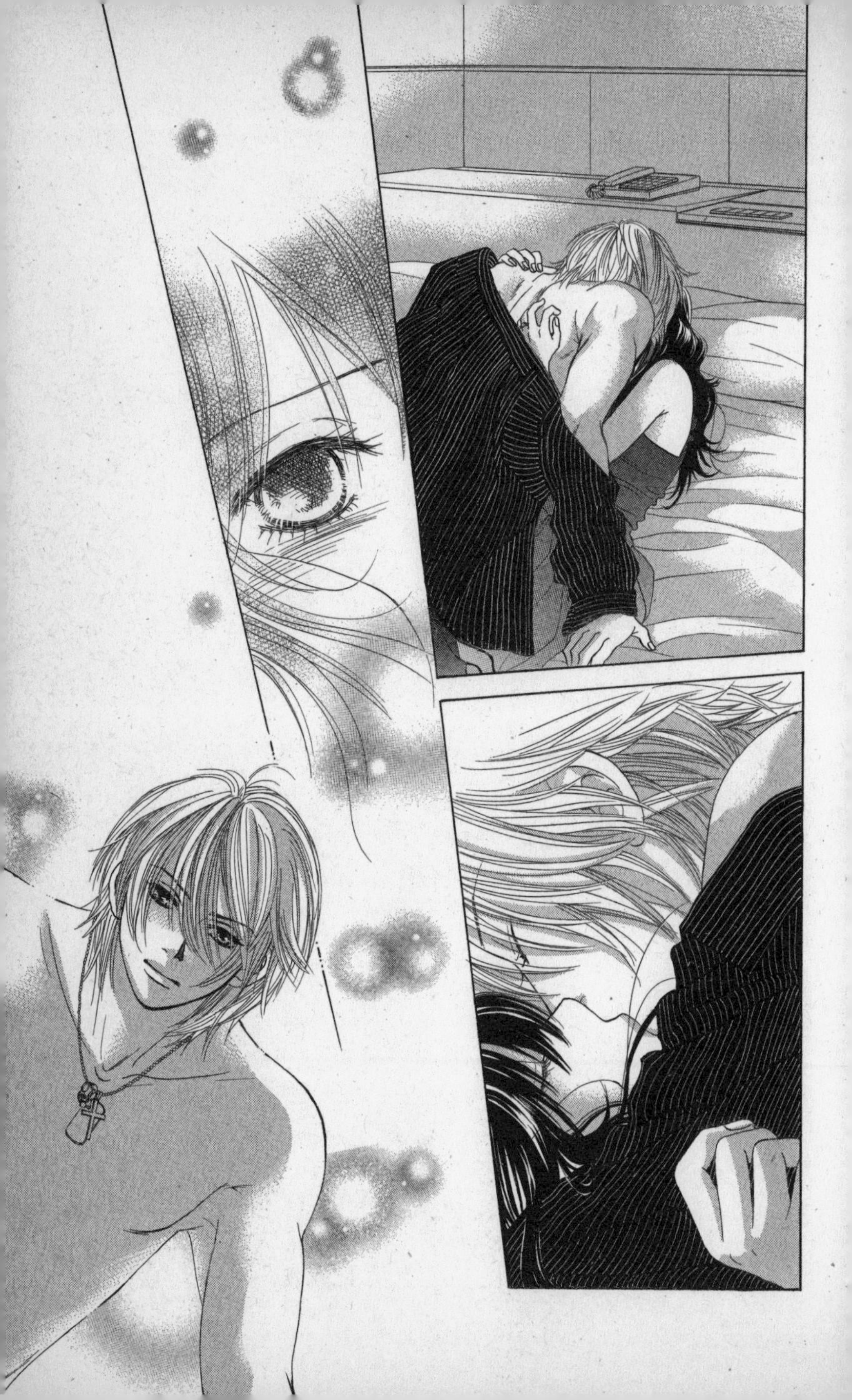

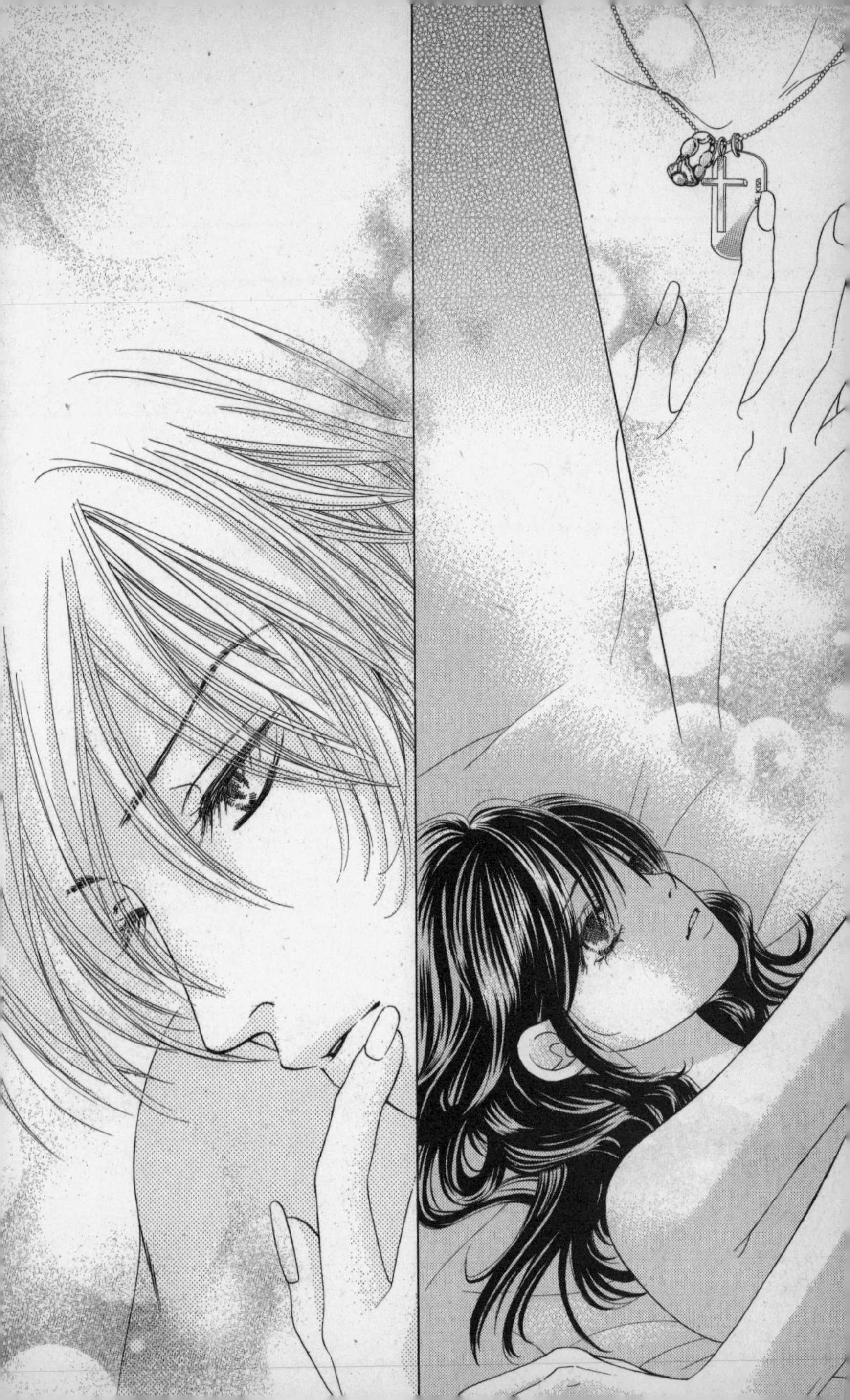

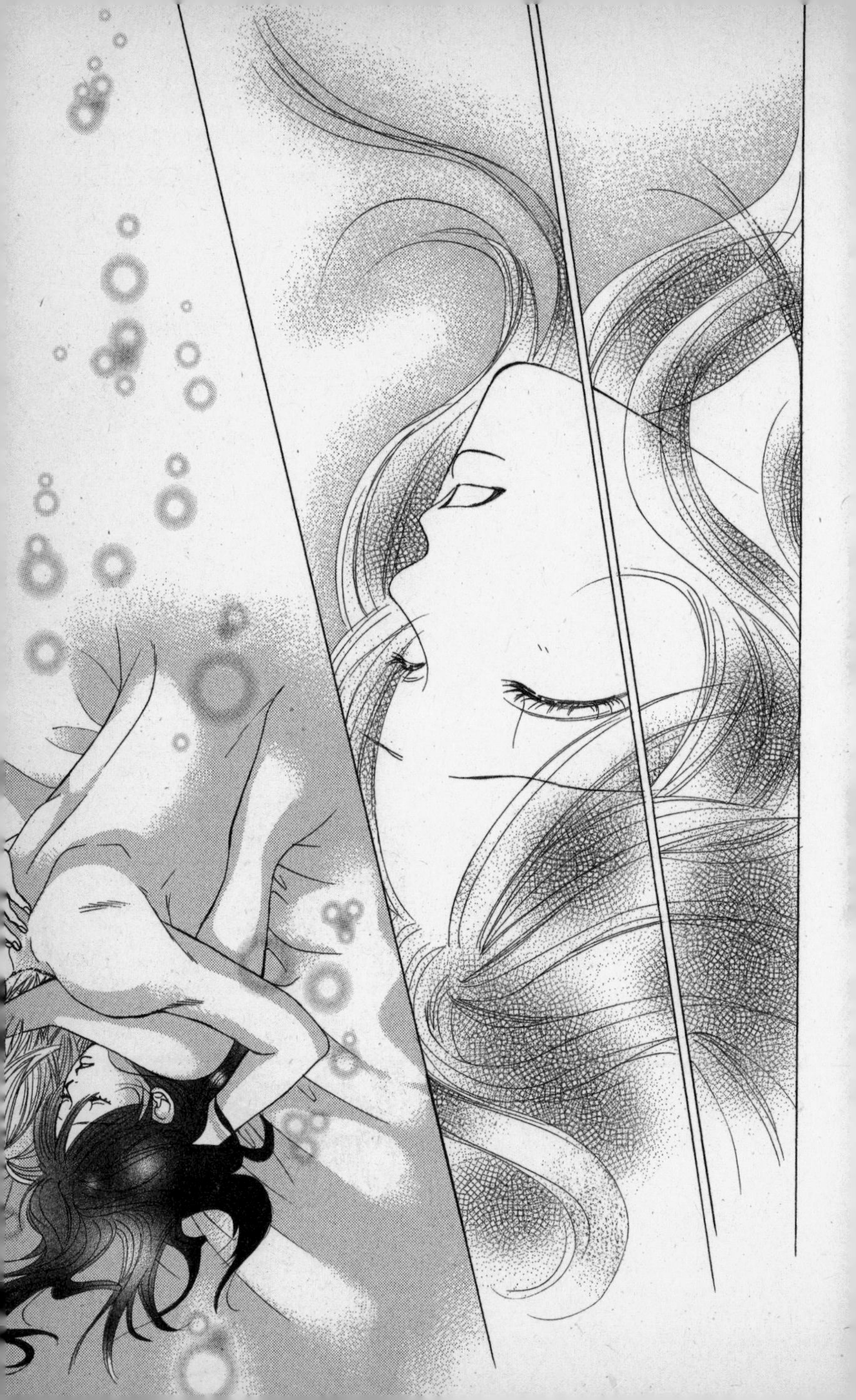

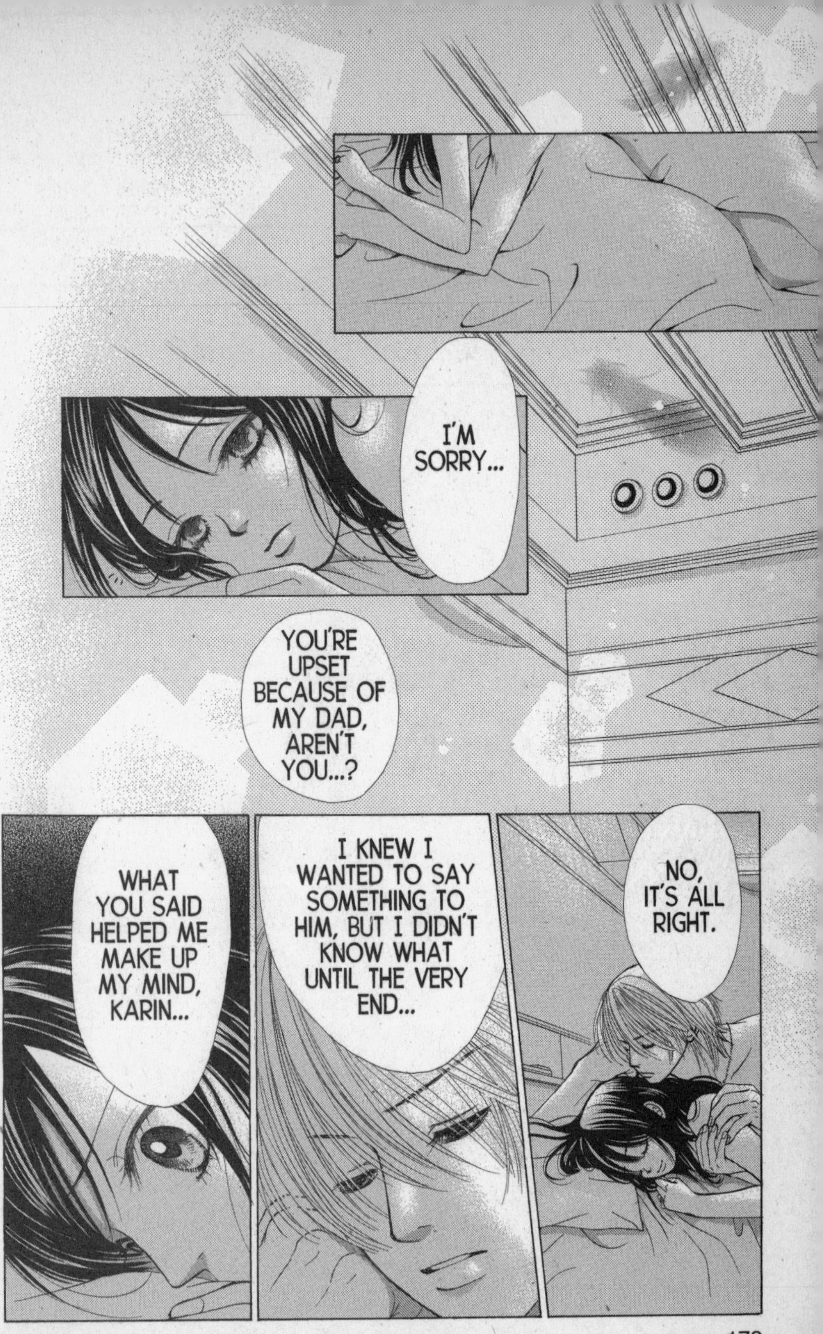
I'M SORRY...
YOU'RE UPSET BECAUSE OF MY DAD, AREN'T YOU...?
NO, IT'S ALL RIGHT.
I KNEW I WANTED TO SAY SOMETHING TO HIM, BUT I DIDN'T KNOW WHAT UNTIL THE VERY END...
WHAT YOU SAID HELPED ME MAKE UP MY MIND, KARIN...

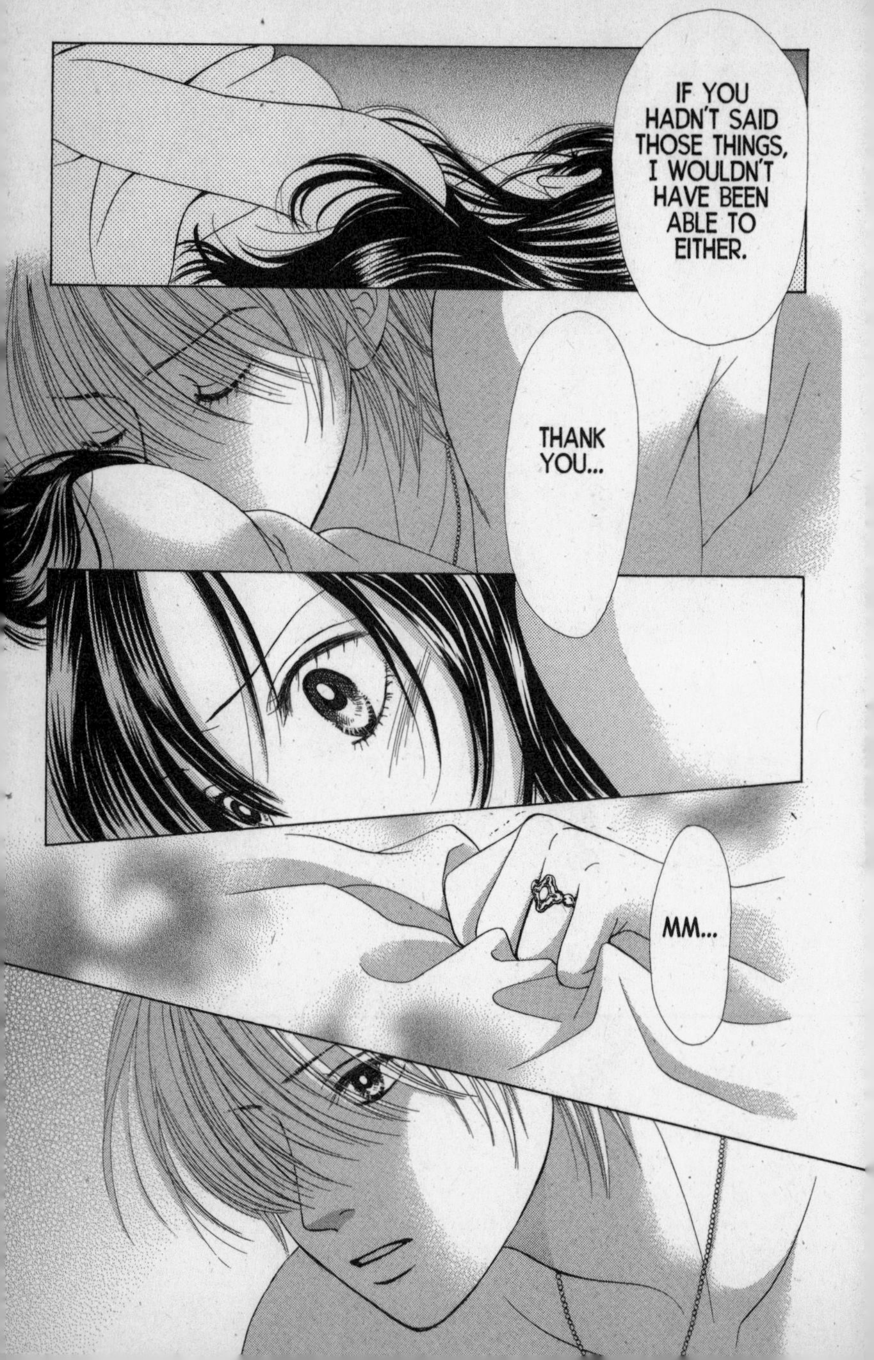
IF YOU HADN'T SAID THOSE THINGS, I WOULDN'T HAVE BEEN ABLE TO EITHER.
THANK YOU...
MM...

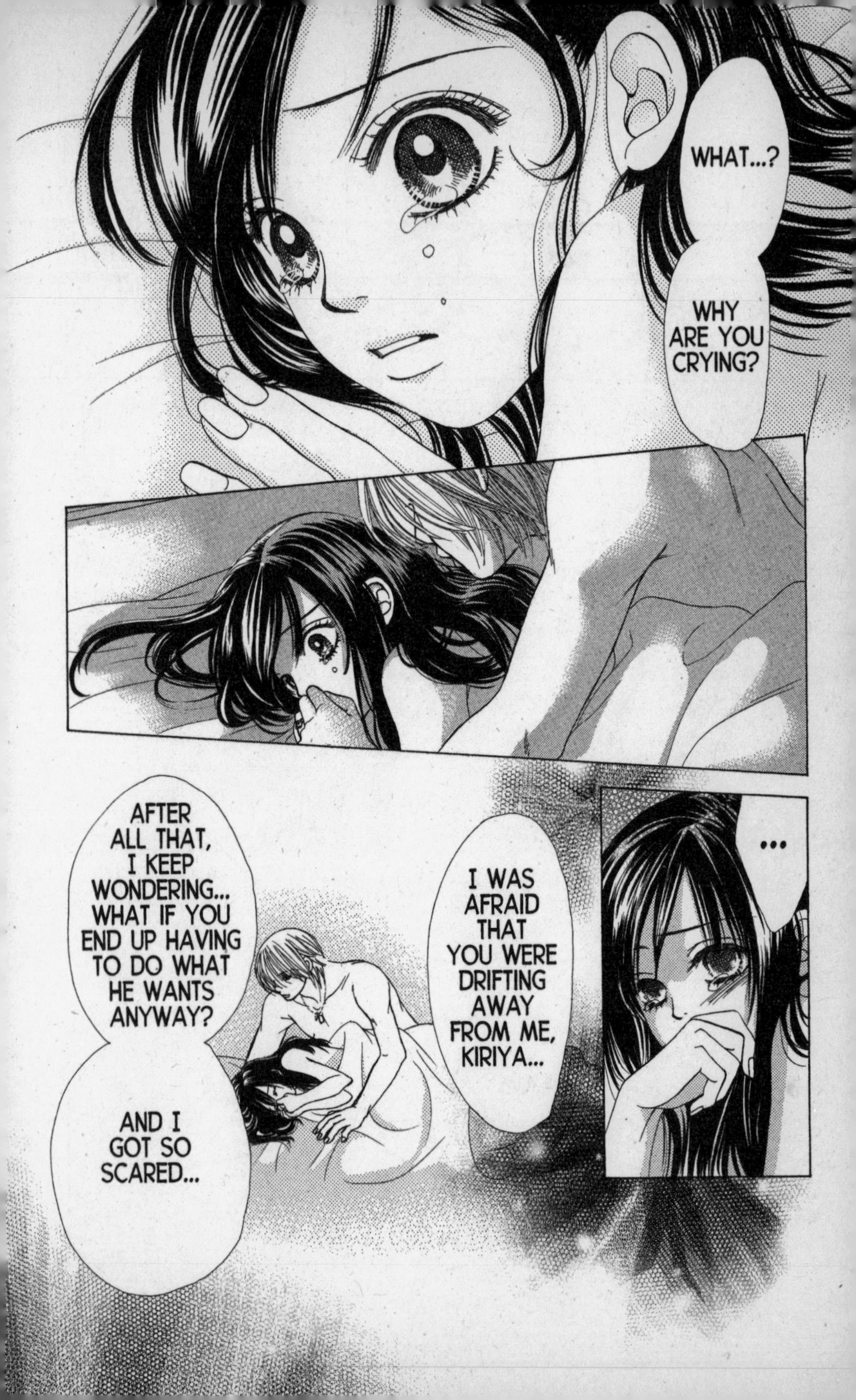
WHAT...?
WHY ARE YOU CRYING?
...
I WAS AFRAID THAT YOU WERE DRIFTING AWAY FROM ME, KIRIYA...
AFTER ALL THAT, I KEEP WONDERING... WHAT IF YOU END UP HAVING TO DO WHAT HE WANTS ANYWAY?
AND I GOT SO SCARED...

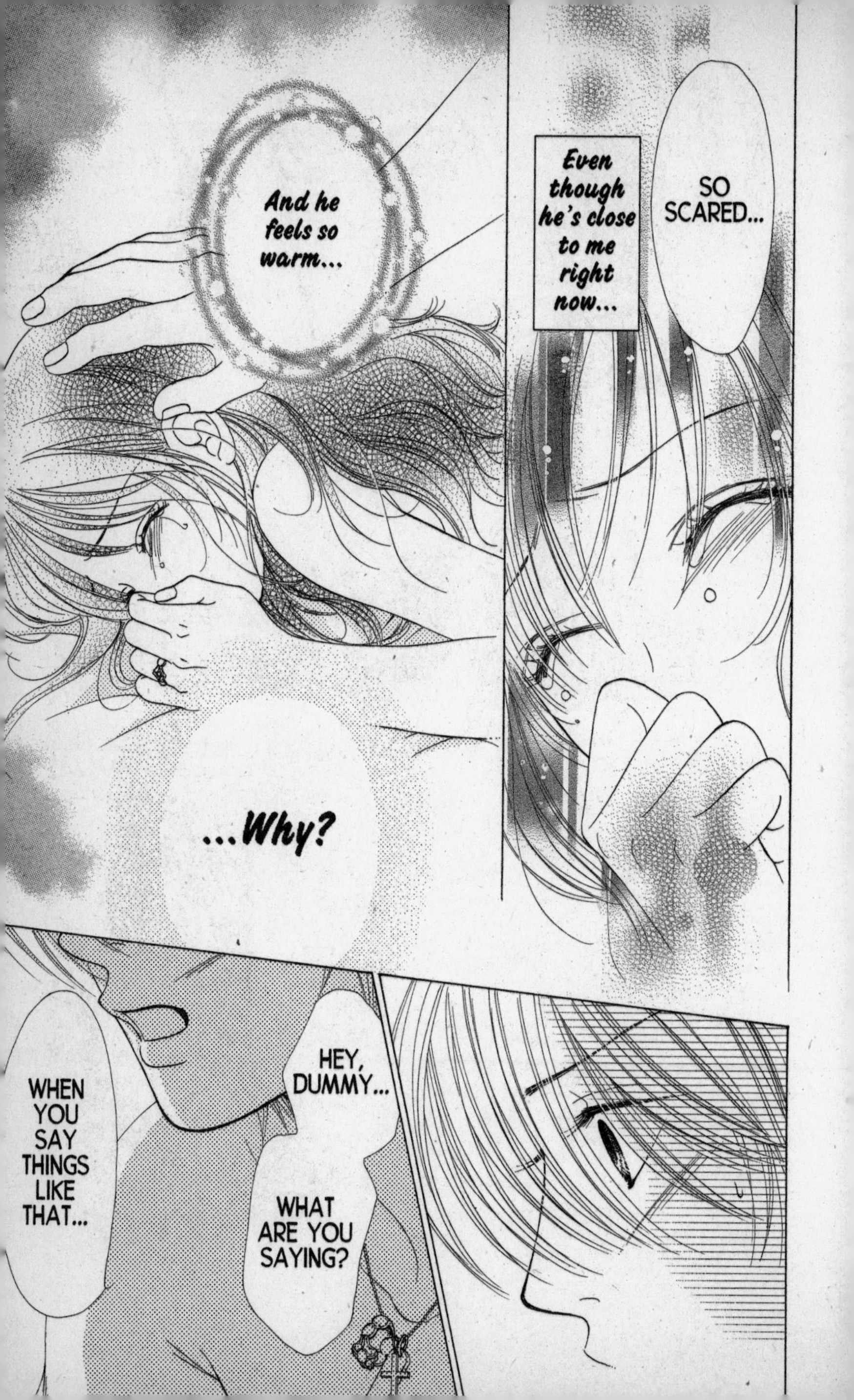

SO SCARED...
Even though he's close to me right now...
And he feels so warm...
...Why?
HEY, DUMMY...
WHAT ARE YOU SAYING?
WHEN YOU SAY THINGS LIKE THAT...

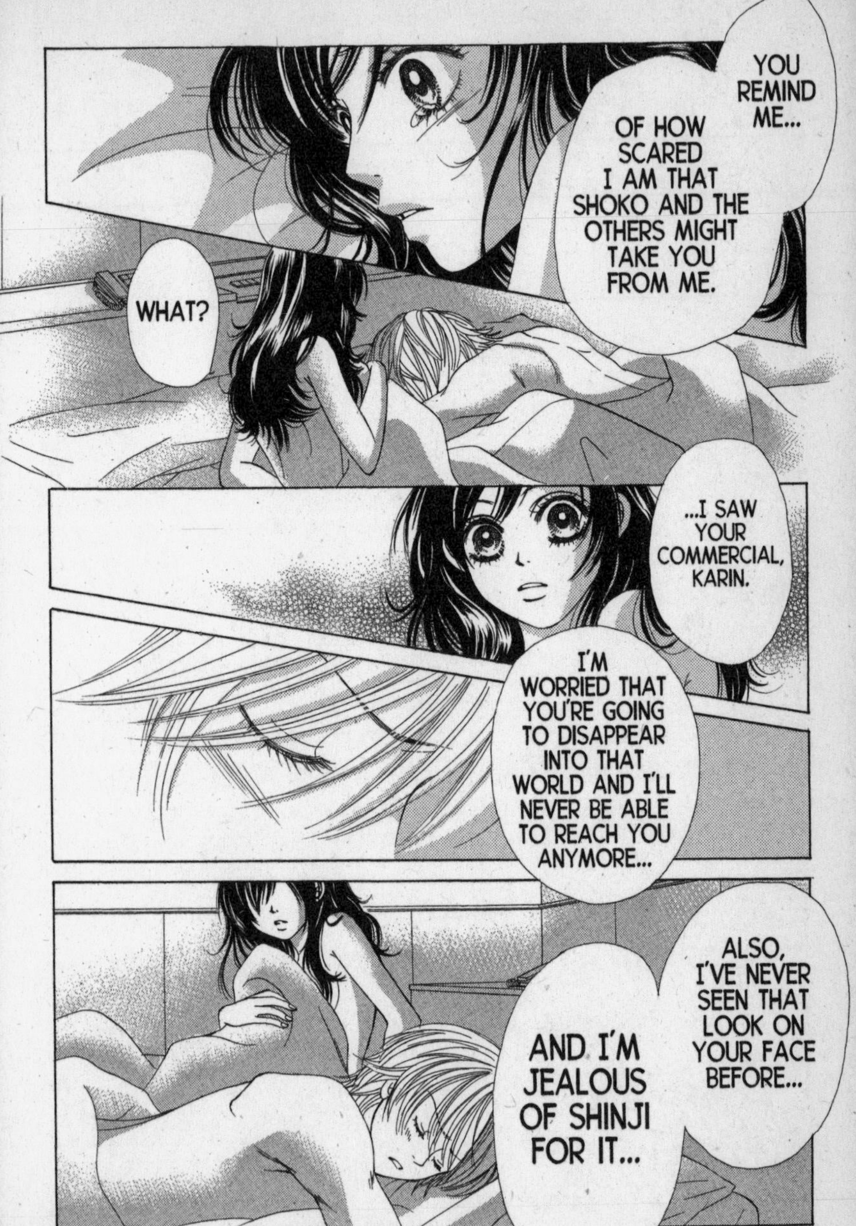
YOU REMIND ME...
OF HOW SCARED I AM THAT SHOKO AND THE OTHERS MIGHT TAKE YOU FROM ME.
WHAT?
...I SAW YOUR COMMERCIAL, KARIN.
I'M WORRIED THAT YOU'RE GOING TO DISAPPEAR INTO THAT WORLD AND I'LL NEVER BE ABLE TO REACH YOU ANYMORE...
ALSO, I'VE NEVER SEEN THAT LOOK ON YOUR FACE BEFORE...
AND I'M JEALOUS OF SHINJI FOR IT...

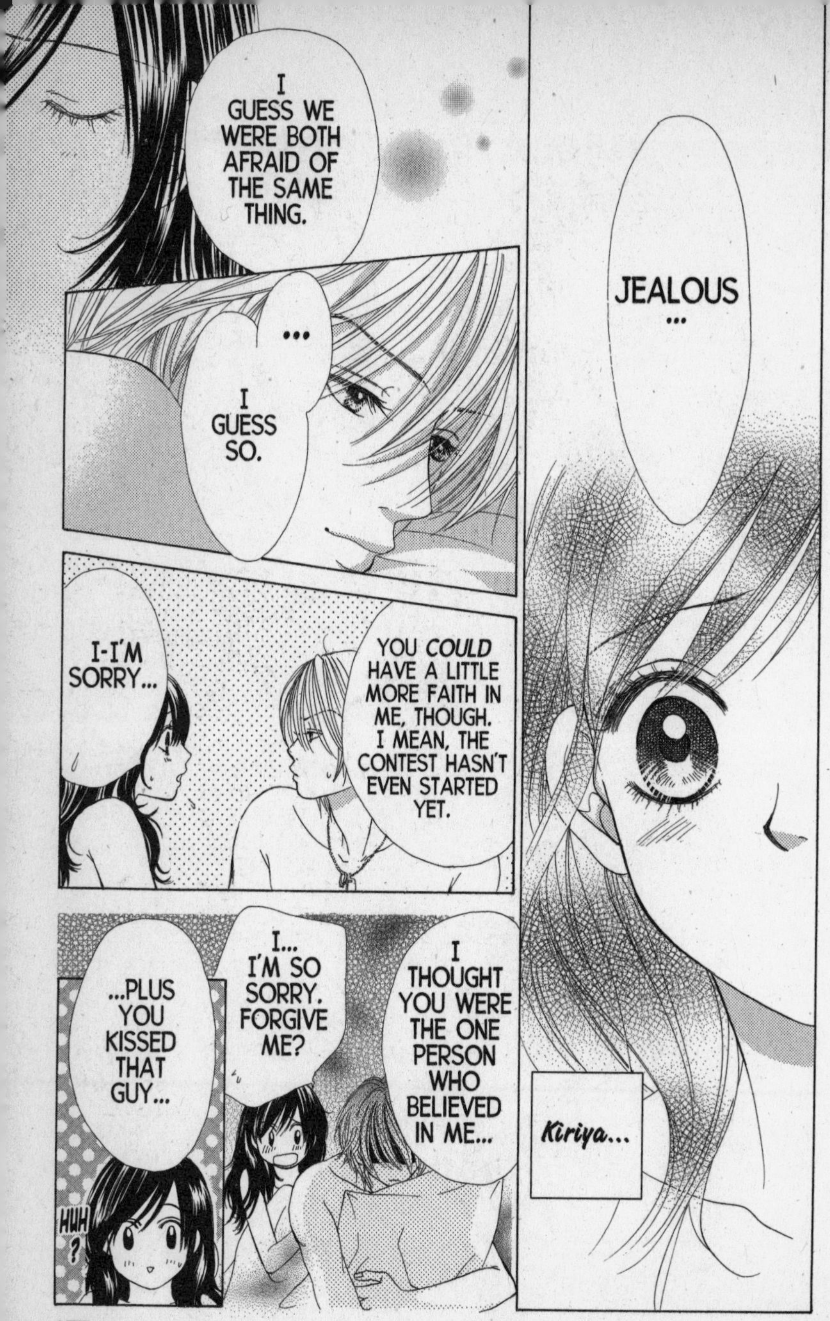
JEALOUS ...
Kiriya...
I GUESS WE WERE BOTH AFRAID OF THE SAME THING.
...
I GUESS SO.
YOU *COULD* HAVE A LITTLE MORE FAITH IN ME, THOUGH. I MEAN, THE CONTEST HASN'T EVEN STARTED YET.
I-I'M SORRY...
I THOUGHT YOU WERE THE ONE PERSON WHO BELIEVED IN ME...
I... I'M SO SORRY. FORGIVE ME?
...PLUS YOU KISSED THAT GUY...
HUH ?

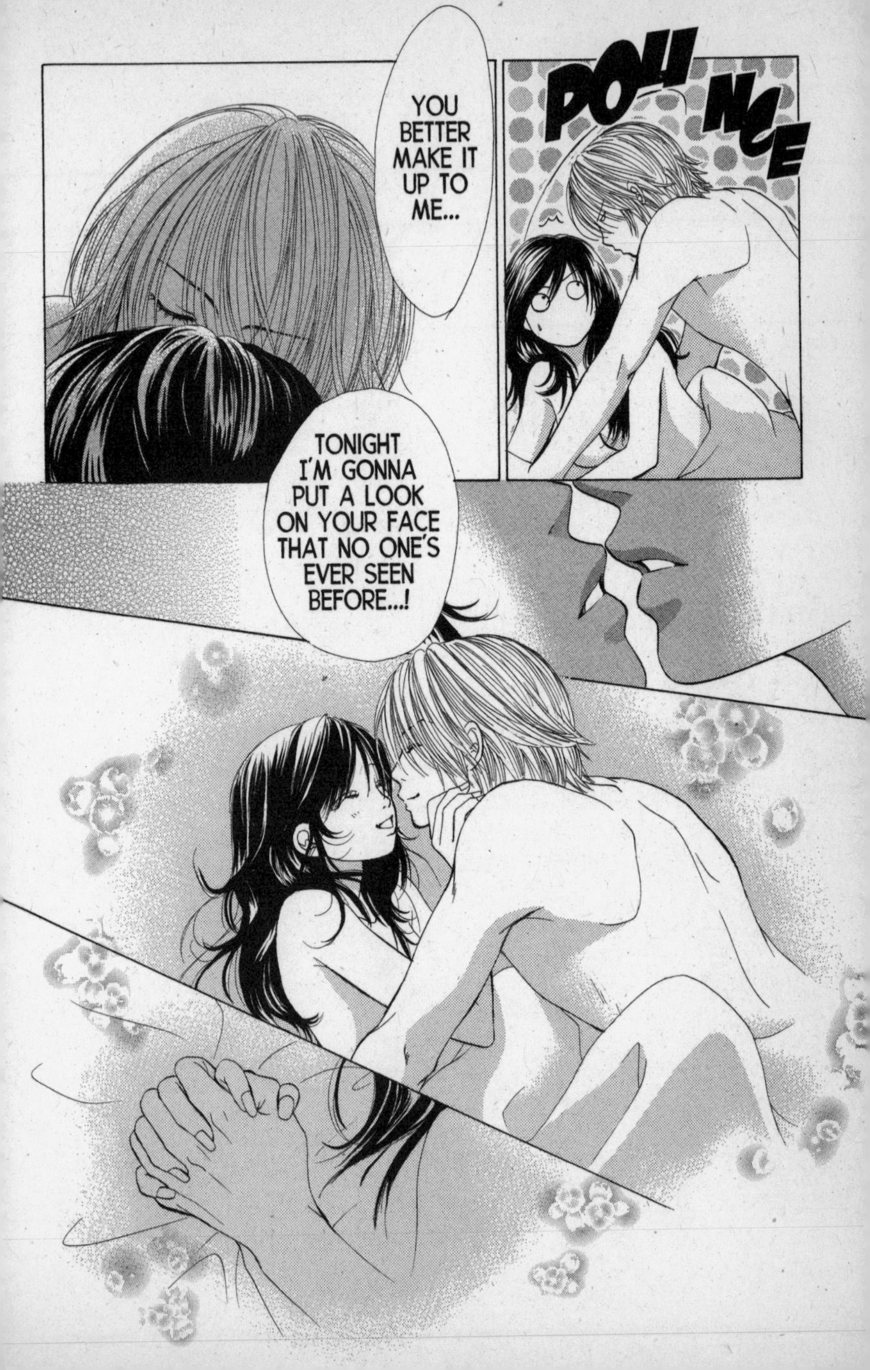
POUNCE
YOU BETTER MAKE IT UP TO ME...
TONIGHT I'M GONNA PUT A LOOK ON YOUR FACE THAT NO ONE'S EVER SEEN BEFORE...!

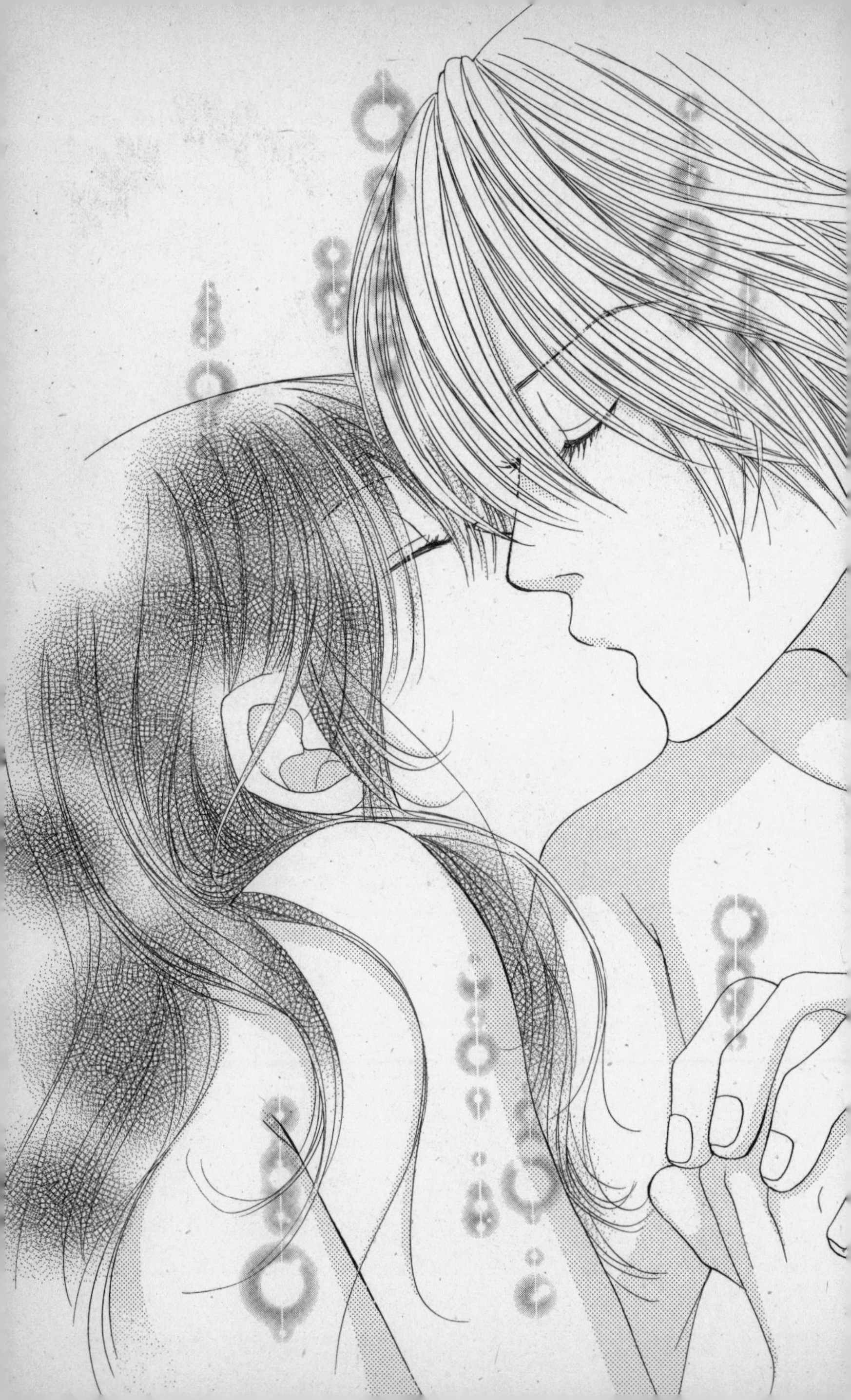

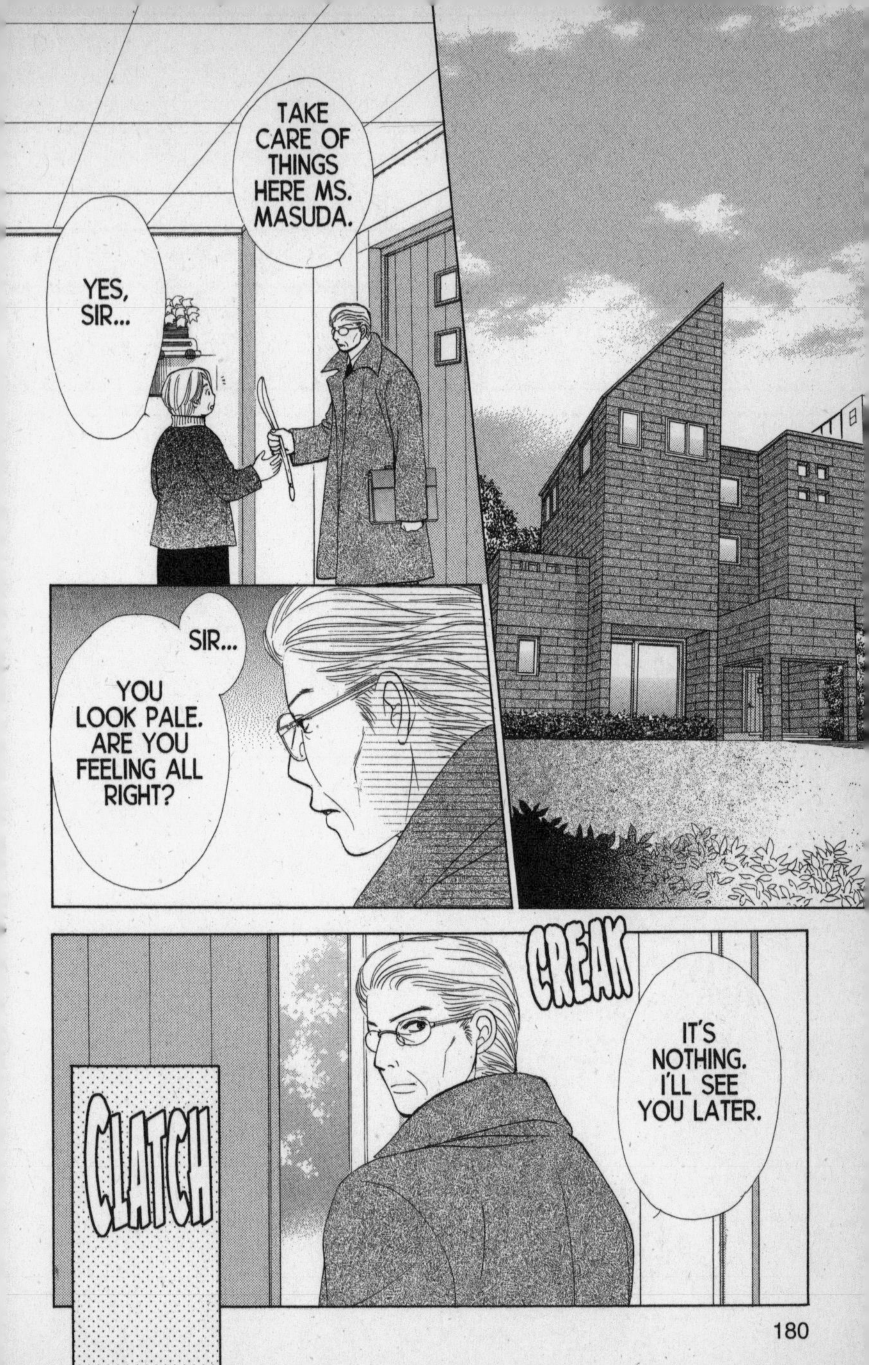
TAKE CARE OF THINGS HERE MS. MASUDA.
YES, SIR...
SIR...
YOU LOOK PALE. ARE YOU FEELING ALL RIGHT?
CREAK
IT'S NOTHING. I'LL SEE YOU LATER.
CLATCH

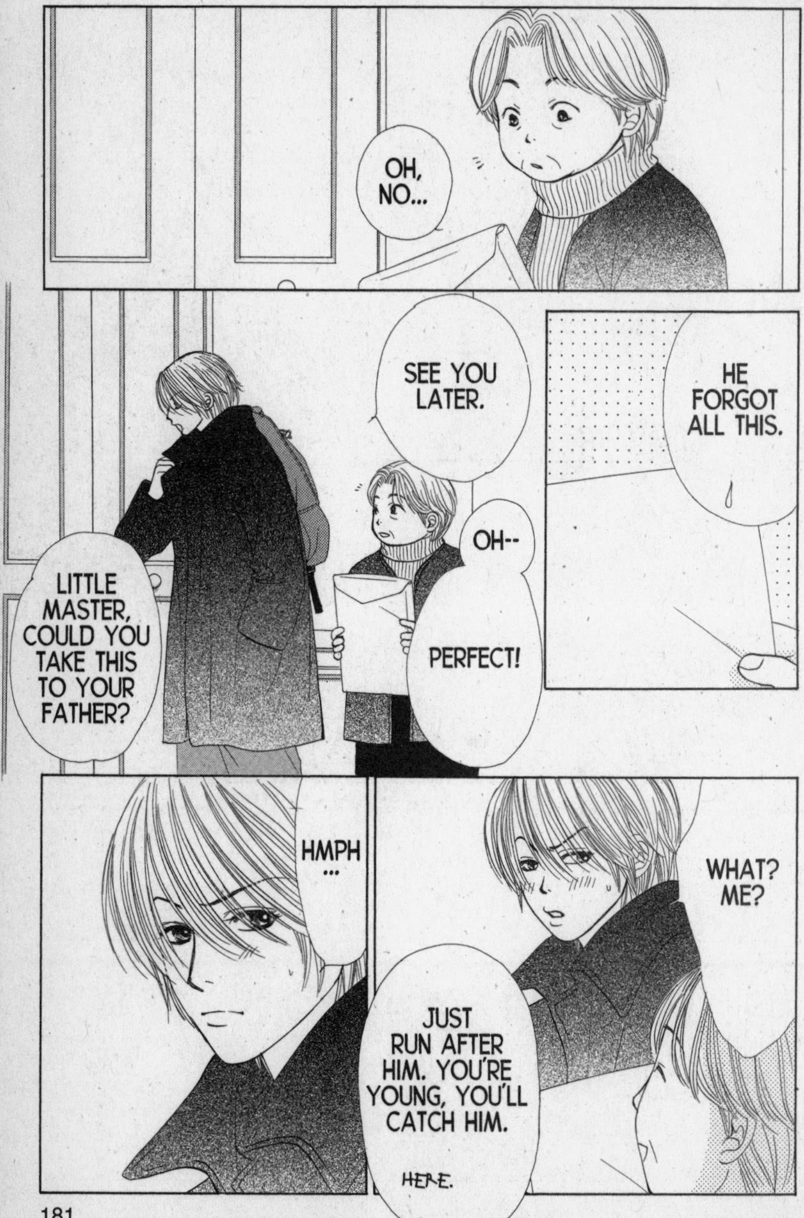
OH, NO...
HE FORGOT ALL THIS.
SEE YOU LATER.
OH--
PERFECT!
LITTLE MASTER, COULD YOU TAKE THIS TO YOUR FATHER?
WHAT? ME?
JUST RUN AFTER HIM. YOU'RE YOUNG, YOU'LL CATCH HIM.
HERE.
HMPH ...

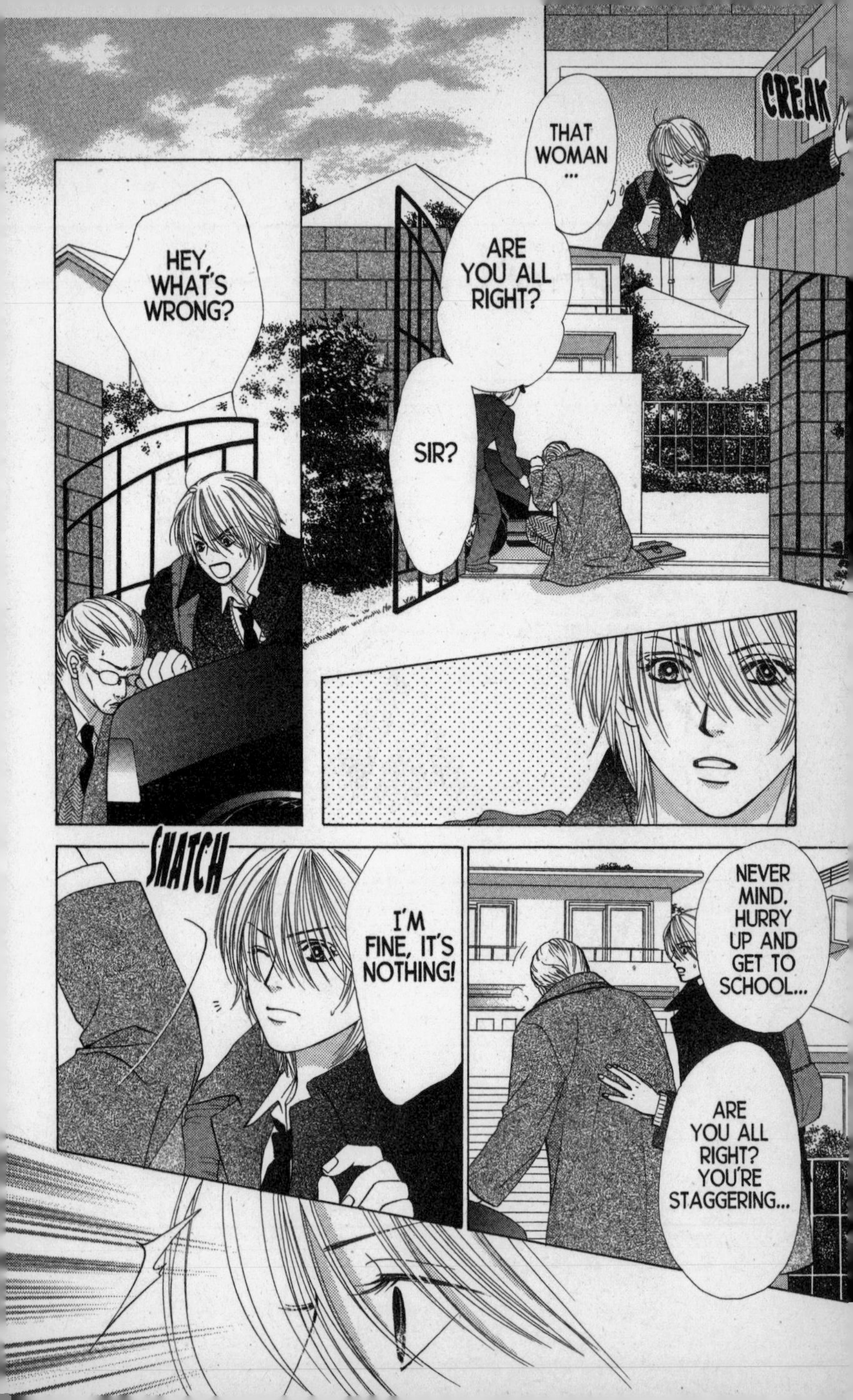
CREAK
THAT WOMAN ...
ARE YOU ALL RIGHT?
SIR?
HEY, WHAT'S WRONG?
NEVER MIND. HURRY UP AND GET TO SCHOOL...
ARE YOU ALL RIGHT? YOU'RE STAGGERING...
SNATCH
I'M FINE, IT'S NOTHING!

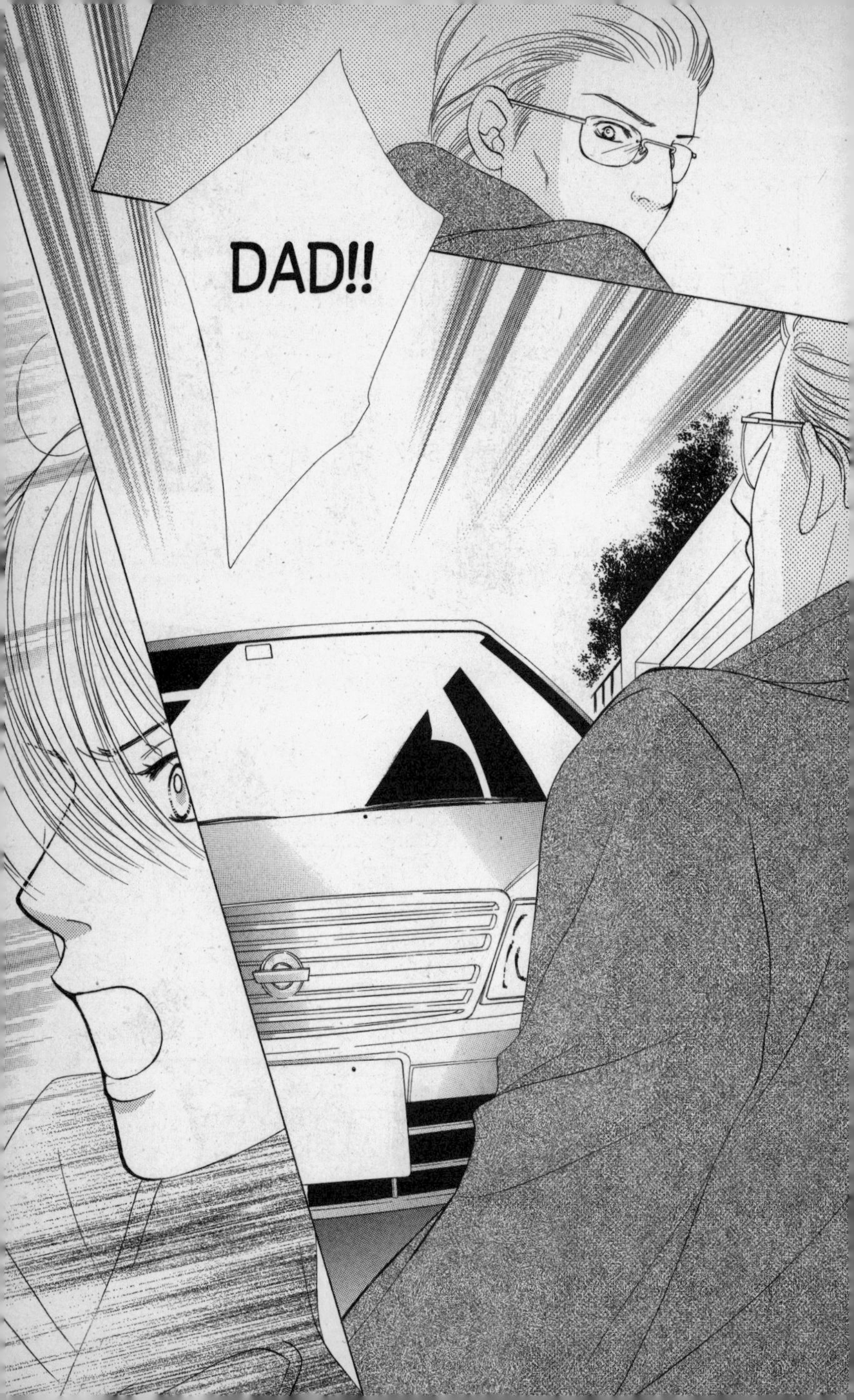
DAD!!

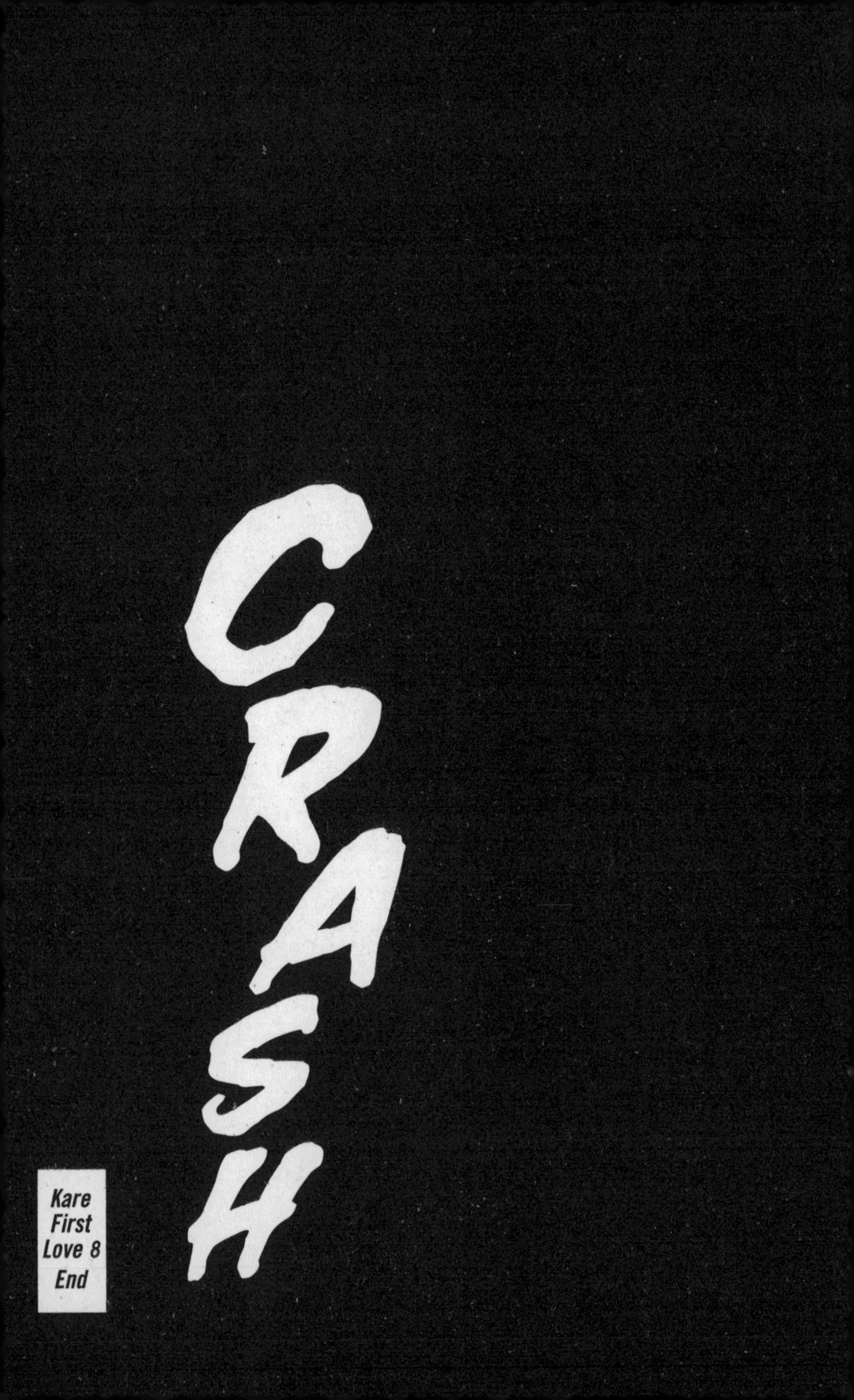
CRASH

Kare First Love 8 End

Official Kaho Miyasaka Site-
Love Factory
http://www.k-miyasaka.com/

Message From the Author

For this volume's cover I decided to feature Kiriya in his outfit from the corporate party scene. Karin's party look appeared on the cover of volume 3. I remember someone wrote to me after that book came out and guessed the designer label of the dress. I was shocked and delighted—it always makes me happy when readers recognize the little extras I put into my work. We're at the point in our story where things are getting more serious. I wish I could maintain a more cheerful vibe, but the plot demands we travel this road. Stick with me, though—I need you!

Kare First Love
Vol. 8
Shōjo Edition
Story and Art by KAHO MIYASAKA

English Adaptation/Kelly Sue DeConnick
Translation/Akira Watanabe
Touch-Up Art & Lettering/Steve Dutro
Cover and Interior Design/Hidemi Sahara
Editor/Andy Nakatani

Managing Editor/Annette Roman
Director of Production/Noboru Watanabe
VP of Publishing/Alvin Lu
Sr. Director of Acquisitions/Rika Inouye
VP of Sales & Marketing/Liza Coppola
Publisher/Hyoe Narita

Printed in the U.S.A.

Published by VIZ Media, LLC
P.O. Box 77010
San Francisco, CA 94107

Shōjo Edition
10 9 8 7 6 5 4 3 2 1
First printing, June 2006

www.viz.com
store.viz.com

A Beauty Who Feels Like a Beast!

To overcome an embarrassing past, teenage Ai gets a makeover and attends a new high school. Soon, the hottest guy at school is chatting her up! But beauty is only skin deep, and Ai learns that fresh makeup and new clothes can't hide her insecurities or doubts.

A tale of high school neurosis at its finest—start your graphic novel collection today!

doubt!!™

Only $9.99!

doubl!!

Story and art by
Izumi Kaneyoshi

vol 1

VIZ MEDIA™

www.viz.com
store.viz.com

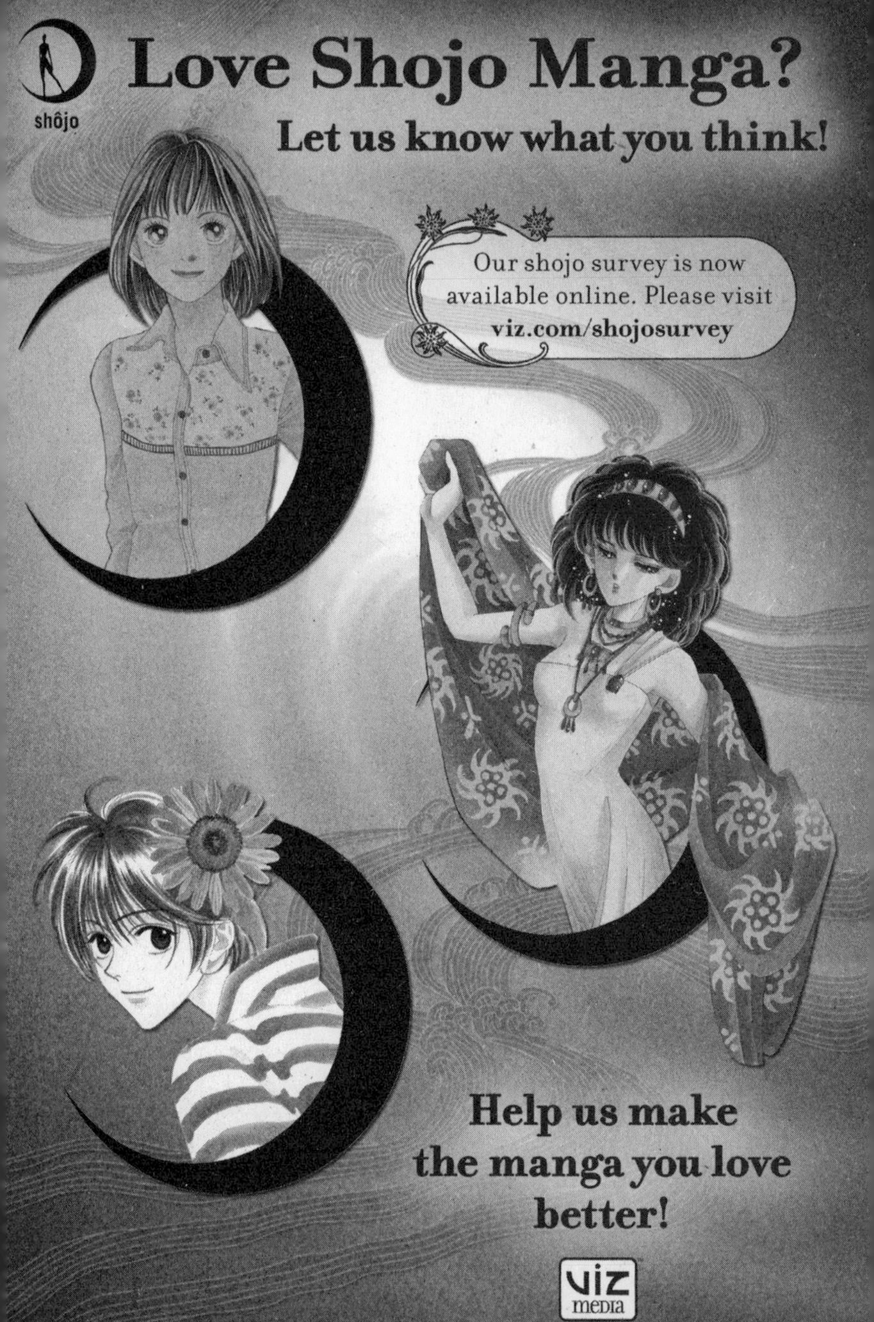
shôjo
Love Shojo Manga?
Let us know what you think!
Our shojo survey is now available online. Please visit viz.com/shojosurvey
Help us make the manga you love better!
VIZ media
ANA-YORI DANGO © 1992 by Yoko Kamio/SHUEISHA Inc. Hanazakari no Kimitachi he © Hisaya Nakajo 1996/HAKUSENSHA, Inc. RED RIVER © 1995 Chie SHINOHARA/Shogakukan Inc.